Glory Yards

Glory Yards

DEREK SMITH

RUTLEDGE HILL PRESS
Nashville, Tennessee

Published in Nashville, Tennessee, by Rutledge Hill Press,
211 Seventh Avenue North, Nashville, Tennessee 37219

Typography by D&T/Bailey, Nashville, Tennessee

Library of Congress Cataloging-in-Publication Data

Smith, Derek, 1956–
    Glory yards / Derek Smith.
        p.   cm.
    ISBN 1-55853-244-7
    1. University of Florida—Football—History.   2. University of
Georgia—Football—History.   3. Florida Gators (Football team)—
History.   4. Georgia Bulldogs (Football team)—History.
5. Football—United States—History.   I. Title.
GV958.U523S65   1993   93-28906
796.332'63—dc20   CIP

Printed in the United States of America
1 2 3 4 5 6 7 8—98 97 96 95 94 93

For Henna

Contents

Preface

FLORIDA AND GEORGIA FANS, OR GEORGIA and Florida fans, if you prefer, have never agreed on much of anything except that each side despises the other.

From the days of leather helmets, two-way players and dusty fields in Macon, Jacksonville, Tampa and Savannah to the eras of Herschel Walker and Shane Matthews, the Orange and Blue has always clashed with the Red and Black.

In this classically-bitter southern football rivalry rooted in the early 1900s, there is even disagreement on the won-loss record between the schools.

Knowledgeable Gators claim Florida doesn't count the 1904 game in Macon because Georgia, a 52–0 winner, actually played Florida Agricultural College. The University of Florida was not established until two years later.

A Georgia "Gator Hater" will staunchly maintain that the Macon game should be included in any history of the gridiron tussles between Saurians (a fancy name for Alligators) and Bulldogs.

Of course, any rhubarb between the two probably will be punctuated by wild cries of "Give 'Em Hell, Florida!" or "How 'Bout Them Dawgs!"

Georgia football was a tradition years before the University of Florida was born, but UF fans christened their team the "Gators" long before there were any "Bulldogs" in Athens.

According to a 1948 *Florida Times-Union* article, a Gainesville, Fla., merchant named Phillip Miller and his son were responsible for Florida's nickname. Miller, while visiting his son, Austin, at the University of Virginia law school in Charlottesville in the fall of 1907, decided to order some UF pennants and banners from the Michie Company, a shop specializing in collegiate paraphernalia. When the store manager asked about Florida's mascot, Miller realized the new school had none.

Austin Miller said he suggested the name "Alligators" because the

9

reptile was native to the state and, apparently, no other school had adopted it.

But the Michie manager said he had never seen an alligator and didn't believe he could design one.

The younger Miller finally found an illustration of the creature in the UVA library.

The first alligator emblems appeared in Miller's drug and stationery store in Gainesville in 1908. The display consisted of a "blue banner measuring six by three feet, showing a large orange alligator, along with several smaller banners and pennants. Some showed the alligator lying down, some rampant; others included only the alligator's head."

The symbol caught on and the nickname was shortened to 'Gators over the next few seasons.

UGA's first president, Abraham Baldwin, was a Yale graduate and the first buildings on the Georgia campus were based on blueprints from Yale.

The tenacity of Georgia's teams, plus the strong ties with the Eli, resulted in the emergence of the nickname "Bulldogs" in 1920.

In a November 3, 1920, *Atlanta Journal* article about collegiate nicknames, reporter Morgan Blake wrote: "'The Georgia Bulldogs' would sound good because there is a certain dignity about a bulldog, as well as ferocity."

After a bruising but scoreless tie between Georgia and Virginia three days after Blake's article, *Atlanta Constitution* writer Cliff Cheatley repeatedly referred to UGA as "Bulldogs" in his game account. The name stuck and has been all but sacred to generations of the Red and Black.

Chartered in 1785, the University of Georgia fielded its first gridiron team in 1892 under Dr. Charles Herty, a chemistry professor who is considered the father of football at the school. On a field near New College, Georgia beat Mercer 50–0 on January 30, 1892, in the first intercollegiate football game played in the South. The Athenians lost 10–0 to Auburn in Atlanta in their only other game that first season.

Ernest Brown coached the second Georgia squad in 1893, opening with a 28–6 loss to Georgia Tech in Athens in the first meeting ever in that historic series. The 1893 Georgians finished 2–2–1.

After Coach Robert Winston guided UGA to its first winning season, 5–1, in 1894, the legendary Glenn S. "Pop" Warner came to Athens. Though his 1895 team struggled to a 3–4 mark, Georgia, under Warner, recorded its first undefeated season, 4–0, in 1896.

Georgia's first football team—1892. Coached by Dr. Charles Herty, a professor of chemistry, the Georgians routed Mercer 50–0 in the first game ever in the Deep South. Herty's boys lost their only other game that year, 10–0 to Auburn, inaugurating the South's oldest football rivalry.

In his only season at Georgia, Coach Charles A. Barnard had a 1–5 record in 1904, the solitary win being a victory in Macon over Florida Agricultural College of Lake City, Fla. Georgia newspaper accounts refer to UGA's victim as the University of Florida, but UF would not officially be established until 1906 with the consolidation of six institutions, including Florida Agricultural College, into a state university.

After the 1904 encounter, Georgia and Florida did not clash until 1915 in what the Gators consider the first game of the rivalry.

With a student body of 102, fledgling Florida fielded its first official football team under Coach Jack Forsythe in 1906. Playing on a base-ball field near the present-day site of Ben Hill Griffin Stadium at Florida Field, the Floridians beat Rollins, 6–0, in their first game ever and went on to a 5–3 record that year.

Forsythe's 1908 eleven was 5–2–1 and was the first UF team to be called the "Alligators."

Charles J. McCoy was hired as the UF coach in 1914 and logged a 5–2 campaign that year. McCoy was at the helm against Georgia in the 1915 game in a season in which Florida finished 4–3.

Charles Barnard was replaced as Georgia coach in 1905 by M. M.

Dickinson, who had coached the 1903 squad and was the first of four head coaches to lead Georgia from 1905 to 1910, when W. A. Cunningham was hired.

Cunningham, a gridiron star at Vanderbilt, was the first Georgia coach to give stability to the football program, molding the beginnings of its winning tradition. Georgia's first All-American, halfback Bob McWhorter, played on Cunningham's 1912 squad.

Cunningham's teams had winning seasons in four of his first five years as head coach going into the 1915 season and the first encounter between Florida and Georgia as state universities.

After the 1904 game, the burgeoning rivalry was an attraction on the order of a traveling circus looking for a home. The teams squared off four times in Athens, three times in Jacksonville, twice in Savannah, and once each in Gainesville and Tampa before settling in Jacksonville where their duels have been waged since 1933.

Year by year the game grew in importance, not only in the Southeastern Conference but in the nation as well. The series developed a reputation for its smash-mouth brand of football on the field and two-fisted, bourbon-laced partying in the stands.

By the late 1950s the game had evolved into such a gridiron bacchanalia that Bill Kastelz, sports editor of the *Florida Times-Union,* described it as the "world's largest outdoor cocktail party," a depiction unique to this football spectacle.

The revelry is bawdy, raucous and always unpredictable; but without the tradition born between the sidelines there would be no party. The fans' antics will never overshadow feats such as those of Don Gaffney passing the Gators to a last-minute victory in 1973 or Georgia back Charley Trippi's five touchdown performance in 1942.

This is the story of "Cannonball" Clyde Crabtree, Cy Grant, Dale Van Sickle, "Fireball" Frankie Sinkwich, Fran Tarkenton, Steve Spurrier, Walter "Tiger" Mayberry, and hundreds of other Dawgs and Gators whose exploits rank this rivalry, with Alabama-Auburn, Texas-Oklahoma, and South Carolina-Clemson, as one of the legendary pigskin bloodlettings in the South.

Acknowledgments

No BOOK SUCH AS *GLORY YARDS* IS PRO-
duced without the generosity and patience of many people.

Special thanks go to Julia Muller, chief librarian of the *Savannah News-Press,* and assistant librarian Sara Wright for their guidance, tolerance and good humor as I coursed through about 100 years of newspaper microfilm.

Joyce Dewsbury, archives coordinator for the University of Florida, was a tremendous help in finding suitable photos and filling in several gaps in the manuscript. The kind assistance of Roy Gatchell, keeper of the University of Georgia athletics archives and a Bulldog lineman for Coach Harry Mehre in 1935–1936, was immeasurable.

Claude Felton, Georgia sports information director, and Norm Carlson, Florida assistant athletic director—communications, along with their staffs, provided pieces of the rivalry's puzzle to make the picture complete. Mary Ellen Brooks of Hargrett Rare Book and Manuscript Library at UGA steered me off a wrong course and back on track in my photos hunt.

I'd also like to thank the staffs of the Duvall County Library in Jacksonville, the Georgia Southern University Library, the Savannah State College Library, the Chatham-Effingham Regional Library and the Georgia Historical Society. Thanks also to Traci Muller of the *Athens Banner-Herald* and to the library staffs of the *Tampa Tribune, Macon Telegraph, Augusta Chronicle* and the *Columbus Ledger.*

Swan Seiler Brannon has my gratitude for helping me over a hurdle in gathering material.

David T. Lock is the consummate Bulldog whose suggestions, exhaustive photo research help, encouragement, and parking prowess at the Gator Bowl were invaluable.

Steve Bisson, chief photographer for the *Savannah News-Press,* and *News-Press* executive sports editor Anthony Stastny, along with manuscript typist Kathy Vanatta, also have my everlasting thanks.

Nothing could have been accomplished without the support and direction of Larry Stone, president of Rutledge Hill Press, Ron

Pitkin, vice president, and their staff. I appreciate the opportunity y'all gave me.

Ultimate thanks go to my wife, Helen Pitts Smith, and my parents, Gordon and Willene Smith. And from the days of gutta-percha nose guards to yacht parties along the St. Johns River, who could forget almost a century's worth of football fans, sportswriters, and the hundreds of boys who wore the Orange and Blue or the Red and Black? Without them, this book would not have been possible.

Glory Yards

The 1904 Georgia team trounced Florida Agricultural College 52–0 in Macon. The Georgians of Coach Charles A. Barnard would not win another game that year. [Hargrett Collection, UGA Libraries]

— 1904 —

Georgia 52, Florida 0

"SONS OF GEORGIA AND FLORIDA ANXIOUSLY awaiting opening of game this afternoon," read the headline in *The Macon Telegraph* on Saturday, October 15, 1904.

"The sons of slug and tackle of the University of Georgia and the Florida State College of Lake City are awaiting anxiously and at the same time nervously, the opening of the gridiron battle," the article began.

Such was the tease for the opening skirmish of a vitriolic rivalry spawned in the Deep South's attraction to what many considered the brutish game of football.

In the autumn of 1904, the Russo-Japanese War raged on the far side of the world, and President Theodore Roosevelt was in the last days of his reelection campaign against Democratic challenger Alton B. Parker.

Thirty-nine years after the Civil War, America was at peace and the gridiron sport was growing in popularity from the Southland to the Pacific shore.

Kickoff at Macon's Central City Park was set for 3 p.m., and a large crowd was expected to turn out for the proceedings.

Charles A. Barnard was opening his first and only season as Georgia's coach. Barnard, a top athlete at Harvard, had been hired to install a strong running game between the tackles, similar to the "Harvard Power System," at Georgia.

The team from the Florida Agricultural College in Lake City had played Auburn and Alabama and had lost by a combined score of 73–0. The state land grant school would be one of six state institutions incorporated to form the University of Florida in 1906. But to the Georgia newspapers and fans, their opponents were from the "University of Florida."

The Floridians were on a suicidal two-game tour of the Peach

17

State. After facing Georgia in Macon on Saturday, they would leave for Atlanta for a Monday afternoon game against Georgia Tech in Piedmont Park.

Georgia was opening its 13th season of gridiron competition and coming off a 3–4 record under Coach M. M. Dickinson in 1903. The Red and Black were heavy favorites in the game.

"Georgians do not expect much opposition from the Florida team," the *Savannah Morning News* said on game day, but the *Telegraph* predicted a tough contest. "The men from the everglades are in as good if not a better condition than the Georgia boys," the newspaper said, but was quick to add that Barnard's squad would be ready: "The (Georgia) players of the first team are all in the pink of condition and no cripples will be in the game."

Fullback and team captain Joseph I. Killorin, Georgia's best weapon, was cautious in assessing the clash. "We will play a fast game and hope to win," he told the *Telegraph*. "Our team realizes the fact that we have strong opponents."

An article by the Georgia coach Barnard, headlined "American Game of Football," appeared in the *Telegraph* on game day and explained the rules of the sport.

The teams arrived in Macon on Friday night and headed to the Plaza Hotel where they turned in early. "Both elevens look husky and are heavy enough to stand many hard knocks that are bound to happen this afternoon," the October 15 *Telegraph* said.

Georgia team manager J. M. Hill had been in Macon several days supervising the erection of goal posts and helping laborers mark off the playing field with lime.

The teams agreed to play two 15-minute halves, and Georgia came out to kick off into the wind after the Floridians won the coin toss. About 700 fans turned out.

Georgia center C. B. Wray kicked off to open the game (and the series, according to Georgia records), although some accounts state the honor went to left end Arthur R. Sullivan. On its first possession, Florida, wearing blue and white, tried unsuccessfully to run through the line and elected to punt on third down.

Left halfback Charles Cox rambled for 35 yards on Georgia's first possession, but a Bulldog fumble was recovered by the Floridians around their 15. Georgia held again, taking over on the enemy 25 after a short punt. Right halfback John Brown then cut outside for 10 and Killorin bulled to the 8. Cox ran into the Georgia record book moments later when he swept end for a touchdown (five points under the rules of the day). The Athenians had their first score with 3:30 gone in the contest.

Sullivan missed the extra point, but he would have plenty of work throughout the afternoon. In the rules of early 1900s football, a team that surrendered a score kicked to the opponent. The squads also switched ends of the field.

On the ensuing Florida kickoff, Georgia quarterback Harry E. Woodruff fielded the "hurdling and twisting" ball at his own 20 and headed upfield. "Aided by splendid interference" the 125-pound Cracker raced 80 yards for Georgia's second touchdown. Several newspapers credited Woodruff with a 90-yard scamper, the second-longest kickoff return in Georgia history. Sullivan's try for goal was good and Georgia led 11–0.

"So it goes on through the game—only faster and faster with Georgia," the *Atlanta Constitution* said.

Georgia scored two more touchdowns in the first half, including a 20-yard run by Cox, and five in the second half. Sullivan converted seven of nine extra points and Georgia won the mismatch, 52–0. On the day, Cox scored four touchdowns, Killorin three and Woodruff two.

"Florida did not attempt an end run, but seemed content to lose in attempts at gains through the line," The *Augusta Chronicle* reported.

The *Atlanta Constitution*'s five-paragraph account in the Sunday paper took on a biting tone. "With a rush the giants of Georgia went down the field (Saturday) afternoon against the little men of Florida . . . the laddies from the Land of Flowers drank the dust of defeat to the tune of 'Nothing—nothing—nothing doing.'"

Including the team line-ups, the game received only a six-paragraph mention at the bottom of the Sunday *Morning News* sports page. The story was overshadowed by the Naval Academy's 10–9 victory over Princeton, the sale of a race horse, and an article headlined "Male Pelvic Diseases Readily Cured."

Florida's battered squad now headed to Atlanta for the Monday tussle with undefeated Georgia Tech. Emotions already ran deep in the Georgia-Georgia Tech rivalry as the Atlantans took aim on UGA's margin of victory over the Florida team. Tech came out in shiny new yellow sweaters, but both elevens fumbled repeatedly in the early going. Tech soon settled down and coasted to a 77–0 win.

According to a *Constitution* account, M. O. Bridges, the Florida captain, was asked to compare Georgia and Georgia Tech. "Why," said he, "Tech could beat her easy. Georgia has a good set of backs, but a line which is too slow for football," the newspaper reported. Florida Agricultural College closed its scoreless season with a 23–0 loss to the Florida State College in Tallahassee.

Georgia headed next to Clemson, where the Tigers were a much more formidable opponent than Florida. The Georgians bowed, 10–0, a week after the massacre in Macon.

The Florida game would be the highlight of the 1904 season for Georgia. Barnard's team lost to South Carolina, Alabama, Georgia Tech, and closed the season with a 17–5 defeat by Auburn.

The Georgia win in Macon is not mentioned in any University of Florida football records which date from the school's establishment in 1906.

Georgia, however, lists the game as the 34th gridiron win in its history. More than 11 years would pass before the University of Florida Alligators faced Georgia for the first time.

And the dispute over 1904 hasn't been settled today any more than the question of which side will have bragging rights after the next Florida-Georgia war.

Georgia: Wray, *center;* Moore, *right guard;* Black, *left guard;* Ritchie, *right tackle;* Arnold, *left tackle;* Hoke, *right end;* Sullivan, *left end;* Woodruff, *quarterback;* Cox, *left halfback;* Brown, *right halfback;* Killorin, *fullback*

Florida: Keene, *center;* T. C. McGuire, *right guard;* Bratton, *left guard;* Rowlett, *right tackle;* Cason, *left tackle;* Dougherty, *right end;* Zelius, *left end;* McDowell, *quarterback;* Bridges, *right halfback;* Cason, *left halfback;* C. H. McGuire, *fullback*

— 1915 —

Georgia 37, Florida 0

JACKSONVILLE WAS EXPERIENCING ITS FIRST Georgia-Florida football frenzy in the days before the big game on November 6, 1915.

"Gridiron Gladiators Ready for Struggle for Pigskin Honors" glared the game day headline in the *Florida Times-Union* proclaiming the first official matchup between the University of Florida Alligators and the "Crackers" of the University of Georgia.

The Peach State gang would be playing its first game ever in Florida before the largest crowd to gather for a football contest in Jacksonville.

"Today promises to mark an epoch in the history of football in this city," the *Times-Union* added.

The nation was watching the ever-spreading war in Europe as well as developments along the Texas-Mexico border where Army units were on alert against Pancho Villa's raiders.

A sports contest between two small southern schools seemed dwarfed in importance compared to the disturbing world events. In addition, there were fans on both sides who had forgotten or not even heard of the gridiron action 11 years earlier in Macon between Georgia and Florida Agricultural College.

Both schools were members of the Southeastern Intercollegiate Athletic Association, the forerunner of the Southeastern Conference. Even then Jacksonville officials were savoring the promise of an annual football extravaganza.

"The dope indicates nothing except that the game will be hard and bitterly fought with either team a possible winner," the *Times-Union* said. "It is hoped that the attendance and spirit manifested at the game will be sufficient to warrant the staging of an annual Georgia-Florida game as the big football event of each season in Jacksonville."

Florida, 1–2 under second-year coach Charles J. McCoy, began the

21

The 1915 Florida team of Coach Charles McCoy was beaten 37–0 by Georgia in the first game between the universities. Fittingly, it was played in Jacksonville. The Alligators went 4–3 in 1915. [UF Archives]

1915 season with 7–0 losses at Auburn and to Sewanee at Jacksonville. The week before the Georgia game, the Alligators chewed Southern, 45–0, in Gainesville.

Many Florida followers knew that Georgia coach W. A. Cunningham's first losing season had been the previous year, at 3–5–1. They also knew Georgia had rebounded strongly in the first part of its 1915 schedule.

Georgia massacred lesser competition in Newberry and Dahlonega before a 6–6 tie with Chattanooga. They beat The Citadel before losing on successive weekends in Athens to Virginia and Auburn.

A Monday report in the *Atlanta Constitution* surely would have been posted in the Florida locker room had it been modern times: "When the University of Georgia football authorities were arranging their football schedule for this season they picked out Florida as a pretty soft thing to put in between their Auburn and Tech games . . . "

Among the Georgia fans attending the game were about 40 members of the University Club of Savannah who left Friday night on a steamship bound for Jacksonville. Other Savannahians headed south by train. "The party will carry along megaphones and other 'rooting' paraphernalia," the *Savannah Morning News* said.

The 20-man Georgia team, arriving by train Friday night, was escorted to their hotel in a motor car cavalcade. Virtually the entire Florida student body, and the Alligators team, arrived in town on Saturday morning aboard the "Florida Special," which trundled in from Gainesville.

The 1915 UGA football squad downed Florida 37–0 in the historic first meeting between the universities in Jacksonville. The Georgians compiled a 5–2–2 mark that year. [Hargrett Collection, UGA Libraries]

Kickoff was set for 3 p.m. at Barrs Field on "an ideal June day in November," the *Athens Banner* said. Many businesses, which had been displaying red and black or orange and blue displays, closed for the day after city fathers declared a half holiday for the afternoon. A "monstrous" automobile parade rattled through the streets with cars decorated in the school colors of Florida or Georgia. The procession snaked north on Durkee Avenue to the playing grounds.

At the field, automobiles were parked to give spectators a view from the end zones and "the sidelines were packed with a solid line of humanity."

Florida won the coin toss and elected to defend the south goal. Georgia center and team captain John Henderson kicked off, but the ball careened out of bounds and the Crackers had to boot it again. The kick was returned by Florida left halfback Harry W. Thompson and the historic game was underway. In quick order, the "Gators," as some reporters already were calling them, were stacked up by Georgia's defense and had to punt.

After a 40-yard Florida kick, Georgia's first offensive series proved just as ineffective. Following an incomplete pass and a five-yard penalty, the Crackers punted back to the Gators.

It was here that Florida quarterback A.W. Ramsdell provided the first of countless spectacular efforts in the rivalry. Ramsdell galloped 45 yards before being pulled down.

Five minutes into the contest, Florida was poised for a score. But the threat flickered out shortly afterward when a Cracker intercepted a pass and returned it 20 yards.

The Gators were outweighed but played feisty defense through the opening quarter.

The Crackers mounted the next serious thrust. After a 20-yard Florida punt, Georgia quarterback David F. Paddock sped around left end for 30 yards. The Alligators foiled a pass attempt and the UGA drive stalled. Florida then failed on downs and kicked to Georgia halfback E. H. Dezendorf, who returned the punt 30 yards. The first quarter ended with the Crackers hunkered on the UF 25.

As the game entered the second period, "the superior weight of the boys from the Empire State of the South began to tell" on the Floridians, the *Morning News* said. The *Constitution* agreed, stating "the game was put in the refrigerator early in that stanza."

Paddock spun loose for 20 yards to the Florida 5. The snap was fumbled on the next play, but Georgia right tackle Bright McConnell grabbed the spheroid and lugged it in for the touchdown. Henderson's kick flew off the mark but Georgia owned a 6–0 lead.

Center John G. Henderson of Ocilla was the captain of the UGA team that beat Florida in 1915. [Hargrett Collection, UGA Libraries]

Despite a 10-yard run by Ramsdell to midfield on Florida's next series, the Gators stalled and were forced to kick. Another exchange of punts and a trade of fumbles followed, with Florida still showing plenty of fight. Indeed, the Gators came up with an interception but lost a fumble deep in their own territory moments later.

Georgia went for the throat with Paddock gaining 10 around right end. The Crackers were penalized five yards before Paddock knifed over left tackle for six yards and a touchdown. Henderson's kick made it 13–0 Georgia.

The third quarter began with Florida unable to advance. With the Gators in punt formation, a wave of Crackers stormed through to block the kick. A series of end runs propelled the Georgians to the UF 15. Dezendorf then darted around left end for the score. Henderson again misfired but UGA led 19–0.

A determined Florida ran for 10 before punting again. The Georgians were using their size advantage to push the Gators back,

Florida center J. R. "Rex" Farrior was a defensive standout in 1915. [UF Archives]

particularly on line plunges. Georgia then drove 25 yards to the Florida 10, where right end Charles Thompson took it over from there. Georgia was now up 25–0, still in the third period.

The Alligators again were stymied on offense, unable to budge the Athenians, and had to punt. From their 30, the Crackers wasted no time in putting up more points. Dezendorf passed to Thompson for 30 yards, but the Georgia end didn't stop there. Finding himself in a "clear field," Thompson raced the remaining 40 yards to pay dirt. Henderson's kick made it Georgia, 32–0.

As late afternoon fell upon Jacksonville, the fourth quarter was cut to eight minutes due to darkness. The lopsided score may have had some bearing on the decision. Most of Cunningham's bench played the final period.

Florida, backed up near its own goal, decided to run a "trick play." The Georgians weren't fooled and swarmed the ball carrier in the end zone for a safety. Georgia, 34–0.

In the last minute of action, John S. Coleman dropkicked a field goal to make the final margin 37–0.

"Georgia, with its beef and brawn, fairly shattered the young 'Gators," the *Times-Union* said. "From the first bleat of the whistle . . . the Georgians were at the wheel of victory . . . "

The play of quarterback A. W. Ramsdell was the only bright spot for Florida.

The teams and alumni from both schools got together on more civilized terms later at a dinner and smoker on the 10th floor of the Seminole Hotel.

Georgia finished its year with a scoreless deadlock against Georgia Tech followed by a triumph over Clemson in Athens to go 5–2–2. Left tackle Tom Thrash garnered all-conference honors for Georgia.

Florida regrouped from the Georgia loss to beat The Citadel, Tulane, and Mercer, for a 4–3 record.

Despite the one-sided score in Jacksonville, a current of excitement pulsed from the north Georgia mountains to Florida Bay. Victors' bragging rights or the bile of defeat for Georgia or Florida would energize millions for years to come.

Scoring:

Georgia	0	13	19	5	—	37
Florida	0	0	0	0	—	0

UGA	TD	McConnell, 5-yard run (kick failed)
UGA	TD	Paddock, 6-yard run (Henderson kick)
UGA	TD	Dezendorf, 15-yard run (kick failed)
UGA	TD	Thompson, 10-yard run (kick failed)
UGA	TD	Thompson, 70-yard pass from Dezendorf (Henderson kick)
UGA	Safety	UF player tackled in UF end zone
UGA	FG	Coleman, dropkick

Georgia: Henderson, Coleman, *center;* Culbreath, *right guard;* McConnell, *right tackle;* Thompson, *right end;* Conyers, *left guard;* Thrash, *left tackle;* Garrard, *left end;* Paddock, *quarterback;* Dezendorf, *right halfback;* Powell, *left halfback;* Neville, *fullback*

Florida: Farrior, *center;* Robles, *right guard;* Golsby, *right tackle;* Lovell, *right end;* Dowling, *left guard;* Lotspiech, *left tackle;* Henderson, *left end;* Ramsdell, *quarterback;* Sparkman, *right halfback;* Thompson, *left halfback;* Fuller, *fullback*

— 1916 —

Georgia 21, Florida 0

FLORIDA WAS EXPECTED TO CLOUD THE AIR with passes when the Alligators played favored Georgia in their first game ever in Athens on Saturday, October 14, 1916.

Georgia, 2–0, was coming off a 26–0 win over Clemson at Anderson, S.C. Coach W. A. Cunningham's team had trimmed The Citadel, 6–0, in its season premiere.

Reports out of Athens contended that several Georgia regulars injured at Clemson would not play against the Alligators.

Star halfback James Reynolds, right guard Bright McConnell, and right halfback W. P. Donnelly, the UGA punter, would be sorely missed, but the Georgians were expected to win.

Florida was opening its season against Georgia and third-year coach Charles McCoy was trying a new tactic in hopes of giving his players an advantage.

"The Alligator athletic authorities have eliminated the so-called practice games and the result of this system will be watched with interest," the Savannah *Morning News* reported. The Boston Red Sox' final victory over the Brooklyn Dodgers in the fifth game of the World Series the previous Thursday dominated the sports pages. In Europe, Allied and German armies embraced in a death grasp along the Somme River.

Cunningham believed the Alligators would go to the forward pass early and often and drilled his men hard to defend against it.

In Gainesville Friday afternoon, the University of Florida student body gathered at Flemming Field to cheer their Gators in a last practice before boarding a train for Georgia.

With the Florida band leading the way, the students escorted McCoy and his 20 Gators to the depot. Amid music and cheers, team captain and fullback J. R. Farrior Jr. made a brief but emotional speech, closing as the train chugged away from the station.

Missing from the Gators squad was quarterback Wakefield Ramsdell, a star in the previous year's loss to Georgia, who had broken a leg in a spring baseball game against Auburn and was still on the mend.

To Georgia's surprise, Florida went to its running game early. The rushes of Farrior and halfbacks F. Hatcher and R. B. Wilson caught UGA off guard. Adding to Georgia's problems, center W. W. Garmany shattered a knee on the game's first play and had to be taken from the field. Still, with the exception of a few long end runs, the Alligators couldn't dent the Georgia defense.

Backs W. H. McLaws, John Coleman, and Walter Neville, along with quarterback E. H. Dezendorf, then pounded to the Florida 10, but a Georgia fumble gave the ball back to Florida.

The Gators early on "presented a defense that was an enigma to the Georgians," the *Athens Banner* said.

The Gators could not advance and punted several times to shove Georgia out of scoring range. Georgia, relying on its runners, muscled "to the shadow of the goal posts" in the second quarter, but Florida held on downs and took possession.

Florida had stunned the Crackers with its rushing game and, on defense, had successfully blunted two UGA marches to enter the intermission heartened by a scoreless half.

"So desperate did the situation become for Georgia that Reynolds and McConnell, both suffering dislocated shoulders, were sent into the game," the *Atlanta Constitution* said. Donnelly, his left hand in a plaster cast, also entered the contest in the third quarter.

With the home crowd screaming, Georgia answered the call after a Florida punt to midfield. Reynolds swept end for 20 yards but the play was called back on a holding penalty. The setback for Georgia was only temporary.

The hard-nosed running of Neville, Reynolds and McLaws pushed the Alligators back. A pass from Reynolds to Dezendorf contributed to the best Georgia drive of the afternoon. Near the Florida goal, Neville smashed through for a touchdown as the stubborn Florida defense broke for the first time. Dezendorf's kick made it 7–0 Georgia.

On the first play of the last quarter, McLaws stomped over left tackle and ran free in the Florida secondary. No Gator could bring him down as he ripped to the enemy end zone. Dezendorf converted to make it 14–0, and Georgia finally had control of the fight.

Late in the game, on a punt from Donnelly, a Floridian fumbled at

Florida coach Charles J. McCoy was the victim of Georgia wins in 1915 and 1916. During his UF tenure from 1914 to 1916, McCoy posted a 9–10 mark, including an 0–5 record in 1916. [UF Archives]

the Florida 10. Georgia team captain Thrash grabbed the ball and lumbered into the UF end zone. Minutes later, the referee's whistle sounded, signaling time had expired.

In what had been a Georgia tradition since the 1890s, students took turns ringing the university chapel bell signifying a Georgia victory.

Florida came to town "with determination to defeat the University of Georgia. . . . " the *Athens Banner* said. "In her supremest effort she failed to accomplish this but if it is any consolation to the Floridians that they made Georgia exert herself to the extent of putting in three players who were out on account of shattered joints then they should see in their defeat much cause for rejoicing."

Georgia beat Virginia the week after Florida but lost its next two games to Navy and Auburn. Wins over Furman and Alabama were sandwiched around a 21–0 loss to Georgia Tech in Athens.

Florida'a misfortune would continue through a winless season. McCoy ended his Florida coaching career 0–2 against Georgia, while Cunningham was 2–0 in facing the Alligators.

Scoring:

Georgia	0	0	7	14 —	21
Florida	0	0	0	0 —	0

UGA   TD   Neville run, yardage unavailable (Dezendorf PAT)
UGA   TD   McLaws, 35-yard run (Dezendorf PAT)
UGA   TD   Thrash, 10-yard return of fumbled punt (Dezendorf PAT)

Georgia: Pew, *left end;* Thrash, *left tackle;* Ferguson, *left guard;* Garmany, *center;* Beasley, *right guard;* Wingate, *right tackle;* Tate, *right end;* Dezendorf, *quarterback;* Coleman, *left halfback;* McLaws, *right halfback;* Neville, *fullback* Substitutes: J. Reynolds, O. Reynolds, Fox, McConnell, Donnelly, Mc-Michael, Ferst, Petree

Florida: Henderson, *left end;* Baker, *left tackle;* O. C. DeVane, *left guard;* Robles, *center;* Golsby, *right guard;* Perry, *right tackle;* Wilkinson, *right end;* Fuller, *quarterback;* Wilson, *left halfback;* Hatcher, *right halfback;* Farrior, *fullback*

— 1919 —

Georgia 16, Florida 0

WITH AMERICA'S ENTRY INTO WORLD WAR I, Georgia canceled its football seasons in 1917 and 1918.

Florida played a six-game schedule in 1917, going 2–4, and had only one game in 1918, losing 14–2 to the doughboys of Camp Johnson.

Tampa was the fourth city to host the Florida-Georgia contest when the teams and their followers reassembled on Saturday, October 25, 1919.

Third-year coach A. L. Busser's Alligators were undefeated entering the fray, having bested Georgia A&M and Mercer in Gainesville.

W. A. Cunningham, in his eighth and last season as Georgia coach, had fielded a squad that was also unbeaten and had not been scored on in its three wins over The Citadel, South Carolina, and Sewanee, all in Athens.

Standout center A. M. "Bum" Day was the pillar of the Crackers' rugged line that averaged 190 pounds per man. Georgia's quarterback, Joe Barchan, was a native Florida son, a graduate of Duval High School in Jacksonville.

Injured halfbacks J. T. Reynolds and H. V. Hartley would miss the Florida contest as would head coach Cunningham, who had tripped and fallen while crossing a railroad track several days earlier, sustaining three cracked ribs. In his absence, the Georgia team would be guided by assistant coach H. J. Stegeman.

Billed by many as one of the strongest Florida squads to date, the Alligators featured right halfback and team captain Jimmy "Tammany" Sparkman of Hillsborough, considered one of the finest defensive players in the South.

"Florida fans are looking for Tammany to show the Crackers that the Peninsula state turns out some stars too," the *Tampa Morning Tribune* said.

Both teams arrived in Tampa by train and settled into the De Soto Hotel. The squads and their bands were honored with a parade through the city on Saturday morning then taken on a car tour of Tampa's cigar factories, shipyards and other points of interest. The UF band played "Florida's new war song so Tampa folks can get used to the stirring tune," the *Morning Tribune* reported.

The game was played on a hot afternoon before about 3,000 at Tampa's Plant Field. Many of the spectators sat in cars lining sections of the sidelines and end zones.

At 3:30 p.m., Georgia's Day kicked off to Florida fullback J. F. Merrin who returned it 10 yards to start the action. An end run by Sparkman was stopped cold, but successive runs by quarterback Rondo Hatton, halfback C. A. Anderson and right tackle E. B. Wuthrich gave Florida a first down. The drive died when Anderson was thrown for a seven-yard loss and Georgia took over on downs.

Florida got an immediate break when Crackers quarterback Barchan fumbled on Georgia's first play from scrimmage and Florida right end Gordon Clemons pounced on the ball.

Stymied by a 15-yard penalty and a fumble by Sparkman which UF recovered, Florida punted back to Georgia. Line plunges by Crackers left halfback E. S. Rothe and Barchan gained a Georgia first down, but the "Gators," as some reporters had dubbed the Floridians, held again. Georgia end D. A. Collings Jr. punted 35 yards to Sparkman who dodged for a five-yard return to the UF 30, where he was shaken up and sidelined for the rest of the half.

The quarter ended with Florida on its 25 after a 15-yard holding call negated runs by Leo Wilson, Sparkman's substitute, and fullback Merrin.

Florida's Hatton punted to begin the second period, the ball going out of bounds at the Georgia 35. Georgia's Rothe fumbled on the first play and Hatton recovered. Short runs by Anderson, Wilson and Hatton put Florida at the Georgia 25 and "the Gator rooters went wild."

But on the next play, Merrin dropped the ball and Georgia left tackle and team captain Artie Pew fell on it to end the threat. Georgia halfback James P. "Buck" Cheves was then hauled down for a loss, and fullback Ed Munn fumbled the ball away to Florida's Anderson. The Crackers had lost their third fumble of the half and put Florida in scoring position for the second time. But the Athenians regrouped, stacking up two Gator line runs for little gain. A forward pass fell incomplete and Georgia took possession on downs.

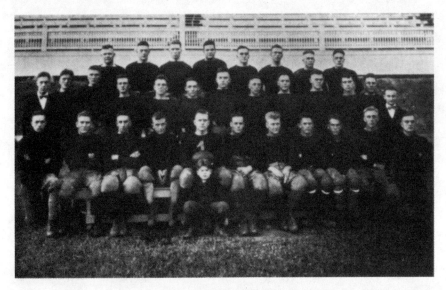

Georgia's 1919 team beat Florida 16–0 in Tampa but finished with a disappointing 4–2–3 record after starting the season 4–0. [Hargrett Collection, UGA Libraries]

A *Morning Tribune* reporter saw the errant pass as the game's turning point: "The passing of the ball marked the end to Florida's superiority," he wrote in his game account. "Up to that time the 'Gators had a clear edge on the Georgia eleven, but after the middle of the second period the Crackers were in the ascendancy."

A 25-yard broken field jaunt by Cheves highlighted the remainder of the quarter and the half expired with the Crackers in possession at the Florida 34.

Taking the second half kickoff, Georgia appeared determined to break the scoreless marathon. After Rothe gained a yard, Cheves skirted left end for 12, then again for 30 yards to the Florida 22.

Line punches by Rothe and senior fullback Neville, along with an end run by Cheves, pushed the Gators back closer to their goal. Neville tore into the line and the ball slipped from his grip. For a brief moment it appeared the Crackers had squandered another scoring chance but Georgia's Collings covered the ball. A 5-yard penalty moved Georgia to the UF 5. Cheves was pulled down for no gain, but Rothe found room around left end and darted in for the touchdown. Collings missed the extra point try but Florida was called for offsides. Again the kick failed, but Georgia led 6–0.

Substitute Florida back B. G. Anderson was tumbled for a disastrous 20-yard loss trying to avoid a tackler "who should have been an easy mark for the interference."

Hatton fell back to punt and drove the ball to Georgia's Joe Barchan at midfield. Following his blockers, the 158-pound quarterback, intent on atoning for his earlier fumble, ripped down the field. "With the precision of clock work the Cracker interference stretched eight Florida players flat on the field," the *Morning Tribune* reported. "Barchan dodged only one man . . . and the two interferers who charged down the field with him swept aside two other 'Gators."

Barchan's touchdown and a successful conversion by Collings put Georgia up 13–0 late in the third quarter and sent the Red and Black fans into hysterics.

As the third period ended, Georgia's Rothe was leveled for a 7-yard loss by a fierce tackle that put him out of the game.

Early in the final period, Collings rolled a punt to the Florida 5. Hatton promptly quick-kicked 35 yards, and the Crackers had the ball at the Gators 40. Three runs netted only a few inches against the weary but tough Floridians. On fourth down, Collings lifted a dropkick from the 40. The ball fell over the Florida goalpost for a field goal and a 16–0 Georgia advantage.

Coach A. L. Busser was 0–1 against UGA while at the Florida helm from 1917 to 1919, losing 16–0 in Tampa in 1919. The series was cancelled in 1917 and 1918 due to World War I. [UF Archives]

Florida halfback and team captain J. K. "Tammany" Sparkman fought in France and returned to play for UF after the war. The Alligators could not defeat Georgia in 1919 but finished 5–3. [UF Archives]

Sparkman, recovered from his first half injury, returned the kickoff 30 yards for Florida, but there would be no more scoring. Georgia faithful reveled in their fourth shutout victory over Florida in as many cities.

For the day, Florida threw the only four passes, all incomplete. The Georgians gained 123 yards in 37 rushes to 38 yards on 29 carries for Florida. The Gators also lost 21 yards trying end runs.

Florida fans took pride in the tenacity of their team's defense and the hard play of 210-pound center Carl E. "Tootie" Perry who matched up well against Day, the Georgia premier center, throughout the game.

"The Florida center, matched against an All-American rival and outplaying him was easily along with Cheeves *(sic)* the star of the game," the *Savannah Morning News* said.

Florida closed the year with road losses to Southern and Tulane, home victories over Stetson and Oglethorpe, and a win against South Carolina in Columbia for a 5–3 record in Busser's last season.

Georgia followed its Florida win with a loss to Auburn, consecutive 7-7 ties with Virginia and Tulane, a 6–0 defeat to Alabama, and a scoreless affair with Clemson to finish at 4–2–3. Georgia end Owen Reynolds was named all-conference.

Cunningham, an Army veteran, left Georgia to rejoin the service and became a career officer. He had winning seasons in seven of his eight years as head coach including a 3–0 record against Florida.

Scoring:

Georgia	0	0	13	3	— 16
Florida	0	0	0	0	— 0

UGA	TD	Rothe, 5-yard run (PAT failed)
UGA	TD	Barchan, 50-yard punt return (Collings kick)
UGA	FG	Collings, 40 yards

Georgia: Day, *center;* Whelchel, *right guard;* Vandiver, *left guard;* Rigdon, *right tackle;* Pew, *left tackle;* O. Reynolds, *right end;* Collings, *left end;* Barchan, *quarterback;* Cheves, *right halfback;* Rothe, *left halfback;* Munn, *fullback*
Substitutions: T. McWhorter for Cheves; Neville for Munn; Highsmith for Whelchel; McWhorter for Rothe

Florida: Perry, *center;* Connell, *right guard;* Baker, *left guard;* Wuthrich, *right tackle;* Golsby, *left tackle;* Clemons, *right end;* Thomas, *left end;* Hatton, *quarterback;* Sparkman, *right halfback;* C. Anderson, *left halfback;* Merrin, *fullback*
Substitutions: Wilson for Sparkman; B. Anderson for Hatton; Ford for Connell; Norton for Baker; Olson for Merrin; Baker for Golsby; Webb for Perry; Warner for Wuthrich

— 1920 —

Georgia 56, Florida 0

THE RUCKUS IN ATHENS ON NOVEMBER 13, 1920, was a meeting of first-year head coaches during a season in which the Georgians became the "Bulldogs."

On the national front 12 days earlier, Ohio newspaper publisher Warren G. Harding rode an avalanche of votes to the presidency.

Guided by Coach William Kline, Florida was visiting Athens for the second time to play Georgia on its home field.

The 1920 Gators had shut out four opponents en route to a 5–1 record (including a game won by forfeit).

But Florida was about to take a step up in competition as they arrived to meet the undefeated, once-tied team of Coach Herman J. Stegeman. Georgia had shutout wins over The Citadel, South Carolina, Furman, and Auburn, while fighting Virginia to a scoreless tie in Charlottesville. The only scoring blemish on Georgia's formidable season record was an Oglethorpe field goal posted in a 27–3 UGA win.

Writers for the *Atlanta Journal* and *Atlanta Constitution* began referring to the Georgia team as Bulldogs during this period, and the nickname caught on. Georgia had adopted Wildcats as its moniker earlier in the season, but the press and popular opinion swayed the school to change to Bulldogs after the tough Virginia game.

Stegeman played for the legendary Amos Alonzo Stagg at the University of Chicago in 1913–14 before coming to Georgia as an assistant coach under W. A. Cunningham. When Cunningham injured himself in a fall the previous year, it was Stegeman who stepped in against Florida, coming away with the 16–0 victory in Tampa.

Aggravating Florida's problems was the fact that the Georgia game would be the Gators' third contest in a week. The Gators lost to Tulane the previous Saturday then defeated Stetson in Gainesville on Thursday before boarding a train for Athens.

The 1920 Alligators ran into a buzz saw in Florida's second trip to Athens, losing 56–0 to a UGA squad that went 8–0–1 and won the Southern Intercollegiate Athletic Association Championship. [UF Archives]

"The Gators are reported to outweigh the Red and Black, but have not made the showing that Georgia has," the *Savannah Morning News* said, adding that the visitors "are hardly expected to be at their best" after their grueling week.

The 17-man Florida squad arrived in the "Classic City" by train about noon on Friday and held an afternoon practice at Sanford Field. Averaging about 190 pounds per man on the line, the Gators were bigger than Georgia. Their leviathan was 225-pound center Carl "Tootie" Perry who had such an outstanding game in the loss to Georgia the previous year. All-conference end Owen Reynolds was Georgia's stalwart.

A crowd estimated at about 5,000 descended on Sanford Field to see if the favored Georgians could hold off the visitors.

Once underway, the game was never really in doubt. Behind their huge line, Florida's fast backs figured to get some yardage, but the Georgia defenders assumed immediate control, firing through to drop the Gators for losses.

On offense, Georgia's line was just as effective, opening holes for quarterback Sheldon Fitts, halfbacks Collings and Hugh Hartley, and fullback W. R. Echols.

Still, it was the defense that put up Georgia's first points. With Florida backed against its goal, quarterback C. A. Anderson dropped

Georgia tackle Artie Pew (left) *captained UGA to a win over Florida in 1919, and center A. M. "Bum" Day* (right) *did the same in 1920. Both earned all-conference honors in 1920.* [Hargrett Collection, UGA Libraries]

back to punt. At the snap, Bulldog right end Paige Bennett stormed through to block and recover the kick for a touchdown.

On the first play of the second quarter, with Georgia knocking on the Florida 7-yard line, Hartley ripped off tackle and raced over the goal line. Pew's kick made it 14–0, Georgia.

Minutes later, the Bulldogs were marching again. Fitts made a fine 20-yard run over tackle before being brought down near the enemy goal. Echols lugged it in from there and Georgia upped the margin to 21–0.

Georgia defenders charged into the Florida backfield time and again, putting immense pressure on the Gators. The rush was so great that Anderson had two more punts blocked with Georgia recovering both of them. When he did manage to get the ball away, the kicks averaged only about 20 yards, giving the Bulldogs good field position each time.

When Fitts scored to make it 28–0 with Pew's conversion, the game was close to being out of hand . . . and it was only in the second period.

Reserve halfback Sam Boney then banged over from the 4 for

Georgia's fourth touchdown of the quarter, increasing the runaway to 35–0 Georgia at halftime.

Stegeman put in his reserves to start the second half, but there was no noticeable letdown in the Georgians' play on either side of the ball.

The score mounted to 49–0 through three quarters before Collings returned to action and rambled for the only touchdown of the last period. Left tackle Joe Bennett's third successive conversion made the final tally 56–0.

"The game was too one-sided to be interesting," the *Morning News* said.

Georgia center A. M. "Bum" Day and tackle Artie Pew were among the standouts on defense, while Echols' line runs and two-touchdown performances by Fitts and Boney headlined Georgia's offensive show.

"Fitts ran the team in true Napoleonic style using the most masterful field generalship," the *Constitution* said. "While the dope has been favoring the Red and Black for the contest, no one expected such an avalanche of touchdowns."

The clanging of the chapel bell reverberated across the campus, ringing out the news of the Crackers' triumph.

C. E. "Tootie" Perry was the monster of Florida's linemen but could not stem the Georgia tide in 1916, 1919, 1920. [UF Archives]

End Owen Reynolds helped Georgia to a 56–0 waltz over the Alligators at Sanford Field in 1920. He and teammates "Bum" Day and Artie Pew were all-conference selections that year. [Hargrett Collection, UGA Libraries]

Florida ended the year 6–3–1 with another win over Stetson and a loss to Oglethorpe.

After the Florida win, Georgia beat Alabama, 21–14, and dismantled Clemson, 55–0, in Athens for an 8–0–1 mark that was good enough to win the Southern Intercollegiate Athletic Association championship.

Georgia end Owen Reynolds, center Day and tackle Artie Pew won All-SIAA honors, Reynolds for the second year in a row.

The new Bulldogs also were ranked ninth in the final postseason polls, the first time either Georgia or Florida had been rated in the nation's top 10.

A month after the Florida game, Georgia and Florida were among the larger SIAA schools to reorganize as the Southern Conference with Dr. S. V. Sanford of Georgia elected as the conference's first president.

Action between Georgia and Florida in the 1920s [UF Archives]

For the next five years, the two schools would wage their gridiron jousts against other opponents. But the seeds of an enduring rivalry had been sown on cleat-torn fields in Macon, Athens, Tampa and Jacksonville.

Scoring:

Georgia	7	28	14	7	—	56
Florida	0	0	0	0	—	0

UGA	TD	P. Bennett, blocked punt in end zone (Pew kick)
UGA	TD	Hartley, 7-yard run (Pew kick)
UGA	TD	Echols run, yardage unavailable (Pew kick)
UGA	TD	Fitts run, yardage unavailable (Pew kick)
UGA	TD	Boney, 4-yard run (Pew kick)
UGA	TD	Fitts run, yardage unavailable (J. Bennett kick)
UGA	TD	Boney run, yardage unavailable (J. Bennett kick)
UGA	TD	Collings run, yardage unavailable (J. Bennett kick)

Georgia: Reynolds, *left end;* J. Bennett, *left tackle;* Whelchel, *left guard;* Day, *center;* Vandiver, *right guard;* Pew, *right tackle;* P. Bennett, *right end;* Fitts, *quarterback;* Collings, *left halfback;* Hartley, Boney, *right halfback;* Echols, *fullback*

Florida: Swanson, *left end;* Baker, *left tackle;* Otto, *left guard;* Perry, *center;* Hodges, *right guard;* Vandergriff, *right tackle;* Coleman, *right end;* C. Anderson, *quarterback;* Pomeroy, *left halfback;* B. Anderson, *right halfback;* Merrin, *fullback*

— 1926 —

Georgia 32, Florida 9

THOUGH OCTOBER 30, 1926, WAS THE FIRST Georgia-Florida meeting in almost six years, football was not on the minds of many Floridians.

When Coach H. L. Sebring and his Gators arrived in Athens for the renewal of the rivalry, they left behind a state recovering from the ravages of a killer hurricane. The massive storm roared into Florida's east coast on September 18, devastating Miami, leaving about 1,000 dead and some 38,000 homeless.

It was homecoming weekend and fans began pouring into Athens Thursday night. The largest crowd ever to jam Sanford Field was expected for the tilt.

Singing "Glory Glory to Old Georgia," the UGA student body and school band paraded to Sanford Field where the Bulldogs were holding their last practice on Friday.

The train carrying the Florida team arrived that afternoon and the Gators received a "most cordial" welcome from Georgia officials and students. The visitors were taken by automobiles to the Georgian Hotel, where the 1–4 Gators had dinner followed by a light practice.

On game day morning, the Florida band arrived by special train and marched through Athens' streets playing "Cheer for the Orange and Blue."

Saturday was sunny and unseasonably hot as about 5,000 fans, including several hundred Florida rooters, took places in the bleachers and additional seating that had been erected for the record-breaking throng.

"The weather was too warm for football and the sun of a clear sky was too much even for Alligators," said the October 31 *Savannah Morning News.*

Sebring, in his second year at Florida after posting an 8–2 record in 1925, took aim at Georgia after losses to Chicago, Mississippi, Mer-

44

Herman J. Stegeman, UGA's head coach from 1920 to 1922, was 1–0 against Florida. As an assistant coach, Stegeman led Georgia to its win over UF in 1919, but UGA records the victory as Coach W. A. Cunningham's, who sat out the game with broken ribs.

cer and Kentucky—each by less than a touchdown—and an opening day victory over Southern.

Georgia, 2–3, was trying to break a three-game losing streak. Coach George "Kid" Woodruff's squad began the season with victories over Mercer and Virginia, but had fallen to powerful Yale, 10–0, in New Haven, Conn., as well as to Furman and Vanderbilt.

Sebring, who starred for the Kansas Aggies in the Missouri Valley Conference, replaced Florida Coach James A. Van Fleet who had guided the Gators to winning campaigns in 1923 and 1924.

Woodruff had been the captain and outstanding quarterback of Georgia's 1911 team. He had made a fortune in business dealings in Columbus and had been Georgia coach since 1923. Because of his love for the university and little need for money, he agreed to coach the team for $1 a year. Woodruff's teams went 5–3–1 in 1923, 7–3 in 1924, and 4–5 in 1925. He succeeded H. J. Stegeman who, in addition to winning the 1920 conference championship, had taken Georgia to successful years in 1921 and '22.

"There will be no walk-away for either team but will be a hard fought battle," the *Florida Times-Union* said. "Should the fighting Gators come through with a victory, Athens, Ga., Gainesville, Fla., and the whole state of Florida won't be functioning again for two or three days."

Florida's Willie DeHoff blocked a UGA punt for a safety in the second quarter of the 1926 game to score Florida's first points in the series' history. [UF Archives]

Georgia's Luke Woodall kicked off to Florida quarterback Ernest J. Bowyer who returned it 19 yards to the Florida 28. On the first play, Gator back Howard "Horse" Bishop, considered Florida's best triple-threat player, fought for a yard over center but went down with a shoulder injury and was out of the game. "Bishop's leaving seemed to sap the Florida spirit to drive and Georgia carried the game to her foe," the *Times-Union* said.

The teams exchanged possessions before Georgia's second punt of the day sailed out of bounds at the Florida 13. Rather than risk a turnover so close to his goal, Florida's James Chaplin punted on first down.

With numerous substitutions, Georgia kept a "fresh driving" team on the field, an important factor this hot afternoon. One of these was halfback Herdis McCrary. With a Georgia first down at its 48, McCrary, who was ejected late in the game for "slugging," found a gap in the Gators' line and reeled off a 34-yard gain to the Florida 18. On the next play, R. G. Hooks raced around right end for 14 more. Quarterback Howell Hollis then plunged over from the 4. The kick was wild but Georgia had the lead, 6–0.

A swap of punts left Florida on the Georgia 43. Bowyer went to the air and connected with Larsen for 22 yards before the left halfback was tackled in the open field by McCrary. The Gators drove to a first down at the Georgia 16 but got no further.

Highlighted by a nine-yard end run by Hooks, the Bulldogs

pushed upfield to the Florida 49 as the first period ended. The second quarter saw two runs by McCrary net 14 yards. Hooks then got six and McCrary five more before Hooks took it to the Florida 12. The attack continued with Hooks hitting right tackle for four, but stalled on third down when McCrary was buried for no gain. On fourth down at the 6, the Bulldogs went to the pass for the first time in the game, Hooks to Woodall for the score. Hollis again missed a drop-kick conversion, and Georgia was up 12–0.

A 20-yard kickoff return by Florida's Bowyer started the Gators out on their own 35. Bowyer slashed for eight on first down before going deep to receiver Willie DeHoff in the clear, but the ball skipped off the end's fingertips.

The drive was rejuvenated by a 15-yard penalty against Georgia and a 15-yard Bowyer completion to left end Frank Oosterhoudt, who made a sensational catch flat on his back at the Georgia 20. Florida had a first down at the Georgia 8 before a Bowyer pass was intercepted by Bulldog end Ivy "Chick" Shiver at the Georgia 7.

The celebration by UGA fans died quickly when McCrary fumbled the ball right back to the Gators at the Georgia 6. Florida ran three times to push inside the Georgia 1 where they faced fourth down. Halfback Tom Owens tried to ram it in around left end, but

Ernest "Goof" Bowyer quarterbacked Florida to its first-ever touchdown against Georgia, but the Alligators were overmatched in the 1926 contest at Sanford Field. [UF Archives]

A track and football star at Illinois, William G. Kline debuted as Florida's athletic director and football coach in 1920. Kline never beat Georgia, going 0–3 from 1920 to 1922. [UF Archives]

the Bulldogs stopped him less than a foot from pay dirt.

The great goal-line stand now left Georgia about eight inches from its own end zone. The Bulldogs elected to punt and substitute back Roy Estes rocketed a long kick downfield. But the Georgians were penalized and forced to punt again, this time with the ball four inches, or half the distance, closer to the goal.

Florida's Willie DeHoff muscled through the Georgia line and blocked Estes' second kick for a safety, Florida's first points ever in the history of the series. Georgia's lead was narrowed to 12–2.

Late in the half, the Bulldogs took over on their 47 and went to work. Estes barreled through the right side of the Florida line, running to daylight for 37 yards to the Florida 20. Robert McTigue circled end to the Gators 6 and a first down. Florida then bunched in to hold Estes for no gain, but on second down the Bulldog substitute swept right end for a 6-yard touchdown. Roy Johnson's placement lengthened the Georgia advantage to 19–2 at intermission.

On the second half kickoff, the Bulldogs' W. J. "Wee Willie" Hatcher grabbed the ball and wove through almost the entire Gator team before being knocked down at the Florida 18. But Georgia was whistled for holding. With the ball placed back on the Georgia 26, Hatcher would not be denied. Taking a handoff, he dodged several Gators and stepped off 25 yards. Morton ran for 12, and a series of short runs brought Georgia to the UF 33. The Florida defense, under the gun and the sun most of the day, then came up with a big play. The Gators halted the drive when end Oosterhoudt leveled Hollis for a 12-yard loss on a pass attempt.

Stirred by the inspired play of the defense, Florida now countered on offense. From their own 49, Bowyer zipped a pass to Oosterhoudt for 28 yards. A Georgia offsides penalty moved the ball five yards before Owens rambled for six over left end for a first down at the Georgia 24. Another rush by Owens and a 13-yard completion from Bowyer to Owens put Florida at the 9. On the next play, Bowyer passed to James Chaplin, who had broken free in the end zone, for the Florida touchdown. Bowyer added the extra point to cut Georgia's lead to 19–9 still in the third period.

The touchdown was the first ever scored on Georgia by a Florida team. When the Gators held the Bulldogs on downs, the small Florida contingent in the stands was loudly heard from.

But Georgia's defense stood firm and Florida had to punt. Taking over at the Florida 48, the Dogs' Hatcher clicked off 14 yards on an end run and fullback Joe Boland shot over tackle for 21 more. Only desperate tackles made by Gator substitute Ion Walker kept Hatcher and Boland from scoring.

H. L. "Tom" Sebring guided Florida fortunes from 1925 to 1927. His teams lost to "Kid" Woodruff's Georgians in 1926 and 1927. [UF Archives]

Tackle James Chaplin snared a pass from quarterback Ernest Bowyer for Florida's first touchdown in the rivalry. [UF Archives]

A holding penalty pushed the Georgians back to the Florida 33, whereupon Hatcher ran for seven. Halfback George Morton then slipped through right tackle, evaded Bowyer at the goal line and scored standing up from 26 yards out. Hollis missed the kick, but Georgia's margin was a comfortable 25–9.

Late in the third quarter, a Florida trick play backfired. Chaplin, back in punt formation, tried to pass instead; but the ball slipped out of his hands and Bulldog tackle Curtis Luckey pounced on it at the Florida 27.

On the bruising runs of Hatcher, Estes, and McCrary, Georgia nosed to the Florida 3. It appeared the Gators were wilting in the autumn heat when McCrary crashed in to the Florida end zone and three Florida defenders were hurt on the play. Johnson's extra point lengthened the Georgia lead to 32–9.

Florida, however, drove to the Georgia 26 early in the fourth quarter but was halted on what would be its last serious offensive of the afternoon.

A *Florida Times-Union* reporter was caught up in the emotion of the closing minutes:

"Whipped to almost a frazzle . . . Florida never once gave an inch in her gallant defensive fight and Kid Woodruff rushing new men into the fray, failed in (his) scoring attempts over the tired but true warriors from Gainesville in the final period of the hectic fray."

The third Florida team to play Georgia in Athens heard the ringing of the university chapel bell signaling another Bulldogs win.

Halloween 1926 brought headlines of Georgia's triumph as well as Army's rout of Yale and Navy's upset of Michigan in Baltimore. The day also brought the death of magician Harry Houdini who succumbed to peritonitis in Detroit.

Florida later routed Clemson but was overcome, 49–0, by Alabama and ended with ties against Hampden-Sydney and Washington & Lee to finish 2–6–2.

Georgia bested Auburn, 16–0, and Georgia Tech, 14–13, before losing, 33–6, at Alabama to complete its season at 5–4. The Bulldogs' halfback George Morton and tackle Curtis Luckey were honored as All-Southern Conference selections.

Scoring:

Georgia	6	13	13	0	—	32
Florida	0	2	7	0	—	9

UGA	TD	Hollis, 4-yard run (kick failed)
UGA	TD	Woodall, 6-yard pass from Hooks (kick failed)
UF	Safety	DeHoff blocked kick in UGA end zone
UGA	TD	Estes, 6-yard run (Johnson kick)
UF	TD	Chaplin, 9-yard pass from Bowyer (Bowyer kick)
UGA	TD	Morton, 26-yard run (kick failed)
UGA	TD	McCrary, 3-yard run (Johnson kick)

Georgia: Woodall, *left end;* Luckey, *left tackle;* Jacobson, *left guard;* Smith, *center;* Rogers, *right guard;* Lautzenhiser, *right tackle;* Shiver, *right end;* Hollis, *quarterback;* Morton, *left halfback;* Sherlock, *right halfback;* Boland, *fullback* *Substitutes:* Estes, McCrary, McTigue, Hatcher, Dudley, Dowis, Bryant, Forbes, Johnson, Morris, Groves, Munn

Florida: Oosterhoudt, *left end;* Clemons, *left tackle;* Ripley, *left guard;* Sarra, *center;* Tucker, *right guard;* Chaplin, *right tackle;* Trogdon, *right end;* Bowyer, *quarterback;* Owens, *left halfback;* Larsen, *right halfback;* Davis, *fullback* *Substitutes:* DeHoff, Fuller, Walker, Townsend, Livingston, Ripley, Greene

— 1927 —

Georgia 28, Florida 0

THE VITAPHONE SONGS OF AL JOLSON IN "The Jazz Singer," America's first "talkie" movie, were the rage of American screen fans in the fall of 1927.

On November 5, the focus of Georgia and Florida devotees who flocked to Jacksonville was the sixth Bulldogs-Alligators confrontation.

George "Kid" Woodruff was in his final year as Georgia coach and had fielded probably the most talent-laden team in the school's history to that time. Led by Herdis McCrary, heralded as one of the premier fullbacks in the South, many observers considered the Bulldogs a national contender. Halfbacks R. G. Hooks, Frank Dudley and quarterback H.F. Johnson Jr. rounded out one of Georgia's finest backfields. The Bulldog lineup also featured ends Tom A. Nash and I. M. "Chick" Shiver, the team captain, who would be honored as All-Americans after the 1927 campaign. To install the Notre Dame box formation at Georgia, Woodruff had hired three of Knute Rockne's former players as coaches, including Harry Mehre and Jim Crowley, one of Rockne's legendary "Four Horsemen."

Gator coach H. L. Sebring was in his third and last season at Florida and coming off a 2–6–2 record in 1926.

The 1927 Gators were 4–2, opening with a win over Southern, a home loss to Davidson and a 33–6 road win against Auburn. Florida then beat Kentucky, 27–6, but lost to N.C. State, 12–6, in Tampa before destroying Mercer in Gainesville a week before the Georgia game.

Georgia shellacked Virginia in its opener and made a statement for Dixie football on October 8th with a 14–10 victory over Yale in New Haven. The Bulldogs then proceeded to crunch Furman, 32–0; Auburn, 33–0; and Tulane, 31–0, to prime themselves for Florida.

The fever of a national championship quest was gripping Georgia

52

George "Kid" Woodruff, who coached UGA for one dollar a year from 1923 to 1927, was 2–0 against Florida.

followers. "Many are pointing to the fact that if the Athenians can make the remainder of the schedule run successfully, they will have a claim on the national collegiate title," the November 4 *Savannah Morning News* said. "This is generally agreed to be a difficult layout but entirely possible for the strong Bulldog squad."

Other than the Yale battle, all of Georgia's games had been so one-sided that Woodruff was able to give his second- and third-stringers significant playing time.

A grand parade stepped off at 11 a.m. on game day and wound through downtown Jacksonville from the Carling Hotel on Adams Street. Frank "Pop" Beddow, perennial grand marshal of Jacksonville parades, led the procession followed by the Atlanta police band, the student bodies, bands and teams from both universities.

A "colorful crowd" of some 15,000 filed into Jacksonville's Fair-field Stadium prior to the kickoff. Georgia's Bob McTigue let the opening kickoff roll into the end zone before deciding to bring it out. He was tackled at the 6 by Florida left end Willie DeHoff, the scorer of Florida's first points in the rivalry a year earlier. Woodruff sent in his second-string backfield to start the game, so confident was he that his star backs would not be needed.

Keeping the ball on the ground, the Bulldogs quickly plowed to three first downs on gains by halfbacks Roy Estes and McTigue, and fullback Bennie Rothstein. Just when it appeared the Georgians were headed for a score, the Gators came to life, stopping them on downs at the Florida 39.

Florida failed to net a first down on its first offensive series and Georgia went back to its running game, with Rothstein, Estes and McTigue carrying the load, before Florida's Brumbaugh intercepted

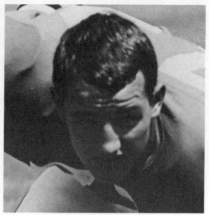

End Tom Nash (left) *was an All-American at Georgia in 1927 when UGA beat Florida 28–0. His son, Tom Jr.* (right), *would star for the Bulldogs as an All-SEC selection in 1970 and 1971.*

a pass at the UF 13 to kill the menace. The rivals traded punts as the quarter ended.

The Gators had proven surprisingly tough in holding the Bulldogs scoreless, and Woodruff put his first-string backfield of McCrary, Hooks, Dudley and Johnson into the game to open the second period.

Beginning at its own 30, Georgia was held short of a first down as Shiver went back in punt formation. Instead of kicking, however, the Bulldog captain raced around end for 16 yards for a Bulldog first down. Georgia was penalized 15 yards for roughing but Hooks got it back with an end run. From the UF 35, Johnson found McCrary on a sharp pass to the end zone for Georgia's first score. Johnson added the conversion for a 7–0 advantage.

Late in the half, Florida put together its best offensive of the day. The Gators' Clyde Crabtree entered the game at halfback and showed some flash on a 35-yard gain to the Georgia 33. DeHoff grabbed a pass from quarterback E. J. "Goof" Bowyer and was tackled at the 17. Bowyer gained another six yards on a pass and the Gators threatened to tie the game.

But on the next play, Georgia left end Tom Nash picked off Bowyer's pass attempt and zig-zagged out to midfield. Moments later, though, right end Will Stanley intercepted a pass for Florida.

The half ended with the Floridians having held the high-powered Bulldogs to a touchdown. Despite their thwarted drive, the Gators went to the locker room knowing they could move the ball against

Georgia. If the defense continued to hold in the second half, Sebring's men knew they had a great chance of pulling the upset.

Florida's opening series in the third quarter was foiled and Bowyer had to hurry his punt, as Georgia took over at midfield. McCrary and Hooks alternated carries as the Bulldogs pounded into Gator land. McCrary hit straight ahead for 3 yards and a first down at the Florida 1 before smacking over center for the score. Johnson's kick put Georgia up 14–0.

Florida's Howard Bishop returned the kickoff 17 yards to the 27. Two bursts by halfback Royce Goodbread netted a Gator first down. Goodbread had two more short gains before Bowyer fumbled the snap from center and Georgia recovered at the Florida 35. Going to the power-running game again, Georgia reeled off yardage on more runs by McCrary and Hooks. On one such carry, Florida's DeHoff was hurt and had to leave the game.

The Bulldogs ran to a first down at the UF 4. Here, the Gators grimly held on, gang-tackling for virtually no gain on three plays. On fourth down, Georgia abandoned the run as Johnson lobbed a pass to McCrary in the end zone. Johnson again converted for a 21–0 Georgia lead late in the third quarter.

An exchange of punts gave Georgia possession at its 34 as the trio of Dudley, McCrary and Hooks went back to work, plowing into the Gator defense and moving the ball steadily downfield.

On the second play of the fourth period, Hooks completed a pass to Tom Nash for 39 yards. Four plays later Hooks found Dudley open behind the Florida goal for a 19-yard touchdown. Johnson's fourth PAT made it 28–0, Georgia.

Florida's offense flickered to life late in the game when Georgia's Johnson fumbled a punt that was recovered by Gator end Justin Clemons and returned to the Bulldog 19. The Gators pushed to within a foot of the Georgia goal line, but Bowyer was stopped short on fourth down. In the game's last minutes, Bowyer went down with a broken leg after a 3-yard run and was lost for the season.

McCrary, with three touchdowns, Hooks, and the Bulldog defense carried the day for the Red and Black. "It was just a case of too much McCrary and too much Hooks waltzing wild behind a line that drove and smashed with a precision and deadliness that was thrilling to behold," the *Times-Union* said.

Florida's DeHoff brothers, Willie and Donald, along with Crabtree and back William Middlekauff, had been the heroes of the Gator defense most of the day even though Florida was whipped. The

Georgia All-Southern Conference fullback Herdis McCrary scored three touchdowns for UGA's "dream and wonder" team against Florida in 1927. [Hargrett Collection, UGA Libraries]

scrappy DeHoffs had to be helped off the field after the game, although not hurt as seriously as Bowyer.

Sebring's Gators closed the season without another loss, beating Alabama, 13–6, in Montgomery and also defeating Washington & Lee and Maryland to go 7–3.

Woodruff's Bulldogs mauled Clemson, 32–0; Mercer, 26–7; and Alabama, 20–6, in Birmingham to enter their traditional year-end bloodletting with Georgia Tech undefeated and with a possible Rose Bowl bid in the making. By this time, Georgia was considered by many to be the top team in the nation.

Tech handed Georgia a 12–0 loss, however, shattering any bowl hopes and ending the Bulldogs' season.

In addition to All-America kudos, Nash and Shiver, along with Bulldog teammates McCrary and right guard Gene Smith, were named to the All-Southern Conference team.

Nash and halfback Roy Estes were drafted by the Green Bay Packers, with Nash garnering All-Pro honors in 1930–31. His son would star for the Bulldogs in later years.

Sebring left coaching and went on to become a judge in Tallahassee. And Woodruff retired with the satisfaction of having coached the greatest Georgia team of the era.

Scoring:

Georgia	0	7	14	7 —	28
Florida	0	0	0	0 —	0

UGA	TD	McCrary, 35-yard pass from Johnson (Johnson kick)
UGA	TD	McCrary, 1-yard run (Johnson kick)
UGA	TD	McCrary, 4-yard pass from Johnson (Johnson kick)
UGA	TD	Dudley, 19-yard pass from Hooks (Johnson kick)

Georgia: Nash, Stelling, *left end;* Morris, *left tackle;* Jacobson, *left guard;* Boland, *center;* Smith, *right guard;* Lautzenhiser, *right tackle;* Shiver, Martin, *right end;* Broadnax, Johnson, *quarterback;* Estes, Hooks, *left halfback;* McTigue, Dudley, Cook, *right halfback;* Rothstein, McCrary, *fullback*

Florida: W. DeHoff, Van Sickle, *left end;* Bryan, D. DeHoff, *left tackle;* Allen, Goldstein, *left guard;* Kirchner, *center;* Reeves, *right guard;* Clemons, Pless, *right tackle;* Stanley, *right end;* Bowyer, *quarterback;* Brumbaugh, Crabtree, Goodbread, Smith, Beck, *left halfback;* Bishop, Cawthon, *right halfback;* Middlekauff, Baldwin, *fullback*

— 1928 —

Florida 26, Georgia 6

"Never before has the orange and blue threat been as strong as the one which rides out of Gainesville at sunrise tomorrow."

The November 8 wire dispatch, two days before the 1928 game, mirrored the optimism in the Florida camp as the Gators prepared to meet Georgia.

The battle would be in Savannah's Municipal Stadium and promised to be one of the best games of the series to date. It also would be a meeting of first-year coaches—Charles Bachman at Florida and Harry Mehre of Georgia.

The Gators were on a 5–0 winning roll coming into Savannah. Bachman's team crushed Southern, 26–0; Auburn, 27–0; and Mercer, 73–0, in Gainesville before nipping N.C. State, 14–7, and slaughtering Sewanee, 71–0, in games in Jacksonville.

Mehre's Bulldogs likewise smashed Mercer, 52–0, in their home opener but fell 21–6 to Yale in New Haven before coming back to whip Furman, 7–0, and Tulane, 20–14, in Athens, plus administer a beating to Auburn, 13–0, in Columbus the week before the Florida game.

Georgia's vaunted backfield of fullback Herdis McCrary, halfbacks Frank Dudley and R. G. Hooks, and quarterback H. F. Johnson, was intact from the previous year when Georgia downed the Alligators, 28–0, in Jacksonville.

But Bachman had the most potent Florida team since the school instituted football, led by eventual first-team All-America end Dale Van Sickle. Most of the squad was composed of sophomores and juniors. Van Sickle, however, had spent most of the week before the Georgia game on the sidelines with the flu.

Ambidextrous quarterback Clyde "Cannonball" Crabtree was one of Florida's backfield linchpins along with halfbacks Carl Brum-

Florida's first All-American, end Dale Van Sickle, was a key player in UF's triumphs over Georgia in 1928 and 1929. He later became a stuntman in Hollywood and died in his late 60s from injuries sustained on the job. [UF Archives]

baugh, Royce Goodbread and Rainey Cawthon. Starting at quarterback for the Gators, though, would be team captain Ernest Bowyer, who had suffered a broken leg in the 1927 Georgia game.

Crabtree had sat out the Sewanee game. "It was feared that Clyde's appendix was thrown out of position when a hearty tackle laid him low" against N.C. State, but he was ready for Georgia.

Both teams arrived by train on the morning of Friday, November 9. The 35-man Florida team and entourage were quartered at the Hotel Savannah while Georgia's 43 players, coaches and managers stayed at the De Soto Hotel.

The opposing squads were feted at a Friday afternoon luncheon at the De Soto where a local orchestra played "pep" songs from both schools. The teams each held light workouts at the stadium later in the day.

Georgia's Mehre had asked Savannah officials not to mark off the field with any white substances containing lime. He was bringing his own chalk concoction from Athens. Mehre said lime irritated cuts and scrapes sustained by the players and his request was granted. Whether the Georgia chalk would give the Bulldogs an advantage remained to be seen.

About 300 Florida fans headed north for the clash, including the

75-member Florida band, coming in on the "Friendship Special" train from Gainesville and Jacksonville.

More than 15,000 spectators packed into Municipal Stadium for the 2 p.m. kickoff. A new scoreboard and loud-speaking system, a rarity among college stadiums at the time, had been installed the week before the game so that each play could be described from the press box. The amplifying equipment was of the same type being installed at Georgia's new $250,000 arena, later named Sanford Stadium, in Athens.

Midway through the first quarter, after the teams exchanged possessions several times, Florida's backs churned through the line on a series of plays that put the Gators at the Georgia 30. On the next play, 172-pound halfback Lee Roy "Red" Bethea scampered up the middle and into the end zone. The extra point attempt failed, but Florida held a 6–0 lead, its first ever in the series, with just under 10 minutes gone in the first quarter.

Play continued in Georgia land with Florida's stingy defense holding the Bulldogs at bay. McCrary, Hooks and the other Georgia backs were being stuffed by the Gators.

Entering the second period, Georgia went to the passing game, a

The 1928 Florida squad of first-year coach Charles Bachman was the first to taste victory over Georgia, beating the Bulldogs in Savannah. [UF Archives]

Action during the 1928 game in Savannah. [UF Archives]

ploy that caught the Gators off guard. Striking quickly, quarterback Johnson completed a 40-yard throw to Dudley, who rambled into the UF end zone to knot the game to the delight of the partisan crowd.

Johnson tensed for the extra point attempt that would put Georgia ahead, but the kick was unsuccessful.

In the dying minutes of the half, Florida again ground close to the enemy goal line. From the Georgia 20, Crabtree, who had replaced Bowyer at quarterback, retreated to pass. Seeing his receivers covered, the 147-pound "Cannonball" tucked in the ball and danced upfield. Reversing his direction and eluding the grasps of four Bulldogs, Crabtree followed a train of blockers into the Georgia end zone. Brumbaugh added the conversion to give Florida a 13–6 advantage at the half.

The Gators increased their margin early in the third period when Brumbaugh found Van Sickle for a 30-yard gain. The 170-pound end then gathered in a Bowyer aerial from 29 yards out for Florida's third touchdown. Brumbaugh's second conversion made it 20–6, Gators.

Georgia could do nothing on offense and Florida set sail again. Cawthon reeled off a 35-yard run to the Bulldog 18 as the third quarter expired.

On the first play of the fourth period, Crabtree drifted back and, throwing left-handed, completed a touchdown pass to Brumbaugh stepping across the UGA goal line. Florida owned the Bulldogs, 26–6.

Georgia's McCrary was injured in the last quarter, his loss enough to "blast the last hope of his team mates," the *Morning News* said.

Ambidextrous quarterback Clyde "Cannonball" Crabtree was a key man in Florida's victories over UGA in 1928 and 1929. In the two games Crabtree ran for two touchdowns and threw for two more. [UF Archives]

The Gators then ran out the clock. Someone in the grandstands set off firecrackers or fired a pistol in the game's closing moments. Believing the final gun had sounded, Florida's frenzied rooters poured out onto the field and had to be cleared away by police.

"And so the game ended with the Floridians ensconced upon a pinnacle they heretofore have failed to reach . . . " the *Morning News* reported.

"The gaping maw of the Saurian, equipped with teeth such as Goodbread, Bethea, Cawthon, Crabtree, Brumbaugh and Company took in the heretofore vicious Bulldog with a gusto," the Associated Press said.

A week later, Georgia fell, 13–12, at home to LSU and closed the year at 4–5 with a 19–0 loss at Alabama and a 20–6 defeat at Georgia Tech. McCrary was drafted by the Green Bay Packers.

Bachman's Gators finished with victories over Clemson and Washington & Lee in Jacksonville, before traveling to Knoxville for the season ender against Tennessee in a battle for the conference championship. On a rain-slick field, the Volunteers pulled out a 13–12 win, ending Florida's season at 8–1, the best ever to that point. The

1928 Gators were the nation's highest scoring team, piling up 336 points in nine games.

Van Sickle was named first-team All-America, the highest honor for a Gator football player since halfback Edgar Jones was chosen to play in the 1925 East-West Shrine game in San Francisco. Van Sickle and Crabtree also were honored as All-Southern Conference selections. Gator back Carl Brumbaugh made the big time, playing defensive back and quarterback for the Chicago Bears for most of the 1930s.

The Gators' first win against Georgia and Van Sickle's personal achievements helped make 1928 a season for Florida to savor and remember.

Scoring:

Florida	6	7	7	6	—	26
Georgia	0	6	0	0	—	6

UF	TD	Bethea, 30-yard run (PAT failed)
UGA	TD	Dudley, 40-yard pass from Johnson (PAT failed)
UF	TD	Crabtree, 20-yard run (Brumbaugh kick)
UF	TD	Van Sickle, 29-yard pass from Bowyer (Brumbaugh kick)
UF	TD	Brumbaugh, 18-yard pass from Crabtree (PAT failed)

Florida: Van Sickle, *left end;* Clemons, *left tackle;* Steele, *left guard;* Clark, *center;* Reeves, *right guard;* Bryan, *right tackle;* Stanley, *right end;* Bowyer, Crabtree, *quarterback;* Brumbaugh, *left halfback;* Goodbread, *right halfback;* Cawthon, *fullback*

Georgia: Maffett, *left end;* Frisbie, *left tackle;* Jacobson, *left guard;* Boland, *center;* Haley, *right guard;* Lautzenhiser, *right tackle;* Smith, *right end;* Johnson, *quarterback;* Hooks, *left halfback;* Dudley, *right halfback;* McCrary, *fullback*

— 1929 —

Florida 18, Georgia 6

WITH A 3–1 RECORD ENTERING THE OCTOBER 26, 1929, Georgia game in Jacksonville, Florida followers expected Coach Bachman's Gators to have a good chance of snatching a second win in a row from the Bulldogs.

Florida debuted with a shelling of Southern, a victory over V.M.I., and a 19–0 win against Auburn in Montgomery before stumbling, 19–6, at Georgia Tech.

The Gators were led by All-America left end Dale Van Sickle and all-conference quarterback Clyde "Cannonball" Crabtree, an effective combination against Georgia the year before.

Harry Mehre's 1929 Bulldogs premiered with a loss to Oglethorpe in Athens, but came back to best Furman before dedicating newly-completed Sanford Stadium on October 12, 1929, with a 15–0 upset of a strong Yale team. End Vernon "Catfish" Smith Jr. scored every point. The stadium's legendary hedges were only about a foot tall at the time and were protected by a wood fence. The Athenians then nipped heavily-favored North Carolina, 19–12, at Chapel Hill to encounter Florida with a 3–1 record.

"Florida's big victory over Georgia last fall in Savannah is still keen in the memory of Bulldogs and their supporters," an October 24 wire report from Athens said. "A strenuous effort will be made to remove this unpleasant recollection."

Georgia scouts who watched the Gators against Tech and Auburn were impressed by the Florida defense, especially the line play. All of Tech's scoring came from their passing game.

Defense was a strength of the Georgia eleven as well, but the Bulldogs also had gotten sparkling play from their sophomore backfield of Austin Downes Jr., Spurgeon Chandler and Jack Roberts. Halfback Armin Waugh had a knee injury and would not play.

By Thursday, classes at Georgia had thinned out with students

64

Charles Bachman's Gators upset Georgia for the second straight year in 1929 at Jacksonville and went on to an 8–2 record. [UF Archives]

hitting the road for "the Land of Flowers" to see the game, "some in their own cars but others starting out on foot with the hope that their red caps will encourage passing motorists to help them reach the big city," the *Savannah Morning News* said.

Slightly favored, Georgia arrived in Jacksonville by special train on Friday and held a workout at the stadium. The Gators remained in Gainesville to escape the pre-game hoopla and arrived by bus a few hours before the 3 p.m. kickoff. A "solid mass of roaring humanity," estimated at 21,000, filled the stadium. Fans who did not have tickets gathered at the corner of Pearl and Adams streets where the *Florida Times-Union* broadcast a running account of the game via a public address system. The afternoon was sunny but a cool breeze wafted off the St. Johns River.

Georgia returned the opening kickoff to their 41 and, after a series of runs by Chandler, including one on a fake quick-kick for 25 yards, was quickly down to the Florida 21-yard line.

But the march sputtered there and Florida took over after stopping a fourth-down thrust by fullback Bennie Rothstein.

Runs by Gators Royce Goodbread, L. R. Bethea and Rainey Cawthon netted a first down but Florida could go no further. After an exchange of punts, the Floridians were set up at the Georgia 48. Two running plays and left halfback Bethea's pass to Harry Greene for 21 yards brought it down to the Georgia 12.

A Crabtree pass to Bethea gained seven and Cawthon ran inside

Fullback Rainey Cawthon was a workhorse in Florida's victories in 1928 and 1929. [UF Archives]

for two more yards before Bethea, on his second attempt, rammed over right end for the touchdown. The conversion attempt was blocked but Florida was up 6–0.

"Between the halves the more bibulous fans betook themselves to the shelters beneath the stand," the *Times-Union* said. "Bacchic? A few. Hilarious? Some. But all in all it was an orderly crowd." Occasionally, fans from one team or the other made "caustic comments" to each other but "these few outbursts were handled by the assembled police and firemen."

Neither squad could move the ball early in the third quarter. Florida's first series ended when Cawthon fumbled the ball away at the UF 44. Again the Bulldogs could not capitalize, and their quarterback, Downes, was lost with a broken collarbone. After another series of exchanges, Chandler dropped back to punt for Georgia, but the kick was blocked by Van Sickle and recovered by Gator left end Jimmy Nolan at the Georgia 28.

Three runs by Cawthon gained 19 yards. Goodbread then circled end for five more. But after a yard gain by Cawthon, Bethea was thrown for a 6-yard loss by Bulldog left end Catfish Smith.

On fourth down, Gator quarterback Crabtree flipped a short pass to Van Sickle for the Gators' second touchdown. Again the Bulldogs blocked the conversion but Florida led 12–0. Van Sickle was hurt on the scoring play but later returned.

On Florida's next possession, Crabtree skirted left end for eight yards. Cawthon plunged for 10 over center and Crabtree gained another first down running over left tackle to the Georgia 45. A short run by Bethea and two gains by Cawthon moved the Gators to the UGA 34. Rushes by Bethea and Cawthon brought the ball down to the 17.

Additional runs by Cawthon and substitute back Charles F. Sauls, and a pass from Crabtree to Goodbread, put the Gators at the enemy 7 as the third quarter closed.

The Georgia defense stiffened to open the final stanza, as Florida's Goodbread was thrown out of bounds for a 3-yard loss. A run by substitute quarterback Luke Dorsett gained nothing and a Dorsett pass fell incomplete, giving possession to the fired-up Bulldogs on their own 20.

Chandler fumbled, falling on the ball for a 2-yard loss, before sweeping left end for 10 yards. Georgia could not gain a first down, though, and Chandler punted away.

After a series of exchanges, Georgia took the ball again on its 20. On first down, Chandler dropped back and threw a short pass, but Crabtree stepped in front of the receiver and made the interception. The Gator star "zig-zagged his way . . . through the entire Georgia team" for the touchdown. Dorsett's conversion attempt failed but Florida led 18–0 midway through the fourth quarter.

When Georgia could not move the ball after the kickoff, Florida pushed to the Georgia 35 on runs by Bethea, Sauls and Dorsett. But Sauls fumbled there and Georgia's Marion Dickens recovered. The turnover ignited the Athenians, even though only a few minutes remained.

Dickens hit Smith on a pass to the Georgia 47. After runs by Dickens and Rothstein, Chandler found Smith again for a 3-yard gain to the Gators 9. Dickens then ran for six yards before Rothstein tore through the middle of the UF line for the touchdown. Rothstein's extra point try failed and the score closed to 18–6 late in the quarter.

Florida, with most of its first string on the bench, threatened to widen the final margin in the last minutes. Sauls took a handoff and galloped 70 yards before being dragged down from behind at the Georgia 6 on the longest run of the day. A penalty against Georgia put the ball at the 1. But from there, the Georgia line stonewalled the Gators.

"Dinner and dance, enthusiastic celebrating, were in order," the *Times-Union* said, "and it was early Sunday morning before many from out of town began the return home."

A week after the Florida loss, Georgia fell to Tulane in its first-ever defeat at Sanford Stadium, then was tripped in an away game at New York University. Mehre's squad returned south to blank Auburn, 24–0, and Alabama, 12–0, before whipping Georgia Tech, 12–6, in

Georgia fullback Bennie Rothstein (27) is pulled down by a Florida defender after an 8-yard gain. [Hargrett Collection, UGA Libraries]

Athens to finish at 6–4. The Tech win was the 150th football victory in Georgia history.

Catfish Smith was named to the All-Southern Conference team.

Bachman's Gators lost 14–0 to Harvard at Cambridge, Mass., then closed the campaign with three road wins over South Carolina, Washington & Lee and Oregon in Miami. The Gators' record was 8–2.

Bachman had faced Georgia twice and come away with upset victories in compiling a 16–3 worksheet in his first two seasons at Florida.

Scoring:

Florida	0	6	6	6	—	18
Georgia	0	0	0	6	—	6

UF	TD	Bethea, 1-yard run (PAT blocked)
UF	TD	Crabtree, 3-yard pass to Van Sickle (PAT blocked)
UF	TD	Crabtree, 20-yard pass interception return (PAT failed)
UGA	TD	Rothstein, 3-yard run (PAT failed)

Florida: Nolan, Clemons, Haines, *left end;* Proctor, Pheil, Waters, *left tackle;* Reeves, Houser, *left guard;* Clark, *center;* Steele, *right guard;* Waters, *right tackle;* Van Sickle, Greene, *right end;* McEwen, Crabtree, Dorsett, *quarterback;* Bethea, M. Smith, *left halfback;* Goodbread, *right halfback;* Cawthon, Sauls, Silsby, *fullback*

Georgia: Smith, *left end;* Bryant, Rose, *left tackle;* Maddox, *left guard;* Boland, *center;* Leathers, *right guard;* Lynn, *right tackle;* Maffett, Kelley, *right end;* Downes, Moran, *quarterback;* Chandler, *left halfback;* Gerdine, Dickens, *right halfback;* Rothstein, *fullback*

68

— 1930 —

Florida 0, Georgia 0

WITH THE GEORGIA STATE FAIR IN FULL SWING
and thousands arriving in Savannah for the November 1 Florida-
Georgia game, a "holiday atmosphere" pervaded the city by Halloween 1930.

Both teams arrived early on Friday, but few knew about the
squads' arrangements which were "shrouded in secrecy," the *Savannah Morning News* said. Both coaches wanted to "get away from the
curious and mildly intoxicated who always want to shake hands and
wish the players luck."

Third-year Florida coach Charles Bachman was hoping his team's
mastery of Georgia the past two years would continue. The Gators
were 4–1, beating Southern, 45–7; N.C. State, 27–0; Auburn, 7–0;
and Chicago, 19–0, before losing to Furman, 14–13, a week before
Georgia.

Backs L. R. "Red" Bethea and Charles Sauls, who tormented the
Bulldogs with their running the previous year, had the tools to
extend the Florida winning streak over Georgia. Bethea, a senior and
the team captain, had scored touchdowns against the Bulldogs in the
1928 and '29 Florida wins. But as they had been the previous two
years, the Gators were underdogs against Georgia.

Coach Harry Mehre was looking for his first win over Florida in
three tries as both teams readied for the action at Municipal Stadium,
the same field where the Gators had claimed their first victory over
Georgia two years earlier.

Again featuring a formidable running game, the Bulldogs were
5–0 entering the Florida contest. Star left end Vernon "Catfish"
Smith was a constant scoring threat; and junior backs Jack "The
Ripper" Roberts, Austin Downes and Spurgeon Chandler were returning for their second shot at the Gators. Quarterback Downes had
recovered from a broken collarbone sustained in the third quarter of
the previous year's game.

Charles W. Bachman coached Florida to consecutive wins over UGA in 1928 and 1929. Bachman was 2–2–1 against Georgia from 1928 to 1932 in compiling a 27–18–3 record at UF. [UF Archives]

Mehre's squad dropped Oglethorpe, 21–6, and Mercer 51–0, in Athens, to open the season, then bested Yale, 18–14, in New Haven to garner national attention. The Athenians defeated North Carolina, 26–0, then beat Auburn, 39–7, in Columbus the week before Florida. Many felt Georgia was on the march to a Southern Conference title.

The Bulldogs were confident, but their enthusiasm was tempered by the pain of two consecutive losses to the Gators and a respect for the Florida backs and rugged line. "The general feeling is that anything may happen this afternoon," the *Morning News* said on game day. "So the football wise . . . refuse to take the threat from the flowery state as anything but a serious one."

The teams held brief practices at the stadium on Friday afternoon. In pre-game interviews, Florida's Bachman lamented the graduation losses of All-American Dale Van Sickle and Gator heroes Clyde Crabtree and Royce Goodbread, kingpins of both Florida victories.

A newspaper correspondent in Brunswick, Ga., about 80 miles south of Savannah, reported early Friday that a steady flow of cars from Miami, Tampa, St. Petersburg and other South Florida locales was clattering north. Florida fans from Orlando, Gainesville and other points closer to Savannah embarked later in the day.

By Friday afternoon, most of the city's hotels, rooming houses and restaurants were teeming with visitors. The game fervor intensified on Saturday morning with the arrival of five special trains, two bringing Gator fans from the Jacksonville area; the others jammed with

Harry Mehre was the first UGA coach to suffer defeat by Florida. He led the Bulldogs to a 6–3–1 record against UF teams from 1928 to 1937 and engineered UGA's shocking up-set of powerful Yale in the dedication game of Sanford Stadium in 1929.

Georgia followers from Athens, Atlanta, Macon and Columbus.

A crowd of some 13,000 settled into the stadium, as Georgia, unable to move the ball on its first possession, boomed a punt that guard Milton "Red" Leathers downed at the Florida 13. Gator full-back Joe Jenkins bulled for two yards and Sauls punted on second down.

Defense continued to rule and a Georgia punt gave Florida posses-sion at midfield. Runs by Bethea and Jenkins and a short pass from quarterback Luke Dorsett to Sauls netted a Gator first down. On the next series, however, Sauls' pass to Bethea was picked off by Bulldog center J. V. McWhorter at the Georgia 35. Fullback James Stoinoff scrambled around right end for 14 yards after a short gain by Dickens, but Georgia was unable to penetrate from midfield. Chan-dler punted again and the Gators took over at their own 17 in the closing seconds of the first quarter.

After an exchange of possessions, Florida took the ball at its own 16. Bethea churned for four on a sweep before "Catfish" Smith rolled him out of bounds. On the next play, UF back Jenkins fumbled and Dickens recovered for Georgia on the Florida 27 for the first scoring chance of the contest.

The Gator linemen held "The Ripper" Roberts for no gain at center. Dickens, bobbling the ball, ran for three. On third down, Roberts fumbled and Florida recovered at its 16.

Herb Maffett was an All-American end at Georgia in 1930. [Hargrett Collection, UGA Libraries]

With neither team able to mount an effective offensive, a defensive grind prevailed through the end of the first half.

Fired by Mehre's halftime talk, the Bulldogs drew a bead on the Florida end zone to open the third quarter.

Roberts scampered off right tackle for 15 yards. Dickens gained a yard but then, on a fake pass play, exploded through the middle for 20. Runs by Roberts and Downes gave Georgia a first and goal at the Florida 7. The Gators' defense would need a supreme effort.

Dickens was walled off in the middle for no gain. Roberts cracked over right guard for three and Dickens for three more to the Florida 1. On fourth down, "The Ripper" smashed off left tackle and was thrown down by Dale Waters and other Gator defenders shy of the goal line.

Despite the defensive lift, Florida could not open the throttle against the tenacious Bulldog defense. The Gators' kick from near their own goal line put Georgia in business at the Florida 20. With the Bulldogs threatening again, UF's Link Silsby stepped in front of a Dickens pass to end the Georgia advance. The Gators had dodged another bullet.

Florida, on a drive highlighted by a 12-yard pass from Dorsett to Sauls, moved to midfield this time before being forced to kick.

The defensive contest continued until the final moments of the third quarter when Silsby dashed 20 yards through the line and the officials added a 15-yard penalty against Georgia for unnecessary roughness. The third period ended with Florida on the Georgia 45.

Silsby opened the final quarter where he had left off, winding 24 yards to the Bulldog 21. On fourth and four at the 15, Silsby muscled for three but came up just short. The Bulldogs had held.

The teams swapped punts and yet another set of fumbles before Georgia got on track with a solid drive.

Chandler twisted around left end for 12 yards. Roberts and Chandler each gained a yard before Roberts burst off right tackle, shooting down the sideline for 42 yards before Dorsett could harness him at the UF 24.

Two plays later, Roberts made another big third-down play, crashing off left tackle for 14 yards to the Florida 8.

A lateral from Roberts to Dickens gained nothing, but a penalty against Florida placed the ball at the 2. Norman "Buster" Mott replaced Dickens, injured on the play, at right halfback.

Four times Roberts hurtled into the line and four times he was thrown back. The stubborn and bloodied Gators had survived another Bulldog foray.

With its backs lined up in the end zone, Florida could not move the ball; and Dorsett was called for a 15-yard grounding penalty. From the 1-yard line, Dorsett punted and Georgia's Downes returned it to the Gators 32.

Roberts dove over left tackle for four yards. Mott then skirted right end for 28 yards and an apparent touchdown. But the celebration of the Georgia followers was cut short—the Bulldogs had been offsides.

Two plays after the penalty, Bethea intercepted a pass by UGA's Chandler and sprinted 35 yards to the Georgia 45 before being pulled down. With about four minutes left in the game, the Gators still had

Georgia guard Ralph "Red" Maddox joined UGA end Herb Maffett as All-American selections in 1930, but the pair could not lead the Bulldogs to a win over Florida that year. [Hargrett Collection, UGA Libraries]

Georgia cheerleaders—1930 [Hargrett Collection, UGA Libraries]

a chance for their third straight win against Georgia. But Florida substitute back Broward McClellan and Bethea could not pierce the Bulldogs' defense and Dorsett punted to Downes, tackled at the Georgia 5.

After a 20-yard pass from Chandler to Smith, the game ended with Chandler struggling over right guard for short yardage. The scoreless deadlock had seen the Bulldogs commit four turnovers, the Gators three. Favored Georgia found some solace in halting the Gators' two-game winning streak in the series.

Georgia went on to edge New York University, 7–6, in New York City the week after, then lost consecutive road games to Tulane, 25–0, and Alabama, 13–0, before ending with a 13–0 victory against Georgia Tech. Mehre closed with a respectable 7–2–1 campaign.

In addition, All-America honors went to Herb Maffett and Ralph Maddox, who, along with the Bulldogs' Roberts, Smith, and guard Milton "Red" Leathers, were named All-Southern Conference, as was Florida guard James Steele.

Florida followed the Georgia game with a 20–6 loss to Alabama in the first game at newly-completed Florida Field in Gainesville. The Gators charged back to take a 27–0 road win against Clemson and bombarded Georgia Tech, 55–7, before a 13–6 loss to Tennessee in Jacksonville, to finish 6–3–1.

Action during the scoreless 1930 game played in Savannah, the first tie in the rivalry. [Hargrett Collection, UGA Libraries]

Scoring:

Florida	0	0	0	0	—	0
Georgia	0	0	0	0	—	0

Florida: Parnell, *left end;* Waters, Pheil, *left tackle;* Steele, *left guard;* Clemons, *center;* James, McRae, *right guard;* Proctor, *right tackle;* Hall, Vickery, *right end;* Dorsett, *quarterback;* Bethea, *left halfback;* Sauls, McClellan, *right halfback;* Jenkins, Silsby, *fullback*

Georgia: Smith, *left end;* Rose, *left tackle;* Maddox, *left guard;* McWhorter, Tassapoulas, *center;* Leathers, *right guard;* Hamrick, *right tackle;* Maffett, *right end;* Downes, *quarterback;* Chandler, Waugh, *left halfback;* Dickens, Mott, *right halfback;* Roberts, Stoinoff, *fullback*

— 1931 —

Georgia 33, Florida 6

As FLORIDA AND GEORGIA PREPARED FOR their 1931 battle on Halloween in Gainesville, collegiate football was in turmoil on the national level.

Army end Richard Sheridan had been fatally injured with a broken neck on a kickoff a week earlier against Yale. Sheridan's death renewed a clamor to abolish the kickoff, considered by some to be the most dangerous play in football. Within the week, however, the football rules committee decided not to ban the play.

All-conference senior end Vernon "Catfish" Smith was the star of a strong 1931 Georgia team expected to challenge Tulane and Tennessee for the Southern Conference crown. The Bulldogs of fourth-year coach Harry Mehre debuted with a whipping of V.P.I. and a 26–7 win against Yale in Connecticut. Georgia then tripped North Carolina, 32–6, and blanked Vanderbilt, 9–0, to enter the Gators' lair undefeated.

Rated a heavy favorite, Georgia had not beaten Florida since the 1927 game in Jacksonville. Indeed, many considered the Gators a jinx team for the Bulldogs. Further inspiring the Florida eleven was the fact they would be playing Georgia for the first time ever in Gainesville before a homecoming throng of some 20,000 at Florida Field. At the time, it would be the largest crowd ever to see a football game in the university town.

But the Gators of fourth-year coach Charles Bachman were a young and injury-plagued bunch. Backs Johnnie Fountain, Shaw Buck and Sam Davis were hurt, forcing Florida to go to its bench for the Georgia meeting. Senior halfback Broward "Bo" McClellan, recovering from a broken leg suffered before the season and still hobbling in practice, was questionable.

Florida began the year with an impressive 31–0 road win over N.C. State then was held to a scoreless tie by North Carolina. The

Georgia back Jack "the Ripper" Roberts' 47-yard touchdown run in the second quarter of the 1931 battle gave UGA a 19–0 lead, and the Gators never recovered. [Hargrett Collection, UGA Libraries]

Gators lost to Syracuse before nipping Auburn, 13–12, in Jacksonville the week before the Georgia game.

Commenting on the unpredictable Gators, W. D. McMillan of the *Savannah Morning News* wrote that Bachman "has the happy faculty of taking a set of players who play dead one Saturday and making bloodthirsty lions out of them the next week-end. Florida may be short on tradition but they are long on fight."

The Bulldogs' train arrived in Gainesville on Friday and the squad took a bus to Ocala, 40 miles away, to escape pre-game attention. The Georgians held a light practice at a local country club in the afternoon and were relatively healthy, although senior halfback Spurgeon Chandler was bothered by a bruised collarbone and quarterback and team captain Austin Downes was limping due to leg cramps. Both would be available if needed.

Georgia fans made their presence known in Gainesville as the weekend approached. "There seemed to be almost as many cars from Georgia jamming the streets as there were Florida cars," the *Florida Times-Union* said. "Everywhere the Georgia colors were in evidence."

The Florida team spent Friday night resting at Keystone Heights outside the city and away from the excited crowds.

Prior to the 3 p.m. kickoff, the stadium "was a Kaleidoscope of vivid color and action," the *Times-Union* reported. In the east stands, the orange caps of the UF freshmen "formed a pool of solid color in a sea of dazzling hues."

Georgia opened the contest by testing its running assault, primarily with second-string backs, but had to punt without earning a first down. Taking over on their 37, the Gators marched to midfield on two fine runs by left halfback Allen Emmelhainz. With the Bulldogs thinking run, Florida went to the air. Right end Joe Hall worked free but dropped a bullet pass from right halfback A. L. Rogero at the Georgia 10. Three plays later, Rogero lost the pigskin and Georgia's Louis Wolfson recovered.

From that point, Georgia unleashed its stable of fine backs, headed by Jack "The Ripper" Roberts, Norman "Buster" Mott and Lloyd Gilmore. Gilmore and left halfback Joe Whire, both second-stringers, carried most of the load in the Bulldogs' first drive. The march climaxed when Gilmore dove over the Florida goal line from the 1. The extra point try failed.

Florida stayed with its air barrage but Rogero was perpetually harassed by Georgia defenders batting down his passes. With their second-string backs still in the game, Georgia had difficulty moving the ball after its touchdown. The great punting of Wendell Sullivan, however, was keeping the Gators contained near their goal.

Homer Key, Mott and Roberts entered the Bulldog defensive backfield to start the second period, with Florida in possession at its 26. Rogero passed to Hughes for a first down at the Florida 40, then sprang loose over center for 13 yards to the Georgia 47. Florida picked up another seven before Georgia's Vason McWhorter tackled C. J. Litherland for an 18-yard loss. Forced to punt, Rogero's kick was fielded by Key who returned it to the Georgia 44.

Runs by Mott and Roberts netted a first down before Mott burst through for 12 to the Florida 30. Four straight carries by Roberts and Key moved the visitors to a first down at the 15. But a penalty against Georgia and Rogero's block of a Sullivan pass gave Florida the ball at its 26. On third down, Rogero went for the bomb, looking for Hall who was in the open. Just as the pass was about to settle into Hall's waiting hands, UGA's Sullivan barely deflected it, breaking up the play.

The ensuing Florida punt left Georgia with a first down at its 29. Line drives by Roberts, Mott and Key reached the 45. On a no-frills off-tackle run, Mott sliced through and galloped 55 yards on a broken field romp for the score. Smith's placement made it 13–0, Georgia.

After an Emmelhainz kickoff return of 24 yards, Rogero passed 16 yards to Hughes. But two plays later, Georgia's Key pulled in an interception on a long pass, and the Bulldogs set to work at the UF 47. Georgia hit back hard and fast.

On a reverse, Roberts bolted around end, winning a foot race to the end zone. Smith converted and Georgia led 20–0 at the half.

The marching bands of both schools highlighted halftime, with UGA playing Florida's fight song in front of the UF grandstand.

The third quarter contained few surprises. Georgia stayed on the ground and Florida's offense was ineffective. There was a brief, but physical, "argument" between Catfish Smith and UF's Rogero on a pass play before Georgia's Key returned a punt to the Bulldog 34. Roberts ran right end for 12 and, two plays later on a reverse, smashed through left tackle to the Florida 20.

The comeback hopes of Florida's homecoming crowd were flickering away as the sun dropped. Key added more gloom for the Gators when he slipped inside right tackle and darted for the sideline. Smith blocked the last Gator defender and Key scored the Red and Black's fourth touchdown. Smith's point after attempt was low, but with a 26–0 lead few Bulldog fans appeared concerned.

Florida's touchdown came in the third quarter. Bogged down on its 30, Georgia decided to quick-kick. Gator senior left tackle Clarence Pheil muscled through the Bulldog line to block the attempt by quarterback Sullivan. Pheil snatched the bounding ball and bulled 15 yards for the score. Still gasping for air after his great play, Pheil was called on to try the conversion kick, but it failed.

Entering the fourth period, Georgia's ground game and strong defense continued to prevail. Roberts and halfback Marion Dickens fueled the Bulldogs' final touchdown drive, stiff-arming paths

Vernon "Catfish" Smith was Georgia's 1931 All-American who scored all of UGA's points in the 15–0 upset of Yale in 1929. He was 1–1–1 against Florida, including the scoreless battle of 1930.

through the Gator defenders. Whire scored on a 9-yard run and Smith's PAT stretched the score to 33–6.

Mehre had won his first victory over Florida in four tries.

Georgia had 336 yards in total offense, all on the ground. The rushing of Roberts, Key, Sullivan, Mott, Whire, Gilmore and Dickens simply trampled the Gators underfoot.

On the day, Georgia snagged three interceptions, holding the Gators to 83 yards on eight pass completions and 134 rushing yards.

Georgia bested New York University a week later, but lost to Tulane, 20–7, in a showdown for the conference title. The Bulldogs then downed Auburn, 12–0, and Georgia Tech, 35–6, before falling 60–0 to Southern California in Los Angeles to finish at 8–2. Catfish Smith capped his great career at Georgia by capturing All-America honors. Smith and Downes were All-Southern Conference, Smith for the third time. Milton Leathers, Jack Roberts and Whire were all drafted by the Philadelphia Eagles.

Florida's campaign continued disastrously. The Gators were pummeled 41–0 at Alabama; tied South Carolina, 6–6; lost 23–0 to Georgia Tech; and 13–0 to UCLA in Los Angeles, before ending the season with a 7–2 loss to Kentucky.

Georgia now led the series 7–2–1, not counting the 1904 game.

The Associated Press summed up the '31 meeting this way: "Florida fought hard all the way, but it was just a case of (a) Bulldog on the bank running circles around the Gator in the pool."

Scoring:

Georgia	6	14	6	7	—	33
Florida	0	0	6	0	—	6

UGA	TD	Gilmore, 1-yard run (PAT failed)
UGA	TD	Mott, 55-yard run (Smith kick)
UGA	TD	Roberts, 47-yard run (Smith kick)
UGA	TD	Key, 20-yard run (PAT failed)
UF	TD	Pheil, 15-yard run (PAT failed)
UGA	TD	Whire, 9-yard run (Smith kick)

Georgia: Wolfson, *left end;* Townsend, *left tackle;* Patterson, *left guard;* McWhorter, Batchelor, *center;* Bennett, *right guard;* Cooper, *right tackle;* Crenshaw, *right end;* Sullivan, Moran, *quarterback;* Whire, Gaston, *left halfback;* Dickens, Key, Mott, *right halfback;* Roberts, Gilmore, Stoinoff, *fullback*

Florida: Parnell, Cherry, *left end;* Pheil, *left tackle;* Forsyth, Bernhard, *left guard;* Ferrazzi, Spiers, *center;* Anderson, *right guard;* Jenkins, Simpson, *right tackle;* Hall, *right end;* Litherland, Treadgold, *quarterback;* Emmelhainz, Kelly, *left halfback;* Rogero, *right halfback;* Hughes, Silsby, *fullback*

— 1932 —

Georgia 33, Florida 12

As THE GREAT DEPRESSION CLOAKED THE country, the grimness of Georgia football fans sank even deeper in the weeks leading up to the Saturday, October 29, 1932, tilt with the Gators in Athens.

Coach Harry Mehre was off to the worst start in his five years at Georgia. The Bulldogs were winless as they prepared for homecoming against Florida. Georgia had lost 7–6 to V.P.I., 34–25 at Tulane, and 12–6 at Vanderbilt. Mehre's team also had struggled to a 6–6 tie with North Carolina in Athens.

The Florida squad owned a 2–1 record. Fifth-year coach Charles Bachman had experienced his first losing season at Florida the year before, including his first loss to the Bulldogs. The Gators premiered in 1932 with victories over Sewanee and The Citadel before losing 17–6 to N.C. State in Tampa the week before the Georgia game.

The Gators had other problems. Right halfback A. L. Rogero, Florida's best passer and punter, suffered a knee injury against N.C. State and would not play. Four other players, Tommy "Memory" Lane, Luke "Monk" Dorsett, W. E. "Pug" Bryan, and Simon Osgood, had been demoted to the Gators' B-squad and would not face the Bulldogs. They had remained in Tampa after the N.C. State game despite strict orders from Bachman that all players were to return to Gainesville with the team. Lane, a sophomore who was having an exceptional year at left guard, would be a significant absence from the Florida line.

Georgia's fortunes revolved around the elusive running of sophomore J. A. "Cy" Grant. Halfbacks Homer Key and Norman "Buster" Mott both had scored touchdowns against Florida in the '31 contest.

Athens bulged with students, alumni and fans of both teams as the game neared and the parties intensified.

The 30-man Florida team arrived in town by train early Friday afternoon and practiced at Sanford Field before retiring to the Georgian Hotel for dinner and a night's rest.

With some 10,000 fans looking on, both teams had little luck on their first possessions, but Georgia found its rhythm after a Florida punt to the UGA 30. Georgia's Leroy Young passed to Mott who was tackled at the Florida 38 after a 24-yard gain. Runs by Marion Gaston and Mott moved the ball to the 18, but Gaston fumbled and Gator quarterback Sam Davis recovered.

After an exchange of kicks, Gator halfback Jack Henderson, on first down from the Florida 40, threw to right halfback George Moye all the way down to the Georgia 25. The play "caught most of the Georgians asleep" as Moye shook away from Mott at the 15 and knifed into the end zone. Junior fullback Jimmie Hughes' conversion failed, but Florida owned the early advantage.

The remainder of the first quarter and the beginning of the second period was a nightmare for the partisan Georgia crowd as the Bulldogs lost two more fumbles when threatening to score.

Midway through the second quarter, Cy Grant eased matters for Red and Black supporters with an electrifying shot through the line at the Florida 37, hitting the open field before being bounced out of bounds at the 3. On the next play, he rammed up the middle to score. Junior right end Graham Batchelor kicked the point after and Georgia led 7–6 at halftime.

During intermission, the Georgia Glee Club and UGA band entertained by performing the fight songs of both schools. And four youngsters, representing Georgia Governor-elect Eugene Talmadge and other state Democrats in attendance, rode mules around the field, much to the crowd's enjoyment.

After both teams failed to move the ball opening the second half, Grant kicked to the Gators' Henderson at midfield. Henderson zigzagged through defenders before being tackled at the Georgia 28. On first down, Henderson passed 22 yards to halfback Moye to the 6. On a reverse, fullback Hughes went to the 2, then pushed forward to the 1-foot line. On third down, Hughes wedged over center and across the Georgia goal line. Again the Gators missed the extra point but they had regained the lead, 12–7.

The score was a redemption of sorts for Hughes who had dropped a pass in the open field early in the 1931 game.

Momentum seemed to have swung to the Gators, but the Florida touchdown was an elixir for the wheezing Bulldogs' offense. Georgia took the kickoff and moved out to its 45 on four plays. Grant then ran wide to the left side of the Gators line, racing for a 45-yard gain to the Florida 10 before being shoved out of bounds. Florida called a time out to regroup but it did little good. After a pass gained a yard, Grant spun through for a 9-yard touchdown and the Bulldogs led again. Batchelor's kick, though wide, still left Georgia with the lead, 13–12.

Florida bowled down to the Georgia 38 on their next incursion but got no further, and Henderson quick-kicked to the 12. Bulldog tackle Bill David skirted right end for 31 yards and Grant ran for seven more. After David banged for five to the Florida 45, Key faked a pass, sprang free of the Gator linemen, and cut to his right in the open field. Left end Fred Miller floored a Florida back with a solid block and Key sprinted to pay dirt. Batchelor's placement was good and Georgia led 20–12.

Entering the fourth quarter, Florida was still within striking distance. But Gator fullback Charles Stolz fumbled and the Bulldogs' Dick Maxwell fell on the ball at the Florida 44.

Gaston got three before Key tore free on a 27-yard scamper to the 14. On first down, Cy Grant piled through the line for the touchdown. Grant added the extra point on a drop kick (his 19th point of the afternoon), and Georgia had iced its win with a 27–12 spread.

Mehre sent in a wave of substitutes after the kickoff, but the demoralized Gators sank deeper when the Bulldogs recovered a UF fumble at the Gators' 40. Georgia drove to the 9 before Mott coughed it up and Florida's George McCampbell recovered.

With less than five minutes to play, the Bulldogs had possession on their 45. Substitute halfback Buck Chapman made a 13-yard gallop to the UF 11 and David muscled to the 1. Mott crowned the march with a touchdown dive. The 33–12 margin for the Bulldogs was insurmountable.

Florida right tackle Carl Shuman sustained a mild concussion in the third quarter and spent the night in the Georgia infirmary.

Never before in the series had the lead seesawed between these increasingly bitter rivals, yet Cy Grant's off-tackle slashes and three scores proved the difference.

Georgia had 448 yards in offense to 109 yards for Florida. The Bulldogs also led in passing yards 80 to 70 and in first downs 24 to 7.

In the Georgia tradition, students rang the school's ancient chapel bell into the night as part of the victory celebration. A bonfire flamed on old Herty Field and red-capped UGA freshmen paraded around it.

Georgia's euphoria over its first victory of the year was shattered a week later when the Bulldogs were beaten in an away game at New York University. Mehre's men rebounded to skin Clemson, 32–18, but lost 14–7 to Auburn and ended the campaign with a scoreless deadlock against Georgia Tech to go 2–5–2. Buster Mott was a draft choice of the Green Bay Packers.

Florida followed the Georgia defeat with losses to North Carolina, 18–13; Auburn, 21–6; Georgia Tech, 6–0; and Tennessee, 32–13, before beating UCLA 12–2 in Gainesville, avenging the 1931 loss to the Bruins in Los Angeles.

Bachman ended his coaching career at Florida with a record of 27–18–3 including a 2–2–1 mark against Georgia.

In December, 13 of the 23 schools in the Southern Conference formed the Southeastern Conference. The charter members of the SEC were Florida, Georgia, LSU, Mississippi, Mississippi State, Tennessee, Vanderbilt, Alabama, Auburn, Kentucky, Georgia Tech, Tulane and Sewanee.

Scoring:

Georgia	0	7	13	13 —	33
Florida	6	0	6	0 —	12

UF	TD	Moye, 40-yard pass from Henderson (PAT failed)
UGA	TD	Grant, 3-yard run (Batchelor kick)
UF	TD	Hughes, 1-yard run (PAT failed)
UGA	TD	Grant, 9-yard run (PAT failed)
UGA	TD	Key, 45-yard run (Batchelor kick)
UGA	TD	Grant, 14-yard run (Grant kick)
UGA	TD	Mott, 1-yard run (PAT failed)

Georgia: Miller, Turbyville, *left end;* David, Gilmore, Townsend, *left tackle;* McCullough, J. Brown, Hazelhurst, *left guard;* McWhorter, Ludwig, *center;* Moorehead, *right guard;* Opper, Cooper, Gunnels, *right tackle;* Batchelor, Maxwell, Crenshaw, *right end;* Young, Griffith, Sullivan, *quarterback;* Key, Chapman, *left halfback;* Mott, Grant, Brown, *right halfback;* Gaston, *fullback*

Florida: McLean, Rogers, *left end;* Shearer, *left tackle;* McCampbell, Shouse, *left guard;* Ferrazzi, *center;* Bernhard, *right guard;* Schuman, Jenkins, Williamson, *right tackle;* Goodyear, *right end;* Davis, Culler, *quarterback;* Henderson, McAnley, *left halfback;* Moye, *right halfback;* Hughes, Stolz, *fullback*

— 1933 —

Georgia 14, Florida 0

THE GRIDIRON COMBAT FOR THE FIRST SEC championship was well underway when Florida and Georgia renewed hostilities in Jacksonville's Municipal Stadium on November 4, 1933.

A week earlier, Georgia's fleet backs and unyielding defense stunned New York University, 25–0, in Athens. The win, coupled with a loss by Alabama to Fordham, meant that undefeated Georgia entered the Florida showdown as the prime contender for the conference title as well as national honors.

The Gators of first-year coach D. K. "Dutch" Stanley were coming off a hard-fought 13–6 loss to a powerful Tennessee eleven in Knoxville in which the favored Volunteers rallied with two fourth-quarter touchdowns. Tennessee coach Bob Neyland praised the work of Florida tackles Hal Starbuck and Bill Stark and said the 1933 Gators appeared to be the best Florida team since the '28 squad that went 8–1.

Despite the rigors of the Depression, a capacity crowd of some 20,000 filled the stadium in Jacksonville to see if the Gators could regroup against the Bulldogs who were a solid pregame favorite.

Florida began the season with a win over Stetson and a 31–0 romp against Sewanee before a scoreless tie with N.C. State and a 9–0 victory against North Carolina in Gainesville. Stanley's team was 3–1–1 facing the Bulldogs.

Sixth-year Georgia coach Harry Mehre had a team brimming with talent. Best known to Florida were headline halfback J. A. "Cy" Grant, who had run for three touchdowns against the Gators in the '32 game, and little Homer Key, another elusive back who stung the Gators with a 45-yard TD run the previous year.

Georgia had clipped N.C. State, 20–10, in its opener; downed Tulane, 26–13; and North Carolina, 30–0, before escaping Mercer,

13–12, in Macon a week before the NYU game.

Florida fans were hoping Georgia would overlook the injury-riddled Gators in anticipation of their November 11 game at Yale. Florida had lost halfback Jack "Sonny" Henderson (injured knee in N.C. State game) and senior center S. W. "Big Bill" Ferrazzi (recovering from a dislocated shoulder). Henderson had thrown a scoring pass to George Moye in the '32 Georgia game. Gator tackle Welcome Shearer and guard Tommy "Memory" Lane were hurt in the Tennessee game but probably would play. Georgia's squad was intact.

Despite his player losses, Florida's Stanley remained defiant. "We're crippled and we won't have our full power but we are going to battle Georgia to the last ditch with the men on hand," he said in a November 3 interview.

Georgia's Mehre was more simplistic in his game assessment: "We fear Florida." He knew the Gators had not been scored on before the Tennessee game and that Florida probably had the best defense his team had played so far. Mehre and his assistants also worried that the Bulldogs would experience a letdown after the emotional win over NYU. He knew his boys would have to contain Gator sophomore halfbacks Billy Chase and Herbert McAnley if the Bulldogs were to win for the third year in a row.

With most of the fans barely in the stadium, Georgia received the 2:30 p.m. kickoff and threatened to score almost immediately. From near midfield, Key flipped a 35-yard pass to right end and team captain Graham Batchelor, who was knocked down at the UF 15. Grant slid through the line to the 6, and Georgia appeared to be in business before the fans had warmed their seats.

The Gators answered their wake-up call, however. Seven times Georgia backs plunged toward the goal, but gained a total of only four yards, including a first down on the 3. The elated Floridians took over on downs but couldn't move the ball and were forced to punt from their end zone. Georgia began its second march from the UF 40.

Key, the 145-pound back whom one writer described as a "midget tartar," slipped over left tackle and raced down the sideline for 33 yards before being knocked out of bounds by Chase at the Florida 7. A running play was stacked up, but on the next play, Key scrambled in his backfield and lofted "a lazy flat pass" toward Grant who had eased across the Florida goal. Grant kicked the point after and Georgia led 7–0 after the first quarter.

"The fox hunter from Cornelia" was UGA halfback "Cy" Grant, who scored three touchdowns in the 1932 Florida game and two more against the Gators in 1933, both Georgia wins. [Hargrett Collection, UGA Libraries]

The Bulldogs got a break early in the second period when Herbert McAnley, the Gator right halfback, fumbled inside the UF 30. Georgia fullback George Chapman fell on it at the Gators' 25. Sam Brown, a second-string halfback, slashed for 18 yards; but a 15-yard penalty pushed the Bulldogs back, and a fourth-down pass was broken up by the Gators.

Florida's offense was almost nonexistent until late in the half when the Gators recovered a Georgia fumble near midfield. Chase, McAnley and substitute halfback Wallace Brown powered through the Bulldogs' line, but time was against the Gators. The clock wound down with Florida at the Georgia 28.

Down by only a touchdown, the Gators had held the Bulldogs to just one score, though Georgia had been inside the UF 10 three times.

In the third quarter, after a Florida punt, Georgia's Chapman ripped off an 18-yard run. From the UF 36 on the third play of the half, Grant cut over tackle and stumbled as a Gator defender snatched at his legs. Regaining his balance and breaking free, he outran two

Florida pursuers to the end zone. Grant added the extra point for a 14–0 Georgia lead. Orange and Blue supporters sat in shocked silence while the Red and Black whooped it up.

The game ended with Georgia nearing the Florida goal again. Halfback Sam Brown circled end for 40 yards to the Gators' 17, but the final gun cracked with Florida's beaten but proud defenders holding Georgia out of the end zone.

In two games against the Gators, Georgia's "Cy" Grant had scored five touchdowns and kicked three extra points, singled-handedly scoring more points than Florida had scored in four games against the Bulldogs dating back to 1930.

Georgia's rushers netted 247 yards to Florida's 79. The Bulldogs held a 37 to 25 passing edge as well.

"In Chase, McAnley and Brown, Florida offered three hard-driving backs who frequently bombarded the Georgia line but all their efforts were of the solo type—gained through sheer punch and with no interference," an Associated Press writer said. "Except in few cases the Florida blockers would have done their runners just as much good had they been squatting on the substitute bench."

The same writer praised the Gators on defense as "a stalwart bunch of courageous fighters."

Florida later fell 19–7 to Georgia Tech; beat Auburn, 14–7; and Maryland, 19–0, to finish the year 5–3–1.

Georgia's glory continued with a 7–0 win over Yale in New Haven, Conn., but a 14–6 upset by Auburn spoiled its SEC crown hopes. It was Alabama who took the inaugural SEC title as the Bulldogs nipped Georgia Tech, 7–6, then were smashed 31–0 by Southern California in Los Angeles to close at 8–2 for Mehre's fourth winning season.

Georgia's Batchelor and 210-pound right guard LeRoy Moorehead were honored as first-team All-SEC selections.

Scoring:

| Georgia | 7 | 0 | 7 | 0 | — | 14 |
| Florida | 0 | 0 | 0 | 0 | — | 0 |

UGA TD Grant, 7-yard pass from Key (Grant kick)
UGA TD Grant, 36-yard run (Grant kick)

Georgia: Turbyville, Maxwell, Ashford, *left end;* Opper, Shi, *left tackle;* McCullough, Cooper, Johnson, *left guard;* Perkinson, Gunnels, *right tackle;* Batchelor, Wagnon, *right end;* Griffith, Young, *quarterback;* Key, Bond, *left halfback;* Grant, S. Brown, *right halfback;* Chapman, Gaston, David, *fullback*

Florida: Rogers, Shearer, *left end;* Starbuck, Hickland, *left tackle;* Bernhard, Lane, *left guard;* A. Brown, Matheny, *center;* Turner, Bryan, *right guard;* Stark, *right tackle;* Moye, Rickett, *right end;* Davis, Bullock, Priest, *quarterback;* Chase, Brown, *left halfback;* McAnley, Gregory, *right halfback;* Hughes, Stolz, Beckwith, *fullback*

	Georgia	Florida
First downs	13	8
Passes	7	10
Passes comp.	2	3
Passing yards	37	25
Punt avg.	36	37
Penalties (yards)	66	25
Fumbles/lost	1/1	3/1
Rushing yards	247	79

— 1934 —

Georgia 14, Florida 0

GEORGIA HAD BEEN THE PRESEASON FAVOR-
ite to win the 1934 SEC title, but their championship hopes already
were shattered by the time the Bulldogs met Florida.

With less than successful seasons, both teams were hoping to gain
some lost respect entering the November 3 game in Jacksonville, the
13th meeting of the schools excluding the 1904 contest.

America was awash in a bloody crime wave of the Depression
gangster era. Earlier in the year, notorious outlaws John Dillinger,
Bonnie Parker and Clyde Barrow, and Charles "Pretty Boy" Floyd
had been killed in shootouts with lawmen. Indeed, on the day of the
game, members of the infamous "Ma" Barker gang were holed up in
a cottage on Lake Weir about 100 miles south of Jacksonville.

As the 2:30 p.m. kickoff neared, a crowd of about 22,000, the
largest ever to watch a football game in Florida, jammed into Municipal Stadium under clear skies in crisp autumn air.

"While neither team has had more than an average season both
have indicated potential power that brings to match two beaten but
eager elevens," the *Savannah Morning News* said on game day.

Under seventh-year coach Harry Mehre, the Bulldogs opened the
season stomping Stetson and edging Furman. But consecutive losses
to North Carolina, 14–0; Tulane, 7–6; and Alabama, 26–6 in Birmingham, shoved the Georgians out of the conference race a week
before the Florida clash.

Second-year UF coach D. K. "Dutch" Stanley was hoping for his
first victory over favored Georgia. The Gators beat Rollins and V.P.I.
before losing 28–12 to Tulane. Florida then defeated N.C. State,
14–0, but fell 21–0 at Maryland to face Georgia with a 3–2 record.

Georgia was without guard Dave McCullough, who was on the
injured list. Gator fullback Charlie Stolz also was hurt and would
be out.

90

Florida made no secret of its intention to pass. The Bulldogs were counting on their reserve strength and usually strong rushing game and also planned to key on Gator halfbacks Billy Chase and Wallace Brown, who had had some success in running against the Bulldogs a year earlier.

The hard-hitting game unfolded with Florida stopping Georgia at the Bulldogs 26. From there, UGA left halfback Maurice Green rocketed a towering punt to the Florida 15. A clipping penalty pushed the Gators back to their 1. Chase tried to punt from the end zone, but Georgia right guard John Brown and left end Charles Turbyville, the team captain, were right on top of him. The kick dribbled out of bounds inches from the Florida goal line. The Bulldogs argued "long and vehemently" for possession, but the officials ruled that the ball had not crossed the line of scrimmage and gave Florida another chance to kick. This time Chase punted out to the UF 36.

The long-range punting of Georgia's Green and John Bond, a sophomore halfback from Toccoa, Ga., kept Florida backed up most of the remainder of the quarter. In what had become a hallmark of the border rivalry, both defenses played ferociously—as if nothing else in the world mattered except keeping the enemy out of their end zone.

Early in the second quarter though, Georgia back Johnny Jones, from his own 35, sprinted for a 22-yard gain around right end. Bond hit substitute left halfback Glenn Johnson on a 1-yard pass, and Johnson followed with a 9-yard run to the UF 22. Bond scrambled for 14 and Georgia had a first down inside the 10.

Twice Bond ripped into the line and twice the Gators threw him back for no gain. On third down, Bond again took the ball and appeared to be headed into the inner pile of bodies. Suddenly, he

Florida halfback Jack Beckwith is the target of the UGA secondary after a long run in Georgia's 14–0 win in 1934. [UF Archives]

faded back and pitched a pass over the lines to Johnson, clear in the end zone. Bond also added the point after and Georgia enjoyed a 7–0 lead midway in the second quarter.

Florida tried to answer. On the running of Chase, right halfback Jack Beckwith, and fullback W. T. "Duke" Warren, the Gators rushed downfield. But the drive ended when Georgia held on its own 8, taking over on downs.

At halftime, the teams and their fans were in much the same shape as they had been at the 1933 game: Georgia was up 7–0 but Florida's defensive showing and the Gators' drive in the second quarter meant the battle still was in doubt.

A golden chance for the Gators came early in the third quarter. Bond fumbled and Florida left end Chuck Rogers wrapped himself around the ball at the UGA 17. The Gators got to the 14 but could go no further. "The Bulldog line became tenacious when the huskies felt the double stripes (of the end zone) drawing uncomfortably close to their backs," the Associated Press reported.

Throughout the game Florida passed with little effectiveness. Chase, a marked man for the Bulldogs, twice was spilled for sizeable losses while attempting to throw. Florida backs Beckwith and Warren also lofted aerials, but the Gator passing offensive netted only 58 yards on the day. In addition, Georgia right halfback Al Minot halted two short-lived Florida drives with interceptions.

The backbreaker for Florida came in the middle of the fourth quarter when Georgia's Bond intercepted a Chase pass and ran it back 32 yards to the UF 42. A 15-yard penalty and a 5-yard loss on a running play put Georgia 20 yards from a first down. Halfback Green faked a punt, racing for 33 yards through an alley at left guard before being snowed under at the UF 30. On the next play, Bond maneuvered into the Florida end zone and Green hit him with the scoring pass. Bond's extra point increased Georgia's lead to 14–0.

The Gators did not threaten again and Georgia owned its fourth victory in a row over Florida. Harry Mehre was now 4–2–1 in meetings with Florida.

Georgia was able to close down Florida's passing, though the Gators' Beckwith led all rushers with 63 yards. Wally Brown, Florida's leading rusher on the season, gained only 15.

The Bulldogs' John Bond clearly was the star of the game with a touchdown pass, touchdown catch, 32-yard interception return, over 40 yards rushing, a 50-yard punting average, and two extra points.

Florida tied Mississippi, 13–13, following the Georgia contest, but

Georgia halfback John Bond was the UGA hero in 1934, throwing a touchdown pass, catching a scoring pass, kicking two extra points, making an interception, and keeping Florida in trouble with his punting. [Hargrett Collection, UGA Libraries]

did not lose again. The Gators dropped Auburn, 14–7; Georgia Tech, 13–12; and Stetson for a 6–3–1 worksheet.

Mehre's Bulldogs finished the season with a display of talent and power, beating Yale 14–7 in Connecticut, then blanking N.C. State, 27–0; Auburn, 18–0; and Georgia Tech, 7–0, to end the year 7–3.

Scoring:

Georgia	0	7	0	7	—	14
Florida	0	0	0	0	—	0

UGA TD   G. Johnson, 9-yard pass from Bond (Bond kick)
UGA TD   Bond, 30-yard pass from Green (Bond kick)

Georgia: Turbyville, *left end;* Shi, *left tackle;* F. Johnson, *left guard;* McKnight, *center;* J. Brown, *right guard;* West, *right tackle;* Wagnon, *right end;* Treadaway, *quarterback;* Green, G. Johnson, *left halfback;* Minot, Bond, *right halfback;* Causey, *fullback*

Florida Rogers, *left end;* Starbuck, *left tackle;* Bryan, *left guard;* Shearer, *center;* Turner, *right guard;* Stark, *right tackle;* Moye, *right end;* W. Brown, *quarterback;* Chase, J. Jones, *left halfback;* Beckwith, *right halfback;* Warren, *fullback*

	Georgia	Florida
First downs	12	8
Pass att/comp/int	8/3/0	9/4/3
Passing yards	50	58
Rushing yards	194	130

— 1935 —

Georgia 7, Florida 0

FLORIDA WAS GIVEN SO LITTLE CHANCE TO whip Georgia in the November 2, 1935, game that Georgia coach Harry Mehre announced he would start second-string backs against the Gators to give his stars John Bond and Al Minot much needed rest.

Other than football, Americans nationwide pondered news reports of Adolf Hitler's diatribes against the Jews and the spear thrusts of Benito Mussolini's Italian army invading Ethiopia in the fall of 1935.

The 4–1 Georgia Bulldogs were having a good season, but a 17–7 loss to Alabama a week earlier in Athens had damaged their conference title hopes. Georgia shelled Mercer and Chattanooga to open the year. The Bulldogs then bashed Furman, 31–7, and N.C. State, 13–0, before meeting Alabama.

At 1–3, the Florida Gators of third-year coach Dutch Stanley were in desperate need of a win.

Florida premiered with a shellacking of Stetson but lost 19–7 at Tulane, 27–6 at Mississippi, and 20–6 to Maryland in Gainesville.

The Gators were expected to pass and were led by senior left halfback W. W. "Billy" Chase, the team captain. Quarterback Bob Ivey could also throw. Florida backs passed for 184 yards and ran for 176 more against Maryland in a balanced offensive display. Georgia scouts at that game were impressed with Chase but not with Florida's line. The Bulldogs would key on Chase, with Mehre announcing that 145-pound end Alex Ashford would have the primary assignment of stopping the Gator hero.

Florida was without injured fullback Herbert McAnley but was bolstered by the return of end Robert Rickett, who had not played since being hurt in the Stetson game. Also in the UF lineup was junior right end Floyd Christian, whose son would play for the Gators in the 1960s.

94

Heading the Bulldogs was senior left halfback and team co-captain John Bond, who had wrecked Florida the year before. Georgia's fullback Ward Holland, halfback Glenn Johnson, and center and co-captain John McKnight were all recovered from injuries and fit to play.

Two days before the game, reports out of Athens indeed said that Mehre would shuffle his backfield to give Bond and right halfback Al Minot a rest against the Floridians. Stanley could not have asked for anything better to incense his Gators, who arrived by bus in Jacksonville on game morning and dressed at the George Washington Hotel.

Sure enough, the game began with Bond and Minot being replaced by Alf Anderson and Johnny Jones in the Georgia backfield.

The first break of the contest went to Florida in the opening minutes of play. Unable to move the ball, Chase kicked to Bulldog quarterback Andrew Roddenbery standing near midfield; but Roddenbery mishandled the ball and Gator center Alton Brown recovered at the UF 48.

Even though Florida's offense was again stymied, the Bulldogs could not get close to the Gator goal line. As Mehre planned, the Georgians were able to pressure Chase and hold the Florida backs to short yardage. The Gator defense was holding its own.

Georgia's backs shot through for several nice gains, but Florida stiffened whenever the Bulldogs threatened to score.

Late in the quarter, UGA halfback Anderson completed a 27-yard pass to Johnny Jones at the Florida 31. Anderson galloped for 10 yards up the middle as the period ended.

Bond entered the game and, on the first play of the second quarter, charged over center to the Gators 12. Desperately, the Floridians dug in. Bond and the vaunted Bulldog offense tried four times to muscle in but were stuffed each time, and the ecstatic Gators took possession. Florida's rejuvenation didn't last long, though, as Georgia's defense again clamped down.

Georgia threatened again in the final moments of the second quarter, forging near the UF goal. Again the determined Gators rallied to keep the Bulldogs out before the timekeeper's whistle sounded, ending the half.

Both defenses had been outstanding. The Gators had withstood two serious Georgia drives and, while the Bulldogs had moved the ball, there was nothing to show for it on the scoreboard. Could the Florida jinx have resurfaced to haunt the Red and Black?

On the second half kickoff, Billy Chase took Frank Johnson's kick

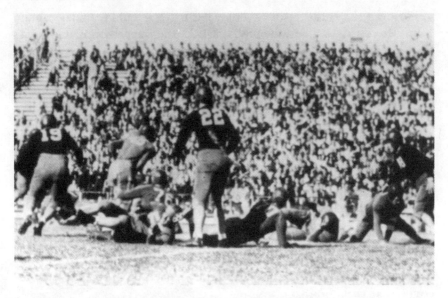

Action "around Georgia's left end" during the 1935 UGA victory.
[Hargrett Collection, UGA Libraries]

at the 9 and twisted upfield, avoiding several lunging tackles by Bulldogs. The Gator halfback raced all the way to the UGA 26 before he was hemmed in and dropped. His dazzling 65-yard run electrified the Florida crowd.

But, proving their mettle in a tough situation, a wall of Bulldogs met the Gators on each play of the series and Georgia regained possession.

Chase's kickoff run proved to be the offensive highlight of the third and much of the final period. Georgia strangled the Gators on defense but, before the afternoon was over, fumbled a total of six times, two of which resulted in turnovers.

With time slipping away in the fourth quarter, Florida had the ball on its 25 and fans on both sides had recollections of the scoreless 1930 game in Savannah.

The "Home State fans were beginning to grow quite a little proud of the scoreless deadlock they believed their team had in its grasp," the *Florida Times-Union* said of the multitude.

It was here that John Bond and Billy Chase, the senior luminaries of their respective teams, were involved in a play that would turn the tide of combat.

With Florida'a offense frustrated again, Chase booted a quick-kick from the Gator 25. The ball traveled low and short to Bond at the UF

40. Before the Gator pursuit could reach him, the Georgia halfback sprinted to the Florida 17 where Kenneth Eppert smashed him out of bounds. Bond had "been a source of grievous trouble to Florida for three years in a row," a Jacksonville reporter wrote.

On the first play from scrimmage, first-string right halfback Al Minot cracked off right tackle, pulled free from a few arm tackles, and sped into the end zone standing up to put Georgia up 6–0. Bulldog fans were in a frenzy as Bond kicked the extra point.

Florida was not finished. With less than a minute left, the Gators had the ball at their 45 when Ivey passed 20 yards to Johnny Burroughs to put Florida at the UGA 25. Successive 5-yard runs by sophomore quarterback Walter "Tiger" Mayberry and Ivey gave the Gators possession at the Bulldog 10 with only seconds left for one last play.

Anticipating Georgia to play the pass, substitute back W. B. Stephens handed off to Ivey, who fired into the line. The Bulldogs spilled forward, piling him under well short of the goal to ice the win.

Despite losing their fifth straight to the Bulldogs and being shut out for the third year in a row, there was no shame for the underdog Gators. No one had given them a chance against Georgia, yet if Chase had broken the kickoff . . . and they had stopped Minot . . .

Bulldog halfback Al Minot came off the bench to score the only touchdown in Georgia's 7–0 win over a determined Florida squad in 1935. [Hargrett Collection, UGA Libraries]

"Outrushed by a mile, the desperate 'Gators nullified gain after gain until the final minutes of the game," the Associated Press reported.

"In fact, doped to lose by almost any margin that Georgia cared to roll up, Coach Dutch Stanley's lads gained a host of admirers by the great and game battle they put up all the way," the *Times-Union* said.

After the Georgia heartbreaker, Florida lost 15–6 to Kentucky in Lexington and won its second game of the year, 20–0, over Sewanee in Gainesville. Georgia Tech destroyed the Gators, 39–6, at Florida Field; and Auburn dusted them, 27–6, in Miami, before Florida ripped South Carolina, 22–0, in Tampa, to end the season 3–7. Stanley ended his coaching career at Florida with an 0–3 record against Georgia.

Mehre's Bulldogs followed the Florida victory with a 26–13 whipping of Tulane in New Orleans but the fun stopped there. Georgia lost, 13–0, to LSU and by 19–7 scores to Auburn and Georgia Tech for a 6–4 mark. Guard Frank Johnson was a first-team All-SEC honoree.

Scoring:

Georgia	0	0	0	7	—	7
Florida	0	0	0	0	—	0

UGA TD   Minot, 17-yard run (Bond kick)

Georgia: Ashford, *left end;* Haygood, *left tackle;* Tinsley, *left guard;* Law, *center;* Hall, *right guard;* Johnson, Gatchell, *right tackle;* Candler, *right end;* Roddenbery, *quarterback;* Anderson, Bond, *left halfback;* J. Jones, Minot, *right halfback;* Green, *fullback*
Substitutes: McKnight, Moorehead, Hartman

Florida: Schucht, *left end;* Hickland, *left tackle;* Root, *left guard;* Brown, Maynard, *center;* J. Lane, *right guard;* Turner, *right tackle;* Christian, *right end;* Eppert, Stephens, Mayberry, Ivey, *quarterback;* Chase, *left halfback;* J. Jones, *right halfback;* Beckwith, *fullback*
Substitutes: Yon, Hughes, Kicliter, Hendricks

	Georgia	Florida
First downs	14	3
Passes/comp	6/3	14/3
Passing yards	55	30
Fumbles/lost	6/2	0/0
Rushing yards	193	61

— 1936 —

Georgia 26, Florida 8

BOTH TEAMS WERE WELL INTO PRACTICE FOR their November 7, 1936, showdown when President Franklin D. Roosevelt was reelected to his second term on Tuesday, November 3.

As the weekend approached, election results faded in the minds of football fans from the Florida Keys to the north Georgia mountains who were gearing up for the 15th Georgia-Florida matchup in Jacksonville.

Neither team was making gridiron headlines. Georgia, 2–4, battered Mercer in its first game and punched Furman before being skinned, 47–7, by LSU in Baton Rouge. Then Rice (13–6), Auburn (20–13), and Tennessee (46–0) all outclassed Georgia in Athens before the Florida game.

The Gators were 3–2 and unpredictable week to week under first-year coach Josh Cody. Florida tamed The Citadel in Gainesville, lost 7–0 at South Carolina, crunched Stetson, fell 7–0 at Kentucky, and nipped Maryland, 7–6, in Gainesville.

The Bulldogs were looking for their 12th victory over Florida, not including the 1904 game, and their sixth win in a row. The rivalry was intensifying with each teeth-rattling encounter. Football forecasters were divided in rating both teams slight favorites.

The fact that Georgia was coming off a blistering defeat and Florida building on a close win convinced some sports writers to predict a Gator win.

"If Josh Cody's 'Gators can maintain the pace they set against Maryland, they should be able to bowl over the Bulldogs," a United Press International dispatch said on November 5.

Injuries to Georgia heightened the chances of a Florida victory. Georgia halfback Glenn Johnson had badly injured an ankle in the Tennessee game and was not expected to play. Guard Walter Troutman and back Lewis Young also had leg injuries and were question-

A Florida defender tries to wrap up UGA halfback Glenn Johnson in the 1936 game. Johnson played despite a badly injured ankle. [Hargrett Collection, UGA Libraries]

able. Two other UGA linemen, Roy Gatchell and co-captain James Hall, were hurt, their status listed as doubtful. Fullback Bill Hartman, though, was returning after being out several weeks; and Forrest "Spec" Towns, the 110-meter high-hurdles champion at the 1936 Olympics in Berlin, was back.

From 20,000 to 22,000 were expected to fill Municipal Stadium, but the threat of rain kept the crowd to about 17,000. Heavy rain had waterlogged the field during the night.

On their own 31, the Georgians moved steadily down the field with Hartman and Sanford Vandiver pounding through the Florida line for big yardage. From the Gator 10, halfback Alf Anderson passed to Vandiver in the end zone for the game's first score. The point after failed but Georgia had an early 6–0 lead.

The effectiveness of the Georgia backs against the strong Florida line took many observers by surprise. Although the Bulldogs did not add to their lead before the second quarter, one writer said, "After the first period the result never was in doubt as Georgia's set of fleet backs took to the air whenever their running attack bogged down."

Yet it was the Gators who were next in the scoring spotlight. Minutes into the second quarter, Georgia was flagged for clipping on a Florida punt, and the Gators took possession at the Bulldog 15. On second down, halfback Walter "Tiger" Mayberry spotted right end Watson Ramsey streaking across the Georgia goal line and hit him for six points. Their conversion also failed but Florida had knotted the score 6–6.

The Bulldogs responded in short order. After substitute quarterback Lewis Young returned the Florida kickoff to the Georgia 36, Hartman found halfback Harry Stevens for a 25-yard gain to the Florida 39. Halfback Glenn Johnson, like Young not expected to play due to injuries, now checked in to the game.

Johnson gouged the Florida defense on two runs that put the ball at the Gator 1. On the next play Hartman crashed over. Again, the point after was no good but Georgia had reclaimed the lead, 12–6.

Florida valiantly fought back in an effort to tie or go ahead before halftime. Bob Ivey connected with Ramsey, then threw to Floyd Christian who was pulled down near the Georgia 10. But the Bulldog defense turned up the heat to stop the Gators, and the half ended.

Florida received the second half kickoff and immediately went to its passing game. The strategy backfired when Bulldog tackle John Davis stepped in front of a Gator receiver, intercepting a Mayberry pass.

Before the stunned Gators could recover, Maurice Green, substituting for Hartman at fullback, lofted a 26-yard pass to junior right end Otis Maffett for the score. Green's kick was true, widening the Georgia lead to 19–6.

Florida's hard-charging Mayberry, halfback Ed Manning and full-

Georgia fullback "Wild Bill" Hartman scored a touchdown in UGA's 1936 win against Florida. He earned All-American honors the next year.

back T. M. "Bugs" Hendricks were being smashed by a dominating Bulldog line. The Gators would rush for only 31 yards on the day.

Late in the third quarter, Georgia went on the march again from its own 36. Halfback Stevens found running room around right end and zipped for 26 yards. Bulldog backs powered into the line and ground down toward the Florida goal as the fourth quarter began.

From the 5, Stevens rifled a pass to Maffett for the receiver's second touchdown of the game. Green's conversion made it 26–6.

In Athens, euphoric students listening to the game by radio began ringing the old chapel bell midway through the fourth quarter, so sure were they of a Bulldog victory.

But the Gators more than played it out. Halfback Ivey, replacing the injured Mayberry, flung a bomb to junior halfback Ken Willis, who was hauled down at the Georgia 2 after a 40-yard gain. Gator runners punished the line but came up short three times. On fourth down, Ben Golden fumbled, the ball dribbling into the UGA end zone where Georgia fell on it.

With under five minutes left, the Gator defense held Georgia, forcing a punt near the UGA goal. Florida end Fonia Pennington

Florida back Walter "Tiger" Mayberry threw for UF's only touchdown in the 1936 Georgia win and was the Gators' first ever All-SEC player in 1937. A marine pilot in World War II, Mayberry earned several medals before being killed in combat.

UGA end Otis Maffett grabbed two second-half touchdown passes in Georgia's 1936 triumph over Florida. [Hargrett Collection, UGA Libraries]

burst through to block the kick, the ball rolling out of the end zone for a Florida safety.

The solid Georgia defense and a mix of running and passing on offense had won the game for the Bulldogs.

"Florida was beaten by a machine which worked too perfectly for any player to stand out as a hero . . ." said an Associated Press account.

Only Towns, the Georgia Olympian, gained mention in the newspapers by recovering a fumbled Florida punt.

One highlight for Florida was the punting of Ivey and halfback Paul Brock who collectively averaged 43 yards per boot, 10 better than the Bulldog kickers. Florida also scored on Georgia for the first time since the '32 game.

Florida "flared brightly in spots but seldom could capitalize on its daring plays," the AP reporter wrote.

The Georgians finished with a 12–6 road win against Tulane, a 7–7 tie with a powerful Fordham eleven in New York City, and a 16–6 decision over Georgia Tech in Athens to go 5–4–1, coach Harry Mehre's worst season since the 1932 team went 2–5–2.

Florida regrouped to beat Sewanee, 18–7, but was pounded 38–14 by Georgia Tech, 13–0 by Auburn, and 7–0 by Mississippi State to finish 4–6.

Scoring:

Georgia	6	6	7	7	—	26
Florida	0	6	0	2	—	8

UGA	TD	Vandiver, 10-yard pass from Anderson (PAT failed)
UF	TD	Ramsey, 15-yard pass from Mayberry (PAT failed)
UGA	TD	Hartman, 1-yard run (PAT failed)
UGA	TD	Maffett, 26-yard pass from Green (Green kick)
UGA	TD	Maffett, 5-yard pass from Stevens (Green kick)
UF	Safety	Pennington blocked UGA punt

Georgia: Towns, *left end;* Davis, *left tackle;* Tinsley, *left guard;* Lumpkin, *center;* Hall, *right guard;* Badgett, *right tackle;* Candler, Maffett, *right end;* Roddenbery, Young, *quarterback;* Anderson, *halfback;* Vandiver, Stevens, *halfback;* Hartman, Green, *fullback*

Florida: Christian, *left end;* Gardner, *left tackle;* Root, *left guard;* Oxford, *center;* Lane, *right guard;* Yon, *right tackle;* Ramsey, Pennington, *right end;* Golden, Manning, *quarterback;* Brock, Ivey, *left halfback;* Welles, Mayberry, Willis, *right halfback;* Hendricks, *fullback*

	Georgia	Florida
First downs	11	9
Rushing yards	194	31
Passes/comp/int	11/7/3	18/8/1
Passing yards	76	168
Fumbles/lost	0/0	3/2
Return yards	39	175
Penalties (yards)	20	40

— 1937 —

Florida 6, Georgia 0

ON NOVEMBER 6, 1937, MORE THAN 22,000 FANS thronged Jacksonville, which had "gone collegiate in its yearly splurge of pennants and chrysanthemums" for the annual Bulldogs-Gators scrap at Municipal Stadium.

One sportswriter later described the contest as "perhaps the most bitterly contested game" of the rivalry to that time.

The Florida team of second-year coach Josh Cody wanted to be the first Gator squad to beat Georgia since 1929 and avoid a seventh consecutive defeat to the Bulldogs. Florida (2–4) lost at LSU, 19–0, to begin the year, beat Stetson, fell to Temple at Philadelphia, shut out Sewanee, 21–0, then lost 14–13 at Mississippi State and 13–7 at Maryland.

Despite the Gators' lackluster showing, halfback and team captain Walter "Tiger" Mayberry, who had thrown Florida's touchdown pass against Georgia in the 1936 game, was being touted for All-America honors.

"He is a fast, sure-footed runner, he can pass and his punting is above the average," said the *Savannah Morning News.* "Down in Florida you have to put up your dukes if you suggest that Mayberry lacks the qualities demanded of an All-American."

As was the case before the 1936 struggle, the game was rated a toss-up.

The 4–2 Georgia Bulldogs had wrecked Oglethorpe in their opener and downed South Carolina, 13–7, and Clemson, 14–0, before being edged 7–6 by Holy Cross in Boston. Georgia then punched Mercer but was demolished 32–0 at Tennessee the week before the Florida matchup. Bulldog coach Harry Mehre was in his 10th and final season at UGA.

Georgia concentrated on shoring up its pass defense, riddled by the Volunteers, in preparation for the Gators. Bulldog end Otis Maffett,

Gator halfback Ken Willis struggles for yards against the UGA defense in Florida's 6–0 win in 1937. [UF Archives]

who caught two touchdown passes against Florida in the previous year's clash, was suffering from tonsillitis but was expected to be ready to play; and Georgia's Quinton Lumpkin was considered one of the best centers in the land. The major question was whether the Bulldogs could regroup after the Tennessee debacle.

Florida practiced behind locked gates in Gainesville and Cody was "silent as a sphinx" about his plans for the game. Like Georgia, the Gators were relatively injury-free and ready to go all out, although quarterback Paul Brock would play with a broken hand in a cast.

Georgia Governor E. D. Rivers occupied a box in the Georgia cheering section while Florida Governor Fred P. Cone rooted for the Gators from the Florida bench on a cool, clear, perfect day for football.

Florida was the first to mount an offensive. Propelled by the running of Mayberry, halfback Ken Willis, and fullback L. D. "Moon" Mullins, the Gators started on their 17 in the opening minutes and surged upfield. Not until the Floridians reached the Georgia 23 did the Bulldogs come to life. The Athenian line suddenly assumed control, hurling Willis then Mayberry for big losses back to the Georgia 41. Mayberry punted from there, the first of 10 Florida punts on the day.

Georgia fullback "Wild Bill" Hartman, a scorer in the '36 game, had some success running, but the Bulldogs could not sustain a drive.

Going into the second quarter, the game had evolved into trench warfare with little offense and plenty of staunch defense.

Then came "the break" of the day. Stopped by the Gators, Georgia was punting from its own 44. As Bulldog halfback Billy Mims took the snap, Florida right tackle Charlie Kreijcier barreled through, "charging like a shot." The kicked ball hit him in the stomach and bounced backward toward the Georgia goal.

In the dust and confusion of the next few seconds, Gator left end Clifford Whiddon scooped up the pigskin at the Georgia 25, broke away from two Bulldogs, and rambled into the end zone standing up. Orange and Blue backers were on their feet, yelling their approval even though left tackle Clark Goff's extra point attempt was low. The half ended with Florida clinging to a 6–0 advantage.

There was little offensive excitement in the third quarter, although Georgia did advance into Florida's domain on one occasion.

With the game hanging in the balance, the fourth quarter would be one of the most exciting of the series. Needing a touchdown and an extra point for victory, the Bulldogs hunkered down.

Georgia began from its 20 as halfback Vassa Cate swung around end for 18 yards. Substitute fullback James Fordham then wrenched free of the lines and fought downfield for 41 yards to the Florida 21. A short pass and runs by Mims and Fordham gave Georgia possession at the Gators 4. But a fourth-down line plunge by Fordham was short and Florida took over.

Cody decided to try a punt, hoping that Tiger Mayberry, whose kicking had been outstanding all day, could drive the Bulldogs back. Standing almost out of the Florida end zone, Mayberry calmly

Florida end Clifford Whiddon recovered a blocked punt for a touchdown in UF's 6–0 defeat of Georgia. The win snapped a six-game winning streak in the series. [UF Archives]

caught the snap and towered a high kick that skipped out of bounds at the Georgia 48.

"Florida fans breathed easier but not for long, " the *Morning News* said. Indeed, the Bulldogs quickly strong-armed their way back into contention.

"Wild Bill" Hartman rumbled wide around left end and wasn't brought down until he reached the Florida 35. With time running out, Georgia's Mims then tried to ignite the Bulldogs' passing attack.

He connected with right end Carroll Thomas at the 18. Retreating again, Mims fired another missile toward a Bulldog receiver at the goal line. This time, Gator quarterback Jack Blalock read the play perfectly and intercepted. With the lusty roar of Gator rooters echoing over the field, Blalock churned down the sideline 67 yards before running out of steam and being pulled down at the Georgia 33. "He probably would have scored had he not been exhausted, " the Associated Press said.

The interception secured the Florida victory, its third in the rivalry and the first over the detested Bulldogs since 1929.

At the final whistle, frenzied Florida fans, "still gasping from the Gators' close call" swarmed onto the field. They overran police and national guardsmen in pulling down the goalposts.

Georgia's Hartman ran for 106 yards but his exploits were overshadowed by Florida's Mayberry, who rushed for 83 yards and whose punting kept the Bulldogs backed up. "Without his great punting Florida could not have held off the surging Georgians, " the *Morning News* said. On several plays, Mayberry had been the last man to pull down a Bulldog runner.

In defeat, Georgia fans wondered what would have happened if a 52-yard run by Jim Cavan to the Gators' 17 in the third quarter had

Josh Cody coached at Vanderbilt and Clemson before becoming head man at Florida in 1936. Cody's Gators were 1–3 against the Bulldogs from 1936 to 1939. [UF Archives]

A Gator runner attracts a rough crowd in the 1937 Florida victory. [Hargrett Collection, UGA Libraries]

not been nullified by an offside penalty.

Georgia went on to nip Tulane, 7–6; fight Auburn to a scoreless tie, and tie Georgia Tech, 6–6, in Atlanta before besting Miami, 26–8, to close at 6–3–2. Harry Mehre ended his career at Georgia with a 6–3–1 mark against Florida.

Florida lost a 10–9 squeaker to Clemson, a 12–0 decision to Georgia Tech, and a 14–0 verdict to Auburn, before a finale 6–0 win over Kentucky, for a 4–7 campaign. Josh Cody had evened his record at 1–1 against Georgia.

Tiger Mayberry was named to the All-SEC first team, the first University of Florida player to be so honored.

Georgia's Hartman was not only named All-SEC but All-America, too. He was a draft pick of the Washington Redskins, while guard Pete Tinsley also turned pro, playing for the Green Bay Packers.

Walter Mayberry joined the Marine Corps, and, as a pilot in World War II, received several medals for battle action before being killed in combat.

The Florida-Georgia rivalry already was a tradition, and a comment from a *Florida Times-Union* reporter showed the mood of the times: "It always has been a pleasure to lose to the good sportsmen of Georgia. And their attitude in defeat made winning a little bit sad."

Scoring:

Florida	0	6	0	0	—	6
Georgia	0	0	0	0	—	0

UF   TD   Whiddon, 25-yard run after blocked punt recovery (PAT failed)

Florida: Whiddon, Pennington, *left end;* Goff, Hassett, *left tackle;* Lightbown, Gardner, *left guard;* Oxford, Williams, *center;* Kocsis, Davis, *right guard;* Kreijcier, Crabtree, *right tackle;* Ramsey, *right end;* Blalock, Stephens, *quarterback;* Mayberry, *halfback;* Willis, *halfback;* Mullins, *fullback*
Substitutes: McGhee, Delaney, Manning

Georgia: Towns, Eldredge, *left end;* Davis, Badgett, *left tackle;* Salisbury, Tinsley, *left guard;* Lumpkin, Milner, *center;* Troutman, *right guard;* Haygood, Decharleroy, *right tackle;* Thomas, Barbre, *right end;* Young, Miler, Roddenbery, *quarterback;* Holland, Mims, *halfback;* Cavan, Cate, *halfback;* Hartman, Fordham, *fullback*
Substitutes: Mathews, Horlick

	Florida	Georgia
First downs	9	10
Rushing yards	152	191
Pass att/comp	1/0	10/3
Passing yards	0	29
Fumbles/lost	0/0	1/0
Penalties (yards)	20	65
Punts/avg.	10/40	8/39

— 1938 —

Georgia 19, Florida 6

THE NOVEMBER 6, 1938, FLORIDA-GEORGIA game in Jacksonville was expected to have little bearing on the outcome of the Southeastern Conference race.

Nevertheless, some 17,000 fans turned out under threatening skies to see if the Gators of third-year coach Josh Cody could beat Georgia for the second consecutive year, a feat that had not been achieved since 1928–1929.

At 2–4 Florida was having far from a banner year. Ambushed by Stetson, 16–14, to begin the season, they were blanked 22–0 by Mississippi State at Starkville before beating Sewanee, 10–6. Cody's troops then fell 19–7 to Miami, lashed Tampa, 33–0, on the road, and were whipped 33–0 by Boston College.

Georgia football was in transition. After a decade, including eight winning seasons, Harry Mehre had left under fire from a substantial number of Georgia supporters who had loftier goals than Mehre attained. He was replaced by Joel Hunt, a former Texas A&M star who had been an assistant coach at LSU. One of Hunt's new assistants at Georgia was a stumpy, barrel-chested young man who had been a lineman at Mercer and a prep school coach—Milledgeville native Wallace Butts.

Hunt's 4–1 Bulldogs debuted with a 20–0 pasting of The Citadel and escaped with a 7–6 win over South Carolina in Columbia. Georgia then whaled Furman, 38–7, and Mercer, 28–19, before a 29–6 loss at Holy Cross the week before the Florida game.

In preparation for Georgia, Cody transferred center and team captain Jimmy Oxford to blocking back in a move to bolster the offense. He was replaced in the line by John Berry, who would be pitted against Bulldog center and captain Quinton Lumpkin, a second-team All-SEC performer in 1937.

Georgia scout Elmer Lampe watched Florida play Boston College

111

and described the Gators as a "dangerous club" that had fallen victim to a number of tough breaks.

Florida's hopes depended heavily on Oxford as well as quarterback Jack Blalock, whose dramatic 67-yard interception return in the 1937 clash had clinched a Gator victory. Three Georgia regulars—end Marvin Gillespie, guard Bob Salisbury and sophomore tailback Earl Hise—were recovering from injuries. Hise was listed as doubtful for the game but the others were expected to play.

The favored Bulldogs featured halfback Vassa Cate and fullback James Fordham, both of whom had run well against the Gators the previous year.

By Friday, Jacksonville's "hotels were packed and jammed and most of the throng is expected to stay overnight (Saturday) either to celebrate or forget," the *Florida Times-Union* said on game day.

After several exchanges of possessions in the first period, Georgia embarked on its first serious drive. Line thrusts by Fordham and halfback Harry Stevens guided the Georgians down the field. With a first down at the UF 5, a Georgia score appeared certain.

Fordham smacked into the line three times but couldn't put the ball in the end zone. On fourth down, Stevens tried his luck but was met by a flood of defenders inside the 1-yard line. The Gators had roused from their hibernation.

The quarter ended with Florida struggling to put yardage between the line of scrimmage and its goal line. Just when it appeared they were getting comfortable offensively, however, fullback W. L. "Bud" Walton fumbled, and UGA guard Walter Wilfong recovered at the Gators' 24.

Fordham spun through a seam in the Florida line, dragging three Gators to the UF 9 before he was pulled down. On second down, halfback Billy Mims tore around right end and was smashed about two feet from the goal line. Fordham then ripped in for the score. The extra point try was wide and Georgia led 6–0 midway through the second quarter.

Florida came back in the closing minutes of the half. Trapped inside its 1 after a downed punt by Florida's Ernest Cody, Georgia's Stevens hurried a quick-kick that caromed out of bounds at the Bulldog 24. The Gators' Bob Johnson completed a pass to Frank Yinshanis at the Georgia 7. Johnson then ran for two on first down. On second down, Oxford's substitute, halfback Tom Scott, cut over left tackle to tie the score. With a chance to give Florida a lead, Gator Paul Eller's kick was low and wide, one of the few conversion attempts he had missed all season. It remained knotted at 6-all at the half.

Florida halfback Tom Scott eyes Bulldog defenders (from left to right) *Harry Stevens, James Skipworth, and Quinton Lumpkin during action in Georgia's 1938 win.* [UF Archives]

The third quarter began with a 15-yard penalty against the Gators on the kickoff for being four minutes late returning from intermission. The stanza was a defensive war, with the Gators continuing to play Georgia to a standstill.

Early in the final quarter, substitute guard Ned Barbre intercepted a Florida pass and was downed at the Georgia 33. The rejuvenated Bulldogs struck quickly. Halfback Vassa Cate worked free on a reverse and bolted to the Florida 49.

Mims faded back and whipped a pass to Cate who hauled it in on the dead run, flashed into the open, and streaked into the Florida end zone. Barbre booted the PAT and Georgia was up 13–6. The touchdown was a measure of revenge for Mims whose punt attempt was blocked for the winning touchdown in the '37 battle.

The sudden turn of events apparently demoralized the Gators who could not stoke their offense against the fired-up Georgians. Mims fielded Walton's punt at the Bulldog 30 and twisted for a 16-yard return. From there Mims, Cate and Fordham ran down to the UF 31. Catching the Gators off guard, Mims backpedaled on the next play and threw to left end Alex McCaskill, who eluded the Gators' secondary and raced into the end zone. Barbre's kick was partially blocked but Georgia's 19–6 tally held up for the final score.

In the 17 Georgia-Florida games through 1938, excluding the 1904 contest, the Bulldogs dominated 13–3–1.

"Neither team appeared up to the class for former Georgia and

Coach Joel Hunt led the Bulldogs for only one season, taking them to a 5–4–1 record in 1938, including a win against Florida. He is best known for bringing Wally Butts to UGA as an assistant coach. [Hargrett Collection, UGA Libraries]

Florida combines but the excessive heat may have had something to do with the listlessness that marked all but a few minutes of the affair," the *Times-Union* said. The teams "hardly could be blamed for playing as if they were in the steam room of a Turkish bath."

Florida followed the Georgia loss with a 21–7 beating of Maryland, a scoreless tie with Georgia Tech in Atlanta, a 9–7 triumph over Auburn, and a 20–12 loss to Temple to finish 4–6–1, Cody's third losing season in as many years.

Joel Hunt's 5–1 start came crashing down after the Florida victory. The Bulldogs were creamed 28–6 by Tulane in New Orleans, lost 23–14 to Auburn, fought Georgia Tech to a scoreless deadlock, and fell 13–7 to Miami. Quinton Lumpkin garnered All-SEC honors, but the Bulldogs' 5–4–1 record resulted in Hunt's ouster. Wally Butts was named the new head coach, a landmark event in Georgia football annals.

Scoring:

Georgia	0	6	0	13	—	19
Florida	0	6	0	0	—	6

UGA	TD	Fordham, 1-yard run (PAT failed)
UF	TD	Scott, 5-yard run (PAT failed)
UGA	TD	Cate, 49-yard pass from Mims (Barbre kick)
UGA	TD	McCaskill, 31-yard pass from Mims (PAT failed)

Georgia: Thomas, McCaskill, *left end;* Badgett, *left tackle;* Hodgson, *left guard;* Lumpkin, *center;* Johnson, Barbre, Wilfong, *right guard;* Williams, *right tackle;* Gillespie, *right end;* Nowell, *quarterback;* Stevens, Mims, *left halfback;* Cate, *right halfback;* Fordham, *fullback*
Substitutes: Eldredge, Brown, Kersey, Wilhite, Matthews, Decharleroy, Rutledge, Hunnicutt, Salisbury, Pinckney, Skipworth, Whelan, McKinney, Shapiro, Cleveland

Florida: Walker, *left end;* Goff, *left tackle;* Kocsis, *left guard;* Berry, *center;* Battista, *right guard;* Lightbown, *right tackle;* Ramsey, *right end;* Blalock, Eller, *quarterback;* Oxford, Scott, *left halfback;* Johnson, *right halfback;* Walton, *fullback*
Substitutes: Yinshanis, Smoak, Reen, Hassett, Piombo, Parnell, Gardner, Mulcahy, Crabtree, Cody, Mullins, Horner, Taylor

	Georgia	Florida
First downs	8	5
Rushing yards	186	82
Pass att/comp/int	11/2/2	12/2/3
Passing yards	80	42
Punt avg. (yards)	38	41
Return yards	110	83
Fumbles/lost	0/0	1/1
Penalties (yards)	78	55

— 1939 —

Georgia 6, Florida 2

WALLY BUTTS WAS TO LEAD GEORGIA TO CON-
siderable gridiron glory, but the first-year head coach was struggling
in the fall of 1939 as the Bulldogs readied for Florida.

In Gainesville, fourth-year coach Josh Cody also was hurting, as
he tried to forge his first winning season.

The November 11, 1939, Armistice Day game at Jacksonville's
Municipal Stadium was tempered by events in Europe, where British
and French armies were steeling to battle the Germans again. World
War II had erupted little more than two months earlier with Hitler's
blitzkrieg into Poland.

Butts debuted with a 26–0 mastery of The Citadel, but the Bulldogs were hammered 20–0 by Furman and 13–0 by Holy Cross
before a 13–6 loss to Kentucky and a heartbreaking 14–13 road loss to
New York University. Georgia beat Mercer, 16–9, to enter the Florida contest at 2–4.

The 1939 Gators thrashed Stetson, 21–0, but fell 12–0 to Texas in
Austin and 14–0 to Mississippi State. Florida came back to down
Boston College, 7–0, on the road; Tampa, 7–0; and Maryland, 14–0,
before an upset loss 6–0 to South Carolina in Columbia, for a 4–3
record.

The Gators' loss to South Carolina had cost them some respect,
and forecasters were rating Georgia "at least a growl better" than
Florida.

Georgia scouts who saw the Florida-Carolina tangle warned of the
Gators' aerial attack and were particularly concerned by the passing of
ace left halfback W. L. "Bud" Walton. In preparation, Butts worked on
the Bulldogs' pass defense and weak punting game.

The Gators, meanwhile, were worried about Georgia halfback
Billy Mims, who had thrown two touchdown passes in the 1938
game. Bullish Bulldog fullback James Fordham had ground out a
touchdown the previous year and also was a threat.

Georgia team captain and halfback Vassa Cate was recovering from an injury, and center Tommy Witt was nursing a bad knee. Cate also had scored, on a pass reception, in the '38 game.

As usual, some 20,000 fans crowded into the stadium prior to the 2:30 p.m. kickoff.

The game, as intense as any Georgia-Florida skirmish, would be one of the most sloppily played in the history of the series. The teams combined for 10 fumbles, four interceptions and 155 yards in penalties on the day. A total of 21 pass attempts resulted in one completion, by Georgia, for a 9-yard gain.

Other than the work of the defense and the turnovers, the first quarter presented little excitement as neither team was able to shift into offensive gear.

Georgia relied on its defense and waited until the second quarter to get its first break. Gator fullback Charlie Tate, who earlier missed a field-goal attempt, fumbled inside the UF 20 and the Bulldogs fell on the ball. Georgia backs Oliver Hunnicutt and Cliff Kimsey sliced into the Gator line for a first down at the 5. It was here that Florida made a goal line stand that was one of the game's best stories.

Hunnicutt shoved for a yard. Two runs by Kimsey netted only two more before he was blanketed by Floridians. On fourth down, Kimsey tried the line again but a mass of Gators threw him back, giving Florida possession at their 6-inch line.

The Bulldogs' defense proved equally stout and Florida could do little. By this time both teams were substituting freely due to the unseasonably hot weather. The half ended with no score.

Cate, appearing in his last game against the Gators, finally came up with the big play in the third quarter. On a Florida punt, the little halfback grabbed the ball at the Georgia 48 and zipped downfield. He was knocked down at the UF 31 after a 21-yard gain, and the Bulldogs had their second scoring chance of the game.

Fordham, Cate and Kimsey plowed into the line for short gains. A 9-yard pass completion from Heyward Allen to left end Alex McCaskill, the only pass completion of the game, pushed the Floridians back to their 1-yard line. From there, Fordham crashed over a mass of Gators for the touchdown.

McCaskill's kick from placement was good but Georgia was called for holding. A pass attempt, then, for the extra point failed, but Georgia had a 6–0 lead.

In the closing moments, Gator back Bobby Johnson punched a perfect "coffin corner" kick out of bounds at the Georgia 1-yard line.

Georgia's 1939 backfield of Vassa Cate, Robert Salisbury, James Fordham, and Billy Mims. [Hargrett Collection, UGA Libraries]

Rather than take a chance that Florida might block a punt for a touchdown, as in the 1937 game, Georgia back Billy Mims deliberately grounded the ball in the Bulldog end zone, giving Florida a safety.

On the ensuing kick, Georgia's Robert Salisbury sailed the ball to Florida right halfback Leo Cahill at the UF 40. Cahill struggled forward to the Georgia 45, and it was do-or-die time for Florida.

Frantically, Gator backs threw four passes, all incomplete. The joyous Bulldogs had notched another victory, Butts' first over Florida.

Georgia pounded South Carolina, 33–6, lost 7–0 to Auburn and 13–0 to Georgia Tech, before beating Miami, 13–0, to finish 5–6. James Fordham was drafted by the Chicago Bears, and Bulldog guard Howard Johnson was picked up by the Green Bay Packers.

Florida scuttled Miami, 13–0, lost 21–7 to Georgia Tech, and closed the year with a 7–7 tie at Auburn, to finish at 5–5–1. Cody ended his coaching career at Florida with a 1–3 mark against Georgia.

Scoring:

Georgia	0	0	6	0	—	6
Florida	0	0	0	2	—	2

UGA	TD	Fordham, 1-yard run (PAT failed)
UF	Safety	UGA's Mims grounded ball in end zone

Georgia: McCaskill, Keltner, Eldredge, *left end;* Williams, McKinney, Greene, *left tackle;* Wilfong, Guest, *left guard;* Hughes, Witt, *center;* Johnson, *right guard;* Posey, Jamison, *right tackle;* Stegeman, Skipworth, *right end;* Nowell, *quarterback;* Kimsey, Mims, *left halfback;* D. Mathews, Cate, *right halfback;* Fordham, *fullback*
Substitutes: Hunnicut, Allen, Salisbury, Nelson

Florida: Ferguson, Piombo, Horner, *left end;* Goff, Cianci, *left tackle;* Hull, Parnell, Vetter, *left guard;* Bucha, Lane, *center;* Battista, Ferrigno, *right guard;* Smith, Kelman, *right tackle;* Smoak, Mitchell, *right end;* Hanna, Bagwell, *quarterback;* Walton, Harrison, *left halfback;* Cahill, *right halfback;* Tate, Mack, *fullback*
Substitutes: Mitchell, Scott, Beno, Houston, Scott, Johnson, Cowen

	Georgia	Florida
First downs	7	4
Rushing yards	99	110
Pass att/comp/int	10/1/2	11/0/2
Passing yards	9	0
Punt avg. (yards)	44	33
Penalty yards	75	80
Fumbles/lost	4/2	6/4

— 1940 —

Florida 18, Georgia 13

JACKSONVILLE'S MUNICIPAL STADIUM WAS jammed with close to 20,000 spectators for the Georgia-Florida meeting on the brisk afternoon of November 9, 1940.

It had been a seesaw season for Florida coach Thomas J. Lieb in his first year in Gainesville.

Mississippi State pasted the Gators, 27–7, in the opener, but Florida rebounded to wallop Tampa, 23–0, before falling 28–0 to Villanova. Florida then beat Maryland, 19–0, and lost 14–0 at Tennessee to meet Georgia at 2–3.

In his second year at Georgia, Coach Wally Butts had yet to prove himself after a mediocre 5–6 campaign in 1939. He had stirred up some excitement by outfitting his boys with silver pants to complement their red jerseys. The "silver britches" would become a Georgia Bulldog trademark.

The 3–2–1 Athenians massacred Oglethorpe, 53–0, and blitzed South Carolina, 33–2, before falling 28–14 to Ole Miss, and 19–13 to Columbia University in New York City. The Bulldogs tied Kentucky, 7–7, but Auburn nipped them 14–13 a week before meeting Florida.

The worst news in the Georgia camp was that star sophomore tailback Frank Sinkwich was hobbled by a sprained ankle from the Auburn game and might not be available. Lieb was skeptical, believing Sinkwich would be on the field.

"We'll be in there—and so will they," he was quoted in a November 7th dispatch in the *Atlanta Constitution*. "They can't scare us with their bear stories."

Football seers forecasted a high-scoring game, with most of them favoring Georgia to come out on top despite the Sinkwich situation.

The ever-widening war in Europe and the Far East was very much on the minds of Americans everywhere. Gator and Bulldog fans were no different in this respect, but the outside world would be forgotten for a few hours while these Southland border foes dueled.

Florida and Georgia were the two most pass-oriented teams in the Southeastern Conference in 1940. The Gators featured the junior combo of halfback Tommy Harrison and his favorite target, left end Forrest "Fergie" Ferguson.

The Gators took to the field, dazzling everyone with their orange jerseys and pants, and navy stockings. "The 'Gators may not be one of the best football teams in America, but certainly they are one of the best dressed," the *Constitution* said.

Tommy Harrison drew the spotlight as the Gators let it be known early that they were firing on all cylinders. The Florida passer dropped back and hit right halfback Fondren Mitchell between the numbers for a 36-yard advance to the UGA 16. Three running plays netted only five yards as the Georgians dug in. On fourth down, Paul Eller calmly kicked an 11-yard field goal from a slight angle to hand Florida an early 3–0 lead.

With time expiring in the first quarter, a Gators' turnover gave Georgia a chance to score. Florida quarterback Hubert Houston dropped a Bulldog punt, and UGA center Tommy Witt pounced on it at the UF 21.

On the first play of the second quarter, halfback Jim Todd threw to right end Van Davis. Davis caught the ball close to the sideline at the Gators 10 and, keeping his balance, tightroped in for the 21-yard touchdown. Center Leo Costa booted the extra point and Georgia led 7–3.

Florida battled back. With Georgia fullback Cliff Kimsey in punt formation, Gator end Fergie Ferguson smashed a Bulldog blocker back into the Georgia punter to block the kick. Florida right end John Piombo then scooped up the ball and galloped 31 yards untouched for the score, with Ferguson blocking the last Bulldog to have a shot at him. With its fans shaking the stadium in their excitement, Florida regained the lead 9–7. Eller's extra point try was wide.

The half ended with no other scoring and, so far, no sign of Sinkwich. Many in the stadium, including the Gators, wondered if he would be in the Bulldogs' huddle when the third period commenced.

He was not. Butts had not been bluffing about his tailback's injury and Sinkwich stayed on the sideline.

The offenses bogged down in the third quarter, with both teams playing choking, snarling defense. Florida missed an opportunity to score on an unusual play. The Gators had the ball on their 39 after a Georgia punt when UF's Pat Reen flew wide on a reverse and got behind the defense. With nothing but open ground between him and the Georgia goal and the closest Bulldog some 10 yards behind, Reen sprinted to the UGA 17 where he turned to check on the pursuit. In doing so, he tripped over his feet and ingloriously fell to the turf. The Bulldogs regrouped to hold off that particular challenge.

A razzle-dazzle play put Georgia in trouble shortly after Reen's misfortune. The Bulldogs' Heyward Allen passed to end Carl Grate who lateralled to fullback Curtis Nelson. The ball tumbled loose and Gator fullback Charlie Tate gathered it in at the UGA 40 on the last play of the third period. The shootout would be decided in the fourth quarter with Florida hugging its two-point lead.

Florida went for broke on the first play of the final period. Gator halfback Bud Walton set up to pass and rifled a strike to halfback Fondren Mitchell standing alone at the Georgia 5. Mitchell made the catch and stepped into the end zone. What had been a tenuous lead suddenly ballooned to 16–7, as Charlie Tate kicked the extra point.

As they had done after Florida's second quarter score, Georgia surged back within minutes.

Opening on their own 20 after the kickoff, Georgia's Jim Todd hummed first-down passes to Paul Kluk and halfback Andy Dudish. A plunge by Nelson put the Georgians on the UF 45. Todd gained a yard, then dropped to pass. Left end George Poschner, weaving through the secondary, made the catch and went in for the touch-down. Georgia had closed to 16–13.

Sparked by the score, Georgia played inspired defense and Florida had to punt. A superb kick by Harrison skidded out of bounds at the Georgia 6. With time running out, Todd drifted back into the end zone, looking to pass to keep the rally alive.

He never had a chance as Gator sophomore left guard Floyd Konesty broke through the line and leveled him for a safety. The two points gave Florida an 18–13 cushion.

Getting the ball back in the closing minutes, Todd desperately went to the air. Florida's Houston, whose fumble led to Georgia's first touchdown, redeemed himself, intercepting a Todd pass and running to the UGA 30 as the final whistle shrilled.

The Gators had won their fourth game of the series and their second in the last four meetings with the Bulldogs. Georgia outpassed Florida 286 to 106, but the Gators won the rushing war, 180 to 80.

The *Atlanta Constitution* lamented the absence of Sinkwich but said Florida coach Tom Lieb had fulfilled his preseason promise in which he stated his Gators would beat Georgia if they did not win another game.

Georgia fell 21–13 to Tulane a week after the Florida defeat but stuffed Georgia Tech, 21–19, and Miami, 28–7, to give Butts his first winning season at Georgia at 5–4–1.

Lieb's Gators coasted to a 46–6 win against Miami and dumped Georgia Tech, 16–7, but lost 20–7 to Auburn and 26–0 to Texas, for a 5–5 finish.

Scoring:

Florida	3	6	0	9	—	18
Georgia	0	7	0	6	—	13

UF	FG	Eller, 11-yard kick
UGA	TD	V. Davis, 21-yard pass from Todd (Costa kick)
UF	TD	Piombo, 31-yard run on blocked punt (PAT failed)
UF	TD	Mitchell, 40-yard pass from Walton (Tate kick)
UGA	TD	Poschner, 44-yard pass from Todd (PAT failed)
UF	Safety	Konesty tackled UGA's Todd in end zone

Florida: Ferguson, *left end;* Hull, *left tackle;* Konesty, *left guard;* Bucha, Parham, *center;* Battista, *right guard;* Lane, *right tackle;* Piombo, *right end;* Latsko, Bagwell, Eller, Houston, *quarterback;* Harrison, *left halfback;* F. Mitchell, *right halfback;* Tate, Mack, *fullback*
Substitutes: C. Mitchell, *end;* Cianci, Klutka, *tackle;* Sauers, Godwin, Parnell, *guard;* Parham, *center;* Latsko, Bagwell, Eller, *quarterback;* Cahill, Walton, Reen, *halfback;* Mack, *fullback*

Georgia: Poschner, *left end;* Greene, *left tackle;* Burt, *left guard;* Costa, Hughes, Witt, *center;* Goodman, *right guard;* Ellenson, *right tackle;* Skipworth, V. Davis, *right end;* Nowell, Kluk, Brown, *quarterback;* Allen, Todd, *halfback;* L. Davis, Blanton, *right halfback;* Kimsey, Nelson, *fullback*
Substitutes: Malone, Grate, *end;* Jamison, *tackle;* Ruark, Horne, *guard;* Blanton, Dudish, *halfback*

	Florida	Georgia
First downs	7	14
Rushing yards	180	80
Pass att/comp/int.	16/6/4	39/18/2
Passing yards	106	286
Fumbles rec.	2	3
Penalties (yards)	35	50

— 1941 —

Georgia 19, Florida 3

"FIREBALL" FRANK SINKWICH WAS BLAZING
a path across the American collegiate gridiron as he and his Georgia
teammates prepared for the November 8, 1941, game against Florida.

Second-year UF coach Tom Lieb was trying to beat Wally Butts'
Bulldogs for the second consecutive year, but the Gators knew they
faced an overwhelming task.

Sinkwich, who had missed the 1940 game with a bad ankle, was
averaging more than 100 yards rushing per game and was a passing
menace as well. The junior tailback, who played high school ball
with Bulldog end George Poschner in Youngstown, Ohio, was
touted for All-America honors. Poschner would miss the Florida
game due to a broken arm.

In its season opener, Georgia butchered Mercer, 81–0. Tragedy
railed at the Bulldogs in their October 3 win over South Carolina
when Sinkwich went down, his jaw broken in two places. Believed
to be done for the year, Sinkwich was back in the Georgia lineup the
next week, protected by a specially-designed face guard that drew
him even more national attention.

Georgia tied Ole Miss, 14–14; beat a strong Columbia eleven, 7–3,
in New York City; lost on the road, 27–14, to Alabama; and clipped
Auburn, 7–0.

Florida, 2–4, premiered with a 26–0 win over Randolph Macon
but lost its second game, 6–0, at Mississippi State. The Gators kicked
Tampa, 46–6, then lost to Villanova, 6–0, Maryland, 13–12, and
LSU, 10–7.

The underdog Gators were paced by the passing combo of left
halfback Tommy "the Red" Harrison to left end Forrest "Fergie"
Ferguson, whose block of a Bulldog kick in the 1940 game led to a
Florida touchdown.

Georgia's 39-man squad spent Friday night in St. Augustine while the Florida team was in Ponte Vedra. The rivals took buses to Jacksonville the next morning.

Florida Gov. Spessard L. Holland and Georgia Gov. Eugene Talmadge were among dignitaries in the overflow crowd of about 21,000 crammed into Municipal Stadium. It was a chilly afternoon, but many of the fans forgot the cold as they tried to catch a glimpse of Sinkwich in his strange headgear during pregame warm-ups.

Sinkwich "runs with more sheer power than any man ever to play on the local field," the *Florida Times-Union* said. "In addition, he has a deceptive style of starting that causes the opposition to lean the wrong way just long enough to give Fireball Frankie an opening."

Georgia received the opening kickoff and looked strong in striking for two quick first downs. When the Gators put a stop to matters, Bulldog quarterback Cliff Kimsey got off a poor punt that careened out of bounds at the UF 37.

Led by team captain and quarterback Charles Tate, playing in front of his hometown crowd, Florida seized the early initiative. Rushes by Tommy Harrison and Joe "Red" Mack, coupled with a pass from Harrison to halfback Leo Cahill, perched the Gators at the Bulldogs' 7. Mack was hurt, however, and the drive stalled.

The Gators brought in left guard and kicking specialist Paul Eller for a field-goal attempt. With the ball set down at the 17, Eller angled it through the goal posts for the game's first points.

To the surprise of many fans, who had expected a Bulldogs track meet hosted by Sinkwich, the Gators continued their tough play and the quarter ended with no other scores. But Georgia got a break in the closing seconds with Florida's Harrison back to punt from his 30. Harrison vainly tried to make a shoestring catch of a low snap and Georgia recovered at the UF 27. The Gators would have their backs to the goal line for the rest of the half.

Early in the second period, Georgia's superior power and reserves began to wear on the Gators. The Bulldogs advanced to the UF 15, before three incomplete passes and an unsuccessful reverse by halfback Lamar Davis turned the ball back over to Florida.

On their next offensive, the Georgians invaded to the UF 14. Sinkwich pummeled the middle three times but only got to the 5. Sophomore fullback Dick McPhee tried his luck on fourth down, but fumbled. The doughty Gators had held again, though they inherited terrible field position.

Georgia end Van Davis partially blocked Harrison's next punt. The ball skittered down at the UF 26. From there the Bulldogs surged to the Gators' 4. Again the scrappy Floridians stacked up Sinkwich and regained possession.

Florida's Harrison rolled to his right in the end zone looking to pass or find a gap to run through. Before he could do either, Dick McPhee knocked him down for a safety, trimming Florida's lead to 3–2.

Though Harrison intercepted a Georgia pass minutes later, neither team threatened during the remainder of the first half. Florida went to the locker room with its startling lead intact, thanks to superb goal line defenses against the super Sinkwich.

Many Gator fans who had tasted victory over the hated Bulldogs in 1940 knew that Florida had not beaten Georgia in consecutive years since 1928–1929.

The second half began with both squads battling ferociously on defense. The passing attacks had been effectively shut down, and the two offenses were relying almost exclusively on the run. Harrison was the Gators' workhorse while Sinkwich and McPhee ripped off runs for Georgia.

Eight minutes into the third quarter, Georgia took possession at the Florida 40 and muscled to the 23, primarily on McPhee's line plunges. Sinkwich finally exhibited some of his considerable prowess. Taking a handoff, he wedged off tackle, shifted clear in the secondary, and dashed 23 yards for the go-ahead touchdown. Leo Costa tacked on the conversion and Georgia had its first advantage, 9–3.

Still in the third quarter, with Florida's offense sputtering, Georgia

Florida coach Tom Lieb instructs his backfield during the early 1940s. [UF Archives]

again surged into the shadow of the Gators' goal. The Floridia defenders, though, blunted the Bulldog attack at the 10. Sinkwich then lined up for a field-goal attempt, splitting the uprights for a 12–3 Georgia lead.

Forced to gamble against time, Florida's Frank Buell attempted a pass from the UF 22, but Bulldog center Clyde Ehrhardt pulled in the interception, returning it to the UF 18 before being tackled.

Sinkwich tore into the Gator line three times to move the yard-sticks inside the 1. On his fourth carry, he bowled into the end zone. Georgia was up 19–3.

But Florida wouldn't go down quietly. Early in the fourth period, on a fake punt, Harrison rambled 52 yards to the Georgia 36 before he was tackled from behind by Walter Ruark.

The Gators clawed to the UGA 22, but Bulldog halfback Andy Dudish smothered the threat by intercepting a Harrison pass in the end zone.

Still Florida refused to wave the white flag. On another fake punt in the closing minutes, halfback Fondren Mitchell dodged 21 yards to the UF 30 for a first down.

The razzle-dazzle wasn't over. Mitchell then passed to fullback O'Neal Hill who lateralled to halfback Eddie Hausenbauer for a 31-yard gain. As the last seconds ticked off, Bulldog halfback Henry Powers grabbed an interception and the Georgia victory was complete.

While the Gators had played tough, Sinkwich lived up to his headlines, rushing for 137 yards on 30 carries and personally account-ing for 15 points on two touchdown runs and a field goal. Harrison gained 90 yards for Florida on 13 rushes. The passing of both squads was negligible. "Georgia is far and away the best club Florida has met and even though (the Gators) were in excellent physical trim they were unable to withstand the continual battering of the Bulldog powerhouse," the *Times-Union* said.

Georgia unequivocally proved it was one of the top teams in the country, but football soon paled in the light of the world crisis. In less than a month America would be at war. Even as Georgia fans celebrated their victory, a Japanese task force was marshalling for a Decem-ber 7 surprise attack on the U.S. Pacific Fleet at Pearl Harbor, Hawaii.

Florida end Forrest Ferguson garnered All-America honors in 1941, the first Gator to be so honored since Dale Van Sickle in 1928. Ferguson entered the service and was severely wounded during the D-Day invasion, where he earned the Distinguished Service Cross for bravery. He died of his war wounds in 1954. Georgia center

Tommy Witt would also lose his life in the imminent conflict.

Florida rallied to beat Miami, 14–0, and Georgia Tech, 14–7, before losing 30–27 to UCLA, to finish the '41 campaign at 4–6.

Georgia found little opposition on its remaining schedule, bombing Centre College, 47–6; Dartmouth, 35–0; and Georgia Tech 21–0. The Bulldogs' 8–1–1 mark earned them their first postseason bowl invitation ever, an Orange Bowl berth against Texas Christian.

On New Year's Day, 1942, in Miami, Sinkwich's legend flourished with an awesome 382-yard running and passing performance that keyed Georgia to a 40–26 victory over TCU. Sinkwich garnered All-America and All-SEC honors, and Georgia finished No. 14 in the 1941 Associated Press poll.

Scoring:

Georgia	0	2	10	7	—	19
Florida	3	0	0	0	—	3

UF	FG	Eller, 17-yard kick
UGA	Safety	McPhee tackled Harrison in UF end zone
UGA	TD	Sinkwich, 3-yard run (Costa kick)
UGA	FG	Sinkwich, 10-yard kick
UGA	TD	Sinkwich 1-yard run (Costa kick)

Georgia: Conger, *left end;* Greene, *left tackle;* Ruark, *left guard;* Ehrhardt, *center;* Kuniansky, *right guard;* Ellenson, *right tackle;* V. Davis, *right end;* Kimsey, *quarterback;* Sinkwich, *left halfback;* L. Davis, *right halfback;* McPhee, *fullback*
Substitutions: Marshall, Anderson, Phelps, *end;* Posey, Lewis, Keltner, *tackle;* Burt, Miller, Lee, *guard;* Hughes, Godwin, Costa, *center;* Maguire, *quarterback;* Allen, Todd, Powers, Dudish, Nunnally, *halfback;* Keuper, Bray, *fullback*

Florida: Ferguson, *left end;* Hull, *left tackle;* Ferrigno, *left guard;* Robinson, *center;* Konesty, *right guard;* Lane, *right tackle;* Klutka, *right end;* Tate, *quarterback;* Harrison, *left halfback;* Cahill, *right halfback;* Mack, *fullback*
Substitutions: C. Mitchell, *end;* Cianci, Lee, *tackle;* McRae, Rayborn, Eller, *guard;* Entzminger, Hausenbauer, *quarterback;* Buell, McNeal, F. Mitchell, Bracken, *halfback;* Cowen, Hill, *fullback*

	Georgia	Florida
First downs	16	8
Rushing yards	276	141
Pass attempt/complete/int	11/2/4	12/2/4
Passing yards	14	39
Punt average (yards)	30	27
Lost fumbles	0	1
Penalties (yards)	40	25

— 1942 —

Georgia 75, Florida 0

NOT SINCE UNION MAJ. GEN. W. T. SHERMAN'S fiery trek from Atlanta to Savannah during the Civil War had an Ohio Yankee put his brand on Georgia like Frankie Sinkwich did in the autumn of 1942.

Pistoned by the All-American running and passing of "Flatfoot Frankie" and a young sophomore back named Charley Trippi, the Bulldogs were unbeaten, untied and ranked number one in the nation going into the November 7, 1942, combat against Florida in Jacksonville.

Sinkwich had personally dismantled the Gators in the 1941 game, scoring 15 points and rushing for 137 yards.

The Gators of third-year coach Tom Lieb knew they were facing a David vs. Goliath situation. The day before the game, Florida students shouted, "Sink Sinkwich!" as they paraded in the rain down Gainesville's University Avenue en route to a pep rally. Florida's chances rode on the passing of backs Jack Jones, Andy Bracken and Billy Mims.

The Gators opened the year with a disappointing 20–7 loss to a squad from the Jacksonville Naval Air Station but came back to pound Randolph Macon, 45–0; Tampa, 26–6; and Auburn, 6–0. The season nose-dived from there as Florida lost 13–3 to Villanova, 26–12 to Mississippi State, and 13–0 to Maryland to enter the Georgia game at 3–4.

At 7–0, Georgia had hardly been tested, other than the season opener when Coach Wally Butts' Bulldogs edged Kentucky, 7–6. Georgia then beat the Jacksonville Naval Air Station, 14–0; Furman, 40–7; Ole Miss, 48–13; Tulane, 40–0; Cincinnati, 35–13; and previously unbeaten Alabama, 21–10.

The Bulldogs were averaging 412 yards of offense per game, second only to Tulsa as the national leader.

Georgia's 1942 backfield (left to right), *Frank Sinkwich, Charley Trippi, Dick McPhee, Lamar "Racehorse" Davis.*

America was in its first year of war, and the 22,000 fans arriving at Municipal Stadium were keeping up with the progress of the Allies. Within hours of the game, news flashes brought word that U.S. forces had invaded North Africa.

Sinkwich had taken quite a pounding against Alabama, according to the *Savannah Morning News:* "Sports writers who saw Sinkwich after the game said he had taken such a beating that his face was hardly recognizable." Yet the Georgia captain, Number 21 in the program, was on the field and ready to go in Jacksonville.

Florida would be without end Joe Graham, who suffered a broken leg in the Mississippi State game, and quarterback Eddie Hausenbauer's broken nose probably would keep him from playing.

Gator Bill Corry returned the opening kickoff to the UF 43. But it was a quick slide to catastrophe for the Gators from there. Florida halfback Jack Jones threw a short pass that Bulldog center Bill Godwin intercepted at the Gators' 47. Sinkwich, usually an inside runner, surprised everyone by thundering around right end to the 36. Lamar Davis then ran a reverse around the other end to the 23, and Dick McPhee shot up the middle to the UF 12. After McPhee added a five-yard run, Sinkwich slanted off right end for the touchdown. Kicking specialist Leo Costa converted and Georgia led 7–0 with three minutes, 30 seconds gone in the quarter. The nightmare for Florida was just beginning.

On second down at the UF 22 after the kickoff, Jones dropped back to pass, but Godwin again was waiting. The Georgia center made his second interception and was hauled down at the Florida 24. Six plays later, Sinkwich bulled in from the 2 on a third-down play. Costa's kick made it 14–0 Georgia.

The Gators penetrated to the Georgia 38 on their next possession, but a fourth-down line run was stopped cold and the Bulldogs took over. On third down at the Georgia 41, Charley Trippi launched a 59-yard bomb to left end George Poschner, who reeled it in at the UF 26 and coasted in for six. Georgia had extended its lead to 21–0.

With time fading in the first quarter, Florida frantically went to the air again. Yet another Jones aerial was picked off, this time by Trippi at the UF 48. The elusive back did not stop till he crossed the Gators' goal. Costa added Georgia's 28th point as the first period ended.

Sinkwich, resting on the bench, was sent back into the fray when the Gators toughened in the second stanza.

With Georgia in possession on its 38, Sinkwich immediately fired a bullet pass to his old high school teammate Poschner at the UF 47. The Bulldog speedster outraced his pursuers to the end zone for Georgia's fifth score. Sinkwich returned to the sideline for the remainder of the half with Georgia comfortably in control, 35–0.

Though Florida displayed better defense in the second quarter, Georgia's crushing interceptions and lightning-quick scoring in the first period had left the Gators shell-shocked.

Midway through the third period, the Bulldogs were at it again.

"To hell with Georgia," Florida players shout during a pep rally in Gainesville prior to the 1942 contest. The Bulldogs paid little heed, skinning the Gators 75–0. [UF Archives]

Frank Sinkwich cuts into the open during Georgia's 75–0 romp over Florida in 1942. Sinkwich's run ended with the Heisman Trophy and a number two ranking for Georgia in the final Associated Press poll. [UF Archives]

Sinkwich ripped off two runs to reach the UGA 48. Todd got eight more before Sinkwich passed to Van Davis at the Florida 23. Runs by Todd and Sinkwich gave Georgia a first down at the 9. Three plays later, Sinkwich flicked a pass to Poschner for another touchdown. Costa's boot made it 42–0 and the affair was turning ugly.

With two scoring runs and two touchdowns passes to his credit, Sinkwich watched the rest of the game from the bench. But Georgia's well-oiled machine relentlessly rolled on.

On Florida's next possession, UGA's Clyde Ehrhardt picked off a fourth pass to give Georgia the ball at the UF 32. Bulldog back Andy Dudish circled left end to the UF 5. Trippi scored from there, crossing the goal line backward after being spun around on a missed tackle. Costa missed the first extra point of the day but, at 48–0, few Georgians complained.

The points orgy continued. Operating from the UF 40, Trippi made the longest run from scrimmage of the day, bolting around right end for his third rushing touchdown. The bulge now stood at 55–0.

At this stage Butts was substituting freely, as was Lieb.

Corralled near their goal line after UGA's kickoff, the Gators went into punt formation, but UF's Fondren Mitchell was rushed hard and the kick went out of bounds at the UF 26. Trippi threw to Joe Polak at the 12, and Mayfield "Sonny" Lloyd put another six on the board, scoring from the 1 two plays later. With Costa's extra point, Georgia was romping 62–0 at the close of the third quarter. "Many of the fans then decided that they had been polite long enough and left before the party was over, " the *Times-Union* said.

Against the Georgia bench warmers, Florida made its best drive of the day at the outset of the final period. Earning three successive first downs, the Gators crawled to the UGA 27, but a 15-yard penalty killed the drive there.

The Bulldogs' thirst for points was not yet slaked. From the UF 41, Lafayette King snared reserve fullback Jim Todd's pass at the 15 and made it into the end zone for Georgia's 10th touchdown. Few fans seemed to notice Costa's failed kick, the massacre standing at 68–0.

A penalty set the Gators back on their 1-yard line on their next series. On second down, quarterback Billy Mims retreated deep into his own end zone to pass. It was here that Frank Riofski, a fourth-string center making his first road trip with the Bulldogs, had his moment in the football sun. Riofski stepped in front of the receiver at the Florida 10, made the interception and trundled in for the score. Costa's ninth extra point was the death-knell postscript to the final 75–0 debacle.

"Indeed, the Bulldogs made everyone happy when the game was over, " the *Times-Union* said.

Charley Trippi ranks with Herschel Walker and Frank Sinkwich as one of UGA's all-time premier backs. Trippi was in on five touchdowns in Georgia's 1942 massacre of Florida. He was All-American and runner-up to the Heisman Trophy in 1946, after being in the service.

Seven Bulldogs had scored, paced by Sinkwich, Poschner with three touchdown grabs, and Trippi's three tallies. Georgia's defenders caught more Florida passes than the UF receivers. The Bulldogs intercepted seven of Florida's 21 throws while the Gators had only six receptions.

It was the most lopsided contest in the history of the series, second only to the Bulldogs' 56–0 win in Athens in 1920. Despite Georgia's bombardment, Florida never surrendered. "Though the action was all in the favor of Georgia, it was plenty hard on both sides," the *Times-Union* reported. "The tackling was vicious, but not frequent enough on the part of the Gators."

Florida finished with a 12–0 loss to Miami and a 20–7 defeat at Georgia Tech, to go 3–7 for Lieb's worst season ever in Gainesville.

The Gators' destruction strengthened Georgia's No. 1 ranking and put the Bulldogs not only in a better position to win their first conference title but a national championship as well. Georgia wrecked Chattanooga, 40–0, but was the victim of a huge 27–13 upset to Auburn in Columbus, Ga., on November 21.

The perfect season was blemished but the Bulldogs demolished nationally-ranked Georgia Tech, 34–0, to win their first Southeastern Conference championship and wrap up a bid to the 1943 Rose Bowl.

Before some 90,000 in Pasadena, Calif., the Bulldogs tripped mighty UCLA, 9–0. Sinkwich was slowed by two sprained ankles

Georgia's All-American end George Poschner, a high school teammate of Frank Sinkwich, hauled in three touchdown passes in UGA's 1942 destruction of Florida.

*Wearing odd headgear to protect his broken jaw,
UGA's Frank Sinkwich plows into the Texas
Christian defense in the 1942 Orange Bowl.*

but Trippi filled in admirably, rushing for 115 yards. Georgia ranked second behind Ohio State in the final Associated Press poll.

Sinkwich crowned the most splendid Georgia gridiron campaign to date by winning the Heisman Trophy, the first Bulldog to do so. He and Poschner also claimed All-America and All-SEC honors. Sinkwich accounted for 2,187 total yards on offense his senior year, an SEC record that stood for years. He was drafted by the Detroit Lions of the NFL and was an All-Pro selection in 1943.

On a somber note, Bulldog left guard Walter Ruark, an alternate captain with Sinkwich in the Rose Bowl, would lose his life in World War II.

Scoring:

Georgia	28	7	27	13	—	75
Florida	0	0	0	0	—	0

UGA	TD	Sinkwich, 7-yard run (Costa kick)
UGA	TD	Sinkwich, 2-yard run (Costa kick)
UGA	TD	Poschner, 59-yard pass from Trippi (Costa kick)
UGA	TD	Trippi, 48-yard interception return (Costa kick)
UGA	TD	Poschner, 62-yard pass from Sinkwich (Costa kick)
UGA	TD	Poschner, 9-yard pass from Sinkwich (Costa kick)
UGA	TD	Trippi, 5-yard run (kick failed)
UGA	TD	Trippi, 40-yard run (Costa kick)
UGA	TD	Lloyd, 1-yard run (Costa kick)
UGA	TD	King, 41-yard pass from Todd (kick failed)
UGA	TD	Riofski, 10-yard interception return (Costa kick)

Georgia: Poschner, *left end;* Ellenson, *left tackle;* Ruark, *left guard;* Godwin, Riofski, *center;* Miller, *right guard;* Williams, *right tackle;* V. Davis, *right end;* Maguire, *quarterback;* Sinkwich, *left halfback;* L. Davis, *right halfback;* Mc-Phee, Todd, *fullback;* Costa, *kicker*
Substitutions: King, Tereshinski, Strother, Vickery, McClure, Pierce, Boyd, Kuniansky, R. Lee, J. Lee, Ehrhardt, Trippi, King, Polak, M. Lloyd, Harrison, Nunnally, Keuper

Florida: W. David, B. Williams, *left end;* H. Miller, *left tackle;* Rayborn, *left guard;* E. Lee, *center;* Konesty, *right guard;* Carey, *right tackle;* Klutka, *right end;* Sutherland, *quarterback;* Jones, *left halfback;* Mitchell, *right halfback;* Corry, *fullback*
Substitutions: Platt, Hausenbauer, W. Godwin, Pratt, Henry, Fields, Wilson, McRae, Kaplan, D'Aguile, Horsey, Hill, Latsko, Hudson, Mims, Bracken, Barrington

	Georgia	Florida
First downs	20	6
Rushing yards	357	81
Passing yards	236	75
Pass att/comp	15/9	21/6
Interceptions	0	7
Punt avg.	47	34
Lost fumbles	1	1
Penalty yards	70	64

— 1944 —

Georgia 38, Florida 12

D∪E TO THE WAR, FLORIDA DID NOT FIELD
athletic teams in 1943, meaning Gators fans had to wait until November 11, 1944, to see if their team could avenge the 1942 slaughter by
the Bulldogs.

Even so, Georgia was a heavy favorite to take its third win in a row
over the Gators. Due to wartime deprivations, the expected capacity
crowd of some 22,000 yielded about 18,000 in the stands of Jacksonville's Municipal Stadium.

In a war-abbreviated schedule, the 4–2 Gators of fourth-year coach
Tom Lieb were closing their season against Georgia.

Florida debuted with a 36–6 shellacking of Mayport Naval Air
Station but fell 26–6 to Mississippi. The Gators beat Jacksonville
Naval Air Station, 26–20; lost 40–0 at Tennessee; beat Maryland,
13–6; and Miami, 13–0.

Georgia played a full schedule in 1943, finishing at 6–4. The '44
Bulldogs were ambushed, 14–7, by Wake Forest in the season opener
but butchered Presbyterian, 67–0, the next week. Georgia then
nipped Kentucky, 13–12; beat a service team from Daniel Field, 57–6;
lost to LSU, 15–7; and defeated powerful Alabama, 14–7, a week
before facing the Gators with a 4–2 mark.

Many Florida fans were still smarting from the 75–0 shelling by
Georgia in 1942. But Frank Sinkwich was finally gone, now with the
Detroit Lions, and Charley Trippi was in the service playing for the
Third Air Force Gremlins. The Gators weren't particularly strong
but they had upset Georgia before when all seemed hopeless.

Both teams played stout defense to open the game, with the
Floridians surprisingly able to stop the Bulldogs' expected passing
attack. Florida made a first down before having to punt. Starting on
their 41, the Bulldogs showed their muscle on the second play from
scrimmage. Halfback C. H. "Rabbit" Smith, a Palatka, Fla., native,

burst over left tackle and sped to the UF 19 before being pushed out of bounds. Georgia runners moved the ball to the 11, but Billy Rutland was swarmed under by Gators before he could make a first down.

On first down, the Gators turned bad field position into a pot of gold in the wink of a running back's eye. With the ball on the UF 10, Gator right halfback Ken McLean hit the enemy line at left tackle and tore into the Bulldog secondary. Cutting back against the pursuit, McLean got a solid block from left end Dewell Rushing and bolted 90 yards for a touchdown. The spectacular play electrified the stadium crowd and, though J. M. Turner's conversion attempt failed, Florida maintained its 6–0 advantage as the contest entered the second period.

Trying to shake up the Georgia defense, the Gators produced a trick play that paid off. Florida quarterback Buddy Carte had intercepted a pass at the UGA 46. On second down at the Georgia 44, Gator fullback Jim Dyer passed to Rushing. As the Bulldogs streamed toward the Gator end, Rushing suddenly lateralled to UF left halfback Bobby Forbes who was speeding to the outside. The play caught the Bulldogs off guard and Forbes raced into the end zone. Turner again missed the extra point but Florida led 12–0 over the disbelieving Georgians.

The lead stood until the closing minutes of the half. Forced to punt from inside their 10, the Gators lined up to kick. On the snap, UGA right end Reid Moseley shot through the Florida line and blocked Reed Bell's punt. Bulldog left end Sam Bailey claimed the ball at the 6. The Gators held the Bulldogs for no gain on three plays, but on fourth down quarterback Billy Hodges rifled a pass to Moseley for the score. Kicker and fullback Billy Bryan's conversion failed but the Bulldogs were on the scoreboard. And the half was not over yet.

With less than a minute left, Georgia held on defense and Florida's Bell punted out of bounds at the UF 44. On the first play of the series, Hodges again found Moseley streaking through the Florida secondary and hit him on the numbers. The Bulldog end raced across the Florida goal, and suddenly the game's complexion had changed to Red and Black. Bryan added the extra point for Georgia's first lead, 13–12.

Halftime found the Gators and their fans wondering if they could survive the sudden turn of events and stay within striking distance in the second half.

But Georgia's onslaught continued. On the opening series of the

Florida back Bobby Forbes tries to break a UGA defender's grasp in Georgia's 1944 win. [UF Archives]

third quarter, left halfback and team captain Billy Rutland skirted left end for a nice gain to the UF 42. George Skipworth then passed to halfback Al Perl all the way down to the UF 4. Rutland hit left end and plunged into the end zone to make it 19–12 Georgia. The extra point kick was wild.

Florida's offense mired and Georgia was able to drive again, reaching the UF 1 as the third quarter ended. Rutland fumbled to open the final period, but again the Gators could not advance and had to punt. Georgia's Perl returned the kick nine yards to the UF 41. On a second down play, Perl took a shovel pass and galloped down to the 25, dragging four Gators with him the last eight yards. A penalty helped the Bulldogs to a first down at the 16. On third down, UGA quarterback Hodges drifted back, drilling a pass to end Sam Bailey in the end zone. Bryan added the point after and Georgia was breathing easier with a 26–12 lead in the fourth quarter.

With less than two minutes left, coach Wally Butts sent in a number of fresh players, a move that spelled more torment for the exhausted Gators. Right halfback Claude Hipps burst over right tackle and ripped 58 yards for another Georgia touchdown.

Up 32–12, Georgia got the ball back seconds later when Florida's Forbes fumbled at the UF 17. Perched on the Gators' 12 with less than a minute to play, reserve Bulldog quarterback Ken McCall, an Orlando native, fired two incompletions. On the last play of the game, he connected with Moseley for Moseley's third touchdown of the day. Red and Black fans could now celebrate a 38–12 final score.

Along with Moseley's 18-point output, Georgia was paced by

freshman Billy Hodges' three touchdown passes. Gator Ken McLean, the big back from Quincy, Fla., was the game's top rusher with 134 yards, including his 90-yard scoring jaunt. Rutland's 127 yards led Bulldog runners.

Georgia ended the year with a 49–13 victory over Auburn, a 21–0 win against Clemson and a bitter 44–0 home loss to Georgia Tech, for a 7–3 record. Butts had his fifth winning season in his first six years at Georgia and was 4–1 versus Florida. Bulldog guard Herb St. John was named to the All-SEC first team, and back Al Perl was drafted by the Pittsburgh Steelers. Georgia now owned a 17–4–1 series record against the Gators.

Scoring:

Georgia	0	13	6	19 —	38
Florida	6	6	0	0 —	12

Florida TD	McLean, 90-yard run (PAT failed)
Florida TD	Forbes, 44-yard run on lateral from Rushing (PAT failed)
Georgia TD	Moseley, 11-yard pass from Hodges (PAT failed)
Georgia TD	Moseley, 44-yard pass from Hodges (Bryan kick)
Georgia TD	Rutland, 4-yard run (PAT failed)
Georgia TD	Bailey, 17-yard pass from Hodges (Bryan kick)
Georgia TD	Hipps, 58-yard run (PAT failed)
Georgia TD	Moseley, 12-yard pass from McCall (PAT failed)

Georgia: Edwards, Bailey, *left end;* Castronis, *left tackle;* St. John, *left guard;* Jackura, *center;* Reid, *right guard;* Perhach, *right tackle;* Wells, Moseley, *right end;* Hodges, *quarterback;* Rutland, *left halfback;* Smith, Hipps, *right halfback;* Bryan *fullback*
Substitutions: Barbas, Phillips, Bailey, Singletary, Green, Sanders, Hiers, Chonko, Furchgott, Bowles, Skipworth, McCall, Deavers, Bradberry, Perl

Florida: Rushing, *left end;* White, *left tackle;* Schmidt, *left guard;* Adams, *center;* Hamilton, *right guard;* Mortellaro, *right tackle;* Graham, *right end;* Carte, *quarterback;* Forbes, *left halfback;* McLean, *right halfback;* Dyer, *fullback*
Substitutions: Mooney, Turner, Hester, Massey, Sapp, Gilmartin, Bell, Belden, Hobbs, K. Hall, Smith

	Georgia	Florida
First downs	12	6
Rushing yards	170	140
Passing yards	121	55
Pass att/comp/int	21/8/1	6/4/0
Punts/avg. yards	6/32	11/31
Fumbles/lost	5/3	6/2
Penalty yards	70	30

— 1945 —

Georgia 34, Florida 0

FOUR GAMES INTO THE 1945 SEASON, A YOUNG
Pennsylvanian named Charley Trippi returned to Athens from the
service and resumed his place in the Bulldogs' lineup.

By the time Florida met Georgia in Jacksonville on November 10,
1945, the Bulldogs had lost two games but still were a formidable foe
for anyone in the country.

Gators' coach Thomas J. Lieb, in his fifth and final year at Florida,
was trying to improve on his 1–3 mark against Georgia.

Florida began the season with a 31–2 sleeper over a squad from the
63rd Infantry Regiment posted at Camp Blanding. The Gators then
beat Mississippi, 26–13; tied Tulane, 6–6; and lost consecutive games
to Vanderbilt, 7–0; and Miami, 7–6. Florida punished Southwestern
Louisiana, 45–0; and lost 19–0 at Auburn to enter the Georgia game
with a 3–3–1 record.

Georgia, 5–2, blasted Murray State, 45–0, in its debut and dusted
Clemson, 20–0. The Bulldogs then beat Miami for the 250th gridiron victory in the school's history. After a 48–6 whipping of Kentucky, Georgia lost 32–0 to LSU and 28–14 at Alabama before
pounding Chattanooga, 34–7, a week before the Florida matchup.
Few forecasters had any doubts that seventh-year Bulldog coach
Wally Butts would add to his 4–1 record against Florida.

Trippi, who had starred with Frank Sinkwich on the 1942 juggernaut, had scored three touchdowns and passed for another score in
the Bulldogs' 75–0 romp over Florida that year. After the '42 season,
he had joined the Army and played for a service team.

The Bulldogs were injury-free facing Florida and Butts was confident in pre-game interviews. "We should play our best game . . . if
we don't win this one we won't have any alibis."

Lieb acknowledged that his Gators would be decided underdogs,
but told reporters the Georgians "will know that we were in the
game."

141

Tom Lieb, "The Old Gray Fox," coached Florida from 1940 to 1945 and was 1–4 against Georgia while compiling an overall record of 20–26–1. [UF Archives]

The Gators faced other woes. First-string guards Horace Drew and Kenneth Hamilton were out; Drew with appendicitis and Hamilton with a leg injury sustained against Auburn. Florida's starting fullback and punter, Fred Hogan, was suffering from the flu and bedridden but was expected to play against Georgia.

Lieb took the opportunity of the pre-game hype to call for an enlargement of the Jacksonville stadium's seating capacity and dressing rooms.

Florida knew it had to stop Trippi, the running of UGA halfback Charles "Rabbit" Smith, and the passing of quarterback Johnny Rauch if it was to have a prayer of winning.

With 21,000 fans settled in, Georgia, on its second possession, seemed to shift into gear. Taking the ball at its 8 after a Florida punt by W. H. Gilmartin, Rabbit Smith circled left end for six and 14 yards on consecutive plays. Rauch pitched to Trippi for a gain to the 44 and Georgia was rolling. Just as suddenly, it rolled to a halt. A center snap went wide and Gator tackle Jack White pounced on the ball at the Bulldog 39.

Minutes later, Florida got to the Georgia 9-yard line, but Gilmartin fumbled and Georgia guard Herb St. John recovered.

On the first play in the second quarter, Trippi raced seven yards around left end to Georgia's 43 but failed to make the needed first down. Florida's White then ripped through to block Trippi's kick and

Gator end Ottis Mooney scooped up the loose ball, running it back 10 yards to the UGA 31. Gator fans were in a frenzy.

After a one-yard run by L. B. Dupree, Thomas Vangelas passed to the left halfback for a 6-yard gain. Two more runs by Dupree put the Gators at the Georgia 15. Back to back passes misfired before Fred Hogan rammed for a first down at the 10.

The Bulldog defenders came to life. Dupree was thrown for a yard loss on first down, then picked up three on the next carry. Vangelas was stopped for no gain and, on fourth down, a Vangelas pass was batted away by a UGA defender. Georgia had withstood the menace but was not yet over its charitable mood. Smith gained nine before Trippi lost the handle, with Vangelas claiming the ball at the Georgia 27. Florida quickly squandered the opportunity when B. S. Carte fumbled, and Michael Cooley fell on the ball for the Bulldogs. Florida never recovered from its missed chances in the early going.

Georgia dominated the remainder of the second period. Trippi took a lateral from Rauch and sprinted for 17. A pass from Rauch to left end Dan Edwards netted nine and a short gain by Smith reached midfield. From the 50, Trippi found an opening at left tackle and, sprinting for daylight, outran most of the Florida team into the end zone for the game's first score. George Jernigan's extra point made it 7–0, Georgia.

Quarterback Johnny Rauch piloted the Bulldogs to four consecutive triumphs against the Gators in 1945 to 1948.

The Gators could not respond but their defense held Georgia off for the remainder of the half. The anticipated Bulldog runaway had not happened and Florida still was in the game as the teams filed to their locker rooms.

After Trippi returned the kickoff 29 yards to the UGA 39, Smith picked up 22 yards on two rushes. Runs by Trippi, Godfrey Steiner and Smith gave the Bulldogs a first down at the Gator 28. The Georgians ground down to the 4 and John Donaldson bucked in from there. Jernigan's PAT put Georgia up 14–0.

Florida continued to self-destruct on offense. On the second play after the kickoff, Gator Tony Occhiuzzi bobbled the pigskin and Rauch pounced on it at the UF 18.

Trippi and Donaldson pummeled the Gators for gains to the 4. Trippi then hauled in a lateral from Rauch and scampered in. Jernigan's boot was true and Georgia extended its lead to 21–0.

Carte ran the kickoff back 40 yards and would have scored if Trippi, the last defender, had not knocked him out of bounds at the UF 46. Unable to move the ball, Florida faced a punting situation. But Bulldog end Reid Moseley poured through to block Hogan's kick, and Georgia had a first down at the Florida 48. Rauch then passed to Moseley at the Gators' 22. On the next play, Rauch shot a lateral to Trippi who darted in for his third touchdown of the afternoon. Jernigan missed the extra point, but Georgia owned a substantial 27–0 advantage and Florida was all but done.

Stifled again on offense, the Gators quick-kicked early in the final quarter with Smith returning the ball from his 23 to the Florida 49. Donaldson, trying to sweep left, was bottled up and reversed his field, running all the way down to the UF 21. Donaldson then whipped a pass to Moseley at the goal line. The end juggled the ball as he was hit by a Gator defensive back but held on as he fell into the end zone to record the final tally, 34–0.

Trippi had returned to the Georgia-Florida series in grand style with three touchdowns and some fine defensive work. His outstanding 239-yard rushing performance was the bulk of the Bulldogs' 317-yard running blitz and still stands as the best single-game rushing total in the series.

With two fumble recoveries and a blocked kick, big Texan tackle Jack White was the Florida hero. But the Gators were haunted by the botched chances to score in the first half when they were in control.

Florida closed with a 41–0 whipping of Presbyterian and a 12–0 loss to a Navy team from the U.S. Amphibs. Lieb finished his

Florida career with a 4–5–1 worksheet and a 1–4 record against Wally Butts' teams.

The Bulldogs romped over Auburn, 35–0, and Georgia Tech, 33–0, and accepted a bid to play Tulsa in the Oil Bowl.

As was the case in the 1943 Rose Bowl, Trippi again was outstanding in postseason play. He passed for a 64-yard touchdown and weaved 68 yards on a punt for another score in what many Georgia faithful consider one of the greatest punt returns of all time. Georgia beat Tulsa, 20–6, for its third bowl victory in as many games. Trippi was honored as an All-SEC selection.

The 9–2 Bulldogs were ranked 18th in the final national Associated Press poll.

Scoring:

Georgia	0	7	20	7 —	34
Florida	0	0	0	0 —	0

UGA	TD	Trippi, 50-yard run (Jernigan kick)
UGA	TD	Donaldson, 4-yard run (Jernigan kick)
UGA	TD	Trippi, 4-yard run (Jernigan kick)
UGA	TD	Trippi, 22-yard pass from Rauch (PAT failed)
UGA	TD	Moseley, 21-yard pass from Donaldson (Jernigan kick)

Georgia: Edwards, *left end;* Castronis, *left tackle;* St. John, *left guard;* Cooley, *center;* Miller, *right guard;* Sanders, *right tackle;* Wells, *right end;* Rauch, *quarterback;* Trippi, *right halfback;* Donaldson, *left halfback;* Smith, Steiner, Jernigan, *fullback*
Substitutions: Phillips, Bailey, Sellers, DeWitt, Lee, Gordon, Reid, Furchgott

Florida: Mooney, *left end;* White, *left tackle;* Martin, *left guard;* Gilbert, *center;* Miller, *right guard;* Sapp, *right tackle;* Chesser, *right end;* Carte, *quarterback;* Vangelas, *right halfback;* Dupree, *left halfback;* Gilmartin, *fullback*
Substitutions: Hall, Vaughn, Pharr, Scarborough, Land, Hobbs, Carter, Williams, Hogan, Vangelas, Occhiuzzi, Odham, Mortellaro

	Georgia	Florida
First downs	17	4
Rushing yards	317	83
Pass att/comp	16/8	7/1
Passing yards	127	7
Fumbles/rec.	4/1	3/1
Punt avg. yards	29	30
Yards penalized	65	15

— 1946 —

Georgia 33, Florida 14

FLORIDA AND GEORGIA WERE TEAMS GOING in opposite directions heading into their November 9, 1946, tussle.

In his first year as Florida's head coach, Raymond B. Wolf had yet to win a game with his squad made up largely of freshmen.

The 0–5 Gators had lost 13–7 to Mississippi; 27–13 at Tulane; 20–0 at Vanderbilt; 20–13 to Miami; and 40–19 at North Carolina.

Eighth-year Georgia coach Wally Butts had one of his finest teams and was seriously in the dogfight for the SEC championship. The undefeated, untied Bulldogs, ranked third in the country, were being considered for bids by the Rose and Sugar bowls.

Georgia began the season with a 35–12 win over Clemson and a 35–7 victory at Temple. The Bulldogs then whipped Kentucky, 28–13; Oklahoma A&M, 33–13; and Furman, 70–0. A week before Florida, the Bulldogs downed defending national champion Alabama, 14–0, in Athens in what many considered the game of the year in the South.

The traditional clash was billed as a passing war, with Florida's quarterback Doug Belden pitted against Georgia's All-America candidate left halfback Charley Trippi and quarterback Johnny Rauch.

The Gators' biggest weapon was right end Broughton "Brute" Williams, the nation's leader in pass receptions and one of the top receivers in the country.

With an open date the Saturday before the Georgia clash, Florida concentrated on finding a way to stop Trippi, the Bulldogs' senior team captain, who had decimated the Gators with his running, passing and defense in the 1942 and '45 games.

Both teams were weakened by injuries. For underdog Florida, passing star Billy Parker and receiver Tommy Bishop were questionable while regulars Fletcher Groves and Cliff Sutton were definitely out. Georgia fullback Dick McPhee and tackle Andy Perhach also would be unable to play.

146

A Florida back looks to pass during action in the 1946 Georgia win. [UF Archives]

Few, if any, in the sellout crowd of about 25,000 at Jacksonville's Municipal Stadium, figured Florida, a 28-point underdog, had much chance of pulling a miracle.

Fired up for the mighty Bulldogs, the young Gators came out snapping. On two fake reverses after the opening kickoff, UF full-back Gaspar "Vic" Vaccaro ran for 13 and eight yards. On the third play from scrimmage, right halfback Charles Hunsinger swept for a first down on a reverse to the Georgia 47. The trick plays had the Bulldogs off balance and Florida fans were starting to get excited. A Belden pass fell incomplete but the Gator quarterback, on another fake reverse, shot through the line for 11 yards. Three plays later, Belden hit "Brute" Williams with a bullet pass to the UGA 21. Jimmy Kynes ran for three but three straight Belden passes, including a fourth-down toss that slithered off Williams' fingers in the end zone, failed; and Georgia took over.

After several exchanges of possession, Florida had the ball at its 14. Carries by Hunsinger and Vaccaro netted a first down at the 24. Belden then connected on a long pass play to Hunsinger to the Georgia 17. Two plunges by Vaccaro and another by Belden brought the ball to the 6. Here again the Bulldogs bristled on defense. A run and two pass attempts gained a half yard and Belden's fourth-down throw was incomplete.

Rushes by Trippi and fullback Joe Geri gave Georgia a first down at its 32. Gator tackle Jack White leveled Trippi for a 16-yard loss on a pass attempt, and Donaldson was dropped for a 6-yard loss by Tommy Bishop and Bill Raborn as the first quarter ended. The underdog Gators, for the moment, were overwhelming Trippi, Rauch and the rest of Butts' powerhouse.

As good teams will do, the Bulldogs created a much needed break for themselves early in the second period. With Florida punting from its own 20, Georgia tackle Jack Bush blocked Bill Gilmartin's kick. Bulldog guard and All-America candidate Herb St. John gathered in the ball and rumbled to the UF 8. Two plays later, Rauch fired a pass to Trippi in the flat for the touchdown, and Red and Black fans finally had something to cheer about. The score was tainted when Georgia kicking specialist George Jernigan, known as the "Springfield Rifle" because of his accuracy, pulled the extra point attempt wide—only his second miss of the season. Georgia led 6–0.

Later, after a 19-yard scamper by Trippi put the Bulldogs near midfield, the frustrated Gators got a Red and Black gift before half-time. Georgia's Geri fumbled and Brute Williams recovered at the Georgia 47.

Belden scratched for four, then passed to Kynes for eight more. Throws to Tommy Bishop and Williams took the Gators to the UGA 17. Fullback Vaccaro bashed straight ahead for nine and Belden pushed over right guard for three. With the Bulldogs defense cornered and ferocious, Vaccaro twice crunched into the middle for two tough yards. On his third carry, the Gator back cracked inside right guard for the tying touchdown. George "Jock" Sutherland's extra point kick flew over the crossbar, and the UF crowd "went wild" as Florida led 7–6 with two minutes left in the half.

The inexperienced Gators were able to hold Georgia at bay for the remainder of the period and almost scored again when halfback Bobby Forbes returned a Trippi punt 32 yards to the UGA 18 on the last play. To the cheers of its faithful, Florida trotted to the dressing room clinging to its slim lead and the knowledge that it had outplayed the Bulldogs. A half remained but the brewings of such a gigantic upset had the fans abuzz. Wally Butts later admitted he was "sick" with fear at halftime as he talked to his boys.

Georgia received the second half kickoff and marched to its 49, primarily on a 12-yard pass from Trippi to Dan Edwards. But Trippi fumbled a Rauch lateral and UF's Williams fell on the pigskin.

This was Florida's high tide. A score now would mire the Bulldogs in serious trouble and add to the victory-starved Gators' surge of emotion. Belden ran for no gain on first down. Hunsinger banged at left tackle for two. Facing third down, Belden drifted back and hurled the ball deep. The pass was intercepted at the Georgia 17 by John Donaldson, who turned upfield for 24 yards before being knocked down. The turnover appeared to take much of the heart out of the young Gators.

Runs by Trippi and Rauch reached the Florida 31. Geri broke free for 11 and Trippi ripped off tackle for nine. Rauch and Geri ran to the 7 before Donaldson dove over right guard for the score. Jernigan's conversion gave Georgia the lead again, 13–7.

Florida railed back after the kickoff, which Bob Gilbert returned to the UF 40. Belden connected on passes to Williams at the Georgia 41 and to Gilbert at the 30. On third down at the 22, Belden tried to pass but Bulldog center Clayton Deavers pulled in the interception at the 20, returning it 24 yards.

Three plays later, Trippi found end Edwards for a 22-yard completion. Trippi then circled left end to the Gators' 17. With the Gators back on their heels, Donaldson loped into the flat to take a pass for six points. Jernigan lengthened Georgia's lead to 20–7.

By early in the fourth quarter, Georgia's defense, fueled by Florida turnovers and resulting UGA scores, began to dominate. The Gators were further weakened when tackle Jack White, a mainstay of their defense, broke his ankle and was carried from the field on a stretcher in the third period. With that, Georgia embarked on two long Gator-tiring, clock-eating scoring drives.

After the Bulldogs' third score, Florida was held without a first down and punted, with the Bulldogs taking over at the UF 45. A naked reverse by Trippi and a pass from Trippi to Donaldson quickly planted Georgia on the Florida 8. Line smashes by Geri, Donaldson and Rauch placed the ball at the 1. Geri went in standing up and Jernigan's conversion made it 27–7.

There was no quit in the Gators, however. Grinding steadily upfield from their own 8, H. H. Griffin passed to Gilbert for 11. Vaccaro, the big back from Tampa, then powered through the Bulldogs for a 22-yard gain. A 15-yard unnecessary roughness penalty against Georgia on an incomplete Florida pass gave the Gators possession at the UGA 11.

On a reverse, quarterback Buddy Carte raced 10 yards around right end for a first down at the 1. Vaccaro skyed over a mass of linemen for the touchdown to climax the impressive 92-yard drive. Sutherland's extra point made it 27–14.

But the Bulldogs still had some points to make. Carries by Don-

Fullback Vic Vaccaro scored two touchdowns for Florida in the Gators' 1946 loss to Georgia. [UF Archives]

aldson, Geri and Trippi reached the Florida 42. Trippi threw to Moseley for a first down at the UF 9 and, three plays later, Trippi piled in from the 1 to settle matters. Jernigan's miss left the final score at 33–14, Georgia.

Had it not been for two turnovers deep in its own territory, Florida may have been in a position to spring one of the monumental upsets in collegiate football history. Georgia fans preferred to chalk it up as the fifth consecutive win over Florida and another step toward an undefeated season.

Charley Trippi had an All-American day, running for a touchdown, catching a scoring pass, and throwing for another TD. He gained 78 yards on 20 carries and completed all seven passes he threw. John Donaldson also had a fine game with two touchdown catches. With his rushing touchdown, the hard-running Vaccaro was the pride of Gainesville even in defeat.

Butts was so unnerved by the Florida effort that he was "sweating and shaking" 30 minutes after the game, as he saluted the Gators. "Those Florida boys simply outbattled us most of the way," he told a *Florida Times-Union* reporter.

Florida's abysmal year ended with a 27–20 loss to Villanova, a 37–6 defeat by North Carolina State, and a 47–12 licking by Auburn. Ray Wolf was 0–9 in his first campaign, the worst record at Florida since the 0–5 mark in 1916. Gator Broughton "Brute" Williams ended his college career and played for the Chicago Bears.

Georgia's bulldozer did not slow down after stopping Florida. The Bulldogs mashed Auburn, 41–0; Chattanooga, 48–27; and Georgia Tech, 35–7, to win their second SEC championship and a Sugar Bowl berth against North Carolina in New Orleans.

Georgia beat the Tar Heels, 20–10, as Trippi closed out his brilliant career with a flourish, playing the entire game and throwing a 67-yard touchdown pass to Dan Edwards. Butts had his first and only undefeated season at Georgia and was 4–0 in his first four bowl games.

Georgia was ranked third in the nation behind undefeated Notre Dame and Army in the final 1946 AP poll.

Trippi and guard Herb St. John garnered All-America honors and were named to the 1946 All-SEC first team. Trippi went on to an All-Pro career with the NFL Chicago Cardinals.

Scoring:

Georgia	0	6	13	14	—	33
Florida	0	7	0	7	—	14

UGA	TD	Trippi, 8-yard pass from Rauch (PAT failed)
UF	TD	Vaccaro, 3-yard run (Sutherland kick)
UGA	TD	Donaldson, 7-yard run (Jernigan kick)
UGA	TD	Donaldson, 17-yard pass from Trippi (Jernigan kick)
UGA	TD	Geri 1-yard run (Jernigan kick)
UF	TD	Vaccaro, 1-yard run (Sutherland kick)
UGA	TD	Trippi, 1-yard run (PAT failed)

Georgia: Edwards, *left end;* Bush, *left tackle;* Hobbs, *left guard;* Cooley, *center;* Johnson, *right guard;* Williams, *right tackle;* Tereshinski, *right end;* Rauch, *quarterback;* Trippi, *left halfback;* Donaldson, *right halfback;* Geri, *fullback*
Substitutions: Moseley, Terry, Hiers, Hobbs, Alexander, Jeffrey, Jernigan, Chandler, Deavers, Deleski, Cook, Smith, Maricich, Bradberry, Bouley

Florida: Turner, *left end;* Mortellaro, *left tackle;* Fields, *left guard;* Hobbs, *center;* Raborn, *right guard;* Dempsey, *right tackle;* Williams, *right end;* Carte, Belden, *quarterback;* Kynes, *left halfback;* Hunsinger, *right halfback;* Vaccaro, *fullback*
Substitutions: Bishop, R. Gilbert, Chesser, Johnson, Robinson, White, Huerta, Lorenzo, J. Gilbert, Griffin, Mims, Forbes, Schanberg, Sutherland, Gilmartin

	Georgia	Florida
First downs	18	17
Rushing yards	140	182
Passing yards	152	102
Pass att/comp/int	26/11/2	13/9/3
Punts/avg. yards	5/29	5/34
Fumbles/lost	1/1	3/2
Penalty yards	35	20

— 1947 —

Georgia 34, Florida 6

FLORIDA WAS DEPENDING HEAVILY ON FLASHY halfback Bobby Forbes, the nation's leading rusher, to avoid losing its sixth straight to Georgia as the November 8, 1947, game neared.

Neither team was setting the football world afire, and ninth-year Georgia coach Wally Butts was struggling to revive the splendors of the previous autumn when Georgia was third-ranked and undefeated. But Charley Trippi was gone now and Georgia was 4–3. The '47 Bulldogs premiered with a 13–7 win against Furman then lost a road game, 14–7, to North Carolina. Georgia bit LSU, 35–19, but was not on the field in a 26–0 thumping at Kentucky. Georgia upset Oklahoma A&M, 20–7, in Stillwater; lost 17–7 to Alabama; and downed Clemson, 21–6.

Under second-year coach Raymond B. Wolf, the 2–6 Gators opened with a 16–14 loss to Ole Miss, a 20–12 beating by North Texas State, and a 20–14 defeat at Auburn, before nipping N.C. State, 7–6. Florida was punchless in a 35–7 loss to North Carolina, but thumped Furman, 34–7, in Tampa a week before meeting Georgia.

Forbes had three long scoring runs against Furman, and everyone knew he would have to have similar success against Georgia if the 14-point underdog Gators were to spring the upset. Florida was also weakened by injuries to ends Dewell Rushing and Bill Turner.

Georgia had the more balanced offense. Quarterback Johnny Rauch had eight touchdown passes, three of them to right end and team captain Dan Edwards, going into Jacksonville. When the Bulldogs ran, they went to backs Johnny Donaldson, Floyd "Breezy" Reid and Al Bodine.

Still, the lackluster seasons of both squads detracted from the rivalry this year. A game-day story in the *Savannah Morning News* said the tilt "will prove nothing to anyone. The Bulldogs have been up and down so many times this season they resemble a fisherman's cork on a summer afternoon." The article also said Florida "couldn't be pleased more than to add the Georgia scalp."

The train carrying the 41-man Georgia contingent chugged into Jacksonville early Friday, where the Bulldogs boarded a bus for the resort at Ponte Vedra where they were headquartered. That afternoon the Florida team checked in at the same hotel, both rivals hoping to avoid the pre-game wildness in nearby Jacksonville.

Despite being favored, Wally Butts shot down Georgia's chances and poor-mouthed his boys in talks with reporters. "They're (Florida) the martyr and we're the monster," Butts told the *Atlanta Constitution*. "That's the way it is every year. I wouldn't mind if we just had a few monsters. . . . I got to looking at those little old Georgia boys this morning at the breakfast table and it just nearly scared me to death to think about having to play them in a football game."

A crowd of about 23,000 watched the contest open with the "little old Georgia boys" overpowering Florida's first offensive effort.

The Bulldogs began their initial possession at the UF 44 and wasted little time in pawing to the Gators' 7. It looked to be the beginnings of a walk in the park for the 'Dogs before Reid fumbled and Gator center Jimmy Kynes fell on the porkhide.

About five minutes into the game, the Bulldogs started to click again after taking a punt at the Florida 37. Three running plays netted seven yards and Georgia had a decision with fourth and three at the 30. The Gators braced for the run and were surprised when Rauch backpedaled and lofted a pass to end Dan Edwards at the 5-yard line. Halfback Billy Henderson got three on a carry and Donaldson forged to the half-yard line. Rauch then sneaked into the end zone. Joe Geri's extra point was good and the Bulldogs broke on top 7–0.

Keying on Forbes, Georgia was able to contain the speedy back, holding him to short gains. Florida played stingy defense and the teams swapped several punts. Late in the first period the Bulldogs took over on their 49 and headed toward pay dirt again. Rauch connected with Bill Henderson for a first down at the UF 34. The Georgians earned another first down on three running plays. Rauch then hurled a strike to Weyman Sellers who was tackled on the 8 on the last play of the quarter. Henderson knifed for a yard before Rauch hooked up with Donaldson in the end zone. Geri's conversion made it 14–0, Georgia.

Though Gator defenders Jimmy Kynes and H. A. "Bam" Webster

Bulldog Bill Henderson powers for yardage during Georgia's 34–6 victory over Florida in 1947, its sixth straight against the Gators. [Hargrett Collection, UGA Libraries]

from time to time pressured Rauch, the Georgia ace was six for six in first half passes.

The Gators showed they weren't skinned yet, though, moving from their own 25 to the UGA 7 before the Bulldogs held on downs. On its next possession Florida struck from the Georgia 31 to the 2, but Forbes lost the ball and Clayton Deavers recovered for the Bulldogs on the last play of the half. Florida, after twice marching inside the UGA 10, had come away with nothing.

The most controversial play of the afternoon occurred in the third quarter when a pass interference call on Florida gave Georgia a first down at the UF 33. The call wildly incensed Florida fans who booed long and loud. Their anger intensified when Georgia's Reid whipped over right tackle and breezed for 26 yards and a first down at the 7. Eli Maricich bulled to the 2, before Rauch ran the quarterback sneak again for his second tally. Geri's kick failed but Georgia was riding high despite the catcalls of Gator rooters still seething over the interference penalty.

Florida needed a spark to get back in the game, and the match was lit a few minutes later. Geri punted for Georgia and the Gators' Hal

Griffin fielded the ball at the UF 32. Griffin faked a handoff to teammate Charles Hunsinger and raced to the sideline. No Bulldog could bring him down as he steamed 68 yards for the touchdown. The conversion attempt by Laz Lewis failed but the Gators were back in the running, trailing 20–6.

About halfway through the fourth quarter, Georgia took possession after a Florida punt went out of bounds at the UF 35. Maricich swept left end for 15 yards and Rauch completed a pass to end Gene Lorendo at the Florida 31. Donaldson then crashed over left guard to the 21, before Rauch retreated in the pocket and arched a pass to Dan Edwards for Georgia's fourth touchdown. Geri's conversion made it 27–6.

The Gators, hurrying, tried to pass, but the strategy backfired shortly after the kickoff. Bulldog center Gene Chandler picked off Vic Vaccaro's pass at the UF 25 and lugged it to the 15 before he was pulled down.

Now the Bulldog bench warmers smelled blood. Stan Nestorak ran over right tackle to the 7. On the next play, Geri bore through the line for the score. His fourth extra point of the day gave Georgia a 34–6 cushion and was the final blow in the Bulldog's sixth consecutive victory over the Gators.

Georgia defenders limited Gator star Forbes to 59 yards in 14

Raymond "Bear" Wolf starred as a player at Texas Christian before being hired as UF head coach in 1946. From 1946 to 1949, Wolf had a 13–24–2 record at Florida, including a 1–3 mark against Georgia. [UF Archives]

carries but he still highlighted the Florida offense.

Johnny Rauch put in a fine performance, running for two scores and passing for two others. He completed 12 of 20 passes for 133 yards, while Joe Geri accounted for 10 Bulldog points with four conversions and a touchdown.

Florida closed with a 7–7 tie at Tulane, a 7–6 win at Miami, and a 25–7 conquest of Kansas State for a 4–5–1 record, leaving Wolf 0–2 against Georgia.

The Bulldogs ended with a 28–6 victory over Auburn and a 27–0 win against Chattanooga, before falling 7–0 at Georgia Tech.

Georgia accepted a bid to play in its first Gator Bowl and tied Maryland, 20–20, for a 7–4–1 mark. Georgia's Edwards received All-America and All-SEC first-team honors. He was drafted by the Pittsburgh Steelers.

Scoring:

Georgia	7	7	6	14	— 34
Florida	0	0	6	0	— 6

UGA	TD	Rauch, 1-yard run (Geri kick)
UGA	TD	Donaldson, 7-yard pass from Rauch (Geri kick)
UGA	TD	Rauch, 2-yard run (kick failed)
UF	TD	Griffin, 68-yard punt return (PAT failed)
UGA	TD	Edwards, 21-yard pass from Rauch (Geri kick)
UGA	TD	Geri, 7-yard run (Geri kick)

Georgia: Sellers, *left end;* Bush, *left tackle;* St. John, *left guard;* Chandler, *center;* B. Reid, *right guard;* Payne, *right tackle;* Edwards, *right end;* Taylor, *quarterback;* Maricich, *left halfback;* Walston, *right halfback;* Bodine, *fullback* *Substitutions:* Geri, Lorendo, Bradberry, Hlebovy, McCall, Johnson, Feher, George, Jeffrey, Pope, Payne, Hobbs, Jackura, Hodges, Field, Prosperi, Lloyd, Nestorak, Brunson, Gatewood, Donaldson, Henderson, Tilliski, F. Reid

Florida: Bishop, *left end;* Carver, *left tackle;* Fields, *left guard;* Kynes, *center;* Groves, *right guard;* Sutton, *right tackle;* Johnson, *right end;* Belden, *quarterback;* Hunsinger, *left halfback;* Forbes, *right halfback;* Parker, *fullback* *Substitutions:* Webster, Lewis, Griffin, Vaccaro

	Georgia	Florida
First downs	16	10
Rushing yards	125	133
Passing yards	133	41
Pass att/comp/int	20/12/1	12/2/1
Fumbles/lost	2/1	2/1
Penalty yards	45	32

— 1948 —

Georgia 20, Florida 12

"WE'RE GOING IN THAT BALL GAME WITH both sleeves rolled up," Florida coach Raymond Wolf told reporters two days before the November 6, 1948, head-banging with Georgia.

The contest would be the first of the series to be played in Jacksonville's newly-completed Gator Bowl.

Riding a four-game winning streak, the Bulldogs were solid favorites to best Florida for the seventh consecutive year. Pre-game hype centered on Gator halfback Chuck Hunsinger, Florida's main weapon, and Georgia passing luminary Johnny Rauch.

In his third year in Gainesville, Wolf was off to his best start with a 4–2 record and was looking for his first win over Georgia.

Ole Miss popped the Gators, 14–0, in UF's season opener, but Florida came back to beat Tulsa, 28–14; Auburn, 16–9; and Rollins, 41–12. The Gators were overpowered 42–7 by Georgia Tech and smashed Furman, 39–14, on the road.

Georgia, 5–1, began the 1948 season by beating Chattanooga, 14–7, but then lost to North Carolina, 21–14. The Bulldogs leaped on Kentucky, 35–12; pasted LSU, 22–0, in a night game in Baton Rouge; outclassed Miami, 42–21; and overwhelmed Alabama, 35–0, in Birmingham the week before the Florida game.

The Bulldogs and Georgia Tech were undefeated and tied for first place in the conference. One forecaster described the Florida contest as "just a workout" for the Bulldogs, who many observers felt were among the nation's elite.

In preparation for Georgia, Wolf spent much time drilling his boys for the expected bullets of Rauch. Florida would be without quarterback Angus Williams, hurt in the Furman game. He was replaced by senior Doug Belden. The Gator line was anchored by stalwart center Jimmy Kynes.

More than 34,000 fans packed the new stadium on a sunny afternoon to see if the 27-point underdog Gators would make a game of it.

From the outset, the Gators, particularly their line, showed the Georgians they weren't just going through the motions, as they fought through blocks to pursue the Bulldog backs. Not until the closing minutes of the first period did the Bulldogs generate any offense.

Relying chiefly on Rauch's shotgun right arm, Georgia took possession at its 25 and marched 75 yards. Rauch found end Bobby Walston for 18 and connected with halfback Floyd "Breezy" Reid who ran to the UF 35. Runs by Lukie Brunson, halfback Joe Geri and Eli Maricich pushed the ball just inside the UF 1-yard line. There Rauch dove in for the score on the last play of the quarter. Geri added the extra point for a 7–0 Georgia lead.

Concentrating on Florida's Hunsinger, the Bulldogs fairly well contained the Gators offensively.

But Wolf had to be pleased with the play of his linemen. With center John Gilbert leading the way, the Gators were controlling the line of scrimmage other than on Georgia's lone drive. Time after time, the blue-uniformed Floridians battled through and smacked Rauch before he could throw.

Florida accounted for the only offense in the second quarter after a Bulldog punt left them with a first down at their own 46. A series of line smashes by Gator backs John Cox, Loren Broadus and Russ Godwin pushed the ball within inches of the Georgia goal line. Cox, a halfback whose father played for Florida in the early 1920s, bulled in from there. The extra point was no good when Belden fumbled the snap, but Florida had pulled to within 7–6 at halftime.

The mighty Bulldogs had all they could handle, and the second half looked promising for "the Sunshiners."

Georgia seized the early momentum in the third quarter on a drive starting at its own 46. For only the second time on the day, the Bulldog linemen ruled the line of scrimmage. Georgia kept the ball on the ground with the running of halfback Geri and headed toward the Florida goal. Bogged down at the UF 35, the Bulldogs had to punt. The play would prove to be the pivotal point in the game.

The Gators' Hunsinger, who had been handled by Georgia most of the day, took the kick at his own 4-yard line and, spinning away from defenders, streaked upfield to the Georgia 40. The Florida contingent went wild until they saw an official signal that the Gators had roughed the kicker. With the boos of Florida followers resounding through the stadium, Georgia was given a first down at the UF 27.

Florida back Chuck Hunsinger braces for a collision with UGA's Johnny Rauch, playing defense, in the 1948 battle. [Hargrett Collection, UGA Libraries]

The Bulldogs moved to the 13 where Geri rambled in for UGA's second touchdown. Geri's conversion put Georgia up 14–6.

The Bulldogs added some insurance in the fourth quarter. Spurred by runs of 30 and 21 yards by sophomore left halfback Billy Mixon, Georgia rammed its way inside the UF 5. Taking a pitchout from Rauch, Reid went in from the 2, avoiding a desperate lunge by the Gators' Jimmy Yancey. A juggled snap resulted in a missed extra point but Georgia widened its lead to 20–6.

Florida's line wearied in the late stages but still outplayed the Georgians, opening holes which forced the Bulldogs' secondary to make a number of tackles. Still Georgia's defense held Florida off the scoreboard in the second half until Hunsinger wove his magic again.

In the most spectacular play of the day, the junior halfback hauled in a Georgia punt at the UF 36, avoided several tacklers, and tore up the field, aided by a fine block from teammate Frank Lorenzo. Sixty-four yards later, Hunsinger was celebrating in the Georgia end zone. The conversion failed and the 20–12 score stood at the final whistle.

Rauch, who ranks as one of Georgia's all-time passing leaders,

Wallace Butts coached Georgia to a 12–9 record against the Gators from 1939 to 1960. Under Butts, the Bulldogs won four SEC championships and appeared in eight bowl games.

ended the game with 118 yards, completing seven of 15 passes. The Gators gained only 39 yards in the air but outrushed Georgia 156 to 120, paced by Hunsinger's 45 yards in 10 tries.

"The Bulldogs had to pull every trick out of the hat to whip Florida," said a dispatch in the November 8 *Savannah Morning News*. Still, Wally Butts was 8–1 against the Gators. Coupled with a Georgia Tech loss to Tennessee, the win against Florida boosted Georgia into the conference lead.

Butts was highly impressed by the exploits of UF's Chuck Hunsinger, calling him "a better running back than I have on my team" in a post-game interview.

Florida never fully recovered from the Georgia loss. The Gators lost 34–15 at Kentucky; beat Miami, 27–13; and fell 34–28 at Alabama. At 5–5, Wolf still was seeking his first winning record.

Georgia shelled Auburn, 42–14; Furman, 33–0; and Georgia Tech, 21–13, to win the SEC championship and gain an Orange Bowl bid against Texas. The underdog Longhorns, led by a lanky back named Tom Landry, battered Georgia, 41–28, as Butts lost for the first time in six bowl trips since 1941. Georgia was ranked eighth in the final Associated Press poll.

John Rauch was named to two All-America teams. He and Florida's Hunsinger were honored as All-SEC first-squad selections. Rauch was selected in the pro draft by the Philadelphia Eagles, while Joe Geri was picked by Pittsburgh and was an All-Pro player for the Steelers in 1950.

Scoring:

Georgia	7	0	7	6	—	20
Florida	0	6	0	6	—	12

UGA	TD	Rauch, 1-yard run (Geri kick)
UF	TD	Cox, 1-yard run (PAT failed)
UGA	TD	Geri, 13-yard run (Geri kick)
UGA	TD	Reid, 2-yard run (PAT failed)
UF	TD	Hunsinger, 64-yard punt return (PAT failed)

Georgia: Chandler, Sellers, Walston, _left end;_ Feher, Bush, _left tackle;_ Hobbs, Greer, _left guard;_ Jackura, Bradshaw, _center;_ B. Reid, Johnson, Love, _right guard;_ Payne, Yelvington, _right tackle;_ Connally, Lorendo, Duke, _right end;_ Walston, Field, Rauch, Prosperi, _quarterback;_ Bradberry, Mixon, McCall, Brunson, Geri, _left halfback;_ Maricich, F. Reid, Donaldson, Bradberry, _right halfback;_ Bodine, Tilliski, Hopp, _fullback_

Florida: Bishop, Turner, _left end;_ Dempsey, Carver, Ewing, _left tackle;_ Huerta, Cole, Brown, _left guard;_ Kynes, Gilbert, _center;_ Groves, Lorenzo, _right guard;_ Sutton, _right tackle;_ Vaccaro, Johnson, Hawkins, _right end;_ Belden, Lewis, Yancey, _quarterback;_ Hunsinger, Montsdeoca, Broadus, Lewis, _left halfback;_ Griffin, Cox, Michael, Gruetzmacher, _right halfback;_ Godwin, Parker, _fullback_

	Georgia	Florida
First downs	13	12
Rushing yards	120	156
Passing yards	121	39
Pass att/comp/int	15/7/0	9/2/0
Punts/avg. yards	6/35	7/33
Fumbles/lost	0/0	3/1
Penalty yards	15	30

— 1949 —

Florida 28, Georgia 7

ODDSMAKERS INSTALLED GEORGIA A 13-point favorite before the November 5, 1949, fracas against Florida, but many observers believed the game would be tighter.

A cold snap blanketed the South yet the Gators-Bulldogs collision was expected to be a barn burner in keeping with the rivalry's tradition since early in the century.

The Gators of fourth-year coach Raymond B. "Bear" Wolf were 3–2–1, opening with a 13–0 win over The Citadel and a 40–7 victory against Tulsa. Florida tied Auburn, 14–14, in Mobile; lost 22–17 to Vanderbilt; and 43–14 to Georgia Tech, before slicing Furman, 28–27.

All-SEC Gator halfback "Churnin" Chuck Hunsinger, who played brilliantly in the 1948 Florida defeat, was back for another shot at the Bulldogs, as was standout center and team captain Jimmy Kynes. Florida quarterback Angus Williams, who missed the '48 game due to injury, was being touted as an all-conference choice.

Wally Butts was in his 11th year as UGA mentor and the 3–4 Bulldogs were defending SEC champions. Georgia bashed Furman, 25–0; Chattanooga, 42–6; lost 21–14 at North Carolina and 25–0 at Kentucky. The Bulldogs took LSU, 7–0; lost 13–9 at Miami and 14–7 to Alabama.

Left halfback Floyd "Breezy" Reid and guard and team captain Porter Payne were the Bulldog leaders, along with end Bobby Walston and tackle Francis "Marion" Campbell. Georgia quarterback Ray Prosperi also was a menace, having passed for almost 700 yards in the first seven games.

Both teams again spent the Friday night before the clash at the beach resort of Ponte Vedra, away from the merry throngs in the city. The players "were about the only people not whooping and hollering in Jacksonville tonight" said a November 4 wire story. "As for the remainder of the football-crazy citizenry, there were dozens of parties

162

and celebrations that gave indications of continuing, if spasmodi-
cally, through breakfast to 2:30 kickoff time . . ."

Traffic choked the city streets, thwarting a scheduled parade on
game day morning. Most of the floats and cars, decorated in colored
bunting of the rivals, made their way to Hemming Park where fans
from both sides gathered.

The Gator Bowl had been expanded so that more than 36,000, the
biggest crowd ever to see a game in the series to that time, were in the
stands.

"The teeming Gator Bowl was a mass of color under a bright
sun," the _Florida Times-Union_ said. The variety of fall and winter
clothing "and a veritable forest of yellow and white chrysanthemums
added to the kaleidoscope of college banners and streamers."

Florida got the ball at its 42 on its second series, and Gator
quarterback Williams immediately rocked the Bulldogs with a 27-
yard completion to left end Don Brown.

Moments later, Hunsinger took a pitch at the UGA 21, cut around
right end behind a block by Bill Turner, and raced down the sideline
for a touchdown. Kicker Laz Lewis added the conversion and Florida
had a stunning 7–0 lead with less than four minutes gone in the
contest.

Georgia barged back six minutes later on a drive that started at
their 47. Slashing runs by Reid and left halfback Billy Mixon took
the Bulldogs down to the UF 7. From there, quarterback Prosperi
flipped a pass to left end Walston who went in for the score. Walston's
kick tied it at 7–7.

With about seven minutes left in the half, Florida halfback Loren
Broadus gathered in a punt at the UGA 35 and ran it back 11 yards,
giving the Gators a chance to regain the lead. Hunsinger crashed
through the line and was tackled just shy of the goal line. On the next
play, Williams called a quarterback sneak and slipped into the end
zone. Lewis' kick put Florida back up, 14–7.

Georgia tried to come back before halftime. Prosperi connected
with Walston on a 27-yard pass. Reid found some room and rambled
to the UF 5, but Georgia was penalized on the play and the ball was
moved back to the UF 34.

With less than a minute left, Prosperi drifted back looking to pass.
But Florida's Broadus drew a bead on it, intercepted and took off
toward the Georgia goal line. He was finally pulled down at the
UGA 29 and Florida fans were in a frenzy. The cheering swelled on
the next play when right halfback Hal Griffin wove through defen-

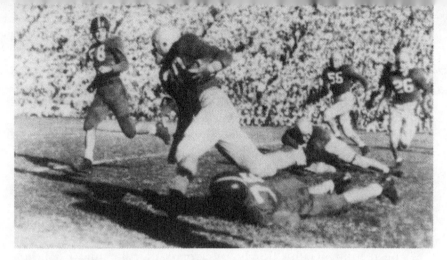

Georgia's "Breezy" Reid gains 17 in the 1949 game, but the heavily-favored Bulldogs were upset 28–7 by "Bear" Wolf's Gators. [Hargrett Collection, UGA Libraries]

ders to the 7. Two plays later, with only 26 seconds till halftime, Hunsinger bulled to pay dirt. Lewis added his third extra point and Florida had a shocking 21–7 advantage.

Intermission supplied some entertaining antics: As the UGA band performed, a Georgia student dressed as a Florida player collapsed on the field. He was carried off on a stretcher by the Georgia cheerleaders to the delight of the Red and Black faction. Meanwhile, Florida fans in the east stands used placards to form a mammoth Gator with a vicious snarl as their band played "We Are the Boys From Old Florida."

The Gators showed no signs of letting up as the third quarter unfolded. With Georgia frustrated on offense, Florida began a drive from its 17. Hunsinger galloped 41 yards and "the crowd smelled more blood," a United Press account said. Runs by Griffin and fullback Russ Godwin pushed the Gators closer to blowing the game open.

Williams was stopped for no gain at the Georgia 15, but, on the next play, Hunsinger crashed over right tackle for his third touchdown. Lewis kicked the conversion and Florida enjoyed a 28–7 bulge with the game still in the third quarter.

With its defense muzzling the Bulldogs, Florida was content to sit on its lead. The gun sounding the close of the game touched off a riotous spectacle. The Gators had bagged one of the biggest upsets in the history of the rivalry, and Ray Wolf rode off the field on the shoulders of his warriors.

"A roar such as never sounded before in the Gator Bowl went up from the sardined crowd . . ." the *Florida Times-Union* said. Hundreds of Florida students and fans swarmed onto the field, mobbing the Gators and vainly trying to pull down the cement-embedded goal-posts.

Florida tasted victory over Georgia for the first time since 1940, snapping a seven-game Bulldog winning streak. The Gators' 28 points were the most ever scored by a Florida team against Georgia at that time.

The "band of hitherto hapless Gators administered a resounding smacking" to the Bulldogs, the _Times-Union_ said.

Hunsinger, with three touchdowns, was the hero of the day. The 185-pound Gator senior from Harrisburg, Ill., outgained the entire Georgia team, running for 174 yards on 18 carries.

He scored a total of four touchdowns in the 1948–49 games against the Bulldogs. On defense, the Gators held Georgia to 77 passing yards and 64 yards on the ground.

The crowds left the stadium and "disgorged from cars, buses and taxicabs in downtown Jacksonville with a resurgence of pep which boded ill for a quiet evening," the _Times-Union_ reported.

Exultant Gator fans celebrated into the night at the annual football dance at the George Washington Hotel and at special races at the Jacksonville Kennel Club.

All-SEC Florida running back Chuck Hunsinger scored three touchdowns in UF's 1949 victory over heavily-favored Georgia, breaking a seven-game losing streak to the Bulldogs. [UF Archives]

Georgia regrouped a week later to batter Duquesne, 40–0; then tied Auburn, 20–20; and ended with a tough 7–6 loss to Georgia Tech in Atlanta, to close at 4–6–1. Breezy Reid was a draft pick of the Green Bay Packers and Al Bodine was chosen by Pittsburgh.

Florida did not follow up on its success. The Gators fell 35–0 to Kentucky in Tampa; 28–13 at Miami; and 35–13 to Alabama, to finish a disappointing 4–5–1.

Florida's Hunsinger and Jimmy Kynes were honored as All-SEC first-team selections. Hunsinger, a first-round draft pick of the Chicago Bears, played in the NFL through 1952.

Wolf closed his UF career 1–3 against Georgia and never had a winning record in Gainesville.

Scoring:

Florida	7	14	7	0	—	28
Georgia	7	0	0	0	—	7

UF	TD	Hunsinger, 21-yard run (Lewis kick)
UGA	TD	Walston, 7-yard pass from Prosperi (Walston kick)
UF	TD	Williams, 1-yard run (Lewis kick)
UF	TD	Hunsinger, 1-yard run (Lewis kick)
UF	TD	Hunsinger, 15-yard run (Lewis kick)

Florida: D. Brown, Bishop, *left end;* Turner, Carver, Ewing, *left tackle;* Sutton, Lorenzo, *left guard;* Kynes, Hazelwood, McDonald, Rozelle, *center;* Huerta, *right guard;* A. Brown, Dempsey, *right tackle;* French, Johnson, *right end;* Williams, Poucher, Lewis, Yancey, *quarterback;* Hunsinger, Montsdeoca, McGowan, Broadus, Gruetzmacher, *left halfback;* Griffin, Cox, *right halfback;* Godwin, Gerber, Parker, *fullback*

Georgia: Walston, Chandler, Duke, McManus, *left end;* Feher, Tanner, Steele, *left tackle;* Greer, Love, Greenway, *left guard;* Pope, Bradshaw, Jackura, McClung, *center;* Payne, Principe, *right guard;* Yelvington, Campbell, *right tackle;* Merola, Lorendo, Duke, *right end;* Prosperi, Field, *quarterback;* Brunson, Mixon, Henderson, Hipps, *left halfback;* Durand, McHugh, Raber, Maricich, Hlebovy, *right halfback;* McCall, Reid, Bodine, Tilliski, *fullback*

	Florida	Georgia
First downs	10	8
Rushing yards	274	64
Passing yards	32	77
Pass att/comp/int	7/3/1	20/8/3
Punts/avg. yards	7/46	9/37
Fumbles/lost	2/1	1/0
Penalties/yards	13/85	6/70

— 1950 —

Georgia 6, Florida 0

UNDER WARM, CLOUDLESS SKIES A SELLOUT crowd of more than 36,000 filled the Gator Bowl on November 11, 1950, to see if Florida could win two in a row over Georgia, a feat not done since 1928–29.

The rivalry's renewal was tempered by the news that Red Chinese divisions had crossed the Yalu River into North Korea three days earlier and were engaging United Nations forces, increasing chances that America might become involved in another global war.

Both teams were trying to shake disheartening losses. Florida had been steamrollered 40–6 by Kentucky a week earlier. A 14–7 defeat by Alabama all but eliminated Georgia from the conference championship race. The 3–1–3 Bulldogs bashed Maryland, 27–7, in their opener, but had been held to a 7–7 tie by little St. Mary's College in San Francisco. A week after the California trip, Georgia and North Carolina fought to a scoreless draw. Georgia then downed Mississippi State, 27–0; tied LSU, 13–13, in Baton Rouge; and beat Boston College, 19–7, before the Alabama loss. The Bulldogs had not had three ties in a year since the 1919 season.

Despite the Kentucky debacle, the Gators of first-year coach Bob Woodruff were off to a surprising 5–2 start. Florida beat The Citadel, 7–3, and Duquesne, 27–14, before falling 16–13 at Georgia Tech. The Gators also scuttled Vanderbilt, 31–27, and Furman, 19–7, before facing Kentucky.

Florida's hopes against Georgia rode with the passing of sophomore quarterback Haywood Sullivan, who had been instrumental in each of the Gators' triumphs in 1950.

Georgia's offense was triggered by the running of left halfback Lauren Hargrove, known to UGA fans as "the Fitzgerald Phantom." Coach Wally Butts' Bulldogs were a touchdown favorite.

The game was savage in intensity from the outset. Neither team

167

established much offense or penetrated the other's domain in the opening quarter. The hard-hitting play on both sides resulted in three fumbles, two recovered by Florida and one by Georgia.

With only seconds left in the first period, UGA senior punter Pat Field got off a coffin-corner kick that skipped out of bounds at the UF 1; but the officials called it back, saying the quarter had expired before the punt. Field tried again on the first play of the second period, lofting another beauty that bounced out at the 10. Field would be a thorn in the hides of the Gators all afternoon.

Midway through the second quarter, Florida's Fred Montsdeoca, the 1949 SEC punting champion, partly shanked a kick. The ball traveled 31 yards, skittering out of bounds at the UF 45. What followed would be remembered as "The Drive" of the 1950 game.

On first down, Georgia quarterback Malcolm Cook started around right end before lateralling to halfback Billy Mixon, who picked up 16 yards. Two rushes by halfback Gus Hlebovy gained 11 more. A cutback run by Lukie Brunson and a keeper by Cook put the ball at the UF 5.

Two line plunges were snuffed out by the Gators. On third down Cook tried to pass, held up and ran for his life toward left end. In the confusion, Georgia end Bobby Walston worked free in the end zone as three Gators bore down on Cook. The Bulldog quarterback saw Walston had been left alone and, in what was described as a "basketball-like" pass, lobbed the ball to the UGA end for the touchdown. Walston's extra point attempt soared wide left but Georgia pulled ahead 6–0.

The Gators raged back as halfback Scott Peek took the kickoff at his 1 and banged out to the 25. Sullivan zipped a pass to left end Bob Horton out to midfield, then threw to end D. E. Brown for a first down at the UGA 32.

Again Sullivan drifted back in the pocket and calmly flipped a pass to right end James French who was in the clear. Apparently startled to find himself so open, French dropped the ball on a play that might have gone all the way.

With the Bulldogs guessing pass, Sullivan handed off to fullback Floyd Huggins who bulled down to the Georgia 14, almost breaking free for the score. Unfortunately for Florida, the final seconds of the half ticked off on the play.

Mixing the running of Huggins with the pass, quarterback Sullivan steered the Gators downfield early in the third quarter. Completing passes to French, left end Robert Knight, and left halfback Buford Long, the Gators were suddenly at the UGA 12.

Just as suddenly, Florida fumbled and Bulldog left guard Jeff Burgamy recovered to end the threat.

Georgia started the final period with a drive of its own. Quarterback Ray Prosperi connected with left end John Duke for a 17-yard gain. Runs of 14 and 13 yards by fullback John Tilliski propelled Georgia inside the UF 30.

Florida halfback John L. Hall stopped the incursion when he leaped in front of a Prosperi pass in the end zone, running it out to the UF 5.

With about five minutes left, Sullivan tried to lift the Gators to victory. As Florida approached midfield, everyone in the stadium knew the game hinged on the next few plays. It was here that Georgia captain and right end Mike Merola made the play of his college career. Sullivan attempted to pass to Huggins behind the line of scrimmage, but Merola swiped the airborne ball and was pulled down at the Florida 25, just when it appeared he was about to break free.

With the fans in Red and Black shaking the stadium, the Bulldogs, chiefly on the running of Billy Mixon, ground to a first down at the Gators' 2 as the game ended.

Florida's Huggins was the game's leading rusher with 128 yards in 19 tries followed by Georgia's Mixon with 97 yards in the same number of carries.

While Georgia's Cook and Walston combined for the winning points, both sides credited Field's punting as crucial to the Bulldogs' victory. "Pat Field's kicking beat us," UF backfield coach Frank Broyles told the *Atlanta Constitution.* "He kept us backed up to our door all day long."

Field, a converted quarterback from Republic, Pa., punted five times, deftly pinning Florida at or inside its 10 with four of them. The fifth punt bounced off a Georgia player's helmet at the UF 25.

"I would not trade him for anybody in the South," Wally Butts had repeatedly told reporters during the season.

The game was the closest in the series since the 6–2 Georgia win in 1939. Joe Lansdell of the *Savannah Morning News* wrote that Georgia "chewed just enough alligator hide off . . . for a traveling bag" to carry home the victory.

Florida lost 20–14 to Miami and closed their campaign at 5–5, taking a 41–13 whipping by Alabama in Jacksonville.

Georgia beat Auburn, 12–10; Furman, 40–0; and lost 7–0 to Georgia Tech. The Bulldogs accepted a bid to play Texas A&M in the first and only Presidential Cup in College Park, Md. Zippy Morocco scored two touchdowns, but the Bulldogs were stampeded 40–20 by the Aggies.

Scoring:

Georgia   0   6   0   0   —   6
Florida   0   0   0   0   —   0

UGA   TD   Walston, 5-yard pass from Cook (PAT failed)

Georgia: McManus, Walston, Duke, *left end;* Campbell, Anglin, Tanner, *left tackle;* Burgamy, Feher, Salerno, *left guard;* Decarlo, Bradshaw, *center;* Principe, Madray, Greenway, *right guard;* Walsh, Yelvington, *right tackle;* Merola, Babcock, *right end;* Rocco, Cook, Field, Prosperi, *quarterback;* Hipps, Mixon, Morocco, Morris, Roberts, *left halfback;* Caprara, Brunson, Hlebovy, Magoni, Hargrove, *right halfback;* Langley, Bilyeu, Tilliski, Raber, *fullback*

Florida: Brown, Davis, Knight, Horton, *left end;* King, Pappas, David, *left tackle;* Rowe, Petry, Reeves, Rozelle, *left guard;* McDonald, Carlton, *center;* Brooks, Morris, Cain, *right guard;* Mitchum, LaPradd, Balas, *right tackle;* French, Patsy, Flowers, *right end;* Sullivan, Williams, Stevens, *quarterback;* Long, Peek, McGowan, Hall, *left halfback;* Reddell, Oosterhoudt, *right halfback;* Huggins, Ware, Montsdeoca, *fullback*

	Georgia	Florida
First downs	14	17
Rushing yards	184	173
Passing yards	48	117
Pass att/comp/int	8/3/1	21/9/1
Punts/avg. yards	5/39	5/39
Fumbles lost	2	2
Penalties/yards	1/5	1/5

— 1951 —

Georgia 7, Florida 6

IN WALLY BUTTS' 13TH SEASON AS GEORGIA coach, many Bulldog fans felt a black cat had run under his ladder and shattered a mirror by the time the November 10, 1951, Florida game rolled around.

Decimated by injuries, the Bulldogs were 3–4 and trying to avoid the conference cellar. Georgia buried George Washington, 33–0, and downed North Carolina, 28–16, at Chapel Hill to begin the year. The UGA eleven then fell, 6–0, at Mississippi State; 43–7 to Maryland; and 7–0 to LSU in Athens, before beating Boston College, 19–7. Georgia lost 16–14 to Alabama a week before the Florida fracas.

The 4–3 Gators of second-year coach Bob Woodruff were a touch-down favorite over Georgia, but knew they had to contend with Bulldog quarterback Zeke Bratkowski and end Harry Babcock, considered to be one of the best passing duos in the country. Georgia tackle Francis "Marion" Campbell, nicknamed for a Revolutionary War hero from South Carolina, was touted as an All-America candidate.

Florida beat Wyoming, 13–0, in the season opener, then downed The Citadel, 27–7, before losing 27–0 to Georgia Tech. Florida pounded Loyola, 40–7, in Pasadena, Calif.; lost 14–13 at Auburn; shelled Vanderbilt, 33–13; and fell 14–6 to Kentucky, before the Georgia clash.

The Gators relied on the passing of quarterback Haywood Sullivan, whose heroics almost led Florida to a win in the 1950 game, the running of halfback Buford Long, and the work of a talented defensive front.

One reporter described downtown Jacksonville as a "menagerie" a few hours before game time, with traffic jammed and Florida students parading through the streets.

A packed Gator Bowl crowd of some 37,000 was on hand on a

171

cloudy, brisk afternoon, with a strong wind that would play a factor in the game's outcome blowing in from the north. The Gators won the coin toss and chose to kick off, so that Georgia would have to drive into the stiff breeze to open the game.

On the second play from scrimmage, Bratkowski hooked up with Babcock for 13 yards. The Bulldogs could do little after that and had to punt.

The second time they got the ball, the Gators used the ground game to move from their 46 to the Georgia 9. Plowing runs by Billy Reddell, Floyd Huggins, Rick Casares and Sam Oosterhoudt put the Gators in position to score.

Sullivan tried to cross up the 'Dogs by going to the pass. He threw toward Casares near the goal line, but Georgia's Bob West was there and intercepted at the 5 to smother the Gator menace.

Florida threatened again on its next series as Sullivan connected with left end Robert Knight for two completions. Again Georgia held, as Marion Campbell burst through to drop Sullivan for a loss. A Casares field goal try failed from the UGA 17.

Inspired by the missed field goal, Georgia went on the prowl with Bratkowski's passing. He threw to James Roberts for 15, Gene White for 11, Babcock for 17, White again for 18, and Roberts for seven in a drive to the UF 9.

But the Florida defense toughened near the goal line. With Georgia facing a third down, UF linemen surged around Bratkowski and someone got a hand up to deflect the pass. Florida end Bob Horton pulled in the wayward ball at the goal line and ran it back to the 14.

With the wind at their backs in the second quarter, the Bulldogs showed some offensive snap. A Florida punt came to Anthony "Zippy" Morocco who lateralled to Conrad Manisera at the UGA 17. Manisera knifed through defenders down the sideline for 33 yards to midfield. Morocco then ripped off 13 yards and halfback Lauren Hargrove hit the line for two more before Bratkowski fired a strike to White at the UF 28. Four plays later, fullback Richard Raber crunched down to the 13. Manisera was blanketed by Gators and lost six. From the 19, Bratkowski rifled a pass that Roberts dropped at the goal line. Bratkowski reloaded on the next down, hitting Morocco, open to his right, at the 6. Despite two Gators trying to haul him down, Morocco zipped in for the score. Sophomore guard Sam Mrvos booted the extra point, and Georgia's 7–0 lead held up till halftime.

The Gators received the second half kickoff and came out running. On a drive starting at the UF 33, Sullivan tore loose on a 24-yard

Edmund "Zeke" Bratkowski was a record-setting UGA quarterback but lost two of three games against Florida from 1951 to 1953, including upsets by the Gators in 1952 and 1953.

romp. Buford Long, Huggins and J. L. "Papa" Hall hit the Georgia line, pushing the yardsticks to the UGA 7.

Hall crunched forward to an apparent first down at the 5, but the Gators were flagged for illegal use of hands and penalized 15 yards. Looking at fourth down, the Gators decided to roll the dice. Sullivan drifted back to pass but was trapped by Bulldogs. He lateralled to Long who zig-zagged through the Georgians down to the 6, two yards shy of the first down. For the third time, a Florida invasion inside the UGA 20 yielded no points.

The devious wind and the defenses reigned for much of the second half although Florida's backs rambled for substantial yardage. Bratkowski found holes in the Gators' secondary but the Floridians held whenever it appeared Georgia was mounting a serious threat.

The game wound into the fourth quarter and Georgia had possession at its 13, when fate smiled on Florida. Bratkowski went deep but Long intercepted at the UGA 41 and dodged to the Bulldogs' 29 with the Orange and Blue backers screaming their support.

Plunges by Oosterhoudt and Casares took the Gators to the UGA 13, but Georgia's Bob West then stormed through to drop Sullivan for a loss back to the 29.

Undaunted on fourth down despite their earlier failures, the Gators went for it. Sullivan whipped a pass toward Oosterhoudt but the ball whistled over his head and it looked as if Georgia had held. They hadn't.

An official called pass interference on halfback Jack Hill, who was guarding Gator end Don French away from Oosterhoudt's vicinity, and Florida had a first and goal at the 7.

Two rushes by the Gators netted a yard against the feisty Georgia defense. On the third down, Long steamed around left end for the score to pull the delirious Gators within a point of a tie. Gator fullback Rick Casares came on for the conversion, but his kick veered wide right and the Georgians clung to their point.

Twice in the closing minutes Florida was compelled to go for big yardage near its goal line. Sullivan was buried by red shirts on fourth down at the UF 20. On the last play of the game, the harassed Gator quarterback backpedaled to pass but was smacked down by victorious 'Dogs at the UF 15.

Florida held a large statistical edge over Georgia in everything but points. The Gators had been able to move on the Bulldogs but only sustained one drive, squandering several scoring chances. Florida had 307 yards total offense and its defense held Georgia to only 22 offensive plays in the second half. It wasn't enough. Georgia had its first conference win of the year by the closest margin in a Florida-Georgia game since the Bulldogs' 6–2 victory in 1939.

In the quarterback duel, Bratkowski was the master, completing 10 of 29 passes for 115 yards compared to Florida's Sullivan, who was 10 of 18 for 94. The Gators were intercepted three times.

Florida ruled the rushing game, gaining 213 yards to the Bulldogs' 79. Gator Sam Oosterhoudt led all runners with 87 yards on 19 carries.

Florida ended the campaign with a 21–6 loss at Miami and a surprise 30–21 win over Alabama in Tuscaloosa for Woodruff's second consecutive 5–5 finish.

Georgia closed with a 46–14 thumping of Auburn in Columbus and a 48–6 rout at Georgia Tech for a 5–5 mark. End Harry Babcock and defensive back and team captain Claude Hipps were named to the All-SEC first team. Zippy Morocco and Marion Campbell were picked in the draft by Philadelphia while Hipps was chosen by Pittsburgh. Campbell later would coach in the NFL, including a stint with the Atlanta Falcons.

★   ★   ★

Scoring:

Georgia   0   7   0   0   —   7
Florida   0   0   0   6   —   6

UGA   TD   Morocco, 13-yard pass from Bratkowski (Mrvos kick)
UF   TD   Long, 6-yard run (PAT failed)

Georgia: Decarlo, Poss, White, *left end;* Anglin, Terrill, Steele, *left tackle;* Burgamy, Salerno, Filipkowski, *left guard;* McClung, Jones, Ragsdale, *center;* Madray, Griffith, Greenway, Mrvos, Beckwith, *right guard;* Yelvington, Campbell, *right tackle;* Babcock, West, Gunn, *right end;* Bratkowski, Morris, *quarterback;* Hargrove, Manisera, Hipps, Cook, *left halfback;* Morocco, Magoni, Hill, Roberts, Madison, Earnest, *right halfback;* Raber, Dipietro, Caprara, Scichilone, *fullback*

Florida: Knight, Horton, Brown, Patsy, *left end;* David, LaPradd, Douglas, Proctor, *left tackle;* Hewlett, Reeves, York, *left guard;* McDonald, D'Agostino, Cummings, *center;* May, Pappas, Brooks, Morris, Medved, *right guard;* Mitchum, Thomas, Hammock, Hatch, *right tackle;* French, Webster, O'Brien, Thomas, *right end;* Sullivan, Nichols, Quinn, *quarterback;* Long, Oosterhoudt, *left halfback;* Hall, Reddell, Long, *right halfback;* Huggins, Jumper, Casares, Webster, *fullback*

	Georgia	Florida
First downs	9	16
Rushing yards	79	213
Passing yards	115	94
Pass/att/com/int	29/10/0	18/10/3
Punts/avg. yards	6/42	6/28
Fumbles lost	1	1
Penalty yards	35	51

—— 1952 ——

Florida 30, Georgia 0

WITH FIVE BACKS DISPLAYING EQUAL RUSH-ing capability, and deadeye passer Zeke Bratkowski, Georgia coach Wally Butts felt he had his most talented offense since the 1948 SEC championship team facing Florida on October 25, 1952.

Yet the 3–2 Gators of third-year coach Bob Woodruff were underestimated, overshadowed and overlooked by the press and the rest of the conference.

Not including the 1904 clash, this was the 30th Georgia-Florida game, with Georgia leading the series 23–5–1.

Georgia Tech, Georgia and Tennessee were considered the cream of the 1952 SEC crop, even though most observers believed Georgia's tough schedule would keep them out of the conference battle. At 4–1, Georgia was playing well, beating Vanderbilt, 19–7; Tulane, 21–16; and N.C. State, 49–0; before losing 37–0 to Maryland. The Bulldogs regrouped to upset LSU, 27–14, in Baton Rouge a week before the Florida game.

The Gators bashed Stetson, 33–6, in their premiere but lost 17–14 at Georgia Tech. Florida dusted The Citadel, 33–0; Clemson, 54–13; and lost at Vanderbilt, 20–13.

Woodruff's squad braced for the expected aerial onslaught of Bratkowski, who was 12th in the nation in passing yardage. Bratkowski's favorite target was All-SEC end Harry Babcock. The underdog Gators were pass-savvy, having defended against Vanderbilt quarterback Bill Krietemeyer, ranked 10th in air offense, a week earlier.

Florida was cheered by the return of halfback Buford Long, who was injured in the Clemson game but was back in full pads and expected to play against the Georgians. The Gators offense depended almost exclusively on the running of Long and backs Rick Casares and J. L. "Papa" Hall. Florida's quarterback was Doug Dickey, who later would return to his alma mater and coach some of the finest Florida teams in history.

Florida tackle Charlie LaPradd was an All-American and All-SEC performer in 1952. His college career was interrupted by service in the army as a paratrooper. [UF Archives]

In Jacksonville, Gator alumni held their annual breakfast at the George Washington Hotel before the pre-game parade, and the party on both sides went into overdrive. The bedlam in the river city was such that one observer described downtown as "a howling animal kingdom." A particularly popular Florida float sported a sign advertising "Bulldog Blood—5 Cents A Quart."

The Gator Bowl was filled to capacity with some 37,000, among whom was Miss America 1953 Neva Jane Langley, a former Floridian who had moved to Georgia and won the title for the Peach State.

A temporary truce was called as the schools' bands joined in playing "The Star-Spangled Banner" prior to the kickoff. "Immediately afterwards, the War Between the States was in full force again," the *Florida Times-Union* reported.

The fire fight on the field was not long in erupting. Two minutes into the game, a brawl broke out between Georgia end Harry Babcock and Gator back Arlen Jumper. Both were ejected. The Bulldogs would have to go without Bratkowski's favorite receiver while Florida would be without its "defensive quarterback," as Woodruff described Jumper.

Most of the first quarter was a defensive battle with the teams swapping possessions a total of five times before Florida drew blood. When a Gator drive died at the UGA 33, Gator halfback Rick Casares set up for a field-goal attempt. Kicking from a slight angle, he split the uprights and Florida led 3–0.

Casares was a man on a mission. His missed extra point in the 1951 game had been the margin of victory in a 7–6 Georgia win. The 205-pound junior was well on his way to redemption against the Bulldogs.

With Babcock out, Bratkowski aimed most of his passes at Art Decarlo, burning the Gators in the middle. Decarlo snared five passes for 56 yards in the first half but the Bulldogs couldn't find the end zone.

Florida went to work again in the second quarter after taking the ball on a Bratkowski interception at the UF 25. Relying mostly on the punishing runs of Casares and Long, the Gators ground out six first downs to the UGA 1. Gator quarterback Doug Dickey sneaked in from there, and Casares' extra point gave Florida a 10–0 advantage that stood at halftime.

The only score of the third period came after the Gators claimed a Georgia fumble at the UGA 28. Runs by Casares, Long and Dickey resulted in two first downs, and Florida coiled for another score at the Georgia 3. Casares careened in from there and his conversion put the Gators in command 17–0 late in the quarter.

The Georgia highlight of the third period was a 50-yard run to the UF 28 by Robert "Foots" Clemens, but the Bulldogs could not capitalize.

Florida took possession at its 23 shortly after the beginning of the final period; and Buford Long, who had scored the only Florida touchdown in the 1951 game, took center stage for the most dazzling play of the afternoon.

Florida back Rick Casares scored a touchdown and kicked a field goal and three extra points in UF's 30–0 win against UGA in 1952. [UF Archives]

Running back Buford Long scampered for a 77-yard touchdown in Florida's 30–0 defeat of UGA in 1952. [UF Archives]

Taking a handoff from Dickey, Long danced over left tackle, swerved to his right and found an open field in the Georgia secondary. Some 10 yards past the line of scrimmage, he reversed field and raced 77 yards for the touchdown to the deafening delight of Gator partisans. Casares tacked on the extra point and Florida's revenge widened to 24–0.

With the game well in hand, Woodruff sent in his reserves and replaced Dickey at quarterback with Fred Robinson, a talented young passer.

On Robinson's third series, Florida rolled to the Bulldogs' 19. From there, the sophomore signal-caller drilled a touchdown pass to Leonard Balas for the cake's icing in the last seconds.

The Gator win touched off "one of the wildest victory parties in Jacksonville history," the *Times-Union* reported. "The celebrating soared on far into the night."

The loss was the worst for Georgia in the series to that time, and the first time since the 1937 Florida 6–0 win that the Bulldogs had been held scoreless against the Gators. Florida's margin of victory would stand until 1990.

Long led the Gators with 116 yards on 10 carries and a touchdown but Casares was the Florida Hercules, rushing for 108 yards on 27 attempts and scoring 12 points. The Gators gained 284 yards on the ground; 59 in the air.

On defense, Florida's heroes included back Steve DeLaTorre who had replaced Jumper and was in on a number of stops, and substitute tackle Howard Chapman.

Georgia rushed for 190 yards, paced by Clemens and back Charley Madison, but Bratkowski had been held to 105 yards passing.

179

Bulldog Connie Manisera lunges for the goal line in the 1952 contest, but the Bulldogs were shut out by Bob Woodruff's underdog Gators. [Hargrett Collection, UGA Libraries]

Woodruff had his first victory over Butts after losing the two previous meetings by a total of seven points, and Florida had its sixth win of the series.

"You don't see backs like Buford Long, Rick Casares and Papa Hall every week," Butts told the *Atlanta Constitution.* "And Florida's defensive line is about as tough as they come."

Bob Woodruff assessed the big win to the *Savannah Morning News:* " . . . while our entire squad was all that anyone could ask, it was obvious that Casares did a really great offensive job."

Georgia was overpowered by Alabama, 34–19, a week later, but beat Pennsylvania, 34–27, and Auburn, 13–7, before falling 23–9 to Georgia Tech and beating Miami, 35–13.

The Gators followed the Georgia win with a 31–21 triumph over Auburn, but lost 26–12 to Tennessee at Knoxville. Florida demolished Miami, 43–6, and Kentucky, 27–0, to earn a bid to the Gator Bowl, the school's first postseason appearance. Florida jumped out to a two-touchdown lead against Tulsa in the Gator Bowl and held on for a 14–13 win. The Gators' 8–3 record was their best season since Charlie Bachman's 1929 team went 8–2, including a 18–6 beating of Georgia.

Florida tackle Charlie LaPradd made first-team All-America, something no Gator had accomplished since end Forrest "Fergie" Ferguson was so named in 1941.

Georgia end Harry Babcock was also selected All-America.

LaPradd, Babcock, Gator guard Joe D'Agostino and Georgia back Art Decarlo were selected to the All-SEC first team. Decarlo later played for the Baltimore Colts while Babcock was drafted by Pittsburgh in the NFL and San Francisco, then of the old All-America Football Conference.

Rick Casares was drafted by the Chicago Bears and also played for Washington and Miami in a pro career lasting until 1966. Buford Long played three years with the New York Giants, but the 77-yard run against Georgia his senior year would be an exploit to savor forever.

Scoring:

Florida	3	7	7	13	—	30
Georgia	0	0	0	0	—	0

UF	FG	Casares, 33-yards
UF	TD	Dickey, 1-yard run (Casares kick)
UF	TD	Casares, 3-yard run (Casares kick)
UF	TD	Long, 77-yard run (Casares kick)
UF	TD	Balas, 19-yard pass from Robinson (PAT failed)

Florida: Kelly, Bilyk, O'Brien, Manning, Horton, Balas, *end;* D'Agostino, May, Morris, Martin, Hammock, York, *guard;* LaPradd, Chapman, David, Winne, Douglas, Medved, *tackle;* Annis, Carlton, Dyal, *center;* Dickey, Robinson, *quarterback;* Casares, Jumper, DeLaTorre, Hall, Long, Haddock, Ives, Scott, Schwartzburg, *back*

Georgia: Decarlo, White, Poss, Carson, *left end;* Anglin, Griffin, *left tackle;* Wimberly, Salerno, Filipkowski, *left guard;* Jones, Ragsdale, Langley, *center;* Griffith, Mrvos, *right guard;* Campbell, Malinowski, *right tackle;* Babcock, West, Gunn, O'Malley, *right end;* Bratkowski, Harper, *quarterback;* Hargrove, Garrard, *left halfback;* Madison, Hill, Roberts, Earnest, *right halfback;* Clemens, Caprara, Scichilone, *fullback*

	Florida	Georgia
First downs	15	15
Rushing yards	284	190
Passing yards	59	105
Pass att/comp/int	10/6/0	19/11/3
Punts/avg. yards	6/46	7/38
Lost fumbles	1	2
Yards penalized	33	65

— 1953 —

Florida 21, Georgia 7

THE NOVEMBER 7, 1953, FLORIDA-GEORGIA game had coach Bob Woodruff's Gators as a slight favorite, despite the fact that Georgia's flying circus of quarterback Zeke Bratkowski and end John Carson was the country's top pass offensive duo.

Bratkowski, the team captain, also was the nation's leading punter. Despite Florida being the oddsmakers' choice, some observers were predicting an aerial field day for the Bulldogs.

Florida supporters knew the Gators had not won consecutive games from Georgia since the 1928–1929 seasons, and that UF rushing leader, running back Tommy Haddock, would have to have a big day if their team was to have a chance. Haddock was also second in scoring in the conference with 42 points.

The Floridians opened 1953 on the road with a 20–16 loss to Rice and held Georgia Tech to a scoreless draw, before losing 26–13 at Kentucky. The Gators stomped Stetson, 45–0, and The Citadel, 60–0, but tied LSU, 21–21, and lost at Auburn, 16–7, to face Georgia with a 2–3–2 record.

The 3–4 Bulldogs of 15th-year coach Wally Butts downed Villanova, 32–19, in their first game, then beat Tulane, 16–14, before falling 14–12 at Texas A&M and 40–14 at Maryland. Georgia then lost 14–6 to LSU, clipped North Carolina, 27–14, and dropped a 33–12 decision to Bart Starr and Alabama. Despite the 21-point margin, Butts described the loss to the Crimson Tide as the Bulldogs' best defensive effort of the season.

Along with the capacity crowd of some 37,000 in the Gator Bowl, thousands more watched the regionally-televised border feud across the South.

Behind the ground-gaining aggregation of running backs Haddock, Joe Brodsky, Fred Cason and Bill Dearing, Florida was quick

182

Florida defenders Jack O'Brien, Don Hatch, and Richard Martin descend on UGA quarterback Zeke Bratkowski in the Gators' 1953 triumph. [UF Archives]

to assert its rushing game. Brodsky, a 215-pound fullback, was especially effective in hammering the Bulldog line.

During the early going, Georgia center Derwent Langley seemed to be stopping the Gator runners almost alone. On the other side of the ball Florida was fiercely rushing Bratkowski, but "the Brat" managed to connect on several passes though Georgia could not get within scoring range.

The stalemate broke in the second period. Georgia started a drive at its 24 and reached the UF 6 before the Gators clamped down on defense with about 5:30 left in the half.

Florida was within the shadow of its goal when Doug Dickey entered the game, replacing Harry Spears at quarterback. That's when things started to happen. The Gators were quickly out of the hole as Dearing blasted off tackle for 27 yards to the Florida 33. The run seemed to take some wind out of the Bulldog defense. Dearing ran for seven more and left halfback Jackie Simpson went wide for five. Two plays later, Haddock swept end for 10. Cason then bolted up the middle on a fullback trap, reeling off 21 yards before he was dragged down at the UGA 24. On second down, Dickey faded back to pass and spotted right end and team captain Jack O'Brien in the end zone, hitting him for the score. Spears' extra point gave Florida a 7–0 advantage and climaxed the 94-yard offensive.

Georgia then started downfield from its 28. Bratkowski connected with left halfback Jimmy Campagna to the UF 42 to bring the Bulldogs' backers to life. The duo clicked again for 11 yards to the Florida 30 with 40 seconds left in the half.

Bratkowski went for the quick strike and whistled a pass to right end Gene White who was open in the end zone. The ball hit White in the chest and popped out. Undismayed, Bratkowski dumped a screen pass for short yardage to halfback Jimmy Williams. With 25 seconds left, Bratkowski swung a pass to Williams again but the halfback dropped it. On fourth down, with only 15 seconds remaining, Bratkowski saw end Cleve Clark break free over the middle and put the ball on the money. But Clark was drilled high and low by Gators and couldn't haul it in, to the delight of the Orange and Blue.

The Gators had the lead and twice had doused Georgia threats inside their 15.

Florida hammered another peg in the Bulldogs' coffin early in the second half. With Georgia in possession, Bratkowski tried a pass but the Gators' Spears grabbed the interception in front of Carson at the UGA 35, fighting to the Bulldogs' 8 before being tackled. From the 1-yard line three plays later, Brodsky cracked into the end zone. Spears' conversion put Florida up 14–0 with 5:05 gone in the third quarter. Boisterous Gator fans, many of whom had not been born when Florida beat Georgia in consecutive years, were sensing that the impossible was about to happen.

The Bulldogs were not rolling over yet. A short kickoff gave them a first down at their 46. Bratkowski went to White for a 10-yard gain, fullback Robert "Foots" Clemens ran for three, and Bratkowski twisted for eight yards and a first down at the UF 33. On third down, the Bulldog passer hit Carson on a 19-yarder to the 9. After the Gators leveled halfback Williams on a sweep attempt, Bratkowski went back to the air, rocketing a pass to end White for the score. Bulldog tackle Joe Graff booted the extra point to trim the Florida lead to 14–7 with 6:45 left in the third.

Any chance Georgia had to pull out a win appeared to vanish when Bratkowski left the field in the third quarter with an injury.

Florida turned up the pressure in the last minutes of the third quarter, shuttling their fullbacks in and out of the game. Starting from the UF 44, Cason shredded the Georgians three times for 19 yards and a first down at the UGA 37. Brodsky punished the 'Dogs for two before tearing free for 15 more down to the 20. Georgia then stockpiled the middle of their defense, expecting another line plunge. Instead, halfback Larry Scott took a handoff from Dickey on a fake to the fullback and swept end to the 2.

Brodsky was knocked backward on first down, but Dickey drove it in on a quarterback sneak. Florida went 56 yards in eight plays and Spears' kick made it 21–7.

As a UF quarterback, Doug Dickey scored touchdowns during Florida wins in 1952 and 1953. He would return as head coach of the Gators from 1970 to 1978. [UF Archives]

In the late stages the Gators rushed only their guards and tackles, effectively setting up a seven-man secondary that snuffed out Georgia's passing. One reporter wrote that Florida's defenders covered star end John Carson "the way bobby soxers surrounded Frankie Sinatra . . . "

Woodruff evened his record against Butts at 2–2, and Florida had won two in a row from the Bulldogs for the first time in more than two decades.

The beefy, bruising running of Brodsky, Dearing and Cason accounted for 146 of Florida's 262 rushing yards, as part of UF's 336 yards in total offense. Second-stringer Doug Dickey had a college kid's dream afternoon, coming off the bench to score a touchdown and pass for another. Dickey also blocked a Bratkowski pass in Georgia's scoreless drive early in the second period.

Bratkowski completed 15 of 25 passes for 220 yards, a touchdown and two interceptions. He also had at least six sure throws slip away from his receivers.

To some observers, Bratkowski seemed to be UGA's only threat in 1953. "The Bulldogs lack speed in the backfield and heft in the line," wrote *Atlanta Journal-Constitution* reporter Harry Mehre, son of the former UGA coach by the same name. "Florida showed more speed, more depth, and more versatility. You can't overcome all three with a lone weapon."

Bratkowski was drafted by the Chicago Bears and was a member of the Green Bay Packers championship teams of 1965–1967.

Georgia did not recover from the Florida loss, dropping a 39–18 contest to Auburn, falling 14–0 to Southern Mississippi, and 28–12 to Georgia Tech. The Bulldogs' 3–8 finish would be Butts' worst ever as UGA coach.

Florida encored with a 9–7 loss to Tennessee and a 14–0 defeat at Miami to finish 3–5–2.

Georgia end John Carson was named to an All-America team, and both he and Bratkowski were selected to the All-SEC squad. Carson was a draft pick of the Cleveland Browns.

Doug Dickey's Florida glory was far from over. He would return as head coach to lead Florida to four bowl seasons from 1970 to 1978.

Scoring:

Florida	0	7	7	7 —	21
Georgia	0	0	7	0 —	7

UF	TD	O'Brien, 22-yard pass from Dickey (Spears kick)
UF	TD	Brodsky, 1-yard run (Spears kick)
UGA	TD	White, 9-yard pass from Bratkowski (Graff kick)
UF	TD	Dickey, 1-yard run (Spears kick)

Florida: Bilyk, Kelly, Lockhart, Barrow, *left end;* Chapman, Hatch, Silver, Winne, *left tackle;* Wright, H. Martin, Thomas, Vosloh, *left guard;* De-LaTorre, R. Martin, Schwartzburg, Eaton, Brooks, *center;* D'Agostino, Haygood, May, Green, *right guard;* Hunter, Cassidy, Fowler, Burke, Wesley, *right tackle;* O'Brien, Brown, Manning, Tatum, *right end;* Spears, Dickey, Allen, Robinson, *quarterback;* Scott, Simpson, Ives, Smith, *left halfback;* Davis, Haddock, Burgess, *right halfback;* Brodsky, Dearing, Cason, Langam, *fullback*

Georgia: Carson, Arthur, Wilkins, Mulherin, *left end;* Griffin, Fruehauf, Luck, *left tackle;* Wimberly, Graff, *left guard;* Cook, Langley, Hastings, Nutt, *center;* Mrvos, Shea, W. Saye, *right guard;* Malinowski, W. White, Anderson, *right tackle;* O'Malley, G. White, Clark, *right end;* Bratkowski, Harper, *quarterback;* Campagna, Garrard, *left halfback;* Madison, Williams, *right halfback;* Clemens, Kelly, *fullback*

	Florida	Georgia
First downs	17	14
Rushing yards	262	105
Passing yards	74	220
Pass att/comp/int	7/4/1	30/16/3
Punts/avg. yards	6/32	4/29
Fumbles lost	1	0
Penalty yards	60	24

— 1954 —

Georgia 14, Florida 13

For THE FIRST TIME IN THE SERIES' HISTORY, the SEC championship was a potential diamond in the booty for the winner of the November 6, 1954, Florida-Georgia collision.

The Bulldogs entered the game in first place in the league while the Gators were snapping at them from a second place tie with Mississippi. The success of both teams was a surprise to the conference's coaches who, in preseason, picked Georgia to finish 10th and Florida eighth. Both teams were very young.

Georgia, 5–1–1, rose to the top with a tough defense that had limited seven opponents to a total of 28 points. The Bulldogs shut out Florida State, 14–0, on the road; beat Clemson, 14–7; lost 6–0 to Texas A&M; defeated North Carolina, 21–7; nipped Vanderbilt, 16–14, and Tulane, 7–0, before fighting heavily-favored Alabama to a scoreless tie in Birmingham.

Florida, 4–3, was favored by less than a touchdown, but coach Bob Woodruff knew that his squad, whom he called the "flaming sophomores," was unpredictable.

The week before the Georgia game, Florida fumbled nine times against Mississippi State but still managed to win 7–0. The Gators began the year with a 34–14 trouncing at Rice, but upset Georgia Tech, 13–12, in Atlanta before beating Auburn, 19–13. Clemson defeated Florida 14–7. The Gators then downed Kentucky, 21–7, and lost at LSU, 20–7, before the Mississippi State victory.

In addition to their chance for the school's first conference crown, the 1954 Florida team had the opportunity to do something no other UF squad had ever accomplished: beat Georgia for the third consecutive year.

The Gators' defense was cemented by center Steve DeLaTorre, who had starred on defense against Georgia in the 1952 Florida win.

187

Big Joe Brodsky was back at fullback and the Gators rotated Bobby Lance, Dick Allen and Fred Robinson at quarterback.

Georgia's strength was in its big front wall, with guard Don Shea and end Joe O'Malley at the foundation. On offense, Georgia relied heavily on the running of fullbacks Bobby Garrard and Bob "Foots" Clemens.

The traditional party on the St. Johns neared feverish intensity as the city crawled with thousands of fans craving annual bragging rights.

Florida held a pep rally in Jacksonville's Hemming Park a few hours before the game. At one point, the UF cheers were interrupted by infiltrating members of the Georgia band who came in screaming "Dog food! Dog food!" The Gators' multitude responded with shouts of "Gator bait! Gator bait!"

As usual, it was standing room only in the Gator Bowl as the teams took the field, the Gators in blue jerseys and white pants and the 'Dogs in their silver britches and red shirts.

The Gators got into immediate trouble on their first possession. Halfback Bob Davis was jarred by several Georgia defenders after a 15-yard run and fumbled. The Bulldogs' John Bell fell on the ball at the UF 40.

Three plays later, quarterback Jimmy Harper floated a pass to end Roy Wilkins, who reached the Gators 11. Despite O'Malley's dropped pass in the end zone, Georgia made another first down inside the 1, chiefly on Garrard's running. On the first snap, Harper sneaked across the goal line. Charles Madison kicked the extra point to make it 7–0 Georgia.

Late in the first stanza, the Gators, on the UGA 44, got a first down the hard way when Joe Brodsky fumbled toward the Bulldogs' goal. The nerve-wracking play ended when a Gator dove on the ball at the UGA 26. Quarterback Dick Allen completed a 9-yard pass to halfback Don Chandler, and Brodsky went for a first down at the 15. Runs by Brodsky and Allen reached the 6 as the quarter ended.

Two plays later, UF halfback Jackie Simpson circled right end, winning a foot race to the corner of the end zone. Allen's conversion knotted matters at 7–7.

The inspired Florida defense held and forced Georgia to punt. The Gators rolled down the field, reaching the UGA 32. Allen went for it all in the end zone but Georgia's Harper batted the pass away. On the next play, the Gators fumbled and a host of Bulldogs piled on the ball at the 32.

The Gators were stunned even more a few minutes later when UGA's Madison tore through a seam in the blue line and juked 40 yards to the UF 28. Runs by Madison, Clemens and halfback Wendell Tarleton gave the Bulldogs a first down at the 5. Two plays later, Clemens banged over. Madison's extra point put Georgia back in front, 14–7, as intermission neared.

Early in the third period, a short Gator punt gave Georgia good field position near midfield. On a second down play, Harper uncorked a pass to Madison for a 23-yard completion to the Florida 29. Garrard, Madison and Bell penetrated to the 12 and, two plays later, Bell was at the Gators 1. The Bulldogs appeared ready to take a two-touchdown lead, but were whistled for offsides and Georgia retreated to the 6.

Three runs into the mouth of the Gators defense gained only three yards. On fourth and goal, Butts went for the touchdown. Harper stepped back and fired a bullet toward O'Malley in the end zone. But the end couldn't pull it in, and the Gators reveled in their defensive stand.

Backed up dangerously close to their goal, the Gators had to punt and Georgia took over at the UF 40. If the Bulldogs were looking for another attack on the Gator goal, Florida halfback Don Chandler had other plans. Harper's simple pass in the flat was snared by Chandler, who began legging it down the sideline from the UF 26.

The play turned into a track meet between Chandler and Harper, the only Bulldog with a shot to keep him from scoring. Chandler clicked off 67 yards before Harper pushed him out of bounds at the UGA 7.

Orange and Blue fans were back in the game, yelling for a touchdown that would tie it.

Two plays after Chandler's run, fullback Davis atoned for his earlier fumble by churning around left end, scoring from seven yards out. Ed Bass came on for the conversion to pull the Gators even. At the snap, Georgia end Roy Wilkins dove and blocked the kick to preserve the Dogs' 14–13 lead. Still, with four minutes left in the third quarter, the gridiron verdict could go either way.

Fred Robinson, probably Florida's best passer, was sent in at quarterback on the Gators' next possession to crank up the offense. On his crisp throwing and the strong running of Brodsky, the Gators looked to be on the move until they fumbled in the dying seconds of the third period.

The teams twice exchanged possessions in the final quarter with

Bob Woodruff was the first Florida coach to post a winning record against Georgia, 6–4 from 1950 to 1959. Woodruff also guided UF to its first bowl game, a win over Tulsa in the 1953 Gator Bowl. [UF Archives]

neither able to sustain any offense. Unable to advance after squeezing out a first down at its 44, Georgia's Garrard got off the key punt of the day. The ball bounded inside the UF 10 and rolled dead at the 1. With about five minutes left, the Gators would have to drive the length of the field to win it. Robinson went to the air but UGA's Bill Saye intercepted on the UF 22, extinguishing the last Gator hope. As the final seconds ticked away, so did Florida's chance of winning its first conference championship.

The game was the closest in the rivalry since the '51 Georgia 7–6 win.

Wally Butts, "the round little man in the brown suit," as a reporter described him, was lifted to the shoulders of his players and given a victory ride to midfield to meet Woodruff.

With 61 yards, Georgia's Madison was the game's top rusher, in addition to kicking the extra point that was the difference in the outcome. The Gators' Brodsky, a juggernaut in the 1953 game, was held to 43 yards on 11 carries.

Georgia's defensive heroes were legion but junior center Bill Saye was the standout, intercepting two passes, deflecting several others, and recovering two fumbles. Wilkins had to be the toughest. Entering the game with a bad ankle, his other foot had been hurt in the day's action. He still was able to block the kick that saved the game for Georgia.

The Gators knocked off Tennessee, 14–0, at Knoxville and lost to Miami, 14–0, to finish at 5–5. Running back Mal Hammack gave the Gators something to cheer about, selected by the NFL Chicago Cardinals and playing 11 years of pro ball.

The win solidified Georgia's position atop the SEC and enhanced its chances for a berth in the Sugar Bowl. But the Bulldogs were subsequently shellacked 35–0 by Auburn, then lost 7–3 to Georgia Tech to miss out on postseason play, despite a 6–3–1 mark.

Scoring:

Georgia	7	7	0	0	—	14
Florida	0	7	6	0	—	13

UGA	TD	Harper, 1-yard run (Madison kick)
UF	TD	Simpson, 4-yard run (Allen kick)
UGA	TD	Clemens, 3-yard run (Madison kick)
UF	TD	Davis, 7-yard run (kick blocked)

Georgia: Wilkins, Roberts, Monti, Arthur, *left end;* Mosteller, Luck, Griffin, *left tackle;* Spadafino, Cushenberry, *left guard;* Saye, Carrollton, Nutt, *center;* Shea, Dye, Fowler, *right guard;* Brown, White, Van Buren, *right tackle;* O'Malley, Clark, *right end;* Harper, Young, *quarterback;* Bell, Tarleton, Pilgrim, Campagna, *left halfback;* Madison, Harris, *right halfback;* Garrard, Clemens, Kelly, Culpepper, *fullback*

Florida: Knight, Bilyk, Lockhart, *left end;* Winne, Hill, Hatch, *left tackle;* H. Martin, Green, Vosloh, *left guard;* DeLaTorre, Purcell, *center;* Barrow, Haygood, *right guard;* Wesley, Burke, *right tackle;* Brown, Burford, *right end;* Lance, Allen, Robinson, Scott, *quarterback;* Simpson, Smith, Chandler, *left halfback;* Davis, Burgess, McIver, *right halfback;* Hammack, Brodsky, Bolton, Bass, Visser, *fullback*

	Georgia	Florida
First downs	12	14
Rushing yards	188	147
Passing yards	51	57
Pass att/comp/int	6/2/1	12/6/2
Punts/avg. yards	7/35	6/41
Fumbles lost	0	3
Penalty yards	50	12

— 1955 —

Florida 19, Georgia 13

A PAIR OF FLEET FLORIDA BACKS AND A
stingy pass defense prompted most sports forecasters to favor the
Gators by a touchdown over Georgia going into the November 5,
1955, game.

Both teams were rated preseason darkhorses in the conference race
but had failed to meet expectations.

Florida, 3–3, defeated Mississippi State, 20–14; lost 14–7 to Georgia
Tech and 13–0 to Auburn; beat George Washington, 28–0, and LSU,
18–14, before falling to Kentucky, 10–7

Georgia, 4–3, lost 26–13 to Ole Miss in its premiere; downed Vanderbilt, 14–13; fell 26–7 to Clemson; beat North Carolina, 28–7, and
Florida State, 47–14, before being upset 14–0 by Tulane. The Bulldogs
trounced Alabama, 35–14, a week before going to Jacksonville.

Georgia coach Wally Butts was using a dual-quarterback system in
1955, with Jimmy Harper coming in to direct the rushing invasion and
Dick Young at the helm in passing situations.

On the Monday before the clash, Florida coach Bob Woodruff went
Butts one better, announcing that he planned to alternate three players,
Jon May, Dick Allen, and Bobby Lance, at quarterback. May, a sopho-
more, had seen little action but some observers already were compar-
ing him to Haywood Sullivan, widely considered to be the finest
Gator passing quarterback to that time.

Speedy Florida halfbacks Jackie Simpson and Jim Roundtree were
expected to give Georgia trouble, particularly on sweeps. Florida's
pass defense was strong and ranked second in the conference. Gator
senior linebacker Steve DeLaTorre was the heart of the defense, and
Don Chandler was the best punter in the country, averaging almost 47
yards per kick.

Georgia was hurting at several positions: Halfback Jimmy Orr injured a shoulder against Alabama, while tackle Alex McDonald and

back Bobby Garrard, though both limping, were expected to face the Gators.

Florida also was not at full strength. Fullback Joe Brodsky and tackle Buster Hill were among several players suffering from the flu that had swept the UF campus.

A capacity Gator Bowl crowd saw the rivals looking tight and trading punts in their first possessions.

Bulldog halfback Wendell Tarleton, on Georgia's second series, scooted over the Florida right side for 12 before gaining six more to the UGA 49.

Garrard fumbled on a third-down call but Bulldog guard Len Spadafino recovered for a first down at the UF 48. Tarleton then darted 30 yards for the day's first scoring threat. The Gators dropped quarterback Harper for a yard loss, but he came right back on a sneak to the UF 4. Another quarterback keeper pushed the markers to the Florida 1 and a Georgia first down. Tarleton barged into the end zone on second down, fumbling after he crossed the goal line, but the touchdown was good. Bulldog end Ken Cooper booted the conversion and Georgia had a 7–0 lead over the favored Gators at the 11:10 mark of the first period.

After the kickoff, on the running of quarterback Lance and halfbacks John Burgess and Simpson, Florida nudged down to the UGA 49. Two rushes by fullback Bob Visser and another by Lance brought the Gators to the 28. Penalties killed the drive after they reached the 17, and Don Chandler hit a coffin-corner kick that went out of bounds at the 11 early in the second quarter.

After swapping punts, a 15-yard roughness penalty on Georgia put Florida on UGA's side of the field. May, UF's promising signal-caller, came in to jump-start the offense but fumbled, and John Bell recovered for the Dogs at the UGA 32.

Georgia set off on a pounding 68-yard drive, thanks to the running of Harper, Garrard, Jefferson Davis and Henry Dukes. Harper started it with an 11-yard run to the UGA 48, and Davis and Dukes combined for another first down to the UF 41. Dukes then sliced through for 15 and Harper tacked on eight more to the Gators 15.

Three plays later from the 5, Garrard went over the right side for the touchdown. Cooper's conversion try was partially blocked, but Georgia's lead mounted to 13–0.

At the half, it appeared the Bulldogs were in firm control and well on their way to a second consecutive upset of the Gators.

But 14 seconds into the third quarter Florida was transformed into a

Don Chandler's punting and blocking helped Florida beat UGA in 1955. Chandler later was an All-Pro with the Green Bay Packers and New York Giants. [UF Archives]

different team from the squad that had been collared in the first half. The catalysts were right halfback Roundtree and star halfback Simpson.

Roundtree snapped up a careening second-half kickoff at the UF 15 and exploded up the middle of the field, running through, and past, most of the Bulldogs. Chandler threw a fine block at the UGA 40, and the Gator sophomore sprinted into the Georgia end zone with UF fans shaking the stadium in exhilaration.

Roundtree's 85-yard run is one of the most brilliant of the series and put Florida back in the fray, 13–6. Chandler's conversion wobbled wide but the Gators were roaring.

Georgia's Roy Wilkins, the hero of the 1954 game, returned a short kickoff to the UGA 43. The Bulldogs showed composure by sticking mainly to the ground and moving the yardsticks. Runs by Tarleton, Garrard, Dukes, and Davis, along with a 10-yard Harper-to-Wilkins pass, put the Dogs at the UF 29. But the Gators held on fourth down, snuffing out the advance.

After Georgia's next possession, Gator halfback Simpson rekindled the fire of Roundtree's big run when he grabbed the punt and dodged upfield for 33 yards before being tackled at the Georgia 40 by Tony Cushenberry.

Simpson and Visser carried for a first down at the UGA 29. Lance gained eight but the Gators faced fourth and two. Woodruff gambled, running Simpson wide for a first down at the 17. Simpson then hit the middle for three before the Gators suffered a five-yard penalty. The Bulldogs hunkered down to put Florida in a fourth-and-nine situation.

Woodruff played Russian roulette one more time. His decision wounded Georgia, as Lance struggled through for a first down at the 6 to end the third period.

Woodruff replaced most of his offensive unit with fresh players to start the fourth quarter. The gritty Georgians flattened May, again in the game at quarterback, for no gain on first down. But Roundtree took a second-down handoff and skirted end for the score. Allen's extra point tied it at 13–13 and noisy Florida fans knew their fortunes had shifted.

At this critical point in the game, Georgia abandoned its running game and went to the pass. The ploy quickly backfired.

Harper set up in the pocket and let fly toward end Red Roberts, but a Florida defender deflected the ball and Gator quarterback Allen, playing defensive back, intercepted at the UF 48 and began sprinting down the sideline.

Allen later told reporters he doubted his chances of scoring because he "saw so many red jerseys in the way." A Bulldog hit him at the 10,

Gator Dick Allen boots the extra point that tied Georgia 13–13 in the fourth quarter of the 1955 game. Minutes later, he returned a pass interception for a 52-yard touchdown to cap one of the greatest UF comebacks in series history. [UF Archives]

but Allen kept his feet and stumbled across the goal line where he and his teammates celebrated the 52-yard scoring run. The touchdown stood despite protests from the Georgia sidelines that Allen had stepped out of bounds.

Allen's attempt at the extra point was blocked by none other than Wilkins, and Florida led 19–13 with 2:55 gone in the fourth.

Georgia was stunned but hardly ready to roll over yet. Halfback Connie Manisera quieted the Florida sections when he tore free on a 17-yard run. A series of rushes by Dukes and Garrard got the Dogs to the UF 24 before the Gators defense halted matters.

Florida took over and went for the throat. Long runs by Lance, Roundtree and fullback Bill Bolton powered the Gators down to the UGA 12, but a Chandler field goal try was wide right.

With 2:25 left in the game, Georgia got the ball at its 20 for one final drive. Butts sent in Dick Young, the passing specialist. The Gators brought down the curtain when Lance picked off a Young pass at the UGA 47 and was run out of bounds at the 31. The Gators ran out the clock to win their third from the Bulldogs in four years.

Florida's 19-point rally from two touchdowns down was the greatest comeback in the rivalry's history to that time. Woodruff later said his team's play in the second half was the result of defensive adjustments made to stop the Georgia ground assault.

"Roun(d)tree's run set the Florida team afire and they took it from there," Wally Butts told the *Atlanta Journal-Constitution* after the contest. He added that his boys had played their best game of the year.

Georgia's Tarleton was the game's top rusher with 61 yards. Yet it was Florida's Roundtree, Allen and Simpson who made Sunday's headlines. Florida defenders Steve DeLaTorre and Ray Brown were standouts, while Don Shea and Len Spadafino led the Bulldogs.

Woodruff downplayed his halftime speech as a factor in Florida's second-half rally. "Listen, if I knew anything that would do that, I'd tell them on Wednesday," he quipped to reporters.

Georgia ended the campaign with a 16–13 loss to Auburn and a 21–3 defeat at Georgia Tech for a 4–6 record.

Florida also finished the year 4–6, losing 21–6 at Vanderbilt and 7–6 at Miami. Gator Steve DeLaTorre garnered first-team All-SEC honors to close his college career. Florida's Don Chandler went on to an All-Pro career as a punter and placekicker for the New York Giants and Green Bay Packers. And Woodruff evened his record against Georgia at 3–3.

Scoring:

Florida	0	0	6	13	—	19
Georgia	7	6	0	0	—	13

UGA	TD	Tarleton, 1-yard run (Cooper kick)
UGA	TD	Garrard, 5-yard run (PAT failed)
UF	TD	Roundtree, 85-yard kickoff return (PAT failed)
UF	TD	Roundtree, 6-yard run (Allen kick)
UF	TD	Allen, 52-yard interception return (PAT failed)

Florida: Burford, Lockhart, Ayers, *left end;* Hamilton, Hill, *left tackle;* Vosloh, Martin, Boney, *left guard;* DeLaTorre, Purcell, Wahlberg, *center;* Barrow, Green, *right guard;* Mitchell, Hicks, Wesley, *right tackle;* Brown, Yeats, Easton, *right end;* Lance, Allen, May, *quarterback;* Simpson, Chandler, McIver, *left halfback;* Burgess, Roundtree, Symank, *right halfback;* Visser, Sears, Bolton, *fullback*

Georgia: Wilkins, Mulherin, *left end;* Griffin, Meatheringham, *left tackle;* Spadafino, Cushenberry, *left guard;* Brown, Saye, *center;* Roberts, Cooper, *right end;* Luck, Mosteller, *right tackle;* Shea, Dye, *right guard;* Dukes, Harris, *right halfback;* Harper, Young, Comfort, *quarterback;* Tarleton, Davis, Manisera, *left halfback;* Garrard, Culpepper, *fullback*

	Florida	Georgia
First downs	14	18
Rushing yards	207	289
Passing yards	26	16
Pass att/comp/int	6/3/0	6/2/2
Punts/avg. yards	4/31	4/43
Fumbles lost	1	0
Penalty yards	50	36

— 1956 —

Florida 28, Georgia 0

"I LIKE IKE" BUTTONS WERE MUCH IN FASH-
ion at the November 10, 1956, Florida-Georgia game as the nation
reflected on President Dwight Eisenhower's landslide re-election over
Adlai Stevenson four days earlier.

The powerful 5–1–1 Gators of seventh-year coach Bob Woodruff
were 13th-ranked in the Associated Press poll and two-touchdown
favorites to whomp the Bulldogs for the second year in a row.

Florida guard and team captain John Barrow, considered one of the
best linemen in the country, was the kingpin of the UF line along
with center Bill Bolton.

Georgia coach Wally Butts was more worried about the Gators'
explosive backfield and its "home run" potential to score from any
part of the field at any time. Halfbacks Jim Roundtree and Jackie
Simpson had bedeviled the Bulldogs in the 1955 Florida victory and
were back, along with battering fullback Joe Brodsky who paced the
Gators to victory in the '53 contest. Butts also knew that the passing
and slick ball-handling of quarterback Jimmy Dunn and the kicking
of specialist Harry Spears could add to Georgia's problems.

The 3–3–1 Bulldogs were sophomore-laden and had been inconsistent. Halfbacks George Whitton, Gene Littleton, and Carl Manning, and quarterback Billy Hearn would have to have big days if
Georgia was to have a chance of whipping Florida. Receiver Jimmy
Orr was hurt and would not play.

Georgia was in the midst of a forgettable season. The Bulldogs lost
14–0 at Vanderbilt; beat Florida State, 3–0; fell 19–7 to Mississippi
State and 26–12 to North Carolina; tied Miami, 7–7; dropped a 14–7
decision to Kentucky; and nipped Alabama, 16–13, in Birmingham.

Florida was in the race for the conference crown. The Gators
opened 1956 with a 26–0 win at Mississippi State, tied Clemson
20–20, and lost 17–8 at home to Kentucky before catching fire.

Halfback Bernie Parrish tears through the UGA line for Florida's first touchdown in 1956. The 13th-ranked Gators prevailed 28–0. [UF Archives]

Florida then clipped Rice, 7–0; beat Vanderbilt, 21–7; won 21–6 at LSU; and downed Auburn, 20–0, at homecoming to meet Georgia with a four-game win streak.

The Gator Bowl was overflowing as usual by the time of the 2:30 p.m. kickoff.

The Gators snapped the defensive skirmish of the initial possessions on their second series as fullback Brodsky, halfback Roundtree and quarterback Dunn combined runs for a first down.

Woodruff then sent in a group of fresh players including a new backfield. Quarterback Harry Spears connected with fullback Ed Sears for 15. Halfbacks John Symank and Bernie Parrish earned a first down on two rushes, and Sears went off tackle for 14 to the UGA 17. Sears got nine more and Spears kept for five to the 3-yard line. The Bulldogs couldn't stop Parrish from diving across for the score. Spears added the conversion for a 7–0 Gators lead.

Georgia ran to a first down but had to punt as the quarter ended. Defense ruled for most of the second period as the teams duked it out around midfield with little result.

At one point in the action, a Bulldog fan in the bleachers yelled a derogatory comment about Butts. From the sideline nearby, Nancy Butts, the Georgia coach's daughter and a UGA cheerleader, called back, " 'He's all right 'cause he's my little fat daddy,' " the *Florida Times-Union* reported.

Florida got the second-half kickoff and presented the Georgians with a great chance to score before the school bands had settled back in their seats. On the third play from scrimmage, "Joltin' Joe" Brodsky was jolted and the ball squirted free. Georgia's Billy Hearn fell on the loose pigskin at the UF 27. The Gators, unfazed by the turnover, proceeded to stuff the Bulldogs.

The Gators crawled back into the quicksand minutes later when Simpson fumbled, and Georgia guard Tony Cushenberry recovered inside the UF 25. After a line plunge and two pass incompletions, Hearn's third heave connected—with Florida's Brodsky at the goal line. Brodsky bulled upfield through the scattered Georgians "like a runaway freight car downhill," a reporter noted. On a dazzling broken-field run, he made it to the UGA 36 before being corralled by Carl Manning.

On the Gators' first play from scrimmage, Roundtree sliced off tackle, cut back against the flow of defenders, and galloped 36 yards for the touchdown. Spears' extra point lengthened the Florida lead to 14–0 with 9:28 left in the third.

Woodruff continued shuttling fresh platoons onto the field.

Early in the fourth quarter, Bulldog halfback George Whitton fielded a punt but fumbled when tackled. The Gators' Simpson

Bulldog George Whitton is hemmed in after a short gain in 13th-ranked Florida's 28–0 blasting of UGA in 1956. The Gators won eight of nine from Georgia from 1955 to 1963. [Hargrett Collection, UGA Libraries]

Guard John Barrow was a mainstay of the Florida line in UF's 28–0 rout of Georgia in 1956. A consensus All-American and SEC lineman of the year, he later starred in the Canadian Football League. [UF Archives]

atoned for his earlier bobble by scooping up the ball at the UGA 25. Moments later Dunn threw a running pass to Roundtree, who wrestled away from several 'Dogs and raced in for a 25-yard touchdown. Spears kicked Florida's 21st point. Georgia fans sensed their party was over, while the Gators were just putting on their dancing shoes.

Georgia, in desperation, went to the air. Under heavy pressure, Hearn passed but Brodsky again intercepted, running it back 14 yards to the UGA 24. Four plays later, Simpson sped around right end for 13 yards and the Gators' fourth touchdown. Spears' boot made it final: 28–0 Florida.

The margin of victory was the greatest in the series for Florida since the Gators' 30–0 win in 1952. Woodruff now owned a 4–3 record against Georgia, while Butts was 11–6 versus Florida. The Gators' Roundtree had personally dismantled Georgia with two touchdowns each in 1955 and 1956. He and Brodsky, with two interceptions, were the Florida heroes of the '56 shutout, and the press corps voted Brodsky the game's most valuable player.

The Gators outrushed Georgia 225 to 88.

Although the Bulldogs had a 24–9–1 edge in the series, Florida had won five of the last eight.

Including the UF debacle, the 1956 Bulldogs did not score in their last three games, losing 20–0 to Auburn and 35–0 to a mighty Georgia Tech squad for a 3–6–1 mark.

Two season-ending losses—28–0 to Georgia Tech and 20–7 to Miami—kept Florida out of postseason play despite a 6–3–1 record. Gator guard John Barrow was a consensus All-American, an All-SEC honoree, and named conference lineman of the year. He later played for Hamilton in the Canadian Football League and was All-CFL. Barrow's son, Greg, lettered as a Gator tackle in 1980.

Scoring:

Florida	7	0	7	14 —	28
Georgia	0	0	0	0 —	0

UF	TD	Parrish, 3-yard run (Spears kick)
UF	TD	Roundtree, 36-yard run (Spears kick)
UF	TD	Roundtree, 25-yard pass from Dunn (Spears kick)
UF	TD	Simpson, 13-yard run (Spears kick)

Florida: Burford, Fleming, Ayers, *left end;* Wesley, Heckman, Schultz, Theodocion, *left tackle;* Vosloh, Boney, Windham, *left guard;* Bolton, Graves, Wahlberg, *center;* Barrow, Johnson, Johns, *right guard;* Midden, Mitchell, Davidson, *right tackle;* Pelham, Yeats, Easton, Jefferson, *right end;* Spears, Dunn, May, *quarterback;* Simpson, Symank, Booker, *left halfback;* Roundtree, Parrish, Newbern, *right halfback;* Brodsky, Sears, Roberts, *fullback*

Georgia: Wilkins, Monti, Bradley, *left end;* Gunnels, Luck, MacDonald, *left tackle;* Brown, Cushenberry, Lucas, *left guard;* Cook, Gilbert, *center;* Dye, Vinesett, Anderson, *right guard;* Monsteller, Meatheringham, Sedlock, *right tackle;* Roberts, Cooper, Watkins, Sealy, *right end;* Hearn, Nunley, Byars, *quarterback;* Whitton, Littleton, Bishop, *left halfback;* Manning, Davis, Bush, Dukes, *right halfback;* Culpepper, Lofton, Strumke, Sapp, *fullback*

	Florida	Georgia
First downs	14	6
Rushing yards	225	88
Passing yards	34	48
Pass att/comp/int	7/2/0	18/6/2
Punts/avg. yards	8/35	9/35
Fumbles lost	3	2
Penalty yards	43	20

— 1957 —

Florida 22, Georgia 0

Enlargement of the gator bowl made it possible for some 42,000 fans to attend the November 9, 1957, Florida-Georgia game as the Gators went for an unprecedented third consecutive triumph over the Bulldogs.

The big international news of the week was the Soviet Union's announcement that it had launched its second orbital satellite in little more than a month.

A hard north wind buffeted the record crowd on a cool and rain-threatening day.

Both teams were injury-riddled and virtually eliminated from the conference championship chase. Florida was 3–2 and favored to whip Georgia after overpowering Wake Forest, 27–0, in their opener, then beating Kentucky, 14–7, on the road. Florida lost 29–20 to Mississippi State; beat LSU, 22–14; and was coming off a 13–0 loss at third-ranked Auburn.

Georgia's starting halfbacks Jimmy Orr and Gene Littleton had been hurt against Alabama and were listed as doubtful for the game. Bulldogs end Gordon Kelley was out.

The Gators' ace halfback Jim Roundtree, who had scored a total of four touchdowns against Georgia in 1955 and 1956, was hampered by a sprained ankle. In a scrimmage on November 6, Roundtree's back-up, Billy Booker, broke an arm. Reserves, fullback Blair Culpepper and Joe Hergert, were also hurt.

Still, both teams had plenty of weapons. Florida's passing defense was ranked fourth nationally and the Gators brandished a balanced offense with quarterback Jimmy Dunn and runners Bernie Parrish, Ed Sears and Charlie Roberts in the backfield.

Georgia junior fullback Theron Sapp was the SEC's second-leading rusher and sophomore quarterback Charley Britt was a passer who Georgia coach Wally Butts described as a future All-American. Britt

203

was expected to give Florida's aerial defense its sternest test of the year.

Adding to the drama, was the unrest in Athens concerning Butts, who had been Georgia's head coach since 1939. The Bulldogs had not had a winning season since 1954 when they went 6–3–1. In addition to a losing record against Florida in the 1950s, Georgia had lost eight in a row to archrival Georgia Tech. Butts' head was in the UGA guillotine.

The Bulldogs began the season with a 26–7 loss to Texas, a 9–6 defeat to Vanderbilt, and a 26–0 pasting at Michigan, before a 13–6 win at Tulane. Georgia then lost 27–14 to Navy; beat Kentucky, 33–14, in Lexington; and fell 14–13 to Alabama.

Neither team could move on its opening possession, but the Gators got good field position at the UGA 47 after Orr's second punt of the afternoon. Runs by Roundtree, Dunn and Parrish netted nine yards. On fourth down, fullback Sears went over the middle for a first down at the 37.

With the Florida linemen tearing holes in the Bulldogs defense, Roundtree, Parrish and Dunn continued to ram the ball to the 9. Dunn's first pass of the day was snagged by end Don Fleming in the end zone for six. Parrish tacked on the conversion and Florida had a 7–0 lead with 2:47 left in the first quarter.

In the second period, a 45-yard kick by Dunn rolled dead at the UGA 2. The Bulldogs failed to get a first down and had to punt from their own end zone. But center David Lloyd's snap was high and the ball flew over punter Ken Cooper's head. The ball bounded out of the end zone for a Florida safety and a 9–0 Florida advantage with 8:58 to play in the half.

The safety apparently rattled the Bulldogs, especially Lloyd who twice toed the ball out of bounds on Georgia's ensuing free kick. The resulting penalties gave Florida a first down at the UGA 30.

The Gators reached the UGA 13 but blew the scoring chance when Bill Newbern lost the ball.

The Bulldogs' good fortune, though, quickly turned. Second-string quarterback Tommy Lewis dropped the ball on a handoff, and Florida's Asa Cox fell on it at the UGA 13. Again the Gators couldn't add to their lead, this time hurt by a holding penalty.

Georgia's Christmas spirit continued. On a second down play, Charley Britt fumbled and Gator tackle Ray Midden recovered at the UGA 18. Florida quarterback Mickey Ellenburg then lofted a pass to Parrish, who dragged UGA's Carl Manning with him into the end zone. Parrish's point after put Florida up 16–0 at the half.

Fullback Theron Sapp was a UGA team captain and had his jersey retired, but he couldn't lead the Bulldogs to a victory over Florida from 1956 to 1958.

Georgia's offensive apogee came in the third quarter after Florida's first possession ended with a punt. Running backs Littleton, Don Soberdash and Sapp crashed up the middle before quarterback Lewis connected with end Aaron Box for 26 yards to the UF 44. A 15-yard jaunt by Sapp rolled the Georgians to the 25. With the Bulldogs threatening, Florida stiffened and Lewis, replacing the injured Britt, was wild on a fourth-down pass.

Early in the fourth quarter, Georgia was dealt another blow when team captain J. B. Davis fumbled, and Florida's Jim Yeats recovered at the UGA 31.

By now, Jim Rhyne, the fourth Gator quarterback of the afternoon, was in. With the game in hand, Woodruff freely went to his bench.

The Gator subs didn't let up on the demoralized 'Dogs. On the fifth play of the offensive, Newbern shot into the Bulldogs' secondary and got behind Lewis and J. B. Davis. Rhyne saw him and lofted the ball over the Georgia defenders for a 20-yard touchdown. The issue was put to rest at 22–0.

At least one UF regular was seen eating a hot dog on the bench as Florida third- and fourth-stringers got a share of the action.

Florida's scoring was diversified, as three quarterbacks threw to three different receivers for touchdowns.

Two Bulldogs look on helplessly as UF's Don Fleming brings in a touchdown pass from Jimmy Dunn for Florida's first score in 1957. The Gators won 22–0. [UF Archives]

Despite his injuries, Roundtree had another sterling day against Georgia, running for 73 yards on 10 carries, and was voted outstanding player of the game by the press corps. In addition to his fine running, his tough blocking drew praise from the opposition and the press alike.

"I've always thought he was one of the most dangerous runners in the conference," Butts said of the Gator runner in a post-game interview. "A great back can do a lot of things on his own, and Roundtree did just that."

The Gators also won the war in the trenches. Much of the credit went to senior guard Howell Boney, tackle and team captain Charlie Mitchell, and end Dan Pelham who bullied the Bulldogs up front. To the Gators' credit, Georgia never penetrated inside the UF 25.

The loss was even tougher for Georgia because they had failed to score against the Gators for the second year in a row, something done neither before nor since 1956–1957.

The loss to Florida intensified calls for Butts' job from many Georgia supporters, and a Bulldogs' 6–0 loss to Auburn the next week didn't help matters.

It's likely that Butts saved face and place on the cold afternoon of November 30, 1957, when Theron Sapp smashed in from the 1 to lift Georgia to a 7–0 win at Georgia Tech. Georgia ended the season at

3–7. Bulldog end Jimmy Orr went on to an All-Pro career with the Pittsburgh Steelers and Baltimore Colts.

Florida followed its victory over Georgia with a 14–7 win against Vanderbilt, a scoreless tie with Georgia Tech, and a 14–0 defeat of Miami for a 6–2–1 year.

Jim Roundtree was selected first-team All-SEC and has to be considered one of the all-time greats of the Florida-Georgia clashes, leading the Gators to three straight wins.

Scoring:

Florida	7	9	0	6	—	22
Georgia	0	0	0	0	—	0

UF	TD	Fleming, 9-yard pass from Dunn (Parrish kick)
UF	Safety	UGA punt snap by Lloyd went out of end zone
UF	TD	Parrish, 19-yard pass from Ellenburg (Parrish kick)
UF	TD	Newbern, 20-yard pass from Rhyne (PAT blocked)

Florida: Fleming, Edgington, McGriff, Pracek, Ayers, *left end;* Heckman, Brantley, Schultz, Hicks, *left tackle;* Boney, Cox, Giannamore, Windham, *left guard;* Wahlberg, Graves, Cansler, Hawkins, *center;* Johns, Miranda, Sheer, *right guard;* Mitchell, Midden, Davidson, Baetzman, *right tackle;* Pelham, Hudson, Yeats, *right end;* Dunn, Rhyne, Ellenburg, Williamson, *quarterback;* Roundtree, Lee, Fannin, Dilts, *left halfback;* Parrish, Newbern, Westbrook, Lucey, *right halfback;* Sears, Roberts, Smith, *fullback*

Georgia: Vickers, Kelley, Towns, *left end;* Meatheringham, Sedlock, *left tackle;* Lucas, Roland, *left guard;* Lloyd, Thompson, Francis, *center;* Vinesett, Anderson, Hutcheson, *right guard;* Dye, Hansen, Leebern, *right tackle;* Cooper, Box, Sealy, *right end;* Britt, Lewis, *quarterback;* Guisler, Littleton, Manning, Davis, *left halfback;* Soberdash, Orr, *right halfback;* Lofton, Sapp, *fullback*

	Florida	Georgia
First downs	18	7
Rushing yards	221	68
Passing yards	63	70
Pass att/comp/int	11/6/0	14/6/1
Punts/avg. yards	5/30	6/37
Fumbles lost	2	3
Penalty yards	51	30

— 1958 —

Florida 7, Georgia 6

WITH FLORIDA A TOUCHDOWN FAVORITE TO beat Georgia for the fourth consecutive year in 1958, the Bulldogs were hoping to catch the Gators looking past them to their first-ever meeting with in-state enemy Florida State.

The Gators were at the apex of their splendor in the Florida-Georgia series as the November 8 game in Jacksonville approached.

Ninth-year coach Bob Woodruff had never had a spectacular season in Gainesville (the closest being an 8–3 mark in 1952), but his teams had consistently beaten Georgia and had shut out the hated Bulldogs the two previous years. *Savannah Morning News* sports editor Tom Coffey wrote, "If ever there was a reason for a team to get itself "up" the Bulldogs certainly have one here."

Florida's year began with a 34–14 drubbing of Tulane, a 14–7 loss at Mississippi State, a 21–14 win over UCLA in Los Angeles, a 6–6 tie with Vanderbilt, a 10–7 loss at LSU, and a 6–5 defeat to powerful Auburn. No one knew how the Gators would react to the bruising loss to Auburn, but many felt Florida outplayed the Plainsmen and earned a moral boost despite the defeat.

The 1958 team of 20-year UGA coach Wally Butts had done little to dispel the ill humor in Athens. Georgia had not come close to a winning season since 1954.

The Bulldogs lost 13–8 at Texas in the season opener, then fell 21–14 at Vanderbilt and 24–14 to South Carolina. Georgia won its first game, 28–13, over Florida State; beat Kentucky 28–0; and lost 12–0 at Alabama a week before the Florida game.

A bright spot for Georgia had been the play of a minister's son from Athens, sophomore quarterback Francis Tarkenton. Playing in his first varsity game, Tarkenton engineered the lone Georgia touchdown in the Texas loss after replacing starter Charley Britt. Butts was under increasing pressure from the fans to give Tarkenton more playing time.

The Bulldogs peaked in performance against Kentucky but had not played well at Alabama, leading many Georgia fans to believe that the off-and-on Bulldogs might have an "on" week against Florida.

For the first time, the Dye brothers, Pat and Nat, would start side by side in the Georgia line. Nat, at left tackle, was a senior; Pat a sophomore at left guard. Pat would go on to be a two-time All-American at Georgia and forge a football dynasty as head coach at Auburn.

Florida looked to the passing and ball-handling deftness of senior quarterback Jimmy Dunn and his favorite target, star receiver and team captain Don Fleming. Tackle Vel Heckman was the stalwart of the Florida line and destined for postseason honors.

The Gators were obviously gearing up for their first meeting with Florida State in what was expected to be a Sunshine State shootout two weeks after the Georgia game. Butts' scouts noted that during the Florida-Auburn clash, many UF fans held up cards stating "Beat FSU" even though the Gators at the time were embroiled in a scoreless game.

Heavy rains during the week meant the rivals would slug it out on a muddy field before a near-capacity Gator Bowl crowd of around 40,000. Gusty winds would toy with the kicking game.

From the outset, the Bulldogs played fierce defense and kept the Gators from getting in sync offensively.

Georgia mounted the first serious threat, driving to the UF 6. But Bulldog halfback Fred Brown was tackled by Dunn and Bob Milby a yard short of a first down, and Florida took over.

With the Gators still unable to move, Georgia took off on another thrust and reached the UF 10. But a pass from Charley Britt fell incomplete and Florida counted its blessings.

Yet a third time the Bulldogs charged downfield, nosing to the UF 12. This march was stalled by a 15-yard penalty for holding and UGA came up with nothing.

Georgia's defense manhandled the Gators again and backed the Floridians even deeper into the shadow of their goal, reaching the UF 4. But again the Gators reared up, as Fleming stuffed quarterback Tommy Lewis at the line of scrimmage on fourth down.

Georgia was far from finished. The Bulldogs surged into Gatorland again. The threat died, however, when Britt's pass to receiver George Guisler fell incomplete in the end zone. How long could the Gators hold on?

With Florida backed up inside its 15 on a fourth down in the second quarter, it appeared Georgia would again get good field position. But Gator kicker Bobby Joe Green boomed a colossal spiral that hung in the wind and rolled dead at the UGA 6. The punt, amazingly, covered 82 yards, the longest in the rivalry's history.

Frustrated Georgia was not content to sit on the ball until halftime, particularly in a scoreless game. Relying mainly on the run, the Bulldogs hammered to the UF 34, where Carl Manning's wind-blasted field-goal attempt soared wide left of the goal post.

The whistle sounded ending the first half and the disgruntled Bulldogs headed for the locker room. Six times Georgia had driven into scoring range, including four offensives that went inside the UF 15, but had nothing to show for it.

Yet, what more could be asked of the Bulldogs' defense? They had kept Florida outside the UGA 40 and held the Gators without a first down for the entire half. Georgia had completely outplayed the Gators and held a lopsided edge in all statistics other than the score. Florida's defense had been battered but had not come unglued.

Continuing its dominance over the Florida offense, Georgia forced a punt by UF's Green with five minutes remaining in the third period. Britt caught the ball, twisting 24 yards to the Gators' 17.

Tarkenton came in at quarterback to a chorus of cheers from Georgia fans. Bulldog fullback "Thundering Theron" Sapp was thrown for a two-yard loss by Gator star Heckman. Brown then rambled five yards to the UF 14 before Tarkenton completed a five-yard throw to end Aaron Box. On the next play, Tarkenton dropped back and hit Brown in the end zone for the score with 3:22 left in the third.

On Carl Manning's extra point attempt, Gator halfback Russell Dilts rushed across to block the kick. The play would be one of the biggest of the day, but the Bulldogs and their fans were enjoying their hard-earned 6–0 lead at the time.

Florida took the kickoff and managed to make its initial first down of the contest with about two minutes left in the third quarter. The offensive quickly flickered out under the intense Georgia defense.

The Gators held Georgia on their next possession, and the Bulldogs' heralded punter, Bobby Walden, came on to kick with less then two minutes gone in the fourth quarter. The scoreboard clock had stopped working earlier and officials were keeping the time on the field to the confusion of the coaches, players and fans.

Walden skyed a 51-yard punt and Florida had the ball at its own 24.

A 75-yard fourth-quarter touch-down run by senior UF quarterback Jimmy Dunn helped Florida edge UGA 7–6 in 1958, the Gators' fourth straight over Georgia. [UF Archives]

It was here that Jimmy Dunn, the 139-pound Gator quarterback, put his name in the Sunday sports section.

On first down, Dunn rolled to his left, got a skull-crunching block from a lineman, and sliced upfield. In seconds he was in the clear and streaking away from lunging Bulldogs who had contained him all day. Outrunning the Georgia secondary, Dunn ticked off the yards and raced into the UGA end zone. The 76-yard scamper was accented by a roaring storm from UF rooters.

Still winded after the marathon run, Dunn was the holder on the all-important conversion that would put Florida ahead. Kicker Billy Booker split the uprights and the Gators were up 7–6 with 13:20 left in the final quarter.

Georgia came back, ramming across the 50, but Dunn intercepted a pass at the UF 24 and took it back to midfield.

At one point in the crucial last minutes, Butts removed Tarkenton and replaced him with Britt, a move that prompted a cascade of boos from the Georgia student section.

Tarkenton was the field general on Georgia's last-ditch drive that started at the UGA 6. The evasive quarterback hit end Norman King on a spectacular 46-yard pass and kept the 11-play march alive with a 16-yard completion to end Bill Herron. With only seconds left, Georgia had the ball on the UF 15.

Florida halfback Russell Dilts blocks the extra point of UGA's Carl Manning in 1958. The play proved crucial as UF won 7–6. [UF Archives]

With confusion on the UGA sideline and in the huddle because of the scoreboard clock problem, the Bulldogs were unsure how much time was left. In field-goal range, Tarkenton surprisingly went to the air again, a fatal mistake for Georgia.

Gator halfback Jack Westbrook darted in front of the receiver at the goal line and hauled in the interception. Florida ran one play and the game was over.

Butts later explained that on the play on which Tarkenton was intercepted, Georgia kicker Carl Manning was in the game and could have tried to kick a winning field goal. "We just didn't know what time it was," Butts told the *Atlanta Constitution,* and Georgia had no time outs left.

The outcome had to be one of the most bitter losses ever for Georgia due, particularly, to the botched first-half scoring opportunities. A rock-ribbed Bulldog defense had only one chink in it. And Jimmy Dunn found it for Florida.

Georgia rolled up 360 yards in total offense to the Gators' 136 and 18 first downs to UF's three. Dunn's jaunt to fame was the only time Florida penetrated inside the UGA 44.

Sportswriters voted Dunn the game's most valuable player, and Gator backers declared he had played his most ferocious defensive game of the year.

Woodruff now owned a 6–3 record against Georgia, becoming the first Florida coach to win four in a row over the Bulldogs.

Team captain Theron Sapp was the Georgia standout, gaining 65 yards in 115 carries and playing like a "demon on defense" the *Morning News* said.

Georgia lost the following week, 21–6, to Auburn; massacred The Citadel, 76–0; and ended with a 16–3 win over Georgia Tech, for a 4–6 record.

Fortune smiled on Florida in the coming weeks. The Gators pounded Arkansas State, 51–7, and downed Florida State, 21–7, in their historic first meeting. Florida then clipped Miami, 12–9, to garner a Gator Bowl bid, the school's second bowl invitation. In a grueling defensive struggle, the Gators lost a 7–3 decision to Ole Miss to finish 1958 at 6–4–1.

Gator tackle Vel Heckman was first-team All-America and made the All-SEC first-team along with Georgia's Sapp. Florida's Fleming, also a first-team All-SEC honoree, played three years for the Cleveland Browns, while Sapp was drafted by the Philadelphia Eagles.

Scoring:

Florida	0	0	0	7	—	7
Georgia	0	0	6	0	—	6

UGA TD Brown, 9-yard pass from Tarkenton (PAT blocked)
UF TD Dunn, 76-yard run (Booker kick)

Florida: Fleming, *left end;* Schultz, *left tackle;* Cox, *left guard;* Hergert, *center;* Johns, *right guard;* Heckman, *right tackle;* Hudson, *right end;* Dunn, *quarterback;* Partin, Westbrook, *left halfback;* Deal, Dilts, *right halfback;* Milby, *fullback;* Booker, *placekicker;* Green, *punter*

Georgia: Vickers, Herron, *left guard;* N. Dye, *left tackle;* P. Dye, *left guard;* Lloyd, *center;* Anderson, *right guard;* Hansen, *right tackle;* Kelley, King, Box, *right end;* Tarkenton, Britt, Lewis, *quarterback;* Guisler, F. Brown, *left halfback;* Soberdash, *right halfback;* Sapp, *fullback;* Manning, *placekicker;* Walden, *punter*

	Florida	Georgia
First downs	3	18
Rushing yards	117	221
Passing yards	19	129
Pass att/comp/int	5/2/0	20/9/2
Punts/avg. yards	10/45	6/46
Fumbles lost	2	0
Penalty yards	43	105

— 1959 —

Georgia 21, Florida 10

EIGHT WEEKS INTO ITS 1959 SEASON, GEOR-
gia was the "surprise" team of the SEC with a 6–1 record and aching
to break a four-game losing streak to Florida. Picked to finish ninth
in the conference, the Bulldogs of coach Wally Butts were 4–0 in the
league and sitting atop the conference standings heading toward the
November 7 brawl with the 3–3–1 Gators.

The Bulldogs were coming off a 42–0 butchery of Florida State
and were bolstered by the return of halfback and team captain Don
Soberdash, who had missed two games with a knee injury.

Georgia premiered with a 17–3 win over Alabama and beat Van-
derbilt, 21–6, before dropping a 30–14 decision at South Carolina.
The Georgians snapped back to pound Hardin Simmons, 35–6;
Mississippi State, 15–0; and Kentucky, 14–7, before Florida State.

Francis Tarkenton who, along with Charley Britt, handled the
Bulldogs' quarterbacking chores, was leading the SEC in passing and
was second in total offense. His primary target was right halfback
Bobby Towns, who was tops in the conference in pass receptions.
Butts had been able to rest most of his first- and second-stringers in
the Florida State blowout, and the Bulldogs were in almost peak
physical condition.

Britt was considered one of the best defensive backs in the South in
addition to his offensive skills. On the Georgia line, a junior guard
named Pat Dye was earning national recognition.

In Gainesville, there was little to cheer about. The Gator camp had
been wracked by injuries, poor play and rampant rumors that 10th-
year coach Bob Woodruff was to be fired.

Florida's year began with a 30–0 pounding of Tulane, a 14–13 win
over Mississippi State, and a 55–10 rout of Virginia. After Rice tied
the Gators, 13–13, Florida fell 13–6 at Vanderbilt, 9–0 at home to

Georgia Coach Wally Butts is shown with quarterback Fran Tarkenton and guard Pat Dye, both All-Americans who starred from 1958 to 1960. They were 1–2 against Florida. Tarkenton became an All-Pro in the NFL while Dye enjoyed success as head coach at Auburn.

defending national champion LSU, and 6–0 at Auburn.

The Gators, on a three-game losing streak, had been battered by the heavier Auburn team. Halfback Bob Milby was hospitalized with a leg injury and probably lost for the year.

A side attraction of the game was the expected duel between two of the nations' top punters: Florida's Bobby Joe Green, considered one of the speediest runners in the league, and Georgia's Bobby "The Toe from Cairo" Walden.

Cloudy skies and a cold, hard rain didn't diminish a throng close to 42,000 from gathering at the Gator Bowl for the rivalry's 37th renewal.

A personal foul penalty against UF on a fourth-down punt gave Georgia its first possession at the UF 48. The Bulldogs penetrated eight yards on three plays. On fourth down, Britt handed off to fullback Bill Godfrey who bulled three yards for a first down. Two runs by left halfback Walden gave Georgia another first down at the Gators' 21. Godfrey ran for two and halfback Towns added five more, circling left end to the 14.

On the next play, Walden took a pitchout from Britt. Giving the appearance of another running play, Walden suddenly pulled up and hurled the ball toward end Gordon Kelley, who was open in the end zone for the touchdown. Durward Pennington kicked the conversion and Georgia led 7–0 with 10 minutes left in the initial quarter.

Florida could not decipher the Bulldogs' defense and Georgia made the Gators pay again late in the first period.

Britt returned a Green quick kick from the UGA 36 to the UF 37. On third down, Britt spotted Towns breaking free near the goal line. The pass was on the money and Towns burst over for Georgia's second TD. Pennington's conversion lengthened the count to 14–0.

Gator runners were being punished by a fired up Georgia line with Dye, guard Billy "Headhunter" Roland, and center Billy Joe "Dude" Thompson causing most of the carnage. Florida quarterback Dick Allen, an Atlantan who headed south to play ball, faced a heated rush on almost every pass attempt. Yet the Gators fought back early in the second quarter.

The Floridians had possession on their 28 when Allen passed to the fleet Green, who snagged the ball and set sail downfield, outlegging most of the Bulldogs' secondary as the yards clicked off. The only man with a chance of catching him was Britt, who pulled Green down from behind at the UGA 2 after the Gator halfback had streaked 70 yards.

The panoramic play left much of the crowd hoarse and breathless as Florida settled in for a first-and-goal. The stage was set for one of the great goal-line stands of the rivalry.

Though Florida had the impetus, the Bulldogs' line of Dye, Roland, Thompson, end Jimmy Vickers, and tackles Don Leeburn and Larry Lancaster was immovable. Four times Gator backs tried to knife through. Each time they were stonewalled. Tom Coffey of the *Savannah Morning News* said one collision between a Florida runner and two Georgia defenders "reminded you of someone diving into a pool in which there is no water."

Georgia took possession on downs at its 2-yard line, but the grim Gators showed their mettle by forcing a Bulldogs' punt in three plays.

Bulldog end Gordon Kelly falls into the end zone with a touchdown pass from Bobby Walden for Georgia's first blood in 1959. Georgia won 21–10, to snap a four-game losing sreak to Florida. [Hargrett Collection, UGA Libraries]

Standing almost out of the end zone, kicker Walden bobbled the wet ball after the snap. Before he could find the handle, the pigskin skittered behind the goal post. Florida end Dave Hudson fell on it, but by then the ball was out of bounds. The Gators had a safety, cutting the Georgia margin to 14–2 with 11:32 still left in the first half.

Until well into the third quarter, the bad weather and both defenses ruled. It appeared Georgia would sleepwalk to its seventh victory of the season after the opening fireworks.

But Florida roused from its lair when Walden got off a wobbly punt from the UGA 42, and the Gators got possession at the UF 46. Florida then put together its best drive of the day. Quarterback Allen hit end Perry McGriff for 10 yards, then completed a 20-yard toss to Nick Arfaras. In seven plays, Florida was at the UGA 9.

Then occurred one of those monumental moments that deepens the intensity of any football rivalry. In a matter of seconds, the dagger was removed from the throat of one antagonist and buried in the heart of the other.

Allen dropped to pass, eyeing a receiver in the end zone. But Charley Britt, the 180-pounder from North Augusta, S.C., claimed the aerial at the goal line and blistered down the sideline with the interception. No Floridian could recover quickly enough to pursue, and Britt splashed 100 yards for the touchdown, raising his arms in triumph as he crossed the goal line. "It was a real-gone dash down the east sidelines and nary a Gator had a chance to get the speeding

Georgia quarterback Charley Britt nabbed a Florida pass at the UGA goal line and rambled 100 yards for a touchdown to seal the Bulldogs' 1959 victory.

one," the *Florida Times-Union* said. Britt's play stands as the longest interception return for a touchdown in Georgia history.

The sudden turnaround effectively pegged the Gators' hide to the wall with 8:24 remaining in the third. Pennington added his third conversion for a 21–2 Bulldogs advantage.

Tarkenton and Britt alternated at quarterback most of the day, but Britt was on the field when Florida fired its last salvo in the fourth period. Due to the cold and rain, many fans had exited the stadium after the start of the final quarter. In the last minutes, Britt tried to pass near midfield, but the Gators' Jack Westbrook intercepted at the UF 46 and streaked 54 yards for Florida's first and only touchdown. The Gators went for a two-point conversion and made it, as quarterback Allen skirted right end. Georgia's lead was cut to 21–10 but the touchdown was little more than window dressing, the game already decided. Florida's four-game winning string over the Bulldogs was broken.

Florida's Allen completed six of 13 passes for 120 yards, including the 70-yard gain by Green.

Tarkenton was five of 12 for 62 yards, while Britt's sole completion was the touchdown throw to Towns.

The win was the 25th for Georgia in the series. Florida had 11 wins and there had been one tie.

Florida found some solace in scalping Florida State, 18–8, a week after the Georgia loss and ended with a 23–14 beating of Miami in

Woodruff's last game as head coach. He was the first Florida coach to have a winning record against Georgia at 6–4. Woodruff went on to be athletic director at Tennessee from 1963 to 1985.

Gator Bobby Joe Green later achieved All-Pro honors as a Chicago Bears punter.

The Bulldogs' final chapter to a fairy-tale season ended with a 14–13 edging of Auburn and a 21–14 win over Georgia Tech to clinch Butts' fourth conference title and a berth in the Orange Bowl against Missouri. The Bulldogs beat the Tigers, 14–0, in their eighth bowl appearance to finish with a 10–1 record and a No. 5 national ranking.

Georgia's Dye was named All-America. Tarkenton, end Jimmy Vickers, and Florida end Dave Hudson were honored as first-team All-SEC selections. Britt was drafted by the Denver Broncos of the AFL and the NFL's Los Angeles Rams, while Georgia end Gordon Kelley and lineman Larry Lancaster were chosen by San Diego. End Bob Towns was a pick of the Houston Oilers.

Scoring:

Georgia	14	0	7	0	—	21
Florida	0	2	0	8	—	10

UGA	TD	Kelley, 14-yard pass from Walden (Pennington kick)
UGA	TD	Towns, 34-yard pass from Britt (Pennington kick)
UF	Safety	Walden fumbled punt snap out of end zone
UGA	TD	Britt, 100-yard interception return (Pennington kick)
UF	TD	Westbrook, 54-yard interception return (Allen run)

Georgia: Vickers, Herron, Pennington, *left end;* Kelley, Box, *right end;* Lancaster, *left tackle;* Lawrence, Leebern *right tackle;* P. Dye, *left guard;* Roland, *right guard;* Thompson, *center;* Britt, Tarkenton, *quarterback;* Brown, Walden, Paris, *left halfback;* Soberdash, Towns, *right halfback;* Godfrey, Galbreath, *fullback*

Florida: McGriff, Patchen, *left end;* Hudson, Edgington, Arfaras, *right end;* Brantley, Dean, Slack, *left tackle;* Royal, Seals, C. Collins, *right tackle;* Cox, Giannamore, Norris, *left guard;* Mills, Senterfitt, *right guard;* Hood, Wehking, *center;* Allen, Williamson, *quarterback;* Green, Butz, *left halfback;* Westbrook, Deal, Partin, *right halfback;* Goodman, *fullback*

	Georgia	Florida
First downs	12	7
Rushing yards	149	59
Passing yards	111	150
Pass att/comp/int	16/6/3	21/10/1
Punts/avg. yards	8/33	10/40
Fumbles lost	2	2
Penalty yards	32	68

— 1960 —

Florida 22, Georgia 14

THE WALLY BUTTS ERA WAS ENDING AT GEOR-
gia and the Ray Graves decade was beginning at Florida as the teams
readied for the November 5, 1960, fray.

Butts was preparing to retire as Bulldogs mentor after 22 years,
but would continue to serve as the UGA athletic director. Graves was
sculpting the first of his Gator teams in a career that would make him
the winningest Florida coach in history.

Yet an elusive passing quarterback and a granite guard, both at
Georgia, were getting most of the ink from the national press.

Francis Tarkenton was expected to be the first or second pick in the
pro football draft, and Bulldog All-America lineman Pat Dye was
also being eyed by NFL scouts.

Georgia, 5–2, was a three-point favorite to thrash Florida for the
second year in a row, though they hadn't accomplished that feat since
1950–51.

Graves, meanwhile, quietly had whipped his Gators into contention for the conference crown. "The circus-style of offense installed
at Gatorland—a maneuver unheard of in the 10 years B. G. (Before
Graves)—has satisfied Florida fans to the fullest of their appetite for
the spectacular," the *Florida Times-Union* said.

Florida, 5–2, cruised over George Washington, 30–6, in its opener;
dropped Florida State, 3–0; and surprised Georgia Tech, 18–17, before
falling to Rice, 10–0. The Gators rallied to down Vanderbilt, 12–0, and
upset LSU, 13–10, before losing to Auburn, 10–7, a week before
heading to Jacksonville.

For the defending SEC champion Bulldogs, 1960 began with a 21–6
loss at Alabama followed by an 18–7 win at Vanderbilt and a 38–6
victory over South Carolina, atoning, somewhat, for the lone loss the
previous year to the Gamecocks. Georgia then lost, 10–3, at Southern
Cal; beat Mississippi State, 20–7; Kentucky 17–13; and Tulsa, 45–7, to
get ready for Florida.

Florida back Don Goodman is buried in a heap of players but burrows for the Gators' first touchdown in the 1960 UF triumph, Ray Graves' first game against Georgia. [Johnston Collection, UF Archives]

The Gator Bowl had been further expanded to accommodate nearly 49,000, and the largest crowd to watch a game in the rivalry would be in the stands for the 2 p.m. kickoff.

An offensive feast seemed in the offing as neither team was particularly strong defensively, Florida ranking seventh in the SEC and Georgia ninth. Offensively, the Bulldogs were second and the Gators fourth.

The chief laborers of the Gators' ground forces were 138-pound quarterback Larry Libertore and power fullback Don Goodman. Libertore was second in the league in rushing, and Gator end Pat Patchen was regarded as a candidate for postseason honors. But Florida was thin in the backfield with losses due to injuries and a flu outbreak. Gator center and team captain Bill Hood was out and would cheer his team from the sideline.

In addition to Tarkenton's passing, Georgia featured a pack of running backs including Fred Brown, Bill McKenny and Billy Jackson.

The Gator Bowl crowd, in addition to the game, was buzzing about the upcoming November 8 presidential election in which Massachusetts Sen. John F. Kennedy was pitted against Vice President Richard Nixon. A reporter noted that fans wearing Kennedy buttons outnumbered those favoring the Nixon-Lodge ticket.

In the 1960 game, quarterback Bobby Dodd, Jr. (11) skirts end for a Florida score in the Gators' 22–14 victory over Georgia, Wally Butts's last game against Florida. [UF Archives]

With a possible bid to the New Year's Eve Gator Bowl hanging in the balance, Florida wasted little time in showing that it was clicking on all cylinders.

The Gators began the game's first drive at their own 23. Libertore ran for 12 on a keeper. As the Bulldogs had feared, Florida kept the ball on the ground, eating up the yards on a possession lasting more than seven minutes of the period.

The Gators pounded to the Georgia 1. Goodman had gained 54 yards in 10 carries during the series as the Floridians now lined up with the Georgia defenders set in their own end zone. Appropriately, Goodman got the handoff and lunged over for the score. Gator Bill Cash culminated the 77-yard, 13-play drive by kicking the conversion for a 7–0 Florida lead with 7:16 gone in the first quarter.

Luck slapped Georgia in the face on Florida's kickoff. Bulldog end Don Tomberlin misplayed the ball and Gator guard Larry Travis corralled the fumble at the UGA 28.

Libertore highlighted Florida's second sustained drive with an 18-yard pass to receiver Tommy Kelley. Goodman's continued stomping and Libertore's five straight carries shoved the ball to the 1, where the workhorse fullback rammed it in for his second touchdown of the quarter. Cash's kick extended Florida's lead to 14–0 with about two minutes left in the first period. The shell-shocked Bulldogs had yet to run a play from scrimmage. Indeed, Georgia had not touched the ball other than on Tomberlin's fumble.

A UGA cheerleader was so frustrated by one of Libertore's option runs that she screamed, "Break his leg off!" according to a newspaper account.

Georgia could not piece together a drive against the inspired Florida defense, as the second quarter unwound and both teams exchanged possessions.

From the UGA 47, Tarkenton hummed a 21-yarder to halfback McKenny of Jacksonville. Fullback Wayne Taylor, also a Floridian, powered to the 22 on two runs. The Gators slammed the door three plays later, however, when halfback Gene Page intercepted a Tarkenton pass at the Florida 12.

The ball changed hands several times, with Georgia turning the ball over on two fumbles and the Gators mishandling it once before leaving for intermission with the score still 14–0, Florida. An injury to Libertore on a punt return late in the second period was a concern to Florida.

Georgia received the second half kickoff but was stopped cold by Gator defenders, including guard Vic Miranda, who dropped Tarkenton for an 11-yard loss.

On Florida's first possession of the second half, reserve quarterback Bobby Dodd Jr., son of the famed Georgia Tech coach, came on to replace Libertore, sidelined with a pulled muscle.

Despite the quarterback change, the Gators didn't miss a beat, grinding away on their third time-consuming drive of the day. Dodd did most of the damage, rushing through and around the Bulldogs' defense in the 10-play series that put Florida at the UGA 1. On a quarterback keeper, Dodd eased over the goal line to the exultation of the Gators and their fans.

With Dodd as holder, Cash got set to kick the extra point to cap the 62-yard march. Dodd took the snap, but pulled in the ball and circled end for the two-point conversion. As the 22–0 Florida lead flashed on the scoreboard, the UF contingent was euphoric.

The Gators' day got even better when halfback Walt Hickenlooper picked off a Tarkenton pass at the UF 11 on the next series.

Late in the third quarter, the snoozing Bulldogs finally stirred, moving downfield from their 40. Tarkenton connected with McKenny for 12, Bobby Walden for 21, then found end Clyde Childers for 17 to the UF 7.

Wayne Taylor then ran twice to reach the 4. After an incompletion,

Georgia All-American quarterback Fran Tarkenton lets a pass fly under pressure by Florida's all-conference defenders Pat Patchen and Vic Miranda in UF's 22–14 victory. [UF Archives]

Georgia had a fourth down and no choice but to go for it. Tarkenton dropped back to pass, retreating all the way to the UF 30 as Gators descended on him from everywhere. With moves that would later notoriously brand him as "The Scrambler," Tarkenton, almost trapped, suddenly tucked in the ball and ran to daylight around end, hugging the sideline on a beeline to Georgia's first touchdown. On the conversion, halfback Walden passed to Fred Brown for two points, and the score was 22–8 with 11:30 left in the game.

Silent most of the afternoon, UGA's rooters came to life, their roar intensifying moments later when Florida's Don Deal fumbled and Georgia tackle Pete Case fell on the ball at the UGA 47. Led by Tarkenton, the Bulldogs battered to the UF 26 in seven plays. Billy Jackson then took a pitchout and lofted a pass to Walden, who made a one-handed catch in the end zone.

Nearly seven minutes remained and the Red and Black sections were in near delirium while Florida fans had gotten deathly quiet.

Trailing 22–14, Georgia naturally went for two. Jackson again tried to hit Walden, but this time the versatile halfback/kicker dropped the ball in the end zone. Florida, desperately needing to reverse momentum, then used up about four minutes, grinding to near midfield before the Bulldogs stopped them on downs.

Jackson did most of the passing now, taking pitchouts from Tarkenton who was unable to throw after suffering a hip injury in the Bulldogs' second scoring series. Still, Georgia rolled to the UF 39 and appeared to be moving toward a possible tying score. But the Gators' defense stiffened at the 31, preserving Ray Graves' first win over Georgia.

After the game, Wally Butts told reporters that Tarkenton had not been at full speed even before the hip injury. Georgia's star quarterback had an asthma attack on Friday night and did not sleep before the game, Butts said.

For Florida, however, nothing could dampen the glow of its fifth win in six games against Georgia. With 86 yards on 21 carries and two touchdowns, Florida's Goodman was named the game's most valuable player.

The contest marked the first time since 1940 that a Florida squad downed both Georgia and Georgia Tech in the same season. The Gators finished second in the conference to Mississippi, Florida's best showing to that time in the SEC.

Butts closed his coaching career with a 9–6 loss at Auburn and a 7–6 victory over Georgia Tech. In 21 meetings with Florida, Butts' teams went 12–9 but had lost seven of the last 10 against the Gators.

Tarkenton and Pat Dye were honored as first-team All-America and All-SEC selections. Tarkenton went on to an All-Pro career with the Minnesota Vikings and New York Giants and still holds several pro passing records, including most TD passes in a career. Both he and Dye were drafted by the AFL's Boston Patriots, but Dye would be better known as the longtime coach of Auburn.

The Gators didn't let up after besting Georgia. They beat Tulane, 21–6, and Miami, 18–0, to gain a berth against Baylor in the Gator Bowl. The Gators took a 13–0 halftime lead and weathered a torrid Bears rally in the last quarter for a 13–12 win in Florida's third bowl game. Graves finished his first season at 9–2 and would always be 1–0 over the legendary Wally Butts.

Florida guard Vic Miranda and end Pat Patchen also made the All-SEC first team.

And Kennedy beat Nixon by a narrow margin.

Scoring:

Florida   14   0   8   0   —   22
Georgia   0   0   0   14   —   14

UF	TD	Goodman, 1-yard run (Cash kick)
UF	TD	Goodman, 1-yard run (Cash kick)
UF	TD	Dodd, 1-yard run (Dodd run)
UGA	TD	Tarkenton, 4-yard run (Walden pass to Brown)
UGA	TD	Walden, 26-yard pass from Jackson (pass failed)

Florida: Patchen, Kelley, Cash, *left end;* Slack, Odom, Dean, *left tackle;* Norris, Collins, Senterfitt, *left guard;* Wehking, Culpepper, *center;* Miranda, Travis, Gill, *right guard;* Beaver, Seals, Stephens, *right tackle;* Holland, Arfaras, Gregory, *right end;* Libertore, Dodd, White, Ringgold, *quarterback;* Deal, Miller, Page, *left halfback;* Hoover, Mack, Hickenlooper, *right halfback;* Goodman, MacBeth, Ewell, Worthington, *fullback*

Georgia: Tomberlin, Clark, *left end;* Case, Vella, *left tackle;* Dye, Allen, Betsill, *left guard;* Ashe, Smith, *center;* Williamson, Davis, *right guard;* Lawrence, Green, *right tackle;* McEachern, Childers, *right end;* Tarkenton, Williams, Pennington, *quarterback;* Brown, Jackson, Paris, Blackburn, *left halfback;* McKenny, Walden, *right halfback;* Godfrey, Taylor, *fullback*

	Florida	Georgia
First downs	17	14
Rushing yards	250	67
Passing yards	53	179
Pass att/comp/int	4/3/0	33/16/3
Punts/avg. yards	5/35	3/49
Fumbles lost	2	2
Penalty yards	122	20

— 1961 —

Florida 21, Georgia 14

FLORIDA WAS A 10-POINT FAVORITE TO BEAT A young Georgia team under first-year coach Johnny Griffith in the November 11, 1961, matchup.

At a time when Chubby Checker's hit "The Twist" and the resulting dance craze were rocking the nation, neither Georgia nor Florida was tearing up the league.

After a fine 9–2 record and a bowl victory in 1960, second-year UF coach Ray Graves' Gators had fallen to middle ground. At 3–3–1, Florida had premiered with a 21–7 win over Clemson; was tied 3–3 by Florida State; beat Tulane, 14–3; lost to Rice, 19–10; and nipped Vanderbilt, 7–0.

Florida had not scored in its two games before Georgia, losing by 23 to LSU and 20 at Georgia Tech.

The Gators still had proven offensive potential. Quarterback Larry Libertore was one of the SEC's best, and bullish fullback Don Goodman had scored two touchdowns against the Bulldogs in 1960. A junior reserve quarterback named Tom Batten had shown some passing ability.

Georgia had a harvest of promising sophomores led by quarterback Larry Rakestraw. But Griffith, a halfback on UGA's undefeated team in 1946, was hard-pressed to produce a winner in Athens.

The 3–4 Bulldogs were pasted, 32–6, by Alabama and 21–0 by Vanderbilt before besting South Carolina, 17–14. Georgia then lost 3–0 at Florida State, clipped Mississippi State, 10–7, and Kentucky, 16–15, before a 32–7 thrashing at Miami. The Georgia camp was saddened by the death of Griffith's father on the Wednesday before the Florida game.

Saturday, a partly cloudy Indian summer day greeted a crowd of some 47,000 crammed into the Gator Bowl.

The teams spent the early going jousting for field position. A

227

Gator quarterback Tom Batten looks to hand off to Don Goodman (45) as Bruce Starling (37) blocks in Florida's 1961 win. [UF Archives]

strong Florida drive was killed by a penalty, and Georgia's Don Blackburn made a fair catch of a Gator punt at the UGA 10.

On the first play of the series, fullback Wayne Taylor dropped the ball and Gator linebacker Tommy Kelley pounced on it at the 'Dogs' 16.

Goodman rumbled for a first down to the Georgia 5. Desperately, the Bulldogs fought back. Halfback Lindy Infante was thrown for a five-yard loss by UGA linebacker Dale Williams. Quarterback Batten was tackled at the 12 by end John Landry, and a delay-of-game penalty knocked the Gators back to the 15. Facing fourth and goal, Graves decided to go for six. Batten rolled out as his receivers sped downfield. The 158-pound thrower lofted a pass toward Infante, who snared it in the corner of the end zone. Bill Cash converted the extra point and Florida led 7–0 with two seconds left in the first period.

Another Georgia turnover put Florida in business again midway through the second quarter. Playing before his hometown crowd, Georgia's Bill McKenny fumbled a punt at the Georgia 14 and Florida tackle Anton Peters recovered.

In a hole, the Bulldogs hurled the Gators back to the 29 with a fury. Cash tried a field goal from the 37, but it fell short and a second Florida threat was averted.

But it only postponed the inevitable. Florida soon had the ball again, this time near midfield.

On first down, Batten whipped a pass to Bob Hoover at the 20. Without breaking stride, the Gator halfback galloped down the sideline untouched into the end zone.

Cash's kick was wide but Florida led 13–0 with 1:45 left in the half. It was the Gators' turn to crow.

At intermission, Georgia tried to figure out a way to awaken its offense. The Bulldogs had not crossed midfield even once and had only 72 yards total offense.

Early in the third period, Georgia's Williams fell on a fumble by Florida's Goodman near the 50. The play jump-started the UGA offense.

On second down, Rakestraw dropped back and saw John Landry unguarded at the UF 20. The Bulldog end made the catch around the 13 and bolted in for the score. Durward Pennington's extra point cut the Florida advantage to 13–7 with plenty of time left in the third quarter.

After the kickoff, Georgia quickly got possession at their 20 after a UF punt bounded into the end zone for a touchback. The Bulldogs came out firing.

On the passing of Rakestraw and the running of fullback Bill Godfrey, Georgia moved down the field. In 12 plays, the Bulldogs were poised on the UF 17.

Runs of seven and nine yards by McKenny pushed Georgia three feet away from a tie. From the 1, Rakestraw dove in to culminate the 80-yard march. Pennington's extra point was good and Georgia had stormed back to lead 14–13 with 48 seconds gone in the final quarter.

The Gators were shaken but certainly not out of it, as Batten

Florida's 1961 coaching triumvirate (left to right): *Pepper Rodgers, Ray Graves, and Gene Ellenson. Ellenson was a UGA lineman in the early 1940s.* [UF Archives]

quickly proved. In eight plays, the UF signal-caller calmly guided the Gators downfield to the UGA 20, but the Bulldogs refused to budge and Florida attempted a field goal. Cash's kick missed the mark from the 27, and the Georgians were closer to the upset with each tick of the clock.

The Bulldogs couldn't generate a drive, however, and Florida got the ball again on its 37. Batten threw two incompletions before finding Sam Holland twice on passes of 10 and 30 yards. The Gator end made a one-handed grab for the big gainer. Haygood Clarke then fought for a yard to the UGA 16.

On the next play, Batten set up to throw to his left and arched a pass to halfback Ron Stoner racing toward the end zone, hitting him for the completion as the Ohioan darted in for the score. The Florida faithful went mad with just under five minutes remaining.

A five-yard penalty forced the Gators to go for the extra point from the 8-yard line. Batten retreated in the pocket and flipped a pass to end Russ Brown for the two-point conversion and a 21–14 Florida advantage.

It appeared that whoever had the ball last would win as Georgia took the kickoff with 4:54 left and headed downfield. With Rakestraw stoking the offense, the Bulldogs pounded 53 yards in eight plays to reach the UF 21 with under a minute left.

It was high drama, the outcome hinging on one last pass. Rakestraw dropped back, then gunned the ball toward a Bulldog in the end zone. But safety Paul White was there to save the day for Florida, grabbing the interception at the UF 11 with 28 seconds remaining. The Gators had captured another one from the adversarial Crackers.

Batten, the 5–11 quarterback from Miami, was honored as the game's most valuable player with his three touchdown tosses and 192 passing yards. In tribute to his play, the Gators presented the game ball to Batten's wife.

Georgia's Godfrey led all rushers with 61 yards on 15 carries while Libertore was Florida's top runner with 43 yards on 12 rushes.

Graves felt the key play of the afternoon was Holland's one-handed circus catch for 30 yards on a third-down pass from Batten on Florida's clinching touchdown drive.

Florida had been unable to stop Rakestraw's passing or the running of McKenny or Godfrey, three elements Graves' staff felt they had to control if the Gators were to win.

"The truth of the matter is, the Gators didn't have to be very smart Saturday for in Tom Batten they had a quarterback who performed

Gator Bob Hoover reaches to catch a 48-yard touchdown pass from Tom Batten over the outstretched arms of UGA's Billy Knowles in Florida's 21–14 victory over Georgia in 1961. [UF Archives]

magic every time he stepped back to throw, " the *Atlanta Constitution* said.

Oddly, cheering was heard coming from the Georgia dressing room after the contest. Griffith later explained that "I told the boys they had nothing to be ashamed of and a lot to be proud of. They knew I was right, so they cheered their approval. I cheered with them."

Griffith's Bulldogs closed the year with a 10–7 loss to Auburn and a 22–7 whipping by Georgia Tech for a 3–7 mark. Georgia's Bobby Walden, who was injured and did not play against Florida, was an All-Pro punter for many years for the Pittsburgh Steelers, including their 1974 Super Bowl championship team.

Florida's campaign ended with a 32–15 beating by Auburn and a 15–6 defeat at Miami for a 4–5–1 record, Ray Graves' only losing season in Gainesville.

Scoring:

Florida	7	6	0	8	—	21
Georgia	0	0	7	7	—	14

UF	TD	Infante, 15-yard pass from Batten (Cash kick)
UF	TD	Hoover, 48-yard pass from Batten (kick failed)
UGA	TD	Landry, 47-yard pass from Rakestraw (Pennington kick)
UGA	TD	Rakestraw, 1-yard run (Pennington kick)
UF	TD	Stoner, 16-yard pass from Batten (Batten pass to Brown)

Florida: Cash, R. Brown, Holland, Dean, Arfaras, Gregory, *end;* Peters, Odom, Beaver, *tackle;* Thompson, Travis, Collins, *guard;* Culpepper, Wehking, *center;* Batten, Libertore, Ringgold, *quarterback;* Hoover, Infante, Hickenlooper, Stoner, Clarke, White, *halfback;* Goodman, Kelley, *fullback;*

Georgia: Childers, Babb, *left end;* Landry, Tomberlin, McEachern, *right end;* Case, Vella, *left tackle;* Holmes, Green, *right tackle;* Cone, Williamson, Allen, *left guard;* Kelly, Vann, *right guard;* Hauss, P. Smith, *center;* Rakestraw, D. Williams, Saye, *quarterback;* Blackburn, Pennington, Woodward, *left halfback;* McKenny, *right halfback;* Taylor, Godfrey, *fullback*

	Florida	Georgia
First downs	10	14
Rushing yards	108	137
Passing yards	192	132
Pass att/comp/int	18/10/0	15/11/2
Punts/avg. yards	6/34	7/36
Penalty yards	40	44

── 1962 ──

Florida 23, Georgia 15

IN THE AUTUMN OF 1952 LARRY "LONG GONE" Dupree was beginning to forge his legend as one of Florida's finest-ever running backs.

Most observers forecast that Dupree and another sophomore, quarterback Tom Shannon, would lift the Gators to a win over Georgia in the November 10 bloodletting in Jacksonville.

The 4–3 Gators were euphoric after a 22–3 shocker over previously-unbeaten Auburn a week earlier. Indeed, UF coaches were worried about a letdown against Georgia even though Florida was favored by two touchdowns.

Excluding the 1904 game, this would be the 40th meeting in the rivalry, with Georgia holding a 25–13–1 edge in victories, although Florida had won eight of the last 10.

The Gators of third-year coach Ray Graves beat Mississippi State, 19–9, in their opener, but followed with a 17–0 loss to Georgia Tech and a 28–21 defeat to Duke. Florida trampled Texas A&M, 42–6; Vanderbilt, 42–7; and lost 23–0 to LSU a week before the Auburn upset. Playing fullback or halfback, Dupree, the 190-pounder from Macclenny, Fla., had established himself as one of the SEC's best runners. And Shannon, a southpaw, was connecting on almost 57 percent of his passes. Despite its three losses, Florida still had an outside chance at a Gator Bowl invitation.

To the north, it had been a gloomy autumn in Athens. The Bulldogs of second-year coach Johnny Griffith were 2–2–3 with two consecutive ties going into the Florida battle.

Georgia opened on the road with a 35–0 shellacking by Alabama but beat Vanderbilt, 10–0, in Nashville. The Bulldogs tied South Carolina, 7–7; dropped Clemson, 24–16; fell to Florida State, 18–0; and tied Kentucky, 7–7, and N.C. State, 10–10. Stellar Bulldog left tackle Ray Rissmiller had badly sprained an ankle in the N.C. State game and was listed as doubtful.

Georgia quarterback Larry Rakestraw, third in the league in passing, had the ability to riddle the Gators. The junior gunner was having a good year despite recurring problems with a serious ankle injury. And UGA fullback Leon Armbrester was the SEC's top runner with a 4.7-yard average per carry.

On the minds of many of the 45,000 fans settling into the Gator Bowl was the supposed end to the "Cuban Missile Crisis," in which the United States and the Soviet Union seemed to be on the verge of nuclear war in late October and early November. President John Kennedy had looked Soviet Premier Nikita Khrushchev dead in the eye and the Russian blinked first, so most Americans thought.

In the game's opening minutes, Georgia's pumped up defense forced a turnover when UF halfback Bob Hoover fumbled a pitchout, and UGA's Kenneth Vann recovered on the Gators' 23.

Armbrester banged for six yards on two carries, and Rakestraw threw to end Mickey Babb for 12 yards to the UF 3. On first down, left halfback Don Porterfield crashed through right tackle to pay dirt. Bill McCullough kicked the extra point and Georgia led 7–0.

A short time later, the Gators fumbled again and the Bulldogs' Carlton Guthrie recovered at the UF 42. On Rakestraw's arm, the Bulldogs marched to the UF 12 before being hemmed in by the Gator defense. McCullough's field-goal attempt into the wind, though, careened wide.

The Gators finally came to life midway through the second quarter when a stiff breeze pushed a Georgia punt out of bounds at the 50.

Quarterback Shannon rifled a completion to Jack Newcomer for nine yards. Minutes later, Dupree took a handoff and found daylight at left tackle. A key block by Tom Gregory put Dupree in the clear, and the Gators' star back raced 41 yards for the touchdown. Going for two on the conversion, Shannon hit Newcomer in the end zone to put Florida up 8–7.

Florida held the Bulldogs after the kickoff and Georgia had to kick. But the wind caught Jake Saye's punt and the 21-yarder gave Florida possession on the UGA 41. With junior fullback Jim O'Donnell running and Shannon passing, the Gators cracked down to the Georgia 11 in nine plays. There, the Florida line opened a gap at right tackle for Dupree, who rambled in for his second touchdown. Jimmy Hall kicked the extra point and Florida widened its lead to 15–7 shortly before halftime.

While Gator backs were finding holes in the Georgia line, the

Bulldogs had been unable to ignite their passing assault due to the wind. The Gators' "Big Blue Line" was destroying the Georgia running game, with Anton Peters leading the charge. Peters punched through to nail Bulldog runners for losses on several plays.

Florida received the second-half kickoff and set sail on its most sustained drive of the afternoon. O'Donnell ran three times for 19. Dupree picked up 23 more on four carries. Shannon ran for 11 on two rushes, then passed to end Sam Holland for 17 more to put Florida inside the UGA 5.

Gator halfback Hoover, avenging his earlier fumble that led to the Georgia score, barged over from two yards out and Florida lengthened its margin to 21–7. The Gators again went for two and Shannon slipped around end to make it 23–7.

Though the Georgians had yet to run a play in the second half, there was plenty of fight left in the Bulldogs, particularly Larry Rakestraw.

Starting at his own 27, Rakestraw put together a drive that breathed life back into the Georgia offense despite the wind. Finding alleys in the UF secondary, he completed five of nine passes to move the Bulldogs to the UF 7. On the 13th play of the drive, Rakestraw backpedaled and lofted a pass to end Barry Wilson in the end zone.

Trailing by 10 points, Georgia gambled on the two-point try. Again Rakestraw went back in the pocket. This time, Don Blackburn worked free in the end zone and Rakestraw hit him for the conversion. With four minutes left in the third quarter, Florida's lead had been pared to 23–15.

Any chances of a Georgia comeback, though, were stomped by the manhandling Florida defense, with Peters, linebacker Roger Pettee, guards Larry Travis and Bill Richbourg, and end Russ Brown leaving their helmet imprints on the Bulldogs.

Georgia spent the rest of the contest backed up near its goal line.

Florida had its ninth win in the last 11 years over the Bulldogs, including three straight for only the second time in the series' history. Dupree was selected the game's MVP, but many sportswriters made an argument for UF's Anton Peters.

The Florida defense had done a phenomenal job holding Georgia to 30 yards rushing, although Rakestraw burned the Gators for 137 yards through the air.

Powered by Dupree's 111 yards on 16 carries and O'Donnell's 80 yards, Florida rolled up 298 yards of total offense.

A week after the Florida loss, Georgia won its most impressive game of the year, stunning Auburn, 30–21, on the road. But Georgia Tech stung the Bulldogs with a 37–6 whipping to end Johnny Griffith's second year at 3–4–3.

Florida mashed Florida State, 20–7, and lost 17–15 at Miami, but still managed to garner a bid to play Penn State in the Gator Bowl. The Gators downed the heavily-favored Nittany Lions, 17–7, in Graves' second bowl victory in his first three seasons at Florida.

Gator guard Larry Travis and Dupree were honored as first-team All-SEC selections. Quarterback Larry Libertore went on to become a state legislator.

Scoring:

Florida	0	15	8	0	—	23
Georgia	7	0	8	0	—	15

UGA	TD	Porterfield, 3-yard run (McCullough kick)
UF	TD	Dupree, 41-yard run (Newcomer pass from Shannon)
UF	TD	Dupree, 11-yard run (Hall kick)
UF	TD	Hoover, 2-yard run (Shannon run)
UGA	TD	Wilson, 7-yard pass from Rakestraw (Blackburn pass from Rakestraw)

Florida: R. Brown, Cash, Gregory, *left end;* Odom, Pearson, *left tackle;* Travis, Thompson, *left guard;* Culpepper, Pettee, *center;* Richbourg, Entzminger, *right guard;* Peters, Dent, *right tackle;* Holland, Dean, *right end;* Shannon, J. Hall, Libertore, *quarterback;* Dupree, Trammell, Skelly, *left halfback;* Hoover, Newcomer, Infante, Starling, *right halfback;* O'Donnell, Kelley, *fullback*

Georgia: B. Wilson, Clark, McEachern, *left end;* Vann, Rissmiller, *left tackle;* Crook, Allen, *left guard;* Hauss, Boynton, *center;* Williamson, Kelly, *right guard;* Holmes, Maddox, *right tackle;* Babb, McCullough, *right end;* Rakestraw, Saye, Hunnicutt, *quarterback;* Porterfield, Lankewicz, Blackburn, Burson, *left halfback;* Knowles, Guthrie, Woodward, McFalls, *right halfback;* Barber, Armbrester, Dukes, Westmoreland, Faircloth, *fullback*

	Florida	Georgia
First downs	19	11
Rushing yards	239	30
Passing yards	59	137
Pass att/comp/int	15/7/1	26/11/2
Punts/avg. yards	6/41	8/36
Fumbles lost	3	0
Penalty yards	15	15

— 1963 —

Florida 21, Georgia 14

FLORIDA AND GEORGIA READIED FOR THEIR
1963 game amid ugly clouds of desegregation violence in the South,
escalated U.S. involvement in Vietnam, and the last days of President
John F. Kennedy, who was within two weeks of a fateful trip to
Dallas.

The November 9, 1963, game was rated a toss-up.

At 4–2–1, Georgia was off to its best start under third-year coach
Johnny Griffith, who had yet to produce a winning season or beat the
Gators. The year began with a 32–7 whipping by Alabama before the
Bulldogs pummeled Vanderbilt, 20–0, and South Carolina, 27–7.
Georgia tied Clemson, 7–7; beat Miami, 31–14, and Kentucky,
17–14, before losing 28–7 at North Carolina.

Florida, 3–3–1, had been a disappointment to the fans in Gainesville, who had grown accustomed to winning under fourth-year
coach Ray Graves. The Gators opened with a 9–0 loss at Georgia
Tech; tied Mississippi State, 9–9; outgunned Richmond, 35–28; won
10–6 at Alabama; beat Vanderbilt, 21–0; and lost 14–0 to LSU and
19–0 at Auburn. The fact that the Gators had not scored in their two
games before Georgia was a major concern in the UF camp.

Florida geared its offense to the running of All-SEC fullback Larry
Dupree who scored twice against Georgia in the 1962 contest. Ray
Graves predicted a high-scoring game, knowing his Gators would be
under intense pressure to contain the Georgia passing duo of quarterback Larry Rakestraw and end Pat Hodgson. Rakestraw was considered the best passing quarterback in the conference and Hodgson was
leading the league in receiving. Rakestraw also was an effective
runner but no other Bulldog had emerged as a solid rusher to balance
his passing.

Spicing the game this year were rumors that Ray Graves was
planning to leave Florida to become head coach at Tennessee, his

Amid a tumble of Bulldogs, Florida's Larry "Long Gone" Dupree (35) edges into the end zone for a first-quarter score in the 1963 UF win, their fourth in a row over UGA. [UF Archives]

alma mater. Graves was denying intentions to go to Knoxville.

Fans on both sides kept up the party tradition, and hundreds of UF backers ate "Bulldog stew" at the Jacksonville Coliseum a few hours before the game. Over 48,000 fans filed into the Gator Bowl for the annual struggle.

Two minutes and 11 seconds into the game the Gators' blitzkrieg struck. On the first play after a UF punt, Rakestraw drifted back from his own 37 and overthrew a short pass. Florida sophomore safety Bruce Bennett, stationed near the sideline, snared the interception and jetted down the sideline, side-stepping a desperation tackle by Rakestraw en route to a 43-yard touchdown. Jimmy Hall kicked the extra point to stake Florida to a quick 7–0 lead.

Graves pulled a surprise on the kickoff. Bob Lyle booted an onside kick and UF's Ken Russell fell on the ball for Florida at the UGA 45.

Mixing the run and pass, quarterback Tom Shannon kept the stunned Bulldogs off guard. The left-hander threw twice to end Russ Brown for gains of eight and seven yards, then connected with receiver Hagood Clarke for 15 more. With about seven minutes left in the first quarter, the Gators were perched on the UGA 4. Dupree iced the 11-play drive, smacking up the middle for the TD. The offensive would be the longest of the day for either team. Hall's conversion put Florida up 14–0.

Though the Bulldogs were feeling snakebit, Florida had been plagued by untimely turnovers all year and the Georgia game was no different. Gator back Jack Newcomer soon fumbled at the UF 21 and the Bulldogs' Leon Armbrester claimed the recovery.

In three plays, Georgia ground to the UF 10 in the face of a vicious eight-man Gator rush. Bulldog sophomore halfback Bob Taylor was knocked down just short of the goal line after slipping through for nine yards. Taylor then twisted outside right tackle for the score with less than two minutes left in what had been an explosive first quarter. Georgia's Bill "The Machine" McCullough tacked on the conversion to cut the UF lead to 14–7.

After a missed Florida field-goal try from 50 yards, Georgia took possession at its 20. Pushed back to its 10 by penalties, Rakestraw catastrophically dropped the pigskin and Florida's Jimmy Morgan fell on it at the UGA 5.

On first down, Dupree was met ferociously by several Georgia defenders. The ball squirted free and wobbled across the goal line, as every player on the field drew a bead on it. In the mad rush of bodies, Gator end Lynn Matthews came up with the bouncing ball for a Florida touchdown. Hall added the conversion and the Gators extended their lead to 21–7.

Florida's defense thwarted Georgia's efforts for the remainder of the half. Indeed, the Gators' strategy to keep Rakestraw in check was paying huge dividends. The Bulldog quarterback had thrown two interceptions, one resulting in a Florida touchdown, and did not have

As referees signal a score, Gator end Lynn Matthews falls on a fumble by a teammate for a second-quarter touchdown. Matthews was honored as an All-American in 1965. [UF Archives]

Johnny Griffith played on Georgia's undefeated 1946 team but was winless as UGA head coach against Ray Graves' Florida squads from 1961 to 1963.

a single completion in six attempts. The Bulldogs had only one first down in the half with a total offense of only 29 yards, all on the ground. Much of the Gators' defensive rampage centered on senior guard Jack Thompson of Savannah, who seemed to be in on almost every play.

Georgia's defense raised its level of play in the third period, a head-knocking 15 minutes with both teams exchanging possession without any major scoring chances.

But late in the period Florida's Dick Kirk fumbled a Georgia punt, and the Bulldogs' Taylor recovered at the Florida 24.

In seven plays, including a 14-yard pass to Pat Hodgson, Rakestraw gunned Georgia to the UF 5. Taking the next snap, the Georgia marksman hit end Mickey Babb on a scoring toss. McCullough's kick narrowed the Florida lead to 21–14 with plenty of time still left in the fourth quarter.

The Gator defenders refused to buckle, though; and the Bulldogs, in time, were down to one last chance.

With just over a minute remaining and Georgia mired on its side of the field, Rakestraw frantically went to the air. But Bruce Bennett again lay in wait like a gridiron Robin Hood to make the interception, his third of the game, near the UGA 26.

As somber Georgia fans headed for the parking lot, the UF crowd whooped it up, savoring four consecutive years of victory over the Bulldogs. Only once before (1955–58) in the storied rivalry had Florida equalled the current win streak.

In the second half, Georgia's defense had played heroically. Other than the final interception by Bennett, Florida reached UGA's side of the field only once, and that drive was stifled by a Bulldog interception.

Most of Georgia's thin offensive production was mute testimony to the savagery of the Florida defense. Rakestraw, Georgia's best runner, had a net loss of 19 yards on 12 rushes. Added to his nightmare were four interceptions.

Florida's Shannon hit nine of 19 passes for 107 yards but threw three interceptions. The Gators' Dupree had a solid, if unspectacular, afternoon, with 74 yards on 19 carries and a touchdown. Indeed, Florida committed seven turnovers, including four fumbles and the interceptions, but was saved by the early touchdowns and its staunch defense.

Graves praised guard Jack Thompson as having played the finest game of his collegiate career and was quick to add accolades for Bennett, his bandit in the secondary, who went on to become Florida's career interception leader.

Florida's defensive back Bruce Bennett, a Georgia native, pulls in one of his three interceptions during the 1963 UF win. [UF Archives]

Georgia's fortunes did not improve after Florida. The Bulldogs fell 14–0 to Auburn and 14–3 to Georgia Tech for a 4–5–1 record. Griffith finished his UGA career without a winning season and was 0–3 against Florida and Ray Graves.

Florida's upswing continued as the Gators beat Miami, 27–21, and Florida State, 7–0, to finish at 6–3–1.

Gator Larry Dupree was honored as a first-team All-SEC selection for the second year in a row. Georgia center Len Hauss was drafted by the Washington Redskins and became a three-time All-Pro.

Thirteen days after the Florida-Georgia madness, America was shattered by the assassination of President Kennedy on a cloudless afternoon in Dallas. In the suddenness of a sniper's action, football was forgotten amid the tears, frustration and anger of a grieving nation.

Scoring:

Florida	14	7	0	0	—	21
Georgia	7	0	0	7	—	14

UF	TD	Bennett, 43-yard interception return (Hall kick)
UF	TD	Dupree, 4-yard run (Hall kick)
UGA	TD	Taylor, 1-yard run (McCullough kick)
UF	TD	Matthews, recovered fumble in the end zone (Hall kick)
UGA	TD	Babb, 5-yard pass from Rakestraw (McCullough kick)

Florida: R. Brown, B. Brown, Thomas, Matthews, Casey, *ends;* Murphy, Whatley, Pearson, Gagner, Lyle, MacLean, *tackles;* Odom, Katz, Pursell, Thompson, Richbourg, *guards;* Morgan, Cliett, Bernhardt, *centers;* Shannon, Clarke, Harper, Dupree, Hall, Bennett, Russell, Seymour, Newcomer, Trammell, Kirk, Lager, Campbell, *backs*

Georgia: Wilson, Babb, Crawford, Nowicki, McCullough, Hodgson, *ends;* Rissmiller, Wilson, Boyd, Winsett, Crook, Maddox, *tackles;* J. Smith, Darden, Scott, Brantley, Evans, *guards;* Hauss, M. Smith, *centers;* Rakestraw, Barber, Knowles, Armbrester, Dickens, Guthrie, Swinford, Taylor, Porterfield, Woodward, McFalls, Hurst, Dukes, Faircloth, *backs*

	Florida	Georgia
First downs	11	9
Rushing yards	142	25
Passing yards	107	94
Pass att/comp/int	19/9/3	29/10/4
Punts/avg. yards	5/46	8/38
Fumbles lost	4	1
Penalty yards	65	22

— 1964 —

Georgia 14, Florida 7

GEORGIA FOOTBALL WAS IMMERSED IN A cauldron of controversy in the months before a young UGA coach named Vince Dooley faced Florida for the first time on November 7, 1964.

There was little sympathy in Gainesville where fifth-year Gators coach Ray Graves was undefeated versus Georgia and was aiming to head the first UF team in history to beat the Bulldogs for five straight years.

Dooley, a former quarterback at Auburn, had come to Athens amid a turmoil that saw coach Johnny Griffith and Athletic Director Wally Butts resign. Butts had been accused of giving information about UGA plays to Alabama coach Paul "Bear" Bryant before a game between the schools in 1962. A magazine printed the story and both Bryant and Butts sued the publication. Butts won a substantial award in the case while Bryant accepted an out-of-court settlement, but the controversy still simmered.

A lanky sophomore quarterback named Steve Spurrier was marshalling the Gators' wide open offense and hitting on 58 percent of his passes, mostly to his favorite receiver, end Charles Casey, who was leading the SEC in receptions.

Florida, 5–1, was ranked ninth in the nation by the Associated Press and was a nine-point favorite to bag the Bulldogs. Bowl hopes were high in Gainesville as was anticipation that Spurrier's aerial exploits would devastate Georgia, which had the worst pass defense in the conference. If the passing barrage faltered, Florida could rely on All-SEC fullback Larry Dupree, even though an ankle injury had slowed the Gator captain.

Florida roared into 1964 with a 24–8 win over SMU, a 16–13 verdict over Mississippi State, a 30–14 decision against Ole Miss, and a 37–0 plucking of South Carolina. The Gators then dropped from the undefeated ranks with a 17–14 loss at Alabama but regrouped to bounce Auburn, 14–0.

As if the blow of the Butts and Griffith resignations weren't enough, Dooley had an inauspicious debut, as the Bulldogs were stomped 31–3 by Alabama and quarterback Joe Namath in Tuscaloosa. Georgia rebounded to nip Vanderbilt, 7–0, and tie South Carolina, 7–7. In his first game in Athens, Dooley's 'Dogs kicked Clemson, 19–7, but followed with a 17–14 loss to Florida State. Georgia then beat Kentucky, 21–7, and North Carolina, 24–8, to face Florida with a 4–2–1 record.

Georgia and Florida were tied for third place in the SEC as the Bulldogs tried for their first winning season since 1960, Fran Tarkenton's senior year. Dooley abandoned the silver britches worn by Georgia teams during the Wally Butts era and went to white pants.

Under sunny skies, the Gator Bowl was packed with some 48,000 for the yearly collision. Making a regal appearance with the UGA cheerleaders was Georgia's mascot, Uga, a white English bulldog dressed in a red sweater. On the opposite sideline pranced Sam, a boxer wearing Florida's colors.

In the early going, the Gators showed why they were included among the nation's elite, gobbling up yardage though unable to penetrate deeply enough to put up any points. On the other side of the ball, they were crushing everything the Bulldogs tried on offense.

Late in the first quarter, Spurrier masterfully mixed his passes with the short running game. Starting on the UF 17, the Gators reeled off 15 plays in reaching the UGA 7. Then Dupree took a Spurrier handoff, knifed over right end, and cut into the end zone to hand Florida the lead with 1:23 gone in the second period. Kicker Jimmy Hall's conversion culminated the 83-yard drive.

After the score, UF cheerleaders tried to fire a small cannon they had been using since the previous year to celebrate Florida touchdowns. But the gun malfunctioned and there was no boom. Unfortunately for Florida, the cannon would not be needed the rest of the day.

The Gators continued their wrecking ball defense and threatened to increase their margin shortly before intermission.

Spurrier rifled passes to Casey, Dupree and Gary Thomas for a total of 45 yards to the UGA 8. But the 'Dogs defense turned ornery and, on fourth and one, Hall missed a field-goal attempt from the UGA 15. The half ended with Florida up by its touchdown and enjoying a wide statistical edge.

The Gator defense had performed superbly. Georgia had been strangled, gaining only one first down on 12 total plays, 40 yards rushing, and nothing through the air. Florida had 11 first downs, 91 yards on the ground, and 90 passing. But Florida only had a touchdown lead to show for its efforts, and Georgia was sure to be pumped up after denying the Gators the field goal before the half.

The Bulldogs' tenacity paid off three minutes into the third period. Georgia senior left tackle Ray Rissmiller jolted Gator halfback Allen Trammell on a first-down run, jarring the football loose. Rissmiller gathered the ball in at the UF 39 and Georgia had its first break. On the play, Rissmiller dislocated his right elbow and was lost for the season but his feat inflamed his teammates.

The Bulldogs drove to the Florida 17 where the Gators' blunted them, taking over the ball when Georgia's Fred Barber fumbled on fourth down.

But Florida couldn't budge the 'Dogs and Spurrier was nailed by tackle George Patton trying a third-down pass. The ball came free and Bulldog tackle Vance Evans came up with it at the UF 11. Again the Gators stood their ground when it counted as Florida linebacker Jimmy Bernhardt intercepted a Preston Ridlehuber pass at the UF goal line.

By now the Bulldogs defense was shutting down Spurrier and Company. Florida could not dig out of the shadow of its goal after Bernhardt's interception and Spurrier had to punt. Georgia's Wayne Swinford returned the kick to the UF 30, and the Bulldogs had their third prime opportunity to score.

Six times Georgia backs banged into the line, reaching the UF 2 in the first minutes of the final period. On the next play, Georgia linemen wedged a narrow opening at right tackle and Barber slanted over for the touchdown. Sophomore Bob Etter added the extra point to tie it at 7–7.

On the second play after the kickoff, Dame Misfortune struck the Gators again. Senior quarterback Tom Shannon, who had come in for Spurrier, and fullback John Feiber fouled up a pitchout, and the ball careened away from them into the hands of Georgia halfback Douglas McFalls at the UF 21.

On the running of Barber and Frank Lankewicz, the Bulldogs used six plays to reach the UF 5 but found themselves in a fourth-and-goal situation. Dooley opted for the field goal and sent Etter onto the field.

With end and team captain Barry Wilson as holder, the Bulldogs lined up for the go-ahead kick with less than 10 minutes left in the game. What appeared to be a sure field goal quickly turned into one of the quirkier plays in the rivalry.

The snap from center was high and got away from Wilson. Desperately, the 150-pound Etter grabbed the ball as the Gators clawed toward him, running for his life wide to the left. A Florida defensive back rolled up to smash Etter, but Wilson leveled him with what probably was the biggest block of his life and Etter scooted untouched into the end zone.

The run left Etter dazed and confused as yelling teammates crowded in around him. "What happened?" he asked.

"You scored, Bobby, you scored!" came the excited replies.

Furman Bisher, then sports editor of the *Atlanta Journal*, wrote of Etter: "It was the first time in his whole life that he ever carried a football, except to get it pumped up."

The thunderous noise of the Georgia fans still shook the stadium as the little kicker from Chattanooga missed the extra point attempt but got another chance when a Gator jumped offside.

On the second kick he crowned his touchdown, booting the extra point. Georgia led 14–7 with 9:25 remaining.

The Bulldog defenders were in a frenzy now and struggling Florida failed to move the ball.

Georgia appeared to be in the clear later when Mack Faircloth's punt was downed by the Bulldogs at the UF 1. But Steve Spurrier had the cool confidence to rally Florida, even though only a minute remained in the contest.

Spurrier zipped a 12-yard completion to Charles Casey. On the next play, he arched a pass to receiver Jimmy Jordan for 44 yards, and the UGA victory celebration suddenly turned to frantic shouts for defense.

Spurrier then called the same play again. This time Jordan was surrounded by three Bulldogs, and McFalls intercepted at the Georgia 10 as the game ended.

Florida's four-game win streak over Georgia was history, and Vince Dooley had his first win over the Gators in one of the bigger upsets of the series. The win was even more surprising because Georgia had only 155 yards total offense, all on the ground.

Etter's run pitted two former teammates at Cairo (Ga.) High School against each other. Florida tackle Dennis Murphy was blocked by UGA end Frank Richter, springing Etter to the outside and giving Richter a story to relish for years.

In Vince Dooley's first game against Florida, Georgia sophomore kicker Bobby Etter scored the winning touchdown on a broken play in a bizarre ending to the 1964 contest.

Stunned by the loss, the Gators fell a week later to Florida State, 16–7, but came back to beat Miami, 12–10, and LSU, 20–6, to finish at 7–3, good for second in the SEC.

Georgia's upset euphoria ebbed in a 14–7 loss at Auburn, but the Bulldogs clipped Georgia Tech, 7–0, to earn a bid to play in the Sun Bowl in El Paso. A two-yard touchdown run by Lankewicz proved the difference as Georgia nipped the Red Raiders, 7–0.

Georgia tackles Jim Wilson and Ray Rissmiller garnered All-America honors as did Florida's Larry Dupree. Wilson, Rissmiller, UGA defensive back Wayne Swinford, and Dupree joined four other Gators—guard Larry Gagner, split end Charles Casey, defensive back Bruce Bennett, and back Bill Richbourg—as first-team All-SEC selections. Dupree made the all-conference first squad for the third consecutive year and is one of the leading UF rushers of all time. Rissmiller was drafted by the Buffalo Bills and Philadelphia Eagles while Wilson was a pro pick by New England and San Francisco.

A Georgia season that began with an untried coach and turmoil in the athletic department ended with a 7–3–1 record and a bowl win for the Bulldogs. At least in his first year, Dooley had made the glass slipper fit.

★   ★   ★

Scoring:

Georgia	0	0	0	14	—	14
Florida	0	7	0	0	—	7

UF   TD   Dupree, 7-yard run (Hall kick)
UGA   TD   Barber, 2-yard run (Etter kick)
UGA   TD   Etter, 5-yard run (Etter kick)

Georgia: Nowicki, Varnado, Handmacher, Richter, R. Crawford, *left end;* Rissmiller, Patton, *left tackle;* Brantley, Kasay, Steely, *left guard;* K. Davis, Darden, Glass, *center;* J. Smith, Dennard, Cooley, Denney, *right guard;* J. Wilson, V. Evans, Harber, Laurent, *right tackle;* Hodgson, B. Wilson, *right end;* Hughes, Ridlehuber, Moore, Dickens, *quarterback;* Barber, Taylor, Bray, McWhorter, *left halfback;* Lankewicz, Hurst, Armbrester, *fullback;* Swinford, McFalls, Porterfield, S. Crawford, *right halfback;* Burson, Hunnicutt, *safety;* Etter, *placekicker;* Faircloth, *punter*

Florida: *Offense:* R. Jackson, *left end;* J. Benson, *left tackle;* Beckman, *left guard;* Carr, Cliett, *center;* Gagner, *right guard;* Preston, Whatley, *right tackle;* Casey, Thomas, *right end;* Spurrier, Shannon, *quarterback;* Dupree, J. Jordan, *tailback;* Feiber, *fullback;* Knapp, Baeszler, *wingback;* J. Hall, *placekicker;* Seymour, Spurrier, *punter*

Defense: Matthews, Barrett, *left end;* MacLean, *left tackle;* Richbourg, *middle guard;* Murphy, Colson, *right tackle;* B. Brown, *right end;* Pettee, Pursell, Card, Bernhardt *linebacker;* Kirk, Trammell, Newcomer, Russell, Grandy, *halfback;* Bennett, *safety*

	Georgia	Florida
First downs	10	13
Rushing yards	155	76
Passing yards	0	145
Pass att/comp/int	2/0/1	18/10/2
Punts/avg. yards	6/39	4/45
Fumbles lost	2	4
Penalty yards	23	40

— 1965 —

Florida 14, Georgia 10

FLORIDA'S PASSING COMBO OF QUARTER-back Steve Spurrier and All-SEC end Charley Casey figured to light up the scoreboard against Georgia's weak secondary when the Gators and Bulldogs met on November 6, 1965.

For an afternoon, many Southerners would try to forget the Vietnam War, which wore on with President Lyndon Johnson trying to negotiate a cease-fire by Christmas.

With two losses each, both teams had their sights set on bowl invitations as well as beating a contemptible rival.

A shakeup in Athens the week before the game added even more drama to the proceedings. On Wednesday, second-year UGA coach Vince Dooley announced that three players—starting defensive back David Cooper, second-string fullback George Demos, and second-unit guard Jiggy Smaha—had been suspended from the team for disciplinary reasons.

Georgia, 5–2, began the year with a bang as the Bulldogs clipped defending national champion Alabama, 18–17; Vanderbilt, 24–10; and mighty Michigan, 15–7, at Ann Arbor. The Bulldogs beat Clemson, 23–9, to remain undefeated, but then fell 10–3 at Florida State and 28–10 at Kentucky. A week before the Florida game, Georgia outscored North Carolina, 47–35.

In Gainesville, sixth-year UF coach Ray Graves was looking to Spurrier, a junior, to pass the Gators over Georgia. And Spurrier appeared to be up to it, having thrown for 1,192 yards and seven touchdowns, five to Casey, in Florida's first six games.

The 4–2 Gators chomped Northwestern, 24–14, to begin the year but lost their home opener, 18–13, to Mississippi State. Florida then won three straight, besting LSU, 14–7; Ole Miss, 17–0; and N.C. State, 28–6, before falling 28–17 at Auburn.

Game day broke windy and drizzly as more than 61,500 fans made their way into the newly enlarged Gator Bowl.

The first quarter pretty much boiled down to a punting duel between Spurrier and Georgia's Kirby Moore.

The pattern was the same for much of the second quarter with the Bulldogs spending most of their time on offense around their 35-yard line.

After UF end Don Barrett recovered a bad pitchout by Georgia quarterback Preston Ridlehuber, the Gators put together a march that reached the UGA 1. There, left halfback Jack Harper hit the line but fumbled, and the Bulldogs' right end Larry Kohn fell on the ball in the end zone to kill the threat.

With about three minutes left before halftime, Florida took possession at the UGA 46 on a punt. Spurrier hooked up with Harper on a screen pass for a 28-yard gain. Fullback Alan Poe ran for nine yards and got the call again for three to put the ball inside the Georgia 10.

Poe then took a pitchout from Spurrier and ripped the last six yards, reaching the left corner of the end zone standing up. Gator kicker Wayne Barfield added the conversion and Florida was on the board, 7–0.

Georgia could not reply and the half ended with Dooley pondering ways to help his Bulldogs advance past their 38, something they had not yet done. Of course, UF defenders Wally Colson, Larry Gagner and Chip Hoye had a lot to do with that.

Florida gave the Georgians some unexpected help in the third quarter. Harper fumbled and Bulldog tackle George Patton recovered at the UF 41. Facing third and eight, halfback Randy Wheeler kept the drive alive with a 12-yard completion from Moore. Two plays gained only three yards but, again on third down, Moore had the hot hand, passing 11 yards to end Pat Hodgson to the UF 13. Wheeler and Moore each ran for three but Ridlehuber lost one back to the 8. Not in a gambling mood, Dooley went for the field goal, sending in kicker Bob Etter, the hero of the 1964 game. Etter's boot was true from the 25 to cut the Florida lead to 7–3 in the waning moments of the third quarter.

The Gators couldn't make any headway and had to punt early in the fourth period. The Bulldogs were playing with noticeable emotion and intensity. They responded with their best drive of the afternoon.

Interference on a Moore pass to Hodgson gave Georgia a first down at the UF 45. Ridlehuber then tore loose on a 21-yard jaunt, the longest run of the day for the Bulldogs. Wheeler inflicted some serious damage inside as Georgia reached the Florida 8. With the Bulldogs in a fourth-down-and-five situation, Dooley elected to go for broke.

Moore drifted back on the wet field and spotted Hodgson breaking free near the goal line. The pass was high but Hodgson leaped, clutched the ball on his fingertips, and fell into the end zone mud for the touchdown. Etter kicked the extra point and Georgia led 10–7 with 12:03 left.

In the rain and wind, both defenses regained their dominance and the clock ticked on. With less than six minutes left, Georgia got another break when a Florida runner was hit and fumbled, the Bulldogs getting possession at the UF 37. Gator fans, and Ray Graves in particular, were experiencing an unpleasant déjà vu of the 1964 clash when Florida turnovers near the UF goal handed Georgia golden opportunities that the Bulldogs cashed in.

For only the third time in the game, Georgia had the ball in Florida territory. This time, however, the Gators defense walled off the Bulldogs and forced a punt. Florida got the ball back at its 23 with just 4:02 remaining in the game.

What followed was a brief, but legendary, drive in the decades of the border war. The Florida thunder began to roll when Spurrier stepped back and drilled a pass to Casey running free near midfield. Casey made the reception after slipping behind Georgia defensive back Joe Burson, then sprinted 18 yards to the UGA 32 before Burson caught him. The pass netted 45 yards and Florida was in business.

On the next play, Spurrier again stepped back to pass, this time connecting with Harper, who made the grab at the UGA 1. Despite two Bulldogs blanketing him, Harper dove across the goal line as Georgia fans sat in disbelief. Florida's rooters, meanwhile, were shaking the stadium with their approval. Many Bulldog supporters believed that if safety Lynn Hughes hadn't stumbled he would have made the interception. Now Barfield's extra point put the Gators back in front, 14–10. Jack Harper had redeemed himself after two earlier fumbles in the game.

Florida used less than 30 seconds for the lightning-quick score, leaving Georgia with 3:37 to pull out a win. There would be no miracle comebacks this year. Shortly after the game, Vince Dooley described the defeat as "the toughest loss of my coaching career."

The win was especially sweet for Gator end Casey, who went to Brown High School in Atlanta and was friends with Georgia's

Ray Graves enjoys a victory cigar in 1965, the year his Gators first beat a Vince Dooley-coached Georgia team. [Johnston Collection, UF Archives]

Hughes, Vance Evans and Jimmy Denney.

Spurrier had missed open receivers on several occasions and had his worst passing day of the season, but nothing dampened the glee of Florida which had avenged the bitter defeat of 1964. Graves had run his record against Georgia to 5–1 and evened matters with Dooley at 1–1.

Georgia's misfortune heightened with a 21–19 loss to Auburn, but the Bulldogs finished with a 17–7 road win over Georgia Tech for a 6–4 mark.

Florida's run continued with a 51–13 drowning of Tulane, but the Gators stumbled in a 16–13 loss at Miami. Graves' team then beat Florida State, 30–17, to earn a trip to the Sugar Bowl and face Missouri. The Tigers sprang to a 20–0 lead before Florida battled back late, falling 20–18. Despite the bowl loss, Graves had a 7–4 worksheet, his fifth winning season in six years at the UF helm.

The 1965 All-America first teams had a decidedly Orange and Blue hue as Steve Spurrier, defensive end Lynn Matthews, defensive back

Bruce Bennett, guard Larry Gagner, and Charley Casey all garnered honors among the nation's best. Georgia tackle George Patton also made several All-America teams. Spurrier, Casey, Gagner, Bennett and Gator guard Larry Beckman joined Georgia's Patton and defensive back Lynn Hughes on the All-SEC first squad.

Bennett later played in the Canadian Football League for a decade and was All-CFL seven times. Gagner went to the NFL and played for Pittsburgh and Kansas City.

Scoring:

Florida	0	7	0	7	—	14
Georgia	0	0	3	7	—	10

UF	TD	Poe, 6-yard run (Barfield kick)
UGA	FG	Etter, 25-yards
UGA	TD	Hodgson, 8-yard pass from Moore (Etter kick)
UF	TD	Harper, 32-yard pass from Spurrier (Barfield kick)

Florida: Casey, Ewaldsen, Matthews, Jetter, *left end;* Preston, Whatley, Gagner, *left tackle;* Beckman, Pursell, Heidt, *left guard;* Carr, Cliett, Card, McCall, *center;* Benson, Sneed, Anderson, *right guard;* Waxman, Thomas, Colson, Splane, *right tackle;* Brown, Hoye, Barrett, *right end;* Spurrier, Bennett, Hungerbuhler, *quarterback;* Harper, Trammell, Manry, *left halfback;* Trapp, Kirk, Williams, *right halfback;* Poe, Baeszler, Grandy, *fullback;* Barfield, *kicker*

Georgia: Richter, Creech, Tootle, *left end;* Pillsbury, Patton, Harber, *left tackle;* Steely, Brantley, *left guard;* K. Davis, J. Davis, Glass, Lawhorne, Dickens, *center;* Denney, Kasay, Phillips, Pennard, *right guard;* Arkwright, Evans, *right tackle;* Hodgson, Ingle, Kohn, *right end;* Moore, Ridlehuber, Hughes, *quarterback;* Wheeler, Wood, Burson, McWhorter, *left halfback;* Mosher, Bray, Sellers, McFalls, *right halfback;* Jenkins, Hurst, Bankston, *fullback;* Etter, *kicker*

	Florida	Georgia
First downs	14	14
Rushing yards	157	95
Passing yards	134	70
Pass att/comp/int	22/9/0	15/1/0
Punts/avg. yards	7/39	10/34
Fumbles lost	3	1
Penalty yards	34	27

— 1966 —

Georgia 27, Florida 10

Florida PASSING MAGICIAN STEVE SPURRIER
was vying for the Heisman Trophy and had dead aim on Georgia
heading into the November 5, 1966, game.

The showdown in the Gator Bowl this year was the high tide of
battle for the SEC championship as both Florida and Georgia were
unbeaten in the league. Florida was undefeated at 7–0 and the Bulldogs were 6–1 overall.

The Gators, ranked No. 7 in the country, were rated a touchdown
favorite.

Spurrier, a first-team All-American in 1965, was putting up numbers that proved to most observers that he was the country's premier
passer. Going into the Georgia contest, the senior from Miami Beach
was hitting on close to 66 percent of his passes and had thrown for 14
touchdowns and almost 1,400 yards.

The 1966 Gators waxed Northwestern, 43–7, to begin the season,
then bashed Mississippi State, 28–7; Vanderbilt, 13–0; Florida State,
22–19; and N.C. State, 17–10. Florida then thrashed LSU in Baton
Rouge, 28–7, and dropped Auburn, 30–27, to draw a bead on the
Bulldogs.

Spurrier was named SEC Back of the Week for his performance
against Auburn, throwing for 259 yards, averaging 48 yards a punt,
and kicking a 40-yard field goal to win the game. The Gators
appeared poised to win their first-ever conference crown if they could
get past despicable Georgia.

In Athens, third-year coach Vince Dooley and his defensive coordinator Erk Russell knew they had to stop Spurrier if the Bulldogs'
best season since 1959 was to continue on a winning roll. The '59
Bulldogs of Wally Butts also started with a 6–1 record, then beat
Florida, and won the Orange Bowl and Georgia's most recent SEC
title.

Georgia trimmed Mississippi State, 20–17, in its initial 1966 outing,

Bulldog offensive guard Edgar Chandler was honored as an All-American in 1966 and 1967 when Georgia and Florida split victories.

then routed VMI 43–7. The Bulldogs edged South Carolina, 7–0, and Ole Miss, 9–3, before a slim 7–6 loss at Miami. Georgia then beat Kentucky, 27–15, and North Carolina, 28–3.

With 17 interceptions, the Bulldogs' secondary was the best in the SEC. Headed by Terry Sellers and All-SEC safety Lynn Hughes, Georgia's defensive backs knew they would get a trial by fire with Spurrier hurling to receivers Richard Trapp and Paul Ewaldsen, among others.

A strong pass rush by tackles George Patton, an All-American, and Bill Stanfill was imperative if Georgia was to have a shot at the upset.

Both fullbacks, Florida's Larry Smith and UGA's Ronnie Jenkins, were dueling for the conference lead in rushing.

A number of bowl scouts were among the more than 62,000 packed into the Gator Bowl for the clash. With all of the pre-game publicity, many fans expected "Superman" Spurrier to burst onto the field from a phone booth.

Florida, receiving the opening kickoff, looked as if it would mash the Bulldogs into the stadium turf. Starting on their 14, the Gators snapped at the Bulldogs with a Spurrier-to-Trapp pass for six and a 7-yard run by Larry Smith. Spurrier shot a pass to tight end John Coons for 28 yards to the UGA 46. The Gator quarterback then kept for five. With the Bulldogs looking for the pass, fullback Graham McKeel bulled through the line and rumbled 38 yards to the UGA 3. Smith wedged to the 1 before Spurrier was stopped for no gain on a keeper. Any ideas of a great goal-line stand died when McKeel muscled over with 5:24 gone in the first quarter. Gator kicker Wayne Barfield's extra point made it 7–0 Florida.

Gator Heisman quarterback Steve Spurrier has unwanted company in UGA's Gerald Varnado, George Patton, and Bill Stanfill in the 1966 Georgia win. [Hargrett Collection, UGA Libraries]

Georgia blazed back minutes later on a drive that began at its 45. With quarterback Kirby Moore running the option and aided by a 19-yard pass interference call, the Bulldogs nosed to the UF 13 before being stopped.

On fourth down, Bobby Etter kicked a 29-yard field goal to narrow the margin to 7–3.

Florida responded on the Georgia kickoff. Harmon Wages tucked the ball in at his goal line and ran through a gap in the advancing Georgians. Wages dug toward the UGA goal, crossing midfield as UF fans turned up the volume. Georgia end Gary Adams finally pulled him down at the UGA 28. Soon after, McKeel banged for a first down at the 4.

Burned by the Gators in the last goal-line situation, Georgia's Stanfill, Patton, Steve Neuhaus, and Edgar Chandler, among others, showed their Red and Black mettle.

Spurrier threw two incomplete passes before he was corralled by

Stanfill for a 6-yard loss. The field-goal unit came on and Barfield hit on a 26-yarder that gave Florida a 10–3 lead with just under 14 minutes left in the second quarter.

The teams traded blows like two punch-drunk boxers. Georgia's Moore flicked a pass over the middle to junior end Frank Richter who bolted to the UF 24 for a 56-yard completion. Two plays later, Moore found Richter for 19 more and a first down at the UF 9. Upon reaching the Gators 3, the Bulldogs went to the air. But Moore's pass was intercepted in the end zone by the Gators' George Grandy.

Florida held its 10–3 advantage at halftime uneasily. Though the Gators' defense was repelling Georgia's offensives, the Bulldogs defense was getting good pressure on Spurrier with almost as much success. Both teams knew the second half would decide bragging rights for another year.

Dooley made a major change in strategy in the UGA locker room. Moore's 12 passes, including two interceptions, had not put UGA in the end zone; so the Georgia head coach decided to go to his rushing game in the second half.

The third quarter, early on, was a mix of hard hits, a Lynn Hughes interception, and punting.

Spurrier got off one kick that slipped out of bounds at the UGA 1, putting Georgia in a hole from which they punted minutes later. Later in the quarter, a Spurrier punt left the Bulldogs with a first down at their own 35.

A dormant UGA offense suddenly sprang to life. Halfback Randy Wheeler sprinted outside on a 25-yard run, then added five more. The 'Dogs shoved down to the UF 30 where they faced fourth and two. Down by seven late in the third, Dooley went for the yardage and Kirby Moore slid through to the 28. Runs by Jenkins, Moore, and Kent Lawrence hammered to the UF 4.

Jenkins bulled in from there and Etter's conversion tied it with 1:07 left in the third period and fans on both sides screaming encouragement in anticipation of the final 15 minutes.

Georgia was rolling now. Pressured in the pocket, a Spurrier pass was picked off by defensive back Terry Sellers at the UF 47. The 'Dogs marched into field-goal range but Etter's 46-yard attempt failed.

Trying to rally his team, Spurrier scrambled back to pass under a torrid Georgia rush, throwing with UGA tackle and team captain George Patton clutching at him.

Spurrier was buried by the Bulldogs' wave and didn't see the resulting disaster. Georgia's Hughes darted in front of the intended Florida receiver near midfield, snaring the interception. The Bull-dogs' all-conference safety then rambled 39 yards for the score and was engulfed in the end zone by a mob of UGA fans and exultant players. Etter's conversion gave Georgia a stunning 17–10 lead.

When the shocked Gators could not move, Georgia again went on the attack starting at its 17. Runs by Jenkins, Lawrence and reserve fullback Brad Johnson helped the 'Dogs down to the UF 17, where Etter kicked a 33-yard field goal to widen the advantage to 20–10 Georgia.

With chances for victory and a conference championship slipping away, the dangerous Spurrier looked to bring his team back from the grave. Georgia's secondary was blanketing the field, however, and the Gators found themselves gambling on a fourth-down play at the UF 30. With Bulldogs bearing down on him, Spurrier threw short and Georgia took possession.

On a sweep from the UF 3 two plays later, Moore followed the blocking of Jenkins to score standing up. Etter added the extra point for a 27–10 Georgia lead with one second left and the upset was complete.

For the second time in three years, Georgia had shocked a Florida squad ranked in the nation's top 10.

Quarterback Steve Spurrier looks over the UGA defensive line in the 1966 game. [UF Archives]

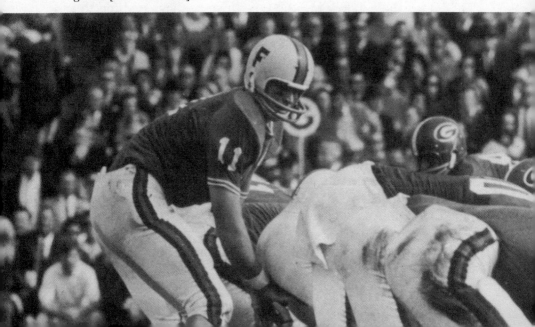

Vince Dooley poses with George Patton, a 1966 All-American tackle who led Georgia to a 10–1 record, including a 27–10 win against Florida.

Spurrier had been intercepted only twice in the Gators' seven victories, but the Bulldogs pulled down three of his passes.

With two interceptions, including one for the deciding touchdown, Hughes atoned for the 1965 game in which he had been beaten on a Spurrier pass that gave the Gators the victory.

The Bulldogs defense held Florida to a single first down in the second half, during which time the Gators' deepest penetration was to the Georgia 43.

The loss tarnished Florida's record but the Gators didn't let it ruin their year. Graves' crew wrecked Tulane, 31–10, and earned a bid to play powerful Georgia Tech in the Orange Bowl, despite a 21–16 loss to Miami. The Gators demolished Tech, 27–12, for Graves' third bowl victory in four trips.

Spurrier earned the Heisman Trophy, the first University of Florida player ever to do so, and ended his collegiate season holding a slew of Florida passing records. He was selected to the All-America and All-SEC first teams for the second consecutive year. Gator center Bill Carr also was a first-team All-America. The two were joined on the All-SEC team squad by teammates guard Jim Benson, flanker Richard Trapp and back Larry Smith.

Spurrier was a first-round draft choice by the San Francisco 49ers and continued a winning football odyssey that eventually would bring him back to Gainesville.

After crushing Florida, the road ahead glittered with gold for Dooley's 'Dogs. Georgia won 21–13 at Auburn to share SEC laurels with Alabama. The Bulldogs then beat highly-ranked Georgia Tech, 23–14, to garner an invitation to the Cotton Bowl against SMU.

Georgia beat the Mustangs, 24–9, for the school's best record since Wally Butts' 1959 team went 10–1. Dooley's squad finished the year ranked fourth in the nation.

Georgia's George Patton, defensive tackle; Larry Kohn, defensive end; Lynn Hughes, safety; Don Hayes, guard; Edgar Chandler, tackle; Bob Etter, kicker; and fullback Ronnie Jenkins were all honored as first-team All-SEC selections, Patton and Hughes for the second year in a row. Chandler, Hughes and Patton (for the second season) were named first-team All-Americans.

Scoring:

Georgia	3	0	7	17	— 27
Florida	7	3	0	0	— 10

UF	TD	McKeel, 1-yard run (Barfield kick)
UGA	FG	Etter, 29 yards
UF	FG	Barfield, 26 yards
UGA	TD	Jenkins, 4-yard run (Etter kick)
UGA	TD	Hughes, 39-yard interception return (Etter kick)
UGA	FG	Etter, 33 yards
UGA	TD	Moore, 3-yard run (Etter kick)

Georgia: *Offense:* Payne, Johnson, *left end;* Pillsbury, Rholetter, *left tackle;* Hayes, Rodrique, *left guard;* Davis, White, *center;* Kasay, Yawn, *right guard;* Chandler, Arkwright, *right tackle;* Richter, *right end;* Moore, *quarterback;* Lawrence, King, *tailback;* Wheeler, McWhorter, *wingback;* Jenkins, Johnson, *fullback;* Etter, *kicker;* Crawford, *punter*

Defense: Varnado, Young, *left end;* Patton, Osbolt, *left tackle;* Cooley, Whiddon, *left guard;* Phillips, Dennard, *right guard;* Stanfill, Rholetter, *right tackle;* Kohn, Adams, *right end;* Neuhaus, Dicks, Lawhorne, Tarrer, *linebackers;* Holmes, Sellers, McKnight, Cooper, *halfbacks;* Hughes, Woodward, *safety*

Florida: *Offense:* Ewaldsen, McCann, *split end;* Preston, Clark, *left tackle:* Dennis, Young, *left guard;* Carr, Barnhart, *center:* Benson, Duven, *right guard;* Pasteris, Morris, *right tackle;* Coons, Yarbrough, *tight end;* Spurrier, Barfield, *quarterback;* Smith, *tailback;* Trapp, Glenn, Wages, *wingback;* McKeel, Christian, *fullback;* Barfield, *kicker*

Defense: Rittgers, Santille, *left end;* Giordano, Foster, *left tackle;* Cutcliffe, Dean, *left guard;* Anderson, Splane, *right guard;* Jetter, Adams, *right tackle;* Barrett, Ely, *right end;* Pippin, Card, Mintom, Hungerbuhler, Downs, Grandy, Manry, *halfbacks;* Rentz, Gaisford, *safety*

	Georgia	Florida
First downs	15	10
Rushing yards	213	61
Passing yards	121	133
Pass att/comp/int	13/5/2	29/16/3
Punts/avg. yards	5/38	6/39
Fumbles lost	0	1
Penalty yards	20	30

— 1967 —

Florida 17, Georgia 16

THE ESCALATING WAR IN VIETNAM AND MAS-
sive anti-war protests gripped the nation as Georgia and Florida tried
to concentrate on their November 11, 1967, gridiron fight.

For the first time in the series' history, the game would be televised
nationally by ABC, and 70,000 jammed into the sun-splashed Gator
Bowl to see it in person.

The 5–2 Bulldogs of fourth-year coach Vince Dooley were serious
contenders to win their second SEC championship in a row and snare
another major bowl bid. Georgia was a touchdown favorite to scalp
the Gators.

The Floridians of eighth-year coach Ray Graves were 2–2 in the
conference and 4–2 overall. Steve Spurrier was gone but Florida
featured a versatile attack with the running of All-SEC back Larry
Smith and the rushing and passing of quarterback Larry Rentz.
Georgia planned to counter with a strong defense.

Florida began the year with a 14–0 victory over Illinois and a 24–7
win against Mississippi State, before being outclassed 37–6 by LSU.
The Gators then thumped Tulane, 35–0, and Vanderbilt, 27–22,
before a 26–21 loss to Auburn.

The Bulldogs began their title defense in fine form, whipping
Mississippi State, 30–0, in the 1967 opener and following with a
24–17 win over Clemson and a 21–0 breather against South Carolina.
Ole Miss ambushed Georgia, 29–20, but the 'Dogs ran over VMI,
56–6, and Kentucky, 31–7. They then lost, 15–14, at Houston before
the showdown with the Gators.

The week before the game, Florida coaches fired up their players
by showing them a war movie, "Never So Few," and films of
Georgia's 27–10 win in 1966.

On Thursday, Georgia received some sad news. "Hood's Ole
Dan," the white English bulldog mascot better known as the original

Gator running back Larry Smith takes on the Vanderbilt defense in 1967. Smith was an All-SEC selection in 1967 and 1968. [UF Archives]

"Uga," died at the home of his owner, Frank "Sonny" Seiler of Savannah. Uga had retired the previous year after 11 years as the official Georgia mascot and had been succeeded by his son, Uga II.

Even if Uga's demise was seen as a bad omen by some Georgia fans, the team did not seem to be especially bothered in the early moments of the first quarter.

The Bulldogs opened running room in the Florida defense and pushed into UF territory on their first two possessions. They suffered a blow early in the game, though, when linebacker Tommy Lawhorne went down with an ankle injury and was lost for the day. On the other side of the ball, the Gators were having trouble cranking up their offense.

Georgia safety Jake Scott ignited the Bulldogs on their third possession, returning a punt to the UF 29. Spurred by a key 11-yard sprint by left halfback Kent Lawrence on a third-down call, Georgia used five plays to reach the Gators 1. Then all-conference fullback Ronnie Jenkins banged across the goal line for first blood.

Florida sophomore safety Paul Maliska leaped high over the lines to bat down the extra-point attempt. The Bulldogs led 6–0, but Maliska's heroics would haunt them.

A Florida fumble gave Georgia possession at the UF 44, and Bulldogs' quarterback and team captain Kirby Moore quickly hurled a 16-yard completion to Jenkins, who then cracked 28 yards to the UF 16. Florida held, however, and the Bulldogs' McCullough came on to hit a 33-yard field goal with 14:56 left in the half.

Trailing 9–0, Florida made some noise with less than five minutes left before intermission. The Gators took six plays to march from their 35 to the UGA 20. Florida All-SEC flanker Richard Trapp caught passes of eight and 18 yards, and Larry Smith snared another for 13 yards to highlight the offensive.

At the 20, a Florida back fumbled and there was a wild melee before a Gator covered the ball at the UGA 33, a 13-yard loss. Georgia fans cheered, as it appeared the Florida drive was blunted.

Florida quarterback Rentz, hobbled by an ankle injury earlier in the period, quickly silenced the Red and Black sections. Rolling out, Rentz hit flanker Mike McCann, who danced away from several Bulldogs and sprinted in for the touchdown. Gator kicker Wayne Barfield kicked the extra point, and Florida closed to 9–7 with 3:12 before halftime.

The teams went to their locker rooms with Georgia looking at missed opportunities and Florida rejuvenated after their score.

Any momentum seized by the Gators seemed to be shattered early in the third quarter. Florida had the ball when Rentz went back to throw, looking for receiver Jim Yarbrough at the UF 32. But Georgia's Scott flashed in from nowhere, pulled in the ball, and sped into the Florida end zone. When McCullough drilled the extra point, Georgia suddenly was up 16–7 and looking comfortable.

Gator All-SEC flanker Richard Trapp looks for daylight on one of his nine pass catches during Florida's thrilling upset of Georgia in 1967. [UF Archives]

At the eight-minute mark of the fourth period, little had changed and the Bulldogs looked to be on their way to a second consecutive win over Florida.

Whether it was the ill fortune of Uga I's death, Maliska's earlier conversion block, or just plain Florida grit and power, Georgia's comet plummeted.

The Gators started a series at their 37 and edged out to their 48 on four plays. From there, Rentz, still hurting from the first-half injury, lobbed a pass to Trapp, who grabbed it at the UGA 40. The star Gator flanker made a reverse spin to get away from a Bulldog defensive back, dodged away from six or eight others, and bolted to pay dirt. The 52-yard play electrified the Orange and Blue faithful, who erupted again when Barfield's conversion sailed through the goal posts to slice the Georgia lead to 16–14 with 6:16 left in the contest.

The doughty Gators mashed Georgia's offense after the kickoff, regaining possession at their 37 inside the four-minute mark. With Trapp hauling in a 24-yard pass and Smith and UF team captain Graham McKeel spearing through the Bulldog line, Florida worked to the Georgia 14 and used up most of the clock in doing so. But facing fourth and one, Graves decided to go for yardage rather than the field goal. Smith then slammed into the line for a first down and the tension intensified. Fullback McKeel hurtled for four, but the Bulldogs poured through to drop Rentz for a six-yard loss with a minute left. Smith swept right for a yard to the UGA 14, but it was fourth down again with 29 seconds left. Time out—Florida.

The stadium trembled with the anxiety, screams and cheers of both sides as senior kicker Barfield, from Albany, Ga., prepared to enter the game for the field-goal try. Graves later told reporters that he had grasped Barfield's hand "and told him that ball had better go right through the uprights if he ever wanted to go back home to Albany, Ga.," the *Florida Times-Union* said. When Barfield trotted onto the field, Rentz, his holder, shook his hand and wished him luck.

"I was as nervous as I've ever been and there we were shaking hands and hoping like hell," the kicker recalled later.

Rentz spotted the ball at the UGA 31 and Barfield stepped into it.

"When I kicked the ball I knew it was straight. I just didn't know if it was far enough," he remembered. But the pigskin split the uprights for the field goal that gave the Gators their first lead of the game at 17–16 and, more importantly, an upset win over the stunned Bulldogs.

Florida kicker Wayne Barfield (48) is swarmed by teammates and fans after his field goal beat Georgia in the last seconds of the 1967 contest. Barfield earned All-SEC kudos that year. [UF Archives]

Exuberant Gator fans swarmed the field, much as UGA rooters had done after the 1966 Georgia win, and Barfield was mobbed by teammates. A fight also erupted on the field, lasting only briefly before it was broken up.

Graves was given the game ball and promptly turned it over to Richard Trapp for his big plays, including nine catches for 171 yards and a touchdown.

Florida not only wrecked the Bulldogs' chances of winning a second consecutive SEC title, but scuttled Georgia's shot at a major bowl bid as well.

Still, Georgia came back strong from that tough day in Jacksonville. The Bulldogs hounded Auburn, 17–0, and beat Georgia Tech for the fourth year in a row, 21–14, in Atlanta. The Bulldogs earned a trip to the Liberty Bowl, Dooley's third postseason bowl in four seasons, but fell 14–7 to N.C. State. Georgia finished at 7–4 and ranked 18th in the final United Press International poll.

Bulldog lineman Edgar Chandler made All-America for the second year in a row. He and defensive tackle Bill Stanfill, fullback Ronnie Jenkins, safety Jake Scott and defensive end Larry Kohn also were named to the All-SEC first team, the second year that Kohn,

Chandler and Jenkins had been so honored. Chandler was later drafted by the Buffalo Bills.

Florida followed the Georgia win with a 28–12 decision over Kentucky, but lost its last two games, 21–16 to arch foe Florida State and 20–13 at Miami, for a 6–4 record.

Florida flanker Richard Trapp and fullback Larry Smith were first-team All-SEC selections for the second year in a row and were joined on the squad of stars by teammates Guy Dennis, guard; and Wayne Barfield, placekicker.

Scoring:

Florida	0	7	0	10	—	17
Georgia	6	3	7	0	—	16

UGA	TD	Jenkins, 1-yard run (kick blocked)
UGA	FG	McCullough, 33 yards
UF	TD	McCann, 33-yard pass from Rentz (Barfield kick)
UGA	TD	Scott, 32-yard pass interception (McCullough kick)
UF	TD	Trapp, 52-yard pass from Rentz (Barfield kick)
UF	FG	Barfield, 31 yards

Florida: *Offense:* Trapp, McCann, *split end;* Amelung, *left tackle;* Steen, *left guard;* Helton, *center;* Dennis, *right guard;* Morris, *right tackle;* Yarbrough, *tight end;* Rentz, *quarterback;* Smith, *tailback;* McCann, *flanker;* McKeel, *fullback;* Barfield, *placekicker*

Defense: Jetter, *left end;* Hadley, *left tackle;* Dorsey, *middle guard;* Healey, *right tackle;* Skrivanek, *right end;* Mann, *left linebacker;* Giordano, *right linebacker;* Gaisford, Tannen, *cornerback;* Downs, Maliska, Hungerbuhler, *safety*

Georgia: *Offense:* Ingle, Lyons, *left end;* Rholetter, *left tackle;* Hayes, *left guard;* Tidmore, Lopatka, *center;* Rodrique, Adkins, *right guard;* Chandler, *right tackle;* Payne, Hughes, Whittemore, *right end;* Moore, Hampton, *quarterback;* King, Woodward, Jenkins, B. Johnson, Kemp, *wingback;* Lawrence, Elrod, *tailback;* McCullough, S. Jones, *kicker*

Defense: Adams, Daniel, *left end;* Stanfill, Handmacher, *left tackle;* Tarrer, Greer, *left guard;* Callaway, Osbolt, *right guard;* Tarrer, Smaha, Young, *right tackle;* Kohn, *right end;* Dicks, Mosher, Lopatka, Lawhorne, Epperson, *linebacker;* Holmes, McKnight, *left halfback;* Scott, Stewart, *safety;* Sellers, Pennington, *right halfback*

	Florida	Georgia
First downs	20	10
Rushing yards	145	135
Passing yards	235	59
Pass att/comp/int	25/13/3	18/6/0
Punts/avg. yards	4/37	8/39
Fumbles lost	3	2
Penalty yards	30	71

— 1968 —

Georgia 51, Florida 0

A DRIVING RAINSTORM DOUSED JACKSON-
ville on November 9, 1968, drenching the more than 70,000 fans
gathered to see if the Gators could pull another miracle against the
powerful Bulldogs.

Defensive backs Jake Scott of Georgia and Steve Tannen of Florida
were expected to be the principal players when the ninth-ranked
Bulldogs met the Gators.

Georgia, 5–0–2, was expected to have little trouble with Florida,
which had been the preseason favorite to win its first SEC crown but
had not lived up to its billing. Most forecasters believed the Bulldogs
were at least a touchdown favorite to best Florida even though the
Gators defense ranked second in the conference and seventh in the
nation.

Georgia visited Tennessee and came away with a 17–17 tie in its
season opener. The Bulldogs then skinned Clemson, 31–13; South
Carolina, 21–20; Ole Miss, 21–7; Vanderbilt, 32–6; and Kentucky,
35–14, before a 10–10 stalemate with Houston a week before facing
Florida.

The 4–2–1 Gators flamed Air Force, 23–20, in their first game,
then beat Florida State, 9–3; Mississippi State, 31–14; and Tulane,
24–7. Then midnight struck for the Gators. Florida lost 22–7 at
North Carolina; tied Vanderbilt, 14–14; and fell 24–13 to Auburn.
The Gators were hungry for their first win in a month when they
faced Georgia.

Florida's two-year All-SEC fullback Larry Smith was the marquee
runner in the league even though he had been hit by injuries and had
not been a factor in the Gators' last two games. A number of other
Gators were also hurt.

Georgia fullback Bruce Kemp, the SEC's second-leading rusher,

A Bulldog sloshes for yardage during the 1968 game played in a heavy rainstorm. Favored Georgia drowned the Gators 51–0. [UF Archives]

was expected to see limited action due to an injury against Kentucky. At quarterback, Georgia was relying on sophomore Mike Cavan, whose father, Jim, had been a UGA halfback in the 1930s. The Bulldog defense was headed by left tackle and team captain Bill Stanfill and safety Jake Scott, both 1967 all-conference selections.

Scouts from the Orange, Sugar and Gator bowls were among the thousands who made their way to the stadium in a steady rain.

Mostly, the teams just muddied their uniforms in the game's first five minutes. The fleet Scott, however, was not one to let the reptilian conditions prevent him from creating an early break for the Bulldogs.

Fielding a line-drive punt near the Georgia 35, Scott splashed 59 yards down the sideline before he was brought down at the Gators' 5. Two plays later, Kemp plowed in for the score. Georgia's Jim Mc-Cullough kicked the extra point and UGA was up 7–0 with 9:14 remaining in the first period.

Florida's offense seemed to be extinguished by the rain, and the Bulldogs got the ball again minutes later. Starting on the UGA 38, Cavan went to the pass despite the weather. He pitched a 17-yard completion to Bill Brice, then launched a 27-yard throw to Kent Lawrence to put the ball at the UF 21. Cavan, calling his own number, slipped around end for 13 to the Florida 7. Three plays later, the Gator defense crunched halfback Steve Farnsworth near the goal line; but, on fourth down, Farnsworth rammed it across. McCullough drilled another conversion to make it 14–0, Georgia with 4:34

still left in the first quarter.

The Bulldogs prowled downfield on their third drive of the period after a personal foul against the Gators put Georgia in possession at the UF 37. Cavan completed a nine-yard pass to end Charles Whittemore, then hit end Dennis Hughes for a first down at the UF 9.

On the first play of the second period, Cavan tossed a pass to Hughes who cradled the ball in the Florida end zone. McCullough's PAT extended the UGA lead to 21–0.

In weather seemingly made for alligators, Georgia was dog-paddling.

Florida's slide steepened. Brian Hipp fumbled near midfield and Georgia cornerback Mark "Craze" Stewart recovered at the UF 46. Cavan found Whittemore for a 16-yard completion and, moments later, connected with Whittemore again, slicing across the middle for a 26-yard Georgia touchdown. The conversion made it 28–0.

The Gators were clawed when they tried to start something on offense, and Georgia's amphibious assault surged forward in the closing minutes of the half.

Georgia had a first down on its 41. Cavan shot a 41-yard waterball through the rain to Hughes, then completed a pass to Farnsworth to the UF 7. With more than three minutes left in the half, many Florida fans started hitting the exits.

Two plays later, Cavan faked a handoff to Farnsworth who was creamed at the line by the Gators. Cavan, meanwhile, scooted around right end and across the UF goal line with 2:14 left in the half. McCullough's extra point ballooned the score to 35–0.

Georgia defensive tackle Bill Stanfill was an All-American and the Outland Trophy winner in 1968. Stanfill and UGA teammate Jake Scott later anchored the Miami Dolphins defense in two Super Bowl wins.

Bulldog quarterback Mike Cavan directed UGA to three touchdowns in UGA's rainy 51–0 romp over the Gators in 1968.

The third quarter began with the rain as unrelenting as the Georgia banzai. The Gators received the second half kickoff and immediately lost their grip. Stanfill slammed into Florida's Larry Rentz at the Gators' 20 and the ball squirmed loose. Bulldog left guard Terry Osbolt claimed the fumble at the UF 5.

Two plays later, Brad Johnson lanced in from the 2. McCullough's kick was wide left, his first PAT miss of the season, but at 41–0 few Georgians were grumbling.

Dooley had pulled out most of his first-stringers when Georgia headed toward the UF goal again halfway through the third period. The Bulldogs used eight minutes with Farnsworth, Johnson and second-unit quarterback Donnie Hampton running at the disheartened Florida defense. Georgia took 14 plays to reach a first and goal at the UF 8 on a sweep by Farnsworth. Hampton then rolled out around left end and legged it in for the touchdown. Soccer-style kicker Pete Rajecki replaced McCullough and made it 48–0 with 1:16 remaining in the third quarter.

By this time, many of the fans of both teams had left the stadium to drown sorrows or to party in victory. On the field, Florida still battled but Jacksonville's version of Custer's Last Stand was over. Even with time winding down, the Bulldogs' bloodlust wasn't yet quenched. The rain poured on and UGA's offense didn't miss a beat, flooding downfield as the scoreboard clock clicked off the last minutes. Georgia raised the ire of many Gators on and off the field when Rajecki come on to drill a 22-yard field goal at the 5:29 mark of the fourth quarter. The ugly affair ended with no other scoring.

Florida's 51-point loss was the worst licking in the rivalry since Georgia won 75–0 in 1942. Ironically, UF assistant coach Gene Ellenson had been a Bulldog tackle that year.

Ray Graves described the massacre as the worst loss he ever suffered as a player or coach but held no grudges due to the blowout. "When you play a rivalry like this you don't ever have enough points," Graves was quoted in the *Atlanta Jounral* and *Constitution*. "They just beat us every way you can get beat. All I can do is congratulate them on a great victory."

Georgia rushed for 293 yards and threw for 188 more for almost 500 yards net offense. Cavan had a fine day with a touchdown run and two scoring tosses. The Bulldogs defense held Florida to 91 yards on the ground, 118 through the air, and intercepted three passes.

Florida awoke from its nightmare in the Gator Bowl to clip Kentucky, 16–14, in Lexington and ease by Miami, 14–10, to end 1968 at 6–3–1.

Gators guard Guy Dennis and running back Larry Smith were selected to All-America and All-SEC first units, the third consecutive year Smith was chosen to the all-conference squad. Dennis made his second appearance on the All-SEC elite team. Defensive back Steve Tannen also was honored as a first-team All-SEC selection.

Through the 1991 season, Larry Smith was Florida's all-time second-leading rusher. He was a first-round draft choice and played in the NFL for the Los Angeles Rams and the Washington Redskins.

A 32-yard interception return for a touchdown by UGA safety Jake Scott propelled Georgia to a 17–16 win over Florida in 1967. A 1968 All-American, Scott won a NFL championship with the Miami Dolphins.

Guy Dennis, the pride of Walnut Grove, Fla., spent a decade in the NFL as an offensive lineman for Cincinnati and later Detroit. Gator tight end Jim Yarbrough was a starting offensive lineman for the Detroit Lions until his retirement in 1977.

Georgia's bubble floated over Auburn, 17–3, and Georgia Tech, 47–8, for Dooley's second SEC championship and a berth against Arkansas in the Sugar Bowl. The Bulldogs fell 16–2 in the New Orleans classic to finish at 8–1–2. In the final collegiate polls, Georgia was ranked fourth by UPI and eighth by the Associated Press.

Georgia defensive tackle Bill Stanfill and defensive back Jake Scott earned All-America honors. They also garnered All-SEC kudos for the second consecutive season and were joined on the squad by defensive end Billy Payne, tackle David Rholetter, end Dennis Hughes and punter Spike Jones. Payne would go on to become president of the Atlanta committee for the 1996 Olympic Games.

Stanfill was a first-round draft choice of the Miami Dolphins, who also selected Jack Scott. The former Bulldogs would be a prominent force in Miami's drive to greatness in the 1970s. Stalwarts of the Dolphins' "No Name Defense," Scott and Stanfill were All-Pro selections from 1971–1974 and helped the Dolphins to two world championships.

Scoring:

Georgia	14	21	13	3	—	51
Florida	0	0	0	0	—	0

UGA	TD	Kemp, 2-yard run (McCullough kick)
UGA	TD	Farnsworth, 1-yard run (McCullough kick)
UGA	TD	Hughes, 6-yard pass from Cavan (McCullough kick)
UGA	TD	Whittemore, 26-yard pass from Cavan (McCullough kick)
UGA	TD	Cavan, 3-yard run (McCullough kick)
UGA	TD	Johnson, 2-yard run (kick failed)
UGA	TD	Hampton, 2-yard run (Rajecki kick)
UGA	FG	Rajecki, 22 yards

Georgia: *Offense:* Hughes, Brice, Green, *tight end;* Rholetter, McGill, Rogers, *left tackle;* Layfield, Adkins, Jennings, *left guard;* Lyons, White, Dupriest, *center;* Rodrique, Yawn, Monk, *right guard;* Byrd, Smith, Baker, *right tackle;* Whittemore, Shaw, Outlar, *split end;* Cavan, Hampton, *quarterback;* Lawrence, Farnsworth, Smiley, *tailback;* B. Johnson, Kemp, *fullback;* Woodward, Elrod, Paine, Allen, *wingback;* McCullough, Rajecki, *placekicker;* Jones, *punter*

Defense: Payne, Daniel, Herlong, *left end;* Stanfill, Saye, Brasher, Woodall, *left tackle;* Callaway, Osbolt, *left guard;* Greer, Wood, Brown, *right guard;* Smaha, Watson, Tucker, *right tackle;* Russell, S. Johnson, Robinson, *right end;* Dicks, Teel, Couch, Tarrer, Huggins, Lopatka, *linebacker;* Stewart, Mc-Knight, Darby, Pennington, Griffin, Shirer, *halfback;* Scott, Swindle, Montgomery, *safety*

Florida: *Offense:* Peek, Maliska, *split end;* Amelung, Griffith, *left tackle;* Steen, Pilcher, *left guard;* Helton, Sinardi, Barnhart, *center;* Dennis, Stephens, *right guard;* Kiley, Morris, *right tackle;* Yarbrough, Dean, *tight end;* Rentz, *quarterback;* Christian, *tailback;* McTheny, Eckdahl, *flanker;* L. Smith, Hipp, *fullback*

Defense: Ghesquiere, Byers, Ely, *left end;* Healey, Youngblood, *left tackle;* Dorsey, Rebol, *middle guard;* Hadley, Foster, *right tackle;* Skrivanek, Hughes, *right end;* Mann, Abdelnour, M. Kelley, D. Williams, *linebacker;* Tannen, Gaisford, Hager, Faix, *cornerback;* Ely, Williamson, Albury, Burns, *safety*

	Georgia	Florida
First downs	23	10
Rushing yards	293	91
Passing yards	188	118
Pass att/comp/int	16/13/0	20/9/3
Punts/avg. yards	4/40	7/34
Fumbles lost	1	2
Penalty yards	58	15

— 1969 —

Georgia 13, Florida 13

THE NOVEMBER 8, 1969, COLLISION WOULD BE between nationally ranked teams both coming off tough losses and hoping to keep alive major bowl hopes.

It also would be the last time Ray Graves would face the Bulldogs, compiling an impressive record against three Georgia head coaches and becoming the winningest coach in Florida history.

More than 70,800 fans would be in the Gator Bowl to see if Florida could avenge the 51–0 plastering administered by the SEC champion Bulldogs in 1968.

In six decades of Florida football, no team had begun a year hotter than Graves' 1969 Gators. Paced by sophomore quarterback phenomenon John Reaves, Florida was 6–0 and ranked seventh nationally before falling in a 38–12 loss at Auburn the week before the Georgia game.

Before the loss, the Gators had upset top-ranked Houston, 59–34; beat Mississippi State, 47–35; Florida State, 21–6; Tulane, 18–17; North Carolina, 52–2; and Vanderbilt, 41–20. The Auburn loss dropped Florida to No. 13 in the national polls.

The 5–2 Bulldogs of Coach Vince Dooley also were on the rebound. Georgia had been 11th-ranked the week before meeting Florida but lost to third-ranked Tennessee, 17–3, in Athens. Georgia began the season by whipping Tulane, 35–0; Clemson, 30–0; and South Carolina, 41–16; before losing 25–17 to Ole Miss. The Bulldogs then beat Vanderbilt, 40–8, and Kentucky, 30–0, before the defeat by Tennessee. Georgia's junior quarterback Mike Cavan, who had destroyed Florida in 1968, was nursing a sore shoulder and would be replaced by Donnie Hampton, although Cavan would play.

Going into Jacksonville, the Bulldogs had slipped to 16th in the rankings, and many fans were worried about a letdown against the Gators, who were a touchdown underdog despite a better record and higher ranking.

274

"Super Soph" Gator quarterback John Reaves confers with UF coaches during the 1969 season. Reaves compiled a 1–1–1 record as a player against UGA and still ranks among the top passing quarterbacks in NCAA history. [UF Archives]

Florida followers believed John Reaves of Tampa to be the second coming of Steve Spurrier, despite the quarterback's horrible day against Auburn when he threw nine interceptions. Still, Reaves was on the brink of breaking the SEC total offense record for a season, a mark set by Georgia legend Frank Sinkwich, who had accounted for 2,187 yards over 11 games in 1942. Sinkwich was in the Gator Bowl for the contest to see if the record would change hands.

Reaves' choice receiver was sophomore flanker Carlos Alvarez, who would become one of Florida's all-time great receivers and hold many UF records. Senior end Paul Maliska, whose block of an extra point had been the difference in Florida's victory in 1967, had been seriously injured in the Auburn contest and was hospitalized.

From the outset, Georgia's secondary cloaked Alvarez and the Bulldogs' line put great pressure on Reaves.

Georgia threatened on its second possession after a punt by Florida's Hunter Bowen left them with a first down at midfield. Hampton threw a 9-yard pass to fullback Julian Smiley, and Cavan came in for a 13-yard completion to halfback Travis Paine. With Smiley and halfback Steve Farnsworth shouldering the load, the Bulldogs reached the UF 8. Farnsworth bolted over the goal line from there, but the Bulldogs were whistled for illegal motion and the score was called back. The march stalled at the 2 where Georgia faced a fourth-down decision. Dooley decided to go for the touchdown but the Floridians crunched fullback Bruce Kemp and the 'Dogs were turned away.

A 16-yard Florida punt gave Georgia another scoring chance with a first down at the UF 23. Smiley cut off left tackle for nine yards before the Gators stopped Georgia cold at the 8. Bulldog kicker Jim McCullough tried a 22-yard field goal but the ball soared wide.

Georgia's quarterback situation was further complicated when Hampton sustained a slight shoulder separation in the first period. He stayed in the game but was hampered by the injury.

Florida got its first break of the afternoon on the first snap of the second period when middle linebacker and co-captain Tom Abdelnour pounced on a fumble by the Bulldogs' Smiley at the Georgia 33. The Gators stuck to the ground with tailback Tommy Durrance and fullback Mike Rich pounding for gains down to the UGA 12. Rich then took a handoff from Reaves, dashed off tackle running over people, and went in for the game's first touchdown. Gator kicker Richard Franco tacked on the extra point, and Florida led 7–0 with 12:48 left in the half.

After the kickoff, spurred by Hampton passes for 18 and 14 yards to split end Charles Whittemore, the Bulldogs perched on the UF 10. Hampton threw again but the pass was intercepted at the goal line by Gator safety Skip Albury, who made a nifty return to the UF 34.

The Bulldogs were stunned and Reaves immediately went to the air. Knowing Alvarez was well covered, he launched completions of 14 and 22 yards to split end Andrew Cheney, then connected with Alvarez for 12 yards. The drive died at the UGA 20 and kicker Franco trotted out on fourth down for the field-goal attempt.

Graves called a pass off a fake kick. On the hike, the Bulldogs smacked reserve quarterback John Schnebly as he tried to throw and it appeared Georgia had averted a score. The Bulldog cheers quickly turned to jeers, as the back judge ruled that the play had been whistled dead before the snap while trying to clear some photographers out of the end zone. Because of the crowd noise, neither team heard the whistle; but Florida had another shot.

Graves now went for three. This time, Franco speared a 36-yarder through the uprights for a 10–0 Florida advantage with 1:34 left in the half. UGA backers referred to the field goal as the "fifth-down play."

The rivals would exchange possession six times in the third quarter before Dooley made a critical personnel change.

With Hampton having little success, the Georgia head coach sent in Cavan. The Bulldogs had a first down on their 44 after a 46-yard punt by UF's Bowen.

As if in a time warp, Cavan resumed where he had left off in the 1968 game, accelerating Georgia's offense and rolling toward the Florida end zone. Blending the run and pass, Cavan hit tight end Mike Greene for gains of 11, six and eight yards. Smiley earned eight on three carries and Cavan sliced for seven on a rollout. Georgia was threatening, the ball's nose on the UF 6.

Farnsworth didn't allow the pressure to build any further as he popped through for a Georgia touchdown. Kicker McCullough missed the extra point but Florida's lead was whittled to 10–6 with about two minutes left in the third period.

After a Gator punt, the Bulldogs took possession at the UF 46. On second down, Cavan handed off to Paine who tore into the line, broke into the secondary, and outraced everyone to the end zone. McCullough converted this time and Georgia had its first lead of the day, 13–10.

On its second possession of the final quarter, Florida found some offensive juice. Starting at their own 16, the Gators meant business, with romps of 34 and 16 yards by Tommy Durrance propelling them. The offensive bogged down at the UGA 16 and this time Graves forewent any trickery. Franco nailed a field goal from the 21 to knot the score with some five minutes to play.

With plenty of time left for either team to decide the issue, the Gators seized the initiative, stopping Georgia on downs. With the Bulldogs double-teaming Alvarez, Reaves concentrated on finding Cheney, a tactic that worked.

The pair clicked for completions of eight, 12 and 15 yards, the latter on fourth down, and Florida was suddenly sitting on the UGA 15 with less than 20 seconds left on the clock.

Franco came on again as Florida stood on the verge of pulling a last-second upset over the damned Crackers. The ball would be spotted at the UGA 22. The snap from center came back low and the holder juggled the ball. The snafu resulted in Franco's kick wobbling wide left of the uprights. What had seemed like a sure Florida win instantly became a reprieve for Georgia.

The tie was only the second of the rivalry, the other occurring in 1930 when the teams fought to a scoreless draw in Savannah.

Cavan was nailed from behind on the next to last play and collapsed leaving the field after the game, but was not injured seriously.

Florida's super sophomores, Reaves and Alvarez, had been the focus of the Georgia defense all day and the Bulldogs' effort paid off.

Ray Graves coached Florida to football prominence from 1960 to 1969. Graves's teams compiled a 6–3–1 record against Vince Dooley, Wally Butts, and Johnny Griffith of Georgia and made five bowl appearances, going 4–1. [UF Archives]

The duo was held to only three completions for 28 yards. Reaves, however, netted 147 yards in total offense to break Sinkwich's 27-year-old season record.

While Florida was disappointed about the botched game-winning field goal, Georgia lamented the three squandered scoring chances in the first half and Florida's "fifth down" field goal. The Gators had another problem. Someone burglarized their locker room after half-time and took money, watches, rings and other valuables. "Only somebody from Georgia would do a thing like that," the *Atlanta Journal* and *Constitution* quoted Florida Gov. Claude Kirk, regarding the thievery.

Georgia's season took a swan dive after Jacksonville. The Bulldogs fell 16–3 at home to Auburn and lost 6–0 at Georgia Tech. Despite a 5–4–1 record, Georgia was invited to play Nebraska in the Sun Bowl. The Bulldogs should have stayed home as the Cornhuskers mowed them down, 45–6.

Florida's victory harvest was to blossom further in 1969. The Gators beat Kentucky, 31–6, and Miami, 35–16, to win a Gator Bowl berth versus Tennessee. Reaves passed for 161 yards and a touchdown as the Gators then beat the Volunteers, 14–13, to finish at 9–1–1.

Florida's Alvarez and defensive back Steve Tannen were honored as first-team All-America selections. They were joined on the All-SEC first team by Reaves, Tommy Durrance, guard Mac Steen and end David Ghesquiere. Tannen finished his career as the second-leading interceptor in Florida history and played for the New York Jets before embarking on an acting career.

Georgia defensive guard Steve Greer and center Tommy Lyons were also named All-America. Greer and punter Spike Jones joined the Floridians on the all-conference squad, Jones for the second consecutive season.

The Ray Graves decade, a golden age in Florida football, ended with the field mentor retiring to concentrate on his UF athletic director duties. Graves led the Gators to gridiron prominence with a 70–31–4 record and four wins in five bowl trips. He also finished 6–3–1 against Georgia's Wally Butts, Johnny Griffith and Vince Dooley.

Scoring:

Florida	0	10	0	3	—	13
Georgia	0	0	13	0	—	13

UF	TD	Rich, 12-yard run (Franco kick)
UF	FG	Franco, 36 yards
UGA	TD	Farnsworth, 6-yard run (PAT failed)
UGA	TD	Paine, 46-yard run (McCullough kick)
UF	FG	Franco, 21 yards

Florida: *Offense:* Cheney, McTheny, *split end;* Griffith, Peek, *left tackle;* Williams, Conrad, *left guard;* Helton, Inardi, *center;* Amelung, Hutcherson, *right guard;* Steen, Kiley, *right tackle;* Dowdy, Yancey, *tight end;* Reaves, Schnebly, *quarterback;* Alvarez, Cheney, *flanker;* Durrance, Vinesett, *tailback;* Rich, Walker, *fullback;* Franco, Bowen, Youngblood, *kicker*

Defense: Coleman, Buchanan, *left end;* Harrell, Cole, *left tackle;* Williams, Paulson, *right tackle;* Youngblood, Shrivanek, *right end;* Ghesquiere, Powell, Abdelnour, Taggart, Kelley, Palahach, *linebackers;* Ely, Sorenson, Tannen, Clark, *cornerback;* Burns, Eckdahl, Albury, Barr, *safety*

Georgia: *Offense:* Whittemore, Robinson, *split end;* Nash, Adkins, *left tackle;* Tucker, Keith, *left guard;* Lopatka, Chamberlain, Keith, *center;* Smith, Gordon, *right guard;* Byrd, McGill, *right tackle;* Greene, Mixon Robinson, Dicharry, *tight end;* Hampton, Cavan, Montgomery, *quarterback;* Farnsworth, Allen, Campbell, *left halfback;* Phine, Elrod, Paine, *right halfback;* Smiley, Kemp, *fullback;* McCullough, Jones, *kicker*

Defense: Heard, Russell, *left end;* Brasher, Wood, Watson, *left tackle;* Callaway, McPipkin, Greer, Rogers, Daniel, Saye, *left guard;* McKnight, Shaw, *right end;* Wisdom, Kitchens, Huggins, Couch, *linebacker;* Sullivan, Shiner, Shirer, Darby, Allen, Griffin, *cornerback;* Swindle, Griffin, *safety*

	Georgia	Florida
First downs	15	20
Rushing yards	175	125
Passing yards	127	155
Return yards	27	52
Pass att/comp/int	23/13/2	42/15/0
Punts/avg. yards	6/44	9/34
Fumbles lost	1	0
Penalty yards	40	39

— 1970 —

Florida 24, Georgia 17

WITH THE PASSING PROWESS OF ALL-SEC quarterback John Reaves and the explosiveness of Georgia's offense, the Gators-Bulldogs tussle on November 7, 1970, was expected to keep the scorekeeper busy.

The Vietnam War raged on but President Nixon promised to continue a withdrawal of U.S. forces and bring 40,000 troops home by Christmas.

Doug Dickey, who played for the Gators in the early 1950s, was on the sideline in his first year as Florida head coach. He and seventh-year Georgia coach Vince Dooley would be trying to improve on the 13–13 tie from the previous year. Some forecasters favored the Bulldogs by two touchdowns.

The 5–3 Gators were trying to break a two-game losing skid in which they were butchered 38–7 at Tennessee and 63–14 in Gainesville by Auburn and a quarterback named Pat Sullivan.

Even though Reaves was leading the conference in passing and had set a new SEC total offense record in 1969, few fans and observers knew what to expect out of the Gators from week to week.

Dickey's team nipped Duke, 21–19, in their 1970 premiere, then dropped Mississippi State, 34–13. Florida was overwhelmed, 46–15, at Alabama but beat N.C. State, 14–6; Florida State, 38–27; and Richmond, 20–0, before the Tennessee and Auburn disasters.

The Gators hurdled the racial barrier in 1970 as Willie Jackson and Leonard George became the first black athletes in Florida history. Jackson's son, Willie Jr., would star for the Gators in the 1990s.

One of Dickey's top priorities was getting his linemen ready to face an extremely tough Bulldog interior. Florida was heartened by the return of junior fullback Mike Rich, who had missed three games due to injured ribs; but All-American flanker Carlos Alvarez was hampered by a bad leg. The game would be a reunion of sorts for Rich, out of Dublin, Ga., and a high school teammate of Ronnie Rogers, a defensive guard for Georgia. The two prepared to butt heads on the Gator Bowl turf.

Georgia, 4–3, had gotten off to a horrendous start as Tulane shocked the Bulldogs, 17–14, in the season opener. Georgia took out its frustration on Clemson the next week, 38–0, but then fell 7–6 at Mississippi State and 31–21 at Ole Miss. The Bulldogs scuttled Vanderbilt, 37–3, and Kentucky, 19–3, before outscoring South Carolina, 52–34, a week before Florida.

Starting quarterback Mike Cavan, injured against the Gamecocks, was replaced by second-stringer Paul Gilbert, who rallied the Bulldogs with three touchdown runs. The effort earned Gilbert Associated Press and SEC Back of the Week honors.

With Cavan still hurt, Coach Vince Dooley announced that Gilbert would get his first start of the year against the Gators.

Though most bowl scouts were elsewhere this sunny, warm Saturday, more than 70,200 wedged into the stands for the sold-out affair.

On the game's opening drive, Georgia immediately went to its power running game, mainly on the legs of sophomore back Ricky Lake. From their own 32, the 'Dogs ran down the field as Lake and backfield mate Robert Honeycutt found holes in the UF line. Gilbert kept the Gators guessing with a 15-yard completion to Rex Putnal. In 11 plays, the Red and Black had a first down at the Florida 2. Lake wasted little time from there, hurdling in for the touchdown. Kicker Kim Braswell's conversion was good and Florida trailed 7–0, having yet to touch the ball.

To almost everyone's surprise, the Gators came out running, though unable to move with any success.

The teams settled into a defensive siege. Reaves, Florida's aerial Houdini, passed little and was ineffectual. The Bulldogs continued to run well but Florida kept them out of scoring range.

Early in the second quarter, Florida marched on the ground to the UGA 12 before the Bulldogs blunted the charge. Dickey sent in Gator junior kicker Jim Getzen who drilled a 29-yard field goal, the first points of his collegiate career, to cut the Georgia lead to 7–3, a score that stood till halftime.

After the Gators were stopped on the initial possession of the second half, Georgia backs pummeled down to the UF 4 before a busted play broke their rhythm, and Braswell come on to kick a 20-yard field goal. Georgia was up 10–3.

Florida got the ball on its 20 after the kickoff and Air Reaves was cleared for takeoff.

He connected with Alvarez, a forgotten man most of the day, for a 20-yard completion, then hurled another strike to the junior receiver for 22 yards. Fullback Mike Rich helped muscle the underdog Gators downfield. A Reaves-to-Alvarez pass for eight pushed them to the UGA 7. Rich smashed across from there for the first Florida touchdown. Getzen's extra point tied it, 10–10.

But Georgia pulled itself together. Staying with the rush, the Bulldogs gobbled up yardage, reaching the UF 39 in five plays. Fullback Honeycutt tore away from several Gator defenders, romped toward the goal line, and was stopped just short of the flag. Gilbert then climaxed the 68-yard thrust with a plunge for the score and Georgia surged back in front. Braswell's kick gave them a 17–10 advantage.

Early in the fourth quarter, Reaves was sacked by Georgia's Chuck Heard and fumbled. The 'Dogs' Larry Brasher pounced on the pigskin at the Florida 37.

Georgia promptly drove to the UF 2. On the next play, Gilbert pitched to Honeycutt running wide. The Bulldog fullback bobbled the ball and was hit by UF's Jack Youngblood. The ball flew free and the Gators' cat-quick defensive end recovered it at the UF 6.

Youngblood later said he concentrated more on stripping the ball than stopping the runner: "I don't know who it was but he had it in his hands and I just snatched it away from him. Heck, the pros do it like that all the time." NFL backs would be victimized by Youngblood in a similar fashion in the coming years.

After the game, the play was considered the crucial point of the struggle but, with time now a factor in the fourth, Florida still trailed by seven.

Both teams swapped punts before Reaves, with a first down at the UF 43, went to the air on almost every play. Three plays had the Gators at the Georgia 32. Reaves then smoked a pass to Alvarez, running between defenders Buck Swindle and Bill Darby in the Georgia secondary. The "Cuban Comet" grabbed the ball at the 7 and raced in for the touchdown. Getzen's kick tied the proceedings at 17 with 5:13 remaining.

Sticking to the run, Georgia retaliated by blasting to the UF 38. Facing fourth down and out of field goal range, Dooley went for the yardage but the Gators defense overwhelmed the play.

Only two minutes showed on the clock, but Reaves and Alvarez

All-American flanker Carlos Alvarez breaks away from two Bulldogs for one of his two touchdowns in Florida's 24–17 victory over Georgia in 1970. [UF Archives]

didn't need a lot of time. On second down, the Gator gunner found back Tommy Durrance on a screen pass that went for 14 yards to the UGA 48. On the next play, Reaves spotted Alvarez again open in the UGA secondary and rocketed the ball toward him. Alvarez snared it on the gallop, reversed his field to pick up a block from split end Willie Jackson, and waltzed in for the score with 1:39 left to play. Getzen's point after handed Florida its first lead of the day, 24–17.

Gilbert went to the long bomb to try to rally the Bulldogs, but Florida's defense was ready and the upset was sealed.

In the on-field Florida celebration after the game, Reaves' jersey was ripped off his back by adoring fans. "I loved it," he later told reporters.

Reaves, though not a banner day by his standards, had come through in the clutch, completing nine of 14 passes for 166 yards, his lowest total of the season. Alvarez caught five for 135 yards and two touchdowns.

The game was a ground war for the most part, with Georgia rushing for 261 yards and Florida 233.

Dooley pointed to Youngblood's fumble recovery in the fourth period as "turning the whole game around" and Reaves agreed. "That was it when they fumbled," the Gator star told reporters. "No doubt about it."

The Gators' 24 points were the most scored by a Florida team in the series since 1956.

A week after the loss to Florida, Georgia upset Auburn, 31–17, but closed with a 17–7 loss to Georgia Tech for a 5–5 record.

Florida's good fortune spilled into the following week as the Gators chomped Kentucky, 24–13, but soured in the campaign finale: a 14–13 loss to Miami. Dickey, though, ended his first season with a respectable 7–4 mark.

Bulldog center Tommy Lyons made All-America for the second consecutive year, and Florida's Jack Youngblood also was an All-American. Youngblood and Lyons were joined on the All-SEC first-team by Florida tight end Jim Yancey and Georgians Royce Smith at guard, tackle Tom Nash, and defensive back Buz Rosenberg.

Youngblood, considered the best defensive end in Florida history, went on to become an All-Pro with the Los Angeles Rams.

This Florida mascot was one happy reptile after the Gators outscored favored Georgia 24–17 in 1970. [UF Archives]

Scoring:

Florida	0	3	7	14 —	24
Georgia	7	0	10	0 —	17

UGA	TD	Lake, 2-yard run (Braswell kick)
UF	FG	Getzen, 29 yards
UGA	FG	Braswell, 20 yards
UF	TD	Rich, 7-yard run (Getzen kick)
UGA	TD	Gilbert, 1-yard run (Braswell kick)
UF	TD	Alvarez, 32-yard pass from Reaves (Getzen kick)
UF	TD	Alvarez, 48-yard pass from Reaves (Getzen kick)

Florida: *Offense:* W. Jackson, *split end;* Dowdy, *quick tackle;* Hutcherson, *quick guard;* Kensler, *center;* Donny Williams, *strong guard;* Abbott, *strong tackle;* Yancey, *tight end;* Reaves, *quarterback;* Alvarez, *flanker;* Rich, Doel, *fullback;* Durrance, *tailback;* Getzen, *placekicker;* James, *punter*

Defense: Youngblood, *left end;* Cole, *left tackle;* Danny Williams, *right tackle;* Buchanan, Taggert, Kelley, *linebacker;* Sorenson, Faix, *cornerback;* Silman, Clifford, *safety*

Georgia: *Offense:* Whittemore, Swinford, Hunnicutt, *split end;* Lopatka, Tucker, Curington, *left tackle;* Jennings, Gordon, Sellers, *left guard;* Lyons, Poss, *center;* R. Smith, McWhorter, *right guard;* Nash, *right tackle;* Greene, *tight end;* Gilbert, *quarterback;* Montgomery, J. Smiley, *tailback;* Honeycutt, Lake, *fullback;* Putnal, *flanker;* Braswell, *placekicker;* Shirer, *punter*

Defense: Heard, Robinson, *end;* Wood, Brantley, *left tackle;* Rogers, Saye, *left guard;* Watson, McPipkin, *right guard;* Brasher, *right tackle;* Wisdom, Couch, *linebacker;* Darby, Sullivan, Rosenberg, *cornerback;* Swindle, Jackson, Shaw, Kimsey, *safety*

	Florida	Georgia
First downs	17	23
Rushing yards	233	261
Passing yards	166	138
Return yards	59	141
Pass att/comp/int	14/9/0	19/12/1
Punts/avg. yards	6/40	4/45
Fumbles lost	1	1
Penalty yards	13	23

— 1971 —

Georgia 49, Florida 7

By THE TIME FLORIDA AND GEORGIA MET ON November 6, 1971, the year was a recurring bad dream for the Gators and a cakewalk almost every weekend for the Bulldogs.

Coach Vince Dooley's Georgians were 8–0, ranked sixth in the country by the Associated Press, and had not allowed a score from three previous opponents before Florida. Only Alabama, unbeaten in SEC play, stood between Georgia and another conference title.

The Bulldogs were 21-point favorites to bury the Gators, but UF rooters were quick to point out that Florida was a two-touchdown underdog in winning the 1970 game. The UGA defense of assistant coach Erk Russell was ranked second in the country.

Georgia began 1971 by overpowering Oregon State, 56–25, then dropping Tulane, 17–7. The victors' march continued in the headlines each Sunday morning: Clemson fell, 28–0; Mississippi State, 35–7; Ole Miss, 38–7; Vanderbilt, 24–0; Kentucky, 34–0; and South Carolina, 24–0.

In Gainesville, the 2–6 Gators of second-year coach Doug Dickey started the season in a free fall to a forgettable season. Five weeks into its schedule, Florida had yet to win, losing 12–6 to Duke, 13–10 to Mississippi State, 38–0 to Alabama, 20–13 to Tennessee, and 48–7 at LSU. Florida clipped Florida State, 17–15, and Maryland, 27–23, before fifth-ranked Auburn and Heisman candidate Pat Sullivan rolled to a 40–7 win.

The Gators still had the record passing combo of quarterback John Reaves and 1969 All-American flanker Carlos Alvarez, but their magic of the past two seasons had vanished in 1971.

Fred Pancoast, the Bulldogs new offensive coordinator, was particularly worried about the Gators' duo. Pancoast had come to Georgia from Florida and had coached during the Reaves-Alvarez blitzkrieg in '69. "I've seen it happen too many times," he told reporters about the Gators' home run threat.

The gridiron fracas would be broadcast regionally by ABC with the perennial throng of some 70,000 going wild in the stadium. Scouts from the Orange and Sugar bowls were also in attendance.

Georgia's quarterback situation was unsettled. Starter Andy Johnson was recovering from a leg injury. Filling in for the talented sophomore signal-caller was senior Jimmy Ray, who had engineered the win over South Carolina.

Injuries had left the Gators without offensive guard Fred Abbott and defensive back Jimmy Barr. Alvarez also was hurting.

The game started with both squads playing fired-up defense on the first few series.

Backed up on its own 4, Georgia advanced out to its 37 before Florida held on downs. Punter Jimmy Shirer then rocketed a 50-yard kick, which gave the Gators possession on the UF 13. The Florida offense lost yardage during the series, and John James came on to punt from the UF 6. James got off a short kick and Georgia had great field position and a first down at the Florida 34 late in the first period.

Running back Jimmy Poulos was the workhorse on the seven-play Bulldog drive, churning for 25 yards on four carries as Georgia reached the UF 1. Poulos got the TD call and went airborne into the end zone for the game's first score. Kicker Kim Braswell tacked on the PAT and Georgia led 7–0 with 59 seconds left in the first quarter.

Buz "Super Frog" Rosenberg fielded a Florida punt early in the second quarter, breaking loose for a 36-yard return to the UF 27 and bringing the Georgia crowd to life.

Ricky Lake, injured and out since the Ole Miss win, entered the game and lit the fuse of the Georgia offense. The junior tailback cracked for 14 yards on six carries as the 'Dogs rammed toward the Florida goal. On the 10th play of the drive, Lake banged over from the 2-yard line. Braswell's conversion put UGA up 14–0 with 9:27 remaining before the half.

The back breaker for the Gators came little more than a minute later. Florida had the ball, first down on its 36. Reaves, under furious pressure all day, retreated to pass but the throw was picked off by Bulldog defensive end Mixon Robinson, who bolted 38 yards into the end zone. Braswell's kick was wide but bedlam still reigned in the UGA sections. Georgia's lead had bulged to 20–0.

Florida, though shaken, came surging back. From his own 20, Reaves promptly hurled his team downfield, reaching the Georgia 9 in 10 plays. The Gator ace then flicked a pass to tight end Jim Yancey alone in a corner of the end zone. Rich Franco kicked the extra point and Florida had trimmed the deficit to 20–7 at the half.

Florida's problems with the Bulldogs' tight defense continued at the outset of the second half and Georgia quickly capitalized. On their second possession, the Bulldogs, with good field position at the UF 48, used seven plays to power to the UF 5 with Ray at the reins. On a quarterback keeper, Ray bolted the remaining yards for the score. Dooley decided to go for two with Ray hitting flanker Shirer uncovered in the end zone—Georgia, 28–7.

The Gators were shut down and a punt gave Georgia the ball at its 42. Three plays punched it to the Florida 38.

Ray then launched a pass to Shirer who pulled away from two defenders and followed an escort of blockers to pay dirt. Braswell's kick extended the Georgia lead to 35–7.

Again the Florida offense was foiled and Georgia took over at its own 48 against a Gators defense that had been on the field most of the day.

The Bulldogs showed no quarter, grinding 52 yards in seven plays with Lake climaxing the drive on a 2-yard plunge. Braswell booted his fourth PAT and Georgia's spread swelled to 42–7 with 16 seconds left in the third.

By now, Dooley was substituting freely. Florida's offense was manhandled and the Georgia celebration was well underway early in the final period. A bright spot for Florida in the fourth quarter was the running of tailback Carey Geiger, a sophomore from Savannah. Geiger ran for 31 yards on three carries, including a 28-yard dash, and caught a Reaves pass for nine more.

Georgia's third-string quarterback, Steve Watson, took over where Ray left off, guiding the Bulldogs from their 48 to the UF 25 in six plays. Flanker Bob Burns, open in the flat, took a Watson pass and sped down the sideline for yet another score. Braswell's kick made the final tally 49–7, the most lopsided win in the series since the 51–0 Georgia victory in 1968.

The 'Dogs had handcuffed Reaves for the first time, limiting the Florida star to 87 yards on nine completions in 21 attempts. He failed to complete a pass to Alvarez, who was playing at less than full speed. The Bulldogs, indeed, had passed Dooley's "Reaves Test."

Georgia ran up 380 yards in total offense, including 228 on the ground, while Florida amassed 202 yards.

Georgia offensive guard and team captain Royce Smith was honored as the Chevrolet Player of the Game.

After Georgia, the Gators strung together two wins, 35–24 over

Kentucky and 45–16 at Miami, to finish 1971 at 4–7. Dickey and Dooley were even at 1–1.

Ironically, the Bulldogs presented the game ball to Pancoast, the UGA offensive mentor who had coached Alvarez and Reaves in their first year at Florida.

Reaves finished his career 1–1–1 against Georgia and was selected a first-team All-American. He left Florida with an impressive resumé. With 7,581 yards, Reaves was the NCAA's all-time leading passer and held the SEC record for touchdown passes with 56. He was a first-round draft pick of the Philadelphia Eagles and also played for Cincinnati, Minnesota and Houston in the NFL. Reaves played for Steve Spurrier's Tampa Bay team in the United States Football League and later returned to Florida as an assistant coach under Spurrier.

Carlos Alvarez graduated as the Gators' career reception leader and top yardage gainer, among other records. Florida punter John James went on to become a 12-year veteran in the NFL for Atlanta, Detroit and Houston.

With the win over Florida, Georgia rose to 9–0, but there was heartbreak in Athens the next week in a showdown with high-powered Auburn. The Bulldogs fell 35–20 as Pat Sullivan's passing onslaught all but cemented his grip on the Heisman Trophy. The loss also paved the way for Alabama to clinch the SEC championship.

Georgia ended the regular season with a 28–24 triumph over Georgia Tech and accepted a bid to play North Carolina, coached by Dooley's brother, Bill, in the Gator Bowl. A 25-yard Poulos touchdown run was the difference as the Bulldogs nipped the Tar Heels, 7–3.

With a sterling 11–1 slate, the Bulldogs finished seventh-ranked in the AP poll and eighth in the UPI standings.

Royce Smith, UGA's captain and an offensive guard, was the Chevrolet Player of the Game in the Bulldogs' 49–7 win over Florida in 1971. He was named All-American and All-SEC.

Georgia's Royce Smith garnered first-team All-America accolades. Smith, tackle Tom Nash and defensive back Buz Rosenberg made the All-SEC first-squad for the second year in a row and were joined by center Kendall Keith, defensive end Mixon Robinson and linebacker Chip Wisdom.

Scoring:

Georgia	7	13	22	7	—	49
Florida	0	7	0	0	—	7

UGA	TD	Poulos, 1-yard run (Braswell kick)
UGA	TD	Lake, 2-yard run (Braswell kick)
UGA	TD	Robinson, 38-yard pass interception (kick failed)
UF	TD	Yancey, 9-yard pass from Reaves (Franco kick)
UGA	TD	Ray, 5-yard run (Shirer pass from Ray)
UGA	TD	Shirer, 38-yard pass from Ray (Braswell kick)
UGA	TD	Lake, 2-yard run (Braswell kick)
UGA	TD	Burns, 25-yard pass from Watson (Braswell kick)

Georgia: *Offense:* Putnal, Hunnicutt, *split end;* Greene, Curington, Tucker, *left tackle;* McWhorter, Jennings, *left guard;* Keith, Hammond, *center;* R. Smith, B. Smith, Jim McPipkin, *right guard;* Nash, Fersen, *right tackle;* Brice, Eskew, *tight end;* Ray, Watson, *quarterback;* Poulos, Lake, Bissell, *tailback;* Honeycutt, Allen, *fullback;* Burns, *flanker;* Braswell, *placekicker;* Shirer, *punter*

Defense: Robinson, Carter, Smoak, *end;* Cagle, Bruce, *left tackle;* P. McPipkin, D. Jones, *left guard;* D. Watson, Burnett, *right guard;* Heard, Hester, McKnight, *right tackle;* Wisdom, Couch, Kitchens, Sleek, *linebacker;* Rosenberg, Swinford, Harper, Milam, *cornerback;* Golden, Jackson, Sullivan, Ellspermann, Conn, *safety*

Florida: *Offense:* W. Jackson, *split end;* Condon, *quick tackle;* Dowdy, *quick guard;* M. King, *center;* K. Anderson, *strong guard;* Padgett, *strong tackle;* Yancey, *tight end;* Reaves, *quarterback;* Alvarez, Boardman, *flanker;* Geiger, Durrance, *tailback;* M. Rich, *fullback;* Franco, *placekicker;* James, *punter*

Defense: M. Moore, *left end;* Buchanan, *left tackle;* Hitchcock, *middle guard;* Fuller, *right tackle;* Harrell, *right end;* Browne, *middle linebacker;* Poff, *weak linebacker;* H. Clark, Sorenson, *cornerback;* Mallory, Revels, *safety*

	Georgia	Florida
First downs	22	11
Rushes/yards	65/228	36/98
Passing yards	152	104
Return yards	127	0
Pass att/comp/int	13/8/0	27/10/1
Punts/avg. yards	4/44	11/38
Fumbles lost	3	2
Penalty yards	32	41

— 1972 —

Georgia 10, Florida 7

FOUR DAYS BEFORE THE GEORGIA-FLORIDA game, President Richard M. Nixon buried challenger George McGovern to win reelection, the latest in a spasm of tumultuous events to mark 1972.

With less than sparkling records, it was highly unlikely that the Gators and Bulldogs could draw much attention away from the Munich Olympics massacre, the Watergate indictments, and B-52 strikes into North Vietnam.

Yet developments on the national and global fronts did not dissuade 67,000 fans from turning out at the Gator Bowl for the November 11, 1972, pigskin proceedings.

Georgia was after its 30th win over the Gators, a duel billed as a matchup between quick-footed Florida running back Nat Moore and Georgia's Jimmy Poulos. Both backs were a similar 5–11 and 180 pounds with running styles that confused tacklers. While Poulos had helped the Bulldogs to victory in the 1971 game, Moore was a junior college transfer who hadn't played football for two years. He had, however, scored nine touchdowns in Florida's first six contests and was the SEC's top rusher.

The 5–3 Bulldogs were not nearly as potent as the 11–1 team of the previous year.

Georgia's season began with a 24–14 win over Baylor but Tulane surprised them, 24–13, in New Orleans. The 'Dogs dropped N.C. State, 28–22; fell 25–7 to Alabama; clipped Ole Miss, 14–13; Vanderbilt, 28–3; and Kentucky, 13–7, before a shutout 14–0 loss to Tennessee prior to meeting the Gators. The defeat by the Volunteers virtually wiped out Georgia's SEC title chances and damaged the 'Dogs' bowl hopes.

The 3–3 Gators of third-year coach Doug Dickey were rated a two-point favorite to avenge the 49–7 shelling administered by Geor-

Gator running back Nat Moore scored a touchdown, but Florida lost to Georgia 10–7 in 1972. After setting several UF rushing records, Moore went on to a stellar career with the Miami Dolphins.

gia in the previous year's contest. With only four seniors, Dickey had a young squad.

Florida lost its opener, 21–14, to SMU, beat Mississippi State, 28–13, and Florida State, 42–13, before losing 24–7 to Alabama on the road. The Gators then toppled Ole Miss, 16–0, and lost 26–20 at home to Auburn.

The battle in Jacksonville was overshadowed in the SEC, and nationally, by the clash between second-ranked Alabama and sixth-rated LSU in Birmingham. But the party on the St. Johns was not dampened by any lack of enthusiasm, and neither team gave a damn about anything outside the Gator Bowl by the 2 p.m. kickoff.

Florida opened on offense pushing the Bulldogs downfield on its first possession. The Gators reached the UGA 13, but quarterback Chan Gailey fumbled and Georgia recovered.

Erk Russell's defenders were doing a good job of containing Moore, but the Georgia offense was being strangled by a snarling Gators defense. Adding pressure was the fact that Georgia hadn't scored a touchdown on offense in seven quarters, dating to the second period of the Kentucky game.

The first quarter ended with neither team mounting a sustained offensive other than Florida's opening incursion.

With two minutes gone in the second period, Gator quarterback Dave Bowden, from the UGA 47, scrambled back and unloaded to

Moore in the clear at the Georgia 25. Both Moore and Bulldog line-backer Keith Harris went up for the ball, but it was Moore who came down with it, streaking the remaining yardage for a 47-yard touchdown that brought the Florida crowd out of its seats. Florida kicker Clifton Aust's extra point was true and the Gators owned a 7–0 advantage.

The struggle settled into a defensive grind until the last minutes of the half, when both teams came up short on field-goal attempts. Florida clung to its touchdown lead going into the locker room.

The third quarter was much like the first half with the Gators, led by middle linebacker Fred Abbott, keeping Georgia pinned with bad field position but unable to kindle anything of their own. Whenever Florida appeared to be about to break out on offense, they fell victim to penalties.

The stalemate ground on into the opening minutes of the final quarter when Dickey attempted a little razzle-dazzle, hoping to catch Georgia napping near midfield. Moore took a handoff, faked a run, then lofted a halfback option pass that Georgia defensive back Buz Rosenberg alertly picked off, returning it 11 yards to the UF 46.

The Bulldogs, banging it out on the ground most of the afternoon, caught the Gators off-guard when quarterback Andy Johnson rolled to his right and passed over the middle to split end Rex Putnal, crossing between two Gators at the UF 10. Thinking run, Florida

Bulldog quarterback Andy John-son hurled a 44-yard pass to Rex Putnal in Georgia's 1972 win over Florida.

Georgia kicker Kim Braswell nailed a 37-yard field goal with 50 seconds left to down the slightly-favored Gators in 1972.

safety Jim Revels had come up on the play; but Putnal streaked by him, snared the pass, and was in the Florida end zone seconds later. Kim Braswell kicked the extra point to tie it at 7–7 and Georgia seemed to have the momentum.

Again the defenses rose up. Several exchanges of punts ultimately gave Florida a first down at its own 10 with 4:17 remaining. Gator back Vince Kendrick slammed for nine and Moore slashed out to the UF 22.

On third down moments later, quarterback Bowden tried to hand off to back Carey Geiger but the ball fell behind him. Georgia defensive guard Joe McPipkin had the pigskin when the players unpiled at the UF 30 and the UGA throng was alive again. With 2:04 left, Braswell began warming up on the sideline.

Georgia's backs plowed down to the UF 21, but it was fourth down and decision time. Dooley called a timeout with 50 seconds left and decided to let Braswell try the field goal. The distance would be about 37 yards and almost exactly on the spot where the left-footed kicker had missed his earlier attempt late in the second quarter.

The stadium fell quiet as Braswell readied to kick.

The ball was set down, Braswell punched it, and the ball fluttered upward. It was not a particularly strong kick and few drew breath as the dying duck wobbled toward the goalpost.

The ball barely skimmed over the crossbar. As the referees signaled three points, the Gator Bowl erupted with Georgians cheering and Floridians jeering.

Soon after, Vince Dooley was given a victory ride on the shoulders of his players to greet Doug Dickey in the midfield pandemonium.

Braswell told reporters the earlier miss had not dismayed him. "I hit it real good, but it didn't go where I wanted it to. I felt real good about the second one and it went through. I don't care if I kick it three yards or 55 yards as long as it goes through."

The Georgia defense, headlined by McPipkin, Tommy Smoak, Dan Jones, and David McKnight, held Moore to 64 total yards. Geiger gained 55 yards for Florida while UGA's Poulos rushed for 52.

The Gators' spiral slowed with a 40–0 breather over Kentucky and a 3–3 tie with LSU, before a 17–6 victory against Miami and a 28–24 defeat to North Carolina. Dickey's 5–5–1 record was only slightly better than the 4–7 worksheet in 1971, and he was 1–2 against Georgia.

Florida's Nat Moore and linebacker Fred Abbott were named first-team All-SEC honorees.

The Bulldogs closed the campaign with a 27–10 defeat at Auburn and a 27–7 win in Athens over Georgia Tech to go 7–4, Dooley's seventh winning season in nine years at Georgia.

Scoring:

Georgia	0	0	0	10	—	10
Florida	0	7	0	0	—	7

UF	TD	Moore, 47-yard pass from Bowden (Aust kick)
UGA	TD	Putnal, 44-yard pass from Johnson (Braswell kick)
UGA	FG	Braswell, 37 yards

Georgia: *Offense:* Putnal, *split end;* Curington, *left tackle;* McWhorter, *left guard;* Hammond, *center;* Jim McPipkin, *right guard;* Fersen, *right tackle;* Hunnicutt, *tight end;* A. Johnson, *quarterback;* Poulos, Bissell, Farnsworth, *tailback;* Honeycutt, Allen, *fullback;* Burns, King, *flanker;* Braswell, *place-kicker;* Golden, *punter*

Defense: Smoak, Ellspermann, *end;* Bruce, Cagle, *left tackle;* Joe McPipkin, Burnett, *left guard;* Jones, Kinnebrew, *right guard;* McKnight, Hester, *right tackle;* Lake, Harris, Pilcher, Sleek, *linebacker;* Swinford, West, Rosenberg, White, *cornerback;* Jackson, Golden, Conn, *safety*

Florida: *Offense:* Jackson, J. Parker, *split end;* P. Parker, Padgett, *quick tackle;* Lawless, Williams, *quick guard;* Kynes, R. Moore, *center;* Stanfield, Iannerelli, *strong guard;* Hackney, Padgett, *strong tackle;* Foldberg, Nugent, *tight end;* Bowden, Gailey, *quarterback;* Boardman, McGriff, *fullback;* N. Moore, Summers, *tailback;* V. Kendrick, Geiger, *flanker;* Aust, J. Williams, *placekicker;* Morrison, *punter*

Defense: Browne, Gowland, *left end;* Lacer, Starkey, *left tackle;* Hitchcock, Griffith, *right tackle;* P. Kendrick, M. Moore, *right end;* Ortega, Boedy, *strong linebacker;* Abbott, Green, *middle linebacker;* Poff, Cameron, *weak linebacker;* Sever, Talbot, George, Dorminy, *cornerback;* Fields, Ball, Revels, Clifford, *safety*

	Georgia	Florida
First downs	14	12
Rushes/yards	57/188	46/137
Passing yards	76	152
Return yards	17	39
Pass att/comp/int	11/4/0	20/8/1
Punts/avg. yards	10/34	8/37
Fumbles/lost	3/1	4/3
Penalties/yards	2/10	6/37

— 1973 —

Florida 11, Georgia 10

WITH 18 STARTERS RETURNING, FLORIDA WAS picked by *Playboy* magazine to win the 1973 national championship, but the Gators' year had been a kamikaze ride to nowhere heading into the November 10 encounter with Georgia.

Seven games into the season, the Gators were 3–4. Many fans were mumbling that *Playboy* should stick to centerfolds and drop its football predictions. Some of Florida's woes were due to star running back Nat Moore being injured and lost for the season.

At 1–4 in the SEC, Coach Doug Dickey's Gators were in the conference cellar, but coming off a startling road upset of 19th-ranked Auburn. No one knew how the erratic Gators would do when they took the field against Georgia.

The 4–3–1 Bulldogs also were hoping to build on an upset, having won the previous week at nationally-ranked Tennessee.

Florida's sophomore quarterback Don Gaffney and UF defensive end Ricky Browne were the heroes of the Auburn win, with Browne being named SEC Lineman of the Week. Gaffney had thrown a touchdown pass against the Tigers, and Dickey tapped him to make his first start of the year against Georgia.

With the preseason hype, all was well in Gainesville in the first two weeks of the year. Florida mastered Kansas State, 21–10, in its first game and edged Southern Mississippi, 14–13. Then the roof collapsed. Mississippi State racked the Gators, 33–12; LSU won, 24–3; and Alabama coasted, 35–14. The slide continued with a 13–10 loss at home to Ole Miss before Florida raised some eyebrows with a 12–8 win at Auburn.

Vince Dooley was observing his 10th anniversary at Georgia, but his Bulldogs were not much cause for celebration in Athens other than the Tennessee victory they had delivered.

Georgia tied Pittsburgh, 7–7, to begin the season, then socked Clemson, 31–14, and N.C. State, 31–12. The Bulldogs lost 28–14 to Alabama in Tuscaloosa and battered Ole Miss, 20–0, but fell 18–14 at Vanderbilt and 12–7 to Kentucky in Athens.

A measure of redemption came the following week when the Bulldogs won a thriller, 35–31, over Tennessee. Georgia, though, came out of it battered, with linebacker Butch Box and flanker Kirk Price lost for the season.

As usual, the Georgia defense was solid, allowing only 15.3 points per game. On the other side of the ball, the Bulldogs were led by senior quarterback Andy Johnson and a rushing offense compiling more than 200 yards per game, featuring tailback Jimmy "The Flying Greek" Poulos and teammates Bob Burns and Horace King.

Saturday broke cold and windy as a sellout crowd of approximately 70,000 filled the Gator Bowl. Thousands more watched the regionally televised game on ABC-TV. Earlier in the year, the network had decided to telecast the contest, but canceled its plans after both teams got off to such mediocre starts. But the rivals' impressive wins the previous week brought ABC back to Jacksonville. The Bulldogs were slight favorites to win their third in a row over the Gators.

In addition to making his first start, Gaffney would be playing in his hometown. Many fans wondered if the pressure would rattle the youngster.

Gaffney quieted those fears shortly after the kickoff. On a fourth-down pass in the game's opening minutes, he hit receiver Joel Parker, loose in the UGA secondary, with a short throw. In what seemed like infinity for Georgia fans, safety Don Golden finally pulled down Parker at the UGA 16. Florida reached the 11 before kicker Larry Williams nailed an 18-yard field goal to give his team first blood at 3–0.

Early in the second period, Georgia began to find some weak spots in the Gators' hides as its commanding running game cranked up. Beginning on their 19, the Bulldogs pistoned downfield and, 79 yards later, were lined up on the Florida 2 in a fourth-down situation.

Quarterback Johnson was piled under by Gator linebacker Ralph Ortega and UF teammate Tyson Sever. The fans in Orange and Blue roared their approval.

Florida's offense, though, was stopped on three plays and Georgia took over at the UF 44 after the ensuing punt. The Bulldogs promptly drove the Gators 15, sticking to the ground. On the next play, Johnson smoked a strike to receiver Richard Appleby, who grabbed the ball just inside the UF end zone and within inches of the sideline. The officials signaled touchdown but television replays indicated that he made the catch out of bounds. To the displeasure of Florida fans, the play stood and Allan Leavitt's conversion made it Georgia, 7–3, with 3:02 remaining in the half.

Both defenses ruled through most of the third quarter but, late in the period, Georgia finally ground into Floridaland. When the 'Dogs were halted seconds into the final quarter, Leavitt, the freshman kicker, came on and speared a 42-yard field goal to lengthen the Georgia lead to 10–3.

After the teams swapped possessions, Florida's Gaffney went to work against the wind. Mixing the run and pass, the Gators approached midfield. Gaffney then connected with wide receiver Lee McGriff running a sideline pattern for a 33-yard reception to the UGA 35.

Faced with fourth and five at the UGA 30 and with time slipping away, Dickey decided to go for it. Gaffney coolly drifted back and connected with Joel Parker for 10 yards. The Gators remained alive.

James Richards slammed off tackle for eight yards, but Thom Clifford was stacked up for no gain. The Gators were then penalized five yards back to the UGA 18 where they faced a third and seven.

With the stadium rocking, Gaffney dropped back in the pocket and flipped a pass toward Vince Kendrick who had open ground in front

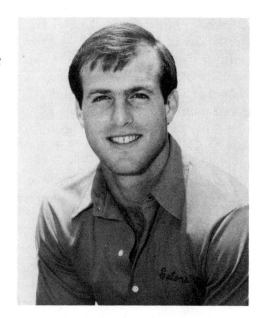

Shown here as a Florida assistant coach, Lee McGriff was one of the heroes of UF's 1973 triumph, hauling in a fourth down touchdown pass from Don Gaffney in the fourth quarter.

Making his first start and in front of a hometown crowd in Jacksonville, UF sophomore quarterback Don Gaffney spurred the underdog Gators to an incredible 11–10 win over Georgia in 1973.

of him at the 15. But the Florida tailback tripped and fell, the ball bounded away, and the Gators had another critical fourth-down decision with four minutes left.

Dickey played out his hand with Gaffney, praying Florida's lucky streak was not over. With the crowd noise at a deafening height, Gaffney handled the snap and stepped back to pass as several Bulldogs clawed toward him.

Looking downfield, he scrambled out of the pocket and shot a pass over the middle. McGriff had a Bulldog draped over his back and two other Georgians crossing in front of him, but Gaffney's throw was on the money and the Florida wide receiver pulled it in for the touchdown.

The Gators were within a point at 10–9, and Dickey decided there would be no tie this blustery afternoon.

Florida lined up to go for the two-point conversion and Gaffney pulled back. Would he run or pass? The Gator took a long look over the field, set up, and rocketed a pass over the middle toward end Hank Foldberg cutting across the back of the end zone. To the thundering of Florida cheers, Foldberg gathered in the ball and the Gators led, 11–10. It was an 80-yard, 13-play drive from which the Bulldogs would not recover. Florida blasted them after the kickoff to preserve one of the sweetest Gator wins in the series' history.

Dickey and Gaffney had played the game like riverboat gamblers, taking home a gutsy victory to avenge the last-minute loss to Georgia in 1972.

"Florida defied all odds and the wind on that final drive," a dejected Vince Dooley said after the game.

Georgia outmanned Auburn, 28–14, a week later and smacked Georgia Tech, 10–3, to face Maryland in the Peach Bowl. The Bulldogs prevailed, 17–16, to end at 7–4–1 and bring Dooley's bowl record at Georgia to 4–3. Bulldog guard Mac McWhorter was honored as a first-team All-SEC selection.

The Gators finished the regular season with a flourish, beating Kentucky, 20–18; Miami, 14–7; and Florida State, 49–0, to wrap up a berth in the Tangerine Bowl against Miami of Ohio. The Redskins ended Florida's five-game winning streak, outscoring the Gators 16–7 in Dickey's first of three consecutive postseason appearances.

Gators selected to the All-SEC first team were defensive end Ricky Browne, defensive back Jim Revels and linebacker Ralph Ortega. Running back Nat Moore left Florida with several rushing records and became an All-Pro receiver with the Miami Dolphins.

There was joy in Gatorland, for not only had Florida won at Auburn but they had beaten their main antagonists—Georgia, Florida State and Miami—all in the same season, a rare feat for the Orange and Blue.

Scoring:

Florida	3	0	0	8	—	11
Georgia	0	7	0	3	—	10

UF	FG	Williams, 18 yards
UGA	TD	Appleby, 15-yard pass from Johnson (Leavitt kick)
UGA	FG	Leavitt, 42 yards
UF	TD	McGriff, 18-yard pass from Gaffney (Foldberg pass from Gaffney)

Florida: *Offense:* McGriff, *split end;* M. Williams, *left tackle;* Loper, *left guard;* J. Stephens, *center;* Lawless, *right guard;* Padgett, *right tackle;* Foldberg, *tight end;* Gaffney, Bowden, *quarterback;* Parker, *flanker;* Richards, V. Kendrick, *tailback;* DuBose, Clifford, *fullback;* Williams, *placekicker;* Morrison, *punter*

Defense: R. Browne, *left end;* Lacer, *left tackle;* Hitchcock, *right tackle;* P. Kendrick, *right end;* Ortega, E. Moore, Cameron, *linebacker;* Sever, A. Butler, *cornerback;* Fields, Revels, *safety*

Georgia: *Offense:* Harper, Christianson, *split end;* Curington, Collier, *left tackle;* McWhorter, Dantzler, *left guard;* Hammond, V. Smith, *center;* Baker, Jim McPipkin, *right guard;* Hertwig, *right tackle;* Appleby, *tight end;* A. Johnson, Davis, *quarterback;* Poulos, Reid, Farnsworth, *tailback;* King, *fullback;* Burns, Harrison, *flanker;* Leavitt, *placekicker;* Golden, *punter*

Defense: McKnight, Russell, *end;* Spivey, Bruce, *left tackle;* Kinnebrew, Joe McPipkin, *left guard;* Jones, Hester, Wiggins, *right guard;* Cagle, *right tackle;* J. Baker, Holt, Harris, *linebacker;* West, Taylor, Conn, Schwak, *cornerback;* Golden, Wilson, Jackson, Ansley, *safety*

	Florida	Georgia
First downs	11	15
Rushes/yards	39/96	62/212
Passing yards	153	29
Return yards	14	2
Pass att/comp/int	21/10/0	7/3/0
Punts/avg. yards	7/36	7/30
Fumbles/lost	0/0	4/1
Penalties/yards	6/62	5/29

— 1974 —

Georgia 17, Florida 16

R**ANKED SIXTH IN THE COUNTRY, SAVORING**
an upset of mighty Auburn, and with a Sugar Bowl invitation in
hand, Florida spirits soared as the Gators girded for the November 9
joust with Georgia.

"It's our bowl game," UGA coach Vince Dooley told reporters
before the fracas in Jacksonville. Florida, 7–1, and Georgia, 5–3,
were both 3–1 in the SEC and still in the romp for the championship.

The hottest player on either team was Georgia sophomore quarterback Matt Robinson who was the SEC total offense leader. Robinson
had passed for 949 yards, run for 215, and thrown or rushed for 13
touchdowns in Georgia's first eight games.

The Gators' offense was versatile and deadly. Quarterback Don
Gaffney ran the wishbone attack like a well-oiled engine and was
complemented by the inside running of Jimmy DuBose and the
outside threat of Tony Green. Gator wide-receiver Lee McGriff led
the conference in receptions and had six touchdowns. Gaffney and
McGriff had teamed together several critical times against Georgia a
year earlier in Jacksonville.

Florida's Achilles heel was pass defense. Although they led the
SEC with 16 interceptions, the Gators were surrendering an average
of 162 yards a game through the air, worst in the conference.

Usually strong on defense, Georgia also had been giving up a lot
of real estate. The offense was averaging 34 points per game, best in
the SEC; but Bulldog opponents were averaging 25 points an outing,
putting Georgia last in scoring defense. The game figured to be an
offensive shootout, with Gaffney and Robinson providing most of
the firepower.

Florida's year began with a 21–17 win over California, a 17–10 victory against Maryland, followed by a 29–13 decision over Mississippi
State. The Gators then beat LSU, 24–14, but were upset, 24–10, at

Vanderbilt. Florida downed Florida State, 24–14, and Duke, 30–13, before ambushing Auburn, 25–14, at Florida Field, the second consecutive win over the Tigers. DuBose rambled for 143 yards on 25 carries in the Auburn game to earn SEC Offensive Player of the Week kudos.

Georgia's run in 1974 had been as unpredictable as a blind date. The Bulldogs outlasted Oregon State, 48–35; lost 38–14 at Mississippi State; bombarded South Carolina, 52–14; fell 28–24 at Clemson; ripped Ole Miss, 49–0; Vanderbilt, 38–31; and Kentucky, 24–20, before succumbing to Houston, 31–24, a week before the Florida game. The Houston loss virtually ended any hope of a postseason bid for Georgia.

What concerned Georgia fans was the ease with which the Gators moved on Auburn, which had one of the best defenses in the nation. Florida gained 361 yards, 324 of it on the ground against the Tigers.

More than 70,000 packed the Gator Bowl to see if favored Florida would win its second consecutive game over Georgia, something the Gators hadn't done since 1962–1963.

The Bulldogs ran with success in the contest's opening minutes and, before many fans were settled in their seats, had swarmed into Gator territory. But UF right cornerback Randy Talbot intercepted a pass at the Gators' 2, halting the drive. With Gaffney's nifty ball handling, the Florida wishbone offense broke down the field, running up four first downs to reach the UGA 24 before the Bulldog defenders came out of the kennel. On fourth down, Dickey decided to try a 44-yard field goal and sent in kicker David Posey. But holder Buster Morrison fumbled the snap and Georgia safety David Schwak recovered at the UGA 34. So far, the fans had seen a track meet with the defenses coming through at the last minute.

On a third and six, Georgia's Robinson hit tight end Richard Appleby for 16. On another third-down play, Robinson faked a run inside, then whipped outside for 31 yards to the Florida 8. Running back Horace King crashed for five yards but lost two on the next play. On third down, Robinson pitched back to King who cut to his right and cruised into the end zone. Kicker Allan Leavitt made the extra point to extend Georgia's lead to 7–0.

Florida decided to go with sophomore Jimmy Fisher at quarterback early in the second period, a move that proved disastrous. The Gators already were in trouble, having started inside their own 10. Georgia guard Chuck Kinnebrew then nailed Fisher for a two-yard loss to the 7. On the next play, Fisher dropped back into his own end

Horace King scored two short-range touchdowns in Georgia's 17–16 upset triumph against the Gators in 1974.

zone to pass, but slipped and fell on the damp turf without being touched. The automatic safety gave Georgia a 9–0 advantage with 13:26 to play in the half.

Gaffney cranked up the Gators' offense in the last minute before intermission. Finding a seam in the UGA secondary, he drilled consecutive 17-yard completions to McGriff to reach the Georgia 18, but the half ended before Florida could do any more damage.

The inflamed Gators burst out of the locker room intent on burying the upstarts in the third quarter. Gaffney immediately went to the air, connecting with McGriff for a 25-yard completion to the UGA 37. DuBose went to work, bruising the Georgians with runs for seven, seven and nine during the drive. With less than five minutes elapsed in the third period, the Gators had the ball on the UGA 3. Gaffney flipped a quick pass to Larry Brinson in the end zone and Florida was back in the game. Posey's conversion trimmed the Bulldog lead to two, 9–7.

Georgia appeared unbothered by the score. The Bulldogs embarked on an assault that quickly put them on Florida's side of the 50. Then Horace King sprang free and looked headed for a Georgia touchdown. But the fleet running back bobbled the ball and UF's Alvin Cowans recovered the fumble. With Gaffney at the controls, the Gators again crashed downfield. Gaffney zeroed in on McGriff for a 15-yard completion to the UF 43. The pair connected on two more passes for 31 yards and a first down inside the UGA 30. The

'Dogs would allow no more, however, and Florida brought on the field-goal unit. Posey's kick was good and Florida led for the first time, 10–9, at the 3:28 mark of the third quarter.

The underdog Georgians had fought the Gators on almost even terms to this point, even though Florida was piling up the yardage. The scoreboard told a tale of a tussle; the Bulldogs were not yet listed in the obituaries.

Taking the kickoff, Georgia began a drive with Robinson going to the pass. Aided by two penalties against Florida, Robinson hit receiver Mark Wilson for a 16-yard gain and a first down at the UF 29.

Georgia nosed to the 5-yard line in the early moments of the fourth period when King, looking for redemption after his third-quarter fumble, took a handoff and tore around right end, escaping the Gators' frenzied rush to cross the goal line. Leading 15–10, Dooley decided to go for two with 13:21 left to play. On the conversion attempt, Robinson drifted back to pass and floated the ball to Appleby running free in the end zone. Georgia 17, Florida 10, with plenty of time left and Gaffney getting the ball again.

The teams swapped possessions and tension heightened as the clock neared the five-minute mark. Florida took over at its 13 and went to work with the game on the line. In nine plays, the Gators reached the UGA 23 and the stadium was on fire.

Gaffney took the snap and backpedaled to pass. He saw McGriff knifing through the UGA secondary at the 3 and hurled the ball toward him, but Bulldog roverback Abb Ansley got a hand on it and pulled it in for the interception. Moments later, Glynn Harrison broke free of the Gators' defense and sprinted 87 yards to the UF end zone. Georgia was offside on the play, however, and the score was nullified.

Florida got the ball back with 2:10 remaining. Gaffney took the Gators in six plays to the UGA 4 with less than a minute left.

From there, Gaffney tried to pass but his receivers were covered. Scrambling to his left, the slippery quarterback tucked in the ball and raced across the goal line as the UF sections exploded.

Trailing 17–16, Dickey went for the two-point conversion and the win. The scene was oddly reminiscent of the previous year's game in which the Gators, down by a point with under four minutes left, went for two. The gamble paid off then with Gaffney finding end Hank Foldberg to give Florida an 11–10 victory. Could Gaffney find another ace in the hole?

Amid the storm of fan noise, Gaffney took the snap and tried to set up a screen pass to DuBose. The Gator fullback got his hands on the ball, but the pass was slightly underthrown and he couldn't hang on to it when slammed by the Bulldogs' Dave Schwak.

With Georgia cheers ringing through the stadium, the Gators tried an onside kick. A personal foul against the Bulldogs meant that Florida's Posey would get to boot the ball from the UGA 45. But the Gators' last hope died when Chip Miller recovered the kick for the 'Dogs. Georgia reveled in one of the biggest upsets in the series' history. Dooley was given a victory ride across the field on the shoulders of his jubilant players.

The Bulldogs had been outrushed and outpassed but the scoreboard showed the bottom line: 17–16, Georgia.

The shock waves of the Georgia uprising apparently had not subsided for Florida a week later as Kentucky walloped the Gators, 41–24, in Lexington. Dickey's squad regrouped to beat Miami, 31–7, and headed to New Orlean's Sugar Bowl with an 8–3 worksheet to meet Nebraska.

The Gators jumped out to a 10–0 halftime lead over the Cornhuskers but couldn't hold on, losing 13–10 to finish at 8–4, Dickey's third winning season in five years.

Gators linebacker Ralph Ortega and guard Burton Lawless garnered first-team All-America honors. Ortega was selected for the second consecutive year to the All-SEC team and was joined by linebacker Glenn Cameron, split end Lee McGriff, defensive end Preston Kendrick and defensive back Randy Talbot.

Lawless was drafted by the Dallas Cowboys and played in the NFL until a serious farm accident ended his career after the 1981 season. Ortega played for the Atlanta Falcons and Miami Dolphins in a pro career lasting until 1980. Cameron was a first-round draft choice and started for the Cincinnati Bengals for a decade.

Georgia fell at Auburn, 17–13, and was humbled 34–14 at home by Georgia Tech, but still received a bid to play Miami of Ohio in the Tangerine Bowl. The Redskins, who handled Florida in the same bowl the year before, topped the Bulldogs, 21–10, to extend their winning streak to 23 games and leave Georgia with a 6–6 record.

Bulldog offensive tackle Craig Hertwig was named All-America and was a member of the All-SEC first team with running back Glynn Harrison and guard Randy Johnson. Hertwig and Horace King were drafted by the Detroit Lions, while linebacker David McKnight was chosen by Baltimore and tackle Barry Collier by San Diego.

The bowl loss resulted in an outburst of anti-Dooley sentiment in Athens and many fans called for the coach's head, some hanging him in effigy. Dooley weathered the typhoon of '74, but remembers it as one of the worst experiences in his coaching career.

Scoring:

Georgia	7	2	0	8	—	17
Florida	0	0	10	6	—	16

UGA	TD	King, 5-yard run (Leavitt kick)
UGA	Safety	Fisher fell in end zone
UF	TD	Brinson, 3-yard pass from Gaffney (Posey kick)
UF	FG	Posey, 25 yards
UGA	TD	King, 5-yard run (Appleby pass from Robinson)
UF	TD	Gaffney, 4-yard run (pass failed)

Georgia: *Offense:* Mark Wilson, Davis, *split end;* Collier, Helms, *left tackle;* S. Wilson, Parrish, *left guard;* Smith, Legg, *center;* R. Johnson, Hendrix, *right guard;* Hertwig, *right tackle;* Appleby, *tight end;* Robinson, Goff, *quarterback;* Harrison, Reid, Pollard, King, Williams, *running back;* Washington, Box, *flanker;* Leavitt, *placekicker;* Dilts, *punter*

Defense: McKnight, *left end;* Reider, Brad Thompson, *left tackle;* Mike Wilson, Spivey, *left guard;* Kinnebrew, Baker, *right guard;* Russell, Saunders, *right end;* Boler, Sanders, Harris, Zambiasi, Cescutti, *linebacker;* Taylor, Mitchell, West, Bob Thompson, *cornerback;* Miller, B. Wilson, Schwak, Ansley, *safety*

Florida: *Offense:* McGriff, Foldberg, *split end;* Parker, Wunderly, *left tackle;* Lawless, Loper, *left guard;* Kynes, *center;* Stanfield, Cain, *right guard;* M. Williams, Mulliniks, *right tackle;* Darby, Anderson, *tight end;* D. Gaffney, Fisher, *quarterback;* Fields, G. Sever, *wingback;* T. Green, Richards, *tailback;* DuBose, Brinson, *fullback;* Morrison, *punter;* Posey, *placekicker*

Defense: Kendrick, M. Smith, Allen, Barber, *end;* Carpenter, Grebe, *left tackle;* Griffith, Wildman, *right tackle;* S. Green, *noseguard;* Ortega, Floyd, Cameron, Reynolds, *linebacker;* T. Sever, H. Davis, Talbot, Butler, *cornerback;* Cowans, Ball, Butler, Summers, Fields, *safety*

	Georgia	Florida
First downs	12	23
Rushes/yards	44/173	66/240
Passing yards	90	180
Return yards	27	8
Pass att/comp/int	12/5/1	19/11/1
Punts/avg. yards	7/36	5/39
Fumbles/lost	4/1	5/1
Penalties/yards	9/66	6/40

— 1975 —

Georgia 10, Florida 7

FLORIDA WAS IN THE COCKFIGHT FOR THE SEC crown, cruising on a six-game winning streak and 11th ranked in the nation when they headed to Jacksonville to clash with Georgia.

Coach Doug Dickey's 7–1 Gators were 10-point favorites to smash the 6–2 Bulldogs, and Dickey described the duel as "my biggest game as the head coach here at Florida." A win over Georgia would put Florida in position to overtake fifth-ranked Alabama in the conference chase and possibly win the Gator's first-ever conference football title.

The clash figured to be a running battle featuring three of the top five rushers in the league. Florida's assault was headed by awesome fullback Jimmy DuBose, who had pounded out a school record 1,055 yards rushing in eight games. The Gators called their offense the "broken bone" because Dickey had added several passing options to his wishbone attack.

The Bulldogs had 1974 first-team All-SEC runner Glynn Harrison, ranked third in the conference in rushing, and sophomore star Kevin McLee, who was leading the SEC in scoring with 60 points. Florida kicker David Posey was second with 50 points.

The Gators were averaging about 100 yards a game more than Georgia and Vince Dooley downplayed his team's chances. "Let me just say this is the best Florida team I've ever seen. . . . Realistically, it's a mighty long shot for us," he told reporters. The Bulldogs were all too aware of Florida quarterback Don Gaffney, who authored the fantastic last-minute Gator win in the 1973 match-up.

But Georgia defensive coordinator Erk Russell had nicknamed his charges the "Junkyard Dogs," and the sobriquet spread like a dry grass fire among the players and fans. Russell was known to butt his bald head against the helmets of his players until blood streamed

Erk Russell was the mastermind of Georgia defensive teams from 1964 through 1980. He left UGA to revive the football program at Georgia Southern College, where he won three national championships.

down his face. It was a ploy that inflamed his defenders and added to his growing legend.

Florida opened 1975 with a 40–14 home win over SMU; lost by only one point, 8–7, at N.C. State; then beat Mississippi State, 27–10; LSU, 34–6; Vanderbilt, 35–0; Florida State, 34–8; Duke, 24–16; and Auburn, 31–14, handily.

Dooley's 'Dogs fell, 19–9, to Pittsburgh in Athens to start 1975, but then dropped Mississippi State, 28–6; South Carolina, 28–20; and Clemson, 35–7. Georgia was surprised, 28–13, at Ole Miss, then wrecked Vanderbilt, 47–3, and Kentucky, 21–13, before surviving a scare to beat Richmond, 28–24. The close call with the supposedly outclassed Spiders embarrassed the Bulldogs who, almost everyone assumed, were looking past Richmond to their date with Florida on November 8.

The afternoon was as bleak as Dooley's pre-game prediction, and the rain showers that had soaked the city earlier in the day were expected to continue.

On the soggy Gator Bowl turf, Georgia's Glynn Harrison ran for nine yards on the first play from scrimmage, but injured a knee and had to leave the game.

With about 10 minutes left in the quarter, Andy Reid lost the ball at the UGA 44 and Florida defensive end Mike Smith recovered. The Gators wasted little time in capitalizing. DuBose ripped downfield for an 18-yard gain and halfback Larry Brinson rambled for 11 more. From the UGA 17, Gaffney shot a pass to tight end Alvin Darby who made a diving catch at the 2. On fourth down, the Gators went for it. Tony Green took a handoff from Gaffney, veered over right tackle, and scored on the 10th play of the offensive. Posey's PAT put the Gators up 7–0.

The remainder of the first quarter, and most of the second period, was a hard-hitting spectacle between old enemies with two of the South's finest defenses.

The Bulldogs' only threat came late in the half when they took over at their 45 after a punt. Split end Gene Washington took a screen pass from quarterback Ray Goff and zipped 22 yards to the UF 33. Harrison then broke free on a 22-yard romp to the Gators' 16. The 'Dogs reached the 4 but were unable to punch it further. Kicker Allan Leavitt drilled a 21-yard field goal and the half ended with Florida up, 7–3.

The intermission served only as a truce for the defensive war that raged in full fury in the third quarter. Georgia marched from its 20 to the UF 35 before Goff was tackled for a 14-yard loss on third down to end the menace. Florida broke through late in the period on a drive that reached the UGA 18. Facing fourth and one, Gaffney handed to Green who was stood up by defensive tackle Jim Baker and stopped short of the first down. Many considered the hit to be the turning point of the game.

Still, Georgia looked helpless against the Gators' defense and Florida's offense seemed out of gas after Green's failure on fourth down. Churning in the stadium mud, both teams' defenders laid vicious hits on their opponents, and the clock ticked deep into the fourth quarter.

Georgia took possession on its 20 and the UGA coaching staff decided to play Houdini. The Bulldogs had gained yards on an end-around play earlier in the game and offensive coordinator Bill Pace decided to embellish. Tight end Richard Appleby would take the handoff from quarterback Matt Robinson as usual, but this time he would pass. Florida remembered Appleby as the Bulldog who had caught the decisive two-point conversion toss to win the previous year's tilt.

Appleby had thrown only one other pass in his college career—earlier in the season against Vanderbilt, running the same play. The ball was intercepted.

Georgia flanker Gene Washington pulled in a spectacular end-around pass from Richard Appleby for an 80-yard touchdown to down favored Florida in 1975.

At the snap, Appleby bolted into the backfield, took the handoff from Robinson, and appeared to be sweeping wide. Gator corner-back Henry Davis ran toward the line to stop Appleby, throwing a brush block at flanker Gene Washington. Suddenly, Appleby straightened, looked downfield and flung the ball. Washington broke into the clear at the UF 30, gathered in the pass, and streaked untouched down the sideline for the touchdown. Leavitt kicked the extra point to extend the Georgia lead to 10–7.

"When I saw that ball coming down, there was no way I was going to drop it," Washington recalled in an interview with the *Atlanta Journal* and *Constitution*. "I watched the ball come right into my hands, and Richard must have done (a) great job of faking the run, because there wasn't a single Florida defensive back around me."

The electrifying score sent Georgia fans into rowdy euphoria, but Vince Dooley was worried that his Bulldogs had scored too early against the explosive Gators' offense with 3:12 left in the game.

Florida's last gasp came with 1:42 left after an exchange of posses-sions. Gaffney made the most of the opportunity, connecting with split end Terry LeCount on two passes as the Gators' lightning offense struck to the UGA 21. But the drive died there and Dickey decided to go for the tying field goal on fourth down. Dickey later said a tie with Georgia, coupled with an Alabama loss, probably would have given the Gators the SEC crown since both teams had 4–0 conference records.

Gator kicker Posey trotted on to try to knot it from 38 yards away. The snap from center was low and Posey's kick never had a chance.

DuBose gained a respectable 96 yards on 19 carries, Brinson had 46 yards on just three rushes, and Green collected 45 in 13 attempts for Florida. Georgia's McLee bulled for 71 yards on 22 rushes while Harrison ran nine times for 57 yards.

Later in the day, Alabama ran over LSU, 23–10, for the key win in the Tide's unprecedented fifth SEC championship in a row.

Florida roused from the bad day in Jacksonville by whipping Kentucky, 48–7, and Miami, 15–11, to earn a berth in the Gator Bowl against Maryland. The Terps won, 13–0, to leave Florida with a 9–3 record, Dickey's fourth winning season in six years.

Gator linebacker Sammy Green was honored as a first-team All-American and made the first-team All-SEC squad along with fullback Jimmy DuBose, offensive tackle Mike Williams and kicker David Posey.

Green played professionally with the Houston Oilers, Seattle Seahawks and New Orleans Saints. DuBose was a running back for Tampa Bay from 1976–1978.

After the win over Florida, Georgia overwhelmed Auburn, 28–13, and Georgia Tech, 42–26, to win a berth against Arkansas in the Cotton Bowl. The Bulldogs led 10–0, but the Razorbacks galloped back to take a 31–10 win. Georgia finished 9–3 and ranked 19th in the AP and UPI polls.

Bulldog offensive guard Randy Johnson was named a first-team

During his 1975 to 1977 career, Ben Zambiasi was Georgia's all-time career tackle leader.

All-American and was joined on the All-SEC first team by running back Glynn Harrison, honored for the second year in a row.

The Appleby-to-Washington touchdown added another chapter to the lore of the Georgia-Florida meetings. "It had happened again in this long and glorious series, " the *Journal* and *Constitution* said. "The unexpected had become the rule rather than the exception."

Scoring:

Georgia 0 3 0 7 — 10
Florida 7 0 0 0 — 7

UF   TD   Green, 2-yard run (Posey kick)
UGA FG   Leavitt, 21 yards
UGA TD   Washington, 80-yard pass from Appleby (Leavitt kick)

Georgia: *Offense:* Mark Wilson, Davis, *split end;* Mike Wilson, Collier, *left tackle;* Parrish, *left guard;* Tereshinski, Legg, *center;* R. Johnson, Hendrix, *right guard;* S. Wilson, Helms, *right tackle;* Appleby, S. Davis, *tight end;* Robinson, Goff, *quarterback;* Harrison, McLee, Reid, Pollard, R. Williams, *running back;* Washington, Box, *flanker;* Leavitt, *placekicker;* Dilts, *punter*

Defense: Craft, Clark, *left end;* Baker, Swoopes, *left tackle;* Sanders, Brad Thompson, *right tackle;* Saunders, *right end;* R. Russell, Lewis, Zambiasi, Cescutti, Griffith, *linebacker;* Schwak, Woods, Mitchell, Henderson, *cornerback;* Krug, R. Johnson, Harris, Miller, Bob Thompson, *safety*

Florida: *Offense:* Chandler, LeCount, G. Sever, *split end;* M. Williams, *left tackle;* Loper, Tribble, *left guard;* Moore, *center;* Pupello, *right guard;* Mulliniks, Forrester, *right tackle;* Darby, Clifford, Enclade, *tight end;* D. Gaffney, Fisher, *quarterback;* T. Green, Carr, *left halfback;* Brinson, Richards, *right halfback;* DuBose, Morgan, *fullback;* Dolfi, *punter;* Posey, *placekicker*

Defense: M. Smith, Kanter, *left end;* Carpenter, King, Grebe, *left tackle;* Hutchinson, Starkey, Wildman, *right tackle;* Allen, Maynor, Adkins, *right end;* Stephens, Logan, S. Green, Flournoy, C. Williams, Barber, *linebacker;* H. Davis, Wright, Ball, Parrish, *cornerback;* Cowans, Fields, Dickey, Blair, *safety*

	Georgia	Florida
First downs	12	20
Rushes/yards	60/212	56/232
Passing yards	109	150
Return yards	0	48
Pass att/comp/int	10/3/2	20/8/1
Punts/avg. yards	8/36	8/36
Fumbles/lost	3/1	5/3
Penalties/yards	3/15	2/10

— 1976 —

Georgia 41, Florida 27

On THE MORNING OF NOVEMBER 6, 1976, President-elect Jimmy Carter flew into Brunswick, Ga., for a few days of relaxation on St. Simons Island four days after his victory over President Gerald Ford.

Of course the election of Carter, the Plains, Ga., native, was a milestone in the year of the nation's bicentennial. But for three hours or so on Saturday, the Southeast focused on Jacksonville, about 80 miles to the south, where seventh-ranked Georgia and 10th-ranked Florida would scrap with the SEC crown at stake.

Coach Doug Dickey's Gators were 4–0 in the conference, 6–1 overall, and as close to an SEC championship as any UF team had ever been. Yet Florida had lost two in a row to Georgia, and the Bulldogs of Coach Vince Dooley were particularly imposing in 1976.

Georgia was 7–1 overall and 3–1 in the league with the fame of the Junkyard Dogs defense growing with every outing. Senior quarterback and team captain Ray Goff was the helmsman for UGA's explosive veer offense.

Florida had a headliner receiver in Wes Chandler, while the Bulldogs featured running back Kevin McLee who would be Georgia's career rushing leader by the time the rivals collided again in 1977.

Georgia began the season with a 36–24 win over California and followed with a 41–0 breather at Clemson. The Bulldogs then beat South Carolina, 20–12, and Alabama, 21–0, before being surprised, 21–17, at Ole Miss. Dooley's men pounded Vanderbilt, 45–0; Kentucky, 31–7; and Cincinnati, 31–17, a week before meeting Florida.

The Gators, coming off three bowl seasons, started 1976 losing, 24–21, to North Carolina in Tampa. Florida then beat Houston, 49–14; Mississippi State, 34–30; LSU, 28–23; Florida State, 33–26; Tennessee, 20–18; and Auburn, 24–19.

315

The Gator Bowl masses of more than 70,000 and thousands more watching ABC's national telecast would see one of the greatest offensive displays in the rivalry's history that afternoon.

With Goff running the option almost flawlessly, the 'Dogs got a first down after starting at their 25. On the fifth play from scrimmage, Goff bucked free and raced 34 yards to the UF 23. In four more plays, Georgia had punched the ball to the 9, using almost five minutes off the clock. On the 10th play of the drive, Goff kept the ball on the option and bolted in for the score. Kicker Allan Leavitt added the extra point and Georgia led 7–0.

Starting from their 29, the Gators quickly displayed their offensive prowess. With UF quarterback Jimmy Fisher at the controls, Florida headed downfield in much the same fashion as the Georgia march. On the 13th play of the possession, UGA's Mark Mitchell was flagged for pass interference when he ran into UF's Wes Chandler at the Georgia 9. On second down from the 6, Fisher hit Chandler in a corner of the end zone to complete the 15-play, 71-yard offensive. David Posey's conversion tied matters at 7–7.

Still in the first period, Florida took over at its 25, only the second time the Gators had had the ball. Running backs Willie Wilder and Earl Carr led the charge as Florida poured through the vaunted Georgia defense like a sieve. In seven plays the Gators romped 70 yards to the UGA 5. On the last play of the first period, Fisher called a quarterback keeper and slipped over the goal line. Posey's extra point put Florida up, 14–7. The long distance scoring marathon was just beginning.

Georgia's veer offense then went on the attack from the UGA 18. Blending the short pass with the option run, Goff steered the 'Dogs over, around and through the Gators defense to reach the UF 8 in 13 plays. He climaxed the 82-yard drive from there, hurling a scoring toss to tight end Ulysses Norris with nine minutes left in the half. UF tackle Dan Grebe got a hand up to block Leavitt's kick and Florida's lead was preserved, 14–13.

On the Gators' third possession of the afternoon, Dickey and his boys found a weakness in the Junkyard Dogs and exploited it like beachfront property. The Gators felt they could run over the left side of the Georgia defensive line and proceeded to do so, with Carr and Wilder heading the stampede. Both backs broke for big yardage and Chandler snared a pass from Fisher for 24 to the UGA 30. On second down, Carr went right instead of left, crossing up the 'Dogs defense. The big back crashed over right guard and charged 29 yards for the touchdown. But this time it was Florida's conversion try that was blocked (by Georgia end Dicky Clark), and the Gators' edge was 20–13 with 6:30 left in the half.

The defenses then stymied both offenses for a series. Goff had suddenly lost his touch and Dooley replaced him with Matt Robinson who ignited the Bulldogs shortly before intermission. Robinson guided the 'Dogs down near the UF goal before drifting back and looking for a target in the end zone. He saw Norris running open across the goal line and released the ball before noticing UF safety Terry LeCount in the vicinity. LeCount grabbed the interception at the 2 and sped upfield on a broken-field run before being dropped at the UGA 43. With 26 seconds left, UF fans were whooping it up. Practically everyone in the stadium got ready for the halftime show—except Dickey and the Florida offense.

Instead of running out the clock, Fisher dropped back to pass and slung the ball to tight end Jimmy Stephens for a 34-yard completion to the UGA 9. With no seconds to spare, Fisher got the snap again, set to pass, and spotted Chandler running maneuvers in the UGA end zone. Trying to cover the speedy receiver, Bulldog defensive back Johnny Henderson stumbled and Fisher zipped the ball in to Chandler for an easy six. Posey's kick made it 27–13 Florida at intermission.

The potent Florida offense had run on high octane the first 30 minutes, scoring on drives of 71, 75, and 80 yards on its first three possessions and using just two plays in the 43-yard scoring blitz to end the half. The Gators seemed well on their way to breaking the two-game losing streak to Georgia and clinching at least a share of their first SEC title.

In the Florida locker room at halftime, some players confidently talked about who would be taking sizes for the rings they would earn for winning the SEC. Despite his team's success, Dickey told his players they likely would need to score more than 40 points to beat the Bulldogs.

After a Georgia turnover and an ensuing, rare punt by Florida, the Bulldogs took possession at their 20. The Georgians sliced downfield, McLee knifing for 32 yards and Goff for 26 more. The 80-yard, seven-play offensive culminated with Goff passing six yards to Norris, who had sprung free in the end zone. Leavitt's kick was good and Florida's lead was trimmed to 27–20.

Starting from their 20 after the kickoff, the Gators gained nine yards on three plays and were looking at a fourth and inches from their 29.

Dickey knew he had to find some way to blunt Georgia's charge. With possibly the game, the SEC crown, and a major bowl invitation hanging in the balance, the Florida field boss decided to roll the dice for the yardage. What turned out to be THE play of the 1976 game would be a left-side sweep with Carr getting the call. The 218-pound fullback got the handoff and rumbled wide. For a split second it looked as though he had running room. Just as suddenly, Bulldog safety Johnny Henderson streaked into the picture and leveled Carr for no gain. Georgia's offensive unit deliriously raced onto the field while the Gators and their fans brooded in disbelieving silence.

"When I was running the play I was asking myself why in the world we were running this play," Carr said after the contest.

It left the Gators reeling. The Bulldogs went for the jugular, with McLee and Goff the primary movers as the 'Dogs reached the UF 2 in five plays. Fullback Al Pollard crashed in from there with 5:32 remaining in the third. Leavitt's kick tied it at 27-all and the Gators were in deep trouble.

As relentless as the Florida offense had been in the first half, it was equally as ineffective in the second half. The Junkyard Dogs were boring in with their ears laid back on every down.

With Florida on the run, Georgia began a time-consuming drive late in the third quarter, starting from its 30. McLee, Pollard and Goff gobbled up yardage inside and outside to lead the Bulldogs into the fourth quarter and close to the Florida goal. From the UF 5, Goff took the snap, ran the option left, and plunged into the end zone. With Leavitt's extra point, the 'Dogs were up 34–27, their first lead since the first quarter.

The vanished Gators offense failed to reappear at this crucial point in the game. As a result, Georgia got the ball back at its own 20 with about 10 minutes left in the game.

Chiefly on the running of McLee, Pollard, and Goff, the 'Dogs embarked on a 16-play drive that melted minutes off the clock and ended with Goff's 1-yard sneak. Leavitt made it a final at 41–27.

With Florida still every bit in the game, Doug Dickey had played a losing hand on the fourth-down run by Carr in the third quarter.

"We took the big gamble and it didn't pay off," he said of the play. "The only way they could have stopped that play was for their safety to make it. He made a super play." Dooley told reporters he probably would have made the same call had he been in the same situation.

Goff had an all-star afternoon, running for 124 yards and three touchdowns, and connecting on five of five passes, including two scoring tosses to Norris.

McLee banged and squirmed for 198 yards to share the marquee with Goff, and Pollard bled the Gators for 84 yards on 22 carries. Florida's Fisher had two touchdown passes and ran for another, while Willie Wilder led the Gators in rushing with 102 yards.

Georgia held Florida, which had the fifth-leading offense in the country, to 65 net yards in the second half. The 68 points scored by the two teams was the most in the series since the 75–0 Georgia win in the 1942 contest.

Florida failed to recover from the defeat in Jacksonville, losing the following week to Kentucky, 28–9, in Lexington to dash its chances of winning its first conference title. The Gators, though, went on to paste Rice, 50–22, and Miami, 19–10, to meet Texas A&M in the Sun Bowl. The Aggies overpowered Florida, 37–14, to end the Gators' year at 8–4.

Dickey had yet another winning season, but was 2–5 against Georgia and 0–4 in consecutive bowls.

Florida receiver Wes Chandler was selected as a first-team All-American, and he and defensive back Alvin Cowans were first-team All-SEC selections. Gator kicker David Posey closed his career as the leading scorer in school history. He played in the NFL for New England and Atlanta.

Georgia's surge continued unabated when, on November 13, the Bulldogs buried Auburn, 28–0, and claimed the SEC crown, Dooley's third conference title. Georgia Tech was UGA's next victim, falling 13–10 in Athens to send now fourth-ranked and 10–1 Georgia to the Sugar Bowl against Pittsburgh.

The Bulldogs had an outside chance at the national championship if they could upset Pitt. But the Panthers and Heisman Trophy running back Tony Dorsett proved too much for Georgia, dropping the 'Dogs, 27–3, in New Orleans to win the national title. Despite the defeat, Georgia was ranked 10th in both polls and Dooley had his finest season since the 11–1 campaign in 1971. Equally as important to many Bulldog fans, he had beaten Florida for the third straight year, something no UGA coach had done since the five-game Georgia winning streak from 1944 to 1948.

Overall in the series, Georgia now held a 33–19–2 advantage.

The 1976 All-SEC first team was colored Red and Black with Ray Goff, Kevin McLee, offensive guard Joel Parrish, offensive tackle Mike Wilson, Leavitt, roverback Bill Krug, linebacker Ben Zambiasi and defensive end Dicky Clark all making the squad.

Wilson, Parrish, Zambiasi and Leavitt also were selected to various All-America teams. Wilson later starred for the Seattle Seahawks,

Quarterback and team captain Ray Goff ran for three touchdowns and threw for two more in UGA's 41–27 win over the Gators in 1976 when he was named SEC Player of the Year.

while Matt Robinson played quarterback for three years with the New York Jets.

Goff's leadership abilities would stand him in good stead, when he would one day succeed the venerable Dooley as head coach at UGA.

Scoring:

Georgia	7	6	14	14	—	41
Florida	14	13	0	0	—	27

UGA	TD	Goff, 9-yard run (Leavitt kick)
UF	TD	Chandler, 6-yard pass from Fisher (Posey kick)
UF	TD	Fisher, 5-yard run (Posey kick)
UGA	TD	Norris, 8-yard pass from Goff (kick failed)
UF	TD	Carr, 29-yard run (kick failed)
UF	TD	Chandler, 9-yard pass from Fisher (Posey kick)
UGA	TD	Norris, 6-yard pass from Goff (Leavitt kick)
UGA	TD	Pollard, 2-yard run (Leavitt kick)
UGA	TD	Goff, 5-yard run (Leavitt kick)
UGA	TD	Goff, 1-yard run (Leavitt kick)

Georgia: *Offense:* Mark Wilson, Davis, *split end;* Mike Wilson, Guest, *left tackle;* Parrish, Kennedy, *left guard;* J. Tereshinski, *center;* Collins, Hendrix, *right guard;* Collier, Helms, *right tackle;* Norris, Striplin, *tight end;* Goff, Robinson, *quarterback;* McLee, Pollard, Young, R. Williams, *running back;* Washington, Box, *flanker;* Leavitt, *placekicker;* Dilts, *punter*

Defense: Craft, G. Williams, *left end;* Swoopes, Petrisko, *left tackle;* Sanders, *right guard;* Clark, *right end;* Lewis, McBride, Griffith, Cescutti, Zambiasi, *linebacker;* Thompson, Hope, Woods, Henderson, *cornerback;* Mitchell, Krug, Gilliam, R. Johnson, *safety*

Florida: *Offense:* Chandler, D. Gaffney, *split end;* Forrester, Sullivan, *left tackle;* Tribble, *left guard;* Moore, Cline, *center;* Pupello, Totten, *right guard;* Mulliniks, Swafford, *right tackle;* Stephens, Rote, *tight end;* Fisher, Kynes, *quarterback;* Carr, *left halfback;* Wilder, Brinson, *right halfback;* Morgan, Enclade, *fullback;* A. Williams, *punter;* Posey, *placekicker*

Defense: Adkins, DuPree, *left end;* Carpenter, Grebe, *left tackle;* Forrester, King, *right tackle;* Kanter, Swanz, *right end;* Logan, Maynor, Flournoy, Hutchinson, C. Williams, Ruth, *linebacker;* H. Davis, Wright, Parrish, W. Gaffney, *cornerback;* Cowans, Aydt, Blair, Walker, *safety*

	Georgia	Florida
First downs	25	19
Rushes/yards	79/432	44/197
Passing yards	70	102
Return yards	29	55
Pass att/comp/int	11/7/1	16/8/4
Punts/avg. yards	3/42	4/37
Fumbles/lost	3/2	2/0
Penalties/yards	8/88	4/35

— 1977 —

Florida 22, Georgia 17

GEORGIA HAD CROWNED A NEW CAREER rushing leader in Kevin McLee by the time the November 5, 1977, conflict erupted with Florida, but neither the Gators nor the 'Dogs were having seasons to put them in the national spotlight.

Expected to vie for the SEC championship, Florida was off to a disappointing 3–2–1 start and trying to snap back from an upset loss at Auburn. The Gators were looking to break a three-game losing streak to Georgia and were after their 20th win in the border war.

As usual, the hotels and motels in Jacksonville and the surrounding region were booked for months in advance of the contest. Many Georgia fans were continuing the tradition of partying on the sea islands near Brunswick and taking charter buses to the game.

Florida's chief offensive weapon was All-American Wes Chandler, one of the best receivers in the land. The gifted Chandler was so valuable to the Gators that Coach Doug Dickey was playing him as both a split end and a running back in UF's wishbone offense.

A side attraction of the game would be the duel between McLee and Florida's best-ever rusher, Tony Green.

McLee had run past fabled Heisman winner Frank Sinkwich during the Vanderbilt game to become Georgia's all-time leading runner. Heading into the feud with Florida, McLee had run for 2,449 yards in less than three years at Georgia. Tony Green would end his UF career, also at the close of 1977, with 2,590 rushing yards to become one of the top runners in Florida history.

Both defenses were strong, particularly at linebacker where Scot Brantley and Charlie Williams anchored Florida and team captain Ben Zambiasi was Georgia's star.

The Gators secondary was banged up but it was questionable whether Georgia's passing offense, ranked last in the league, could exploit the weakness.

Running back Kevin McLee had become UGA's new career rusher when Georgia met Florida in 1977, but the Gators prevailed 22–17.

Florida's year began with a 48–3 pounding of Rice and a 24–22 verdict over Mississippi State. The Gators then lost, 36–14, at LSU and were tied, 17–17, by Pittsburgh at Florida Field before besting Tennessee, 27–17. Florida visited Auburn the next week and was surprised, 29–14.

Georgia opened with a 27–16 win over Oregon but then lost, 7–6, to Clemson, the first time the Tigers had won in Athens since 1914. The Bulldogs beat South Carolina, 15–13; lost 18–10 at Alabama; then defeated Ole Miss, 14–13, and Vanderbilt, 24–13, before a 33–0 spanking by Kentucky. Georgia eased by Richmond, 23–7, a week before Florida.

Even though neither team was ranked in the polls, the game was televised nationally and close to 70,000 were in the stands.

The first scoring action came after UF's Alan Williams punted the ball out of bounds at the UGA 6. On first down, Willie McClendon burst over right tackle and broke loose in the Florida secondary, galloping 53 yards before being tackled at the UF 41.

On third and nine, quarterback Jeff Pyburn connected with Jesse Murray on a sideline route that gave Georgia a first down at the Florida 14. The 'Dogs used four plays to put the ball at the 2. On second and goal, Pyburn pitched to McClendon sweeping left and the quick, powerful back smashed across the goal line. Kicker Rex Robinson added the conversion and Georgia led 7–0 with 3:17 left in the period.

The Bulldogs got the ball back on their 30 late in the quarter. Pyburn and McClendon led the move again as they crossed midfield.

On the first play of the second quarter, Pyburn scrambled 11 yards down the sideline to the UF 37, but injured his right knee and had to leave the game. His replacement, Steve Rogers, a local boy from Jacksonville, fumbled his first snap and the Gators' Melvin Flournoy fell on the ball at the UF 31.

Again the Junkyard Dogs held Florida's wishbone in check and Williams had to punt. Rogers returned at quarterback for Georgia but, on third down at the UGA 24, he was hit hard by UF middle guard Scott Hutchinson and the ball popped loose. Gator defensive tackle Sylvester King claimed the pigskin at the UGA 12 and Florida had another break. On second down, Gator quarterback Terry Le-Count lofted a pass toward Chandler, running in the middle of the end zone. The star split end leaped, snared the ball with one hand, and pulled it in for the touchdown. Florida kicker Berj Yepremian's extra point tied it at 7–7 with 11:30 left in the half.

Georgia needed less than a minute to retaliate. Rogers appeared to have shaken his jitters, as he swept right end for a six-yard gain on first down.

On the next play, Rogers started to his left and looked as if he wanted to turn upfield. A split second before being hit, he pitched to McClendon running full-throttle behind him. The swift Bulldog running back caught the ball in stride and steamed down the sideline. Tight end Ulysses Norris threw a vital block and McClendon left everyone else in the dust, sprinting 74 yards for the score. Robinson booted the extra point to extend UGA's margin to 14–7.

Florida took over and quickly moved out to midfield, where the strangest play of the afternoon occurred. LeCount tried a pass but Georgia linebacker Jim Griffith intercepted at the UGA 37. With Gators closing in on him at the Florida 42, Griffith tried to lateral to roverback Bill Krug who was trailing him. The pitch was wild and the Gators' Tony Green pounced on the ball near the sideline. With new life, Florida continued its offensive, reaching the Georgia 26 before the 'Dogs could stop them. Yepremian then came on and speared a 43-yard field goal to pull the Gators to 14–10 with 4:18 before intermission.

Florida, now with impetus, went to the air in an attempt to score again before the half. Unfortunately for the Orange and Blue, Georgia's Billy Woods intercepted a LeCount pass at the Gators 32 and, in turn, put the Bulldogs in position to add points in the last minutes.

Georgia used seven plays to reach the 13 but could go no further. With 15 seconds remaining, Robinson notched a 29-yard field goal to give Georgia a 17–10 lead at halftime.

A first-team All-American in 1976 and 1977, UF split Wes Chandler burned the Bulldogs with three touchdowns in 1977. He earned All-Pro honors with the San Diego Chargers.

Starting from their own 22 on their second possession of the second half, the Gators gained short yardage on two plays. But on third down, LeCount, a converted defensive back, kept the ball and zig-zagged to daylight, racing 48 yards to the UGA 26 before being brought down. On third down from the UGA 18, Chandler, lined up in the backfield, got the call, and ripped into the Georgia line. Before the 'Dogs could react, he had sped past and was celebrating in the end zone. Yepremian came on for the extra point that would tie the issue at 17. But holder Alan Williams mishandled the snap; and the kicker, trying to pick up the ball, was slammed by UGA's Krug. Georgia 17, Florida 16.

With their defense again crushing Georgia on offense, Florida had a first down on its 27 after a Bulldog punt. The Gators forged all the way down to the UGA 38 before Green fumbled. The ball was picked off in midair by the omnipresent Krug and Georgia held its one-point lead.

The Bulldogs had gotten emotional lifts from both the fumble and the botched extra point, but the Gators had a death grip on the Georgia offense, shutting it down completely. Dooley inserted Randy Cook at quarterback, but the third-stringer was as ineffective as Rogers against the torrid Florida rush.

Florida regained possession on its 43 and, once more, put offensive pressure on the Junkyard Dogs, clawing to the UGA 27 early in the final period before the drive halted. Yepremian trotted on for a 43-yard field goal attempt to give the Gators their first lead. But the kick careened away from the uprights and many of the Red and Black faithful were beginning to savor their fourth straight win over the jinxed Gators.

Georgia got the ball on its 20 and Kevin McLee, who had done little all afternoon, cracked for five yards, but lost the ball when hit. Linebacker Brantley was there to pull it in for Florida.

The revived Gators knew this might be their last chance. Three times in the second half they had been inside the UGA 40 and had come away with no points. Would they be denied again?

With less than 10 minutes remaining in the fourth, Florida pounded to the UGA 1 in seven plays. Chandler was the man to handle the ball, and the New Smyrna Beach, Fla., senior did not disappoint. Thrusting over left guard, Chandler landed in the end zone and Florida suddenly had its first lead of the afternoon, 22–17.

Ahead by less than a touchdown, Dickey decided to go for two. LeCount dropped to pass, found no one open, and took off running, but was buried by 'Dogs short of the goal line.

The way the Gator defense had dominated the second half, most of the nails were in the coffin when Georgia got the ball on its 33 for a last-chance effort with 2:44 remaining. Rogers brought the sputtering Bulldogs offense to life, punching to the UF 47, the first time Georgia had crossed midfield in the half. But the 'Dogs would get no closer as Florida defenders regained control. After being sacked for a 5-yard loss and throwing an incompletion, Rogers, with little time left, went back to pass, was hit, and fumbled after a 17-yard loss. Florida's victory was complete when defensive end Michael DuPree recovered at the UGA 31.

The Gators had captured the elusive 20th win over Georgia, and there was jubilation from Key West to Pensacola.

Florida's defense in the second half held Georgia to eight yards net rushing and no yards passing in one of the greatest defensive efforts of the rivalry. Much of the credit went to Hutchinson and linebackers Brantley and Charles Williams.

Offensively, the top Gators were Chandler and LeCount. Chandler scored three touchdowns, caught three passes for 50 yards as a split end, and ran for 57 yards on 15 carries as a halfback. LeCount was UF's top rusher with 108 yards on 16 attempts, with much of his yardage coming on scrambles that averted losses.

McClendon was the Bulldogs' ground leader, carrying 10 times for 162 yards. All but nine of his yards came on nine carries in the first half. McClendon was seemingly forgotten in the second half, carrying only once.

Tony Green helped the Gators to victory in 1977 and scored a touchdown in the 1975 battle. He played for Washington, Seattle, and the New York Giants in the NFL.

Eight Georgia fumbles, five of which were scooped up by the Gators, contributed to the UGA demise.

Florida's bowl hopes were shot out of the clouds a week later with a 14–7 home loss to Kentucky, but the Gators regrouped to outscore Utah, 38–29. They then closed with a 31–14 triumph over Miami before losing, 37–9, to Florida State in Gainesville. At 6–4–1, Dickey had his fifth consecutive winning season, although there would be no bowl trip this year.

Wes Chandler garnered first-team All-American honors for the second consecutive year. He and defensive back Alvin Cowans also became two-time first-team All-SEC selections. Gators' linebacker Scot Brantley, middle guard Scott Hutchinson and Tony Green also received first-team All-SEC recognition.

The 1977 Gators were well represented in the pros. Chandler left Florida after catching a school record 22 touchdown passes and notching a UF record 28 total touchdowns in his career. A first-round draft choice, Chandler went on to a fine career in the NFL as an All-Pro wide receiver with the San Diego Chargers and once was named NFL Player of the Year. Terry LeCount played wide receiver for San Francisco and Minnesota, and Derrick Gaffney was a wide receiver for the New York Jets for several years. Lineman Scott Hutchinson also turned pro with the Buffalo Bills and later was with Tampa Bay. Tony Green played two years in the NFL.

The folks in Athens had no holiday gridiron plans for the first time in five seasons. Auburn crunched Georgia, 33–14, a week after the loss to Florida, and the Bulldogs bowed, 16–7, at Georgia Tech to finish 5–6. Georgia's offensive guard George Collins and roverback

328 • Derek Smith

Bill Krug were honored as All–Americans and were named to the All–SEC first team along with linebacker Ben Zambiasi and defensive tackle Ronnie Swoopes. Collins was a draft choice of St. Louis.

Scoring:

Florida	0	10	6	6	—	22
Georgia	7	10	0	0	—	17

UGA	TD	McClendon, 2-yard run (Robinson kick)
UF	TD	Chandler, 12-yard pass from LeCount (Yepremian kick)
UGA	TC	McClendon, 74-yard run (Robinson kick)
UF	FG	Yepremian, 43 yards
UGA	FG	Robinson, 29 yards
UF	TD	Chandler, 18-yard run (run failed)
UF	TD	Chandler, 1-yard run (run failed)

Florida: *Offense:* Chandler, D. Gaffney, *split end;* Forrester, Guido, *left tackle;* Bennek, Hough, *left guard;* Totten, Schroeder, *center;* Kiefer, Midden, *right guard;* Forrester, Lenard, *right tackle;* Swafford, Gilbert, *tight end;* LeCount, *quarterback;* T. Green, *left halfback;* Wilder, Coburn, *right halfback;* Carr, Portale, *fullback;* A. Williams, *punter;* Yepremian, *placekicker*

Defense: Ruth, Adkins, DuPree, Blair, Kanter, *end;* Flournoy, Luckie, *left tackle;* Hutchinson, Coleman, *middle guard;* King, Tennell, *right tackle;* Brantley, Pratt, C. Williams, Kreis, *linebacker;* Peek, Skalaski, Wright, Aydt, *cornerback;* H. Davis, Cowans, James, Hatch, Brodsky, *safety*

Georgia: *Offense:* Murray, Veal, *split end;* Guest, Parks, *left tackle;* Mandray, Fruehauf, *left guard;* Braswell, *center;* Collins, Milo, *right guard;* Collier, Kennedy, *right tackle;* Norris, Hodge, *tight end;* S. Rogers, Pyburn, Cook, *quarterback;* McLee, Young, McClendon, *running back;* Prince, *flanker;* R. Robinson, *placekicker;* Garrett, *punter*

Defense: G. Williams, *left end;* Boersig, Freedman, *left guard;* Swoopes, Petrisko, *right guard;* Dennis, Terry, *right end;* Lewis, Donaldson, Zambiasi, D. Rogers, Griffith, McBride, *linebacker;* Thompson, Woods, Hope, *cornerback;* Krug, Henderson, Hipp, Collins, *safety*

	Florida	Georgia
First downs	19	11
Rushes/yards	77/258	49/233
Passing yards	79	33
Return yards	2	28
Pass att/comp/int	12/5/2	12/2/0
Punts/avg. yards	5/40	7/39
Fumbles/lost	5/2	8/5
Penalties/yards	2/20	1/5

— 1978 —

Georgia 24, Florida 22

$\mathbf{F}$LORIDA COACH DOUG DICKEY WAS THE bullseye for many dissatisfied UF fans calling for his ouster in the weeks prior to the November 11, 1978, brawl with 11th-ranked Georgia.

The players signed a petition supporting their coach amid a cyclone of intense criticism from several Florida newspapers and a growing number of Gator rooters. The outcry subsided slightly when Florida upset Auburn, but everyone knew it probably would take an unexpected win against powerful Georgia to save Dickey's job. The Gators were 3–4 and five-point underdogs.

The situation was far rosier in Athens where Vince Dooley's 'Dogs were a serious contender for another SEC title and a berth in the Sugar Bowl.

Georgia's kennel king was senior tailback Willie McClendon, whose average of 139 yards rushing a game was the best in the SEC. Against Virginia Military a week earlier, McClendon surpassed Frank Sinkwich's single-season UGA rushing record. The irrepressible Bulldog star would play against Florida with a fractured left hand and a strained left knee.

The game looked to be a struggle between the Gators' passing offense and a Georgia defense that was the stingiest in the league against scoring. Bulldog defensive coordinator Erk Russell described his philosophy as "intelligent fanaticism."

The Gators' air bombardment, led by quarterback John Brantley and sophomore split end Cris Collinsworth, was second in the conference, averaging 183 yards a game and accounting for 10 touchdowns.

Dickey's team debuted with a 35–25 loss to SMU before mashing Mississippi State, 34–0. The Gators then lost, 34–21, at home to

330 • Derek Smith

LSU and 23–12 on the road to Alabama; beat Army, 31–7; lost to Georgia Tech, 17–13; and then shocked Auburn 31–7, at Florida Field.

Baylor was Georgia's first victim of 1978, falling 16–14. The Bulldogs then bested Clemson, 12–0, in Death Valley before South Carolina dropped the 'Dogs, 27–10, in Columbia. Georgia came back to cream Ole Miss, 42–3; LSU, 24–17; Vanderbilt, 31–10; Kentucky, 17–16; and VMI, 41–3, to meet Florida with a five-game winning streak.

The day dawned with gray skies, but the sun seared through the overcast about an hour before game time.

On the opening possession, Georgia receiver Lindsay Scott fumbled after taking a pass from quarterback Jeff Pyburn, and Gator linebacker Dave Little came up with the ball at the UGA 29.

Collinsworth gathered in a Brantley pass at the UGA 13, but the highly regarded Bulldogs defense stiffened and Florida had to settle for a 30-yard Berj Yepremian field goal. The advantage didn't last long.

Georgia embarked on a grueling 88-yard march after UF's kickoff, with McClendon and fullbacks James Womack and Ronnie Stewart doing the dirty work. Womack tore free on a 23-yard jaunt and Pyburn passed, completing throws of 15 and 24 yards to flanker Anthony Arnold. From the UF 3, McClendon capped the drive with a sweep around right end. Rex Robinson kicked the conversion and Georgia was up 7–3.

Still in the first period, the Gators defense was flagged for having 12 men on the field. The penalty gave the 'Dogs a first down, and Georgia reached the UF 16 before things stalled. Robinson then kicked a 32-yard field goal to extend Georgia's lead to 10–3.

Florida found the range in the initial minutes of the second quarter, taking the kickoff and promptly forging to the UGA 33 on the passing of Brantley and the running of tailback David Johnson of St. Augustine. From there, Brantley spotted Collinsworth wheeling toward the end zone and unloaded the ball to the future Gator All-American. Despite the lunging grasp of defensive back Scott Woerner, the lanky wide receiver made the reception for six. Yepremian punctuated the 80-yard drive with the extra point to knot it at 10–10.

Suddenly, Florida was surging. With the pressure on, Georgia's Womack returned the kickoff 32 yards. Bulldog backs then ripped for big yards on a 55-yard offensive and Georgia was perched on the UF

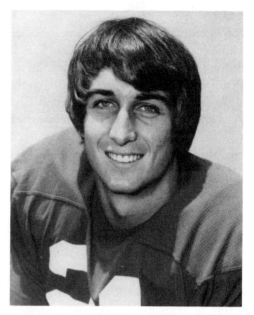

Wide receiver Cris Collinsworth was a UF All-American who scored touchdowns in the 1978 and 1979 Georgia wins. He was an All-Pro receiver for the Cincinnati Bengals.

3. To the surprise of almost everyone except the Georgia team and coaches, Pyburn lofted the ball to tight end Mark Hodge in a corner of the end zone. Robinson's conversion regained the lead for Georgia, 17–10, with about seven minutes left in the half.

But trouble was not over for Florida. On first down after the kickoff, Brantley's pass was tipped by a Bulldog lineman and picked off by Georgia roverback Chris Welton at the UF 44.

Dooley caught the Gators napping on Georgia's first offensive play. UGA's Arnold sped into the backfield on an apparent end around. But instead of running wide after taking the handoff from Pyburn, Arnold, a former high school quarterback from Athens, passed to Lindsay Scott tearing downfield, hitting him on the numbers for a touchdown despite three Gators in the vicinity. Robinson kicked the PAT and Georgia had tallied 14 points within a 26-second span to take a 24–10 lead.

The UGA scoring barrage didn't dishearten Florida. Aided by a pass interference call and a personal foul penalty, the Gators drove 78 yards to the UGA 2. When Brantley missed a third-down pass, Yepremian came on to kick a 19-yard field goal, hacking the Georgia margin to 24–13 at the half.

Georgia, despite a couple of surprise contributions from its passing game, had racked up 216 yards on the ground in the first half.

The only serious scoring threat of the third quarter came when

UGA's Woerner fielded a Bill Conover punt and raced 63 yards before Florida tight end Ron Enclade made a diving, stretching, touchdown-saving tackle at the UF 28. Though in scoring position, Pyburn, on first down, threw an interception to linebacker Scot Brantley, brother of the UF quarterback.

Stymied for most of the second half, Florida drove to a first and goal at the UGA 6 early in the fourth quarter, the big play coming on a Brantley pass of 31 yards to receiver John Smith. Tailback Johnson ran twice to move the ball to the 2. But on third down, Brantley was dropped for a yard loss.

To the boos of many UF fans wanting the Gators to go for it, Dickey sent in his field-goal unit. Yepremian was true from 20 yards out. Twice Florida had been inside the Georgia 5 and come away with only two field goals. Regardless, the Gators trailed by only eight, 24–16, with 11:54 to play.

Resurrected by the field goal, the Gators swallowed the Bulldogs offense after the kickoff and forced a punt. Florida got the ball back on its 12 and, in eight plays, muscled to the UGA 35.

The clock reached the seven-minute mark when Brantley pulled out from center and fired a 20-yard overhand lateral to Collinsworth, who had been in motion at the snap. Collinsworth, converted to split end from quarterback, spotted tight end Enclade downfield. The surprised 'Dogs, unable to recover, saw Collinsworth's pass sail over their heads to a wide-open Enclade, who caught the ball at the 5 and scored easily. On the happy Florida sideline was Steve Spurrier who, in his first and only year as the Gators' quarterback coach, had helped diagram the trick play.

The 35-yard touchdown narrowed Georgia's lead to 24–22, and Florida elected to go for the two-point conversion.

Over 70,000 Georgia-Florida zealots turned the stadium into a bowl of deafening noise as Brantley took the snap and rolled out, looking for an open blue shirt. He spied split end Tony Stephens and fired, but Georgia linebacker Steve Dennis was among several 'Dogs converging on Brantley to deflect the pass. The ball landed in the hands of UGA roverback Chris Welton in the end zone, and Georgia hugged its two-point lead with more than six minutes left in the game.

Florida had used its last timeout to set up the two-point conversion, but there was still plenty of clock to work with if they could shut down the Georgia offense.

The geared-up Gators defense had been keying on Willie McClendon all day and nothing changed on this series. But Dooley had other weapons. Womack rammed the line three times for 11 yards and a first down. McClendon then sliced off tackle for 11 more before Womack plowed for a third consecutive first down to the Florida 42. The Georgia ground juggernaut was keeping the Gators offense off the field, and Florida couldn't stop the clock as it ticked under three minutes to play.

The 'Dogs rolled to the UF 18, where they faced a fourth and one with 1:49 left. If the Gators were to have a chance, they had to stop Georgia here. Instead of going for an almost sure field goal and a five-point lead, Dooley decided to go for the first down to ice the win. Behind guard Matt Braswell's block, Stewart banged into the Florida defense and fell forward to the 16. The first down assured that Florida would not touch the ball again, as Pyburn now knelt for intentional losses to kill the clock and hand Georgia the win.

Dooley later called the offensive "one of the greatest gut drives in the history of Georgia football."

Dickey and Dooley met and embraced at midfield and joyous Bulldog backers lingered in the stadium, as the UGA Redcoat Band blared fight songs to lead the victory celebration. The Gator Bowl emptied in about an hour, but winners and losers partied in their campers and RVs outside the stadium or at Jacksonville night spots into the early morning hours.

A target of UF defenders all day, McClendon registered an admirable 76 yards on 30 carries while playing hurt, and sustained the clock-killing drive with 20 yards on four rushes.

Pyburn hit seven of 11 passes for 86 yards and a touchdown. His Florida counterpart, Brantley, was 10 of 23 for 192 yards and a TD but had two interceptions. Georgia's Welton, who came up with those two interceptions, was the defensive standout.

Georgia fullbacks Womack and Stewart spiced up the post-game commentary, telling reporters they had played with a vengeance because Dickey once indicated they were not big enough or good enough to play for Florida when both were being recruited in high school.

Florida won its fourth game of the season a week later, downing Kentucky, 18–16, but fell 38–21 to Florida State. The axe fell in Gainesville and Dickey was fired on November 29, though he was on the sideline for the Gators' 22–21 loss to Miami. Florida ended at 4–7.

Gator linebacker James Harrell spent almost a decade in the NFL playing for Detroit and Kansas City.

Coach Doug Dickey, a former UF quarterback, led Florida to a 58–43–2 record from 1970 to 1978 but was winless in four bowl games. He was 3–6 against Vince Dooley's Bulldogs. [UF Archives]

Doug Dickey ended his nine years at Florida with a 58–43–2 record, including a 3–6 mark against Georgia. The former Gator quarterback went on to become athletic director at Tennessee.

Georgia was tied by Auburn, 22–22, the following week, then nipped Georgia Tech, 29–28, to earn a berth against Stanford in the Bluebonnet Bowl in Houston. In the bowl, the Bulldogs struck for a 22–0 lead but could not contain the Cardinal and All-American quarterback Steve Dils, losing 25–22. With a 9–2–1 worksheet, Georgia was ranked 15th by UPI and 16th by AP in the final polls.

The Bulldogs' Willie McClendon, offensive tackle Mack Guest, linebacker Ricky McBride, offensive guard Matt Braswell and kicker Rex Robinson joined Florida's Cris Collinsworth and Berj Yepremian as first-team All-SEC honorees.

Scoring:

Georgia	10	14	0	0	—	24
Florida	3	10	0	9	—	22

UF	FG	Yepremian, 30 yards
UGA	TD	McClendon, 3-yard run (Robinson kick)
UGA	FG	Robinson, 32 yards

UF	TD	Collinsworth, 33-yard pass from Brantley (Yepremian kick)
UGA	TD	Hodge, 3-yard pass from Pyburn (Robinson kick)
UGA	TD	Scott, 44-yard pass from Arnold (Robinson kick)
UF	FG	Yepremian, 19 yards
UF	FG	Yepremian, 20 yards
UF	TD	Enclade, 35-yard pass from Collinsworth (pass failed)

Georgia: _Offense:_ Scott, Russell, _split end;_ Milo, Blakewood, _left tackle;_ Hudson, Akacki, _left guard;_ Donaldson, Parrish _center;_ Braswell, Harper, _right guard;_ Guest, Morrison, _right tackle;_ Norris, Hodge, _tight end;_ Prince, Arnold, _flanker;_ Pyburn, Belue, _quarterback;_ W. McClendon, S. Kelly, _tailback;_ Womack, Stewart, _fullback;_ R. Robinson, _placekicker;_ Garrett, _punter_

Defense: Dennis, Ros, D. Rogers, Miller, McBride, Middleton, _linebacker;_ Goodwin, Cook, _left end;_ Petrisko, Parks, _left guard;_ Freedman, Payne, _right guard;_ Terry, McShea, _right end;_ Woerner, Bell, B. Kelly, Hope, _cornerback;_ P. Collins, Welton, Archer, B. Kelly, _safety_

Florida: _Offense:_ Stephens, J. Gaffney, _split end;_ Bennek, Wickline, _left tackle;_ Subers, Midden, _left guard;_ Schroeder, Lawrence, _center;_ Galloway, J. Johnson, _right guard;_ Swafford, Mabardy, _right tackle;_ Bell, Enclade, _tight end;_ Collinsworth, D. Jones, _flanker;_ Brantley, Groves, _quarterback;_ C. Davis, D. Johnson, Waters, _halfback;_ T. Williams, Portale, T. Robinson, _fullback;_ Yepremian, _placekicker;_ Conover, _punter_

Defense: Sutton, Brooks, Brantley, Harrell, Kreis, D. Little, Golden, _linebacker;_ Pratt, Voor, _left end;_ Luckie, Hough, _left tackle;_ Fisher, Harrell, _right tackle;_ Dupree, Hinton, _right end;_ Fiorillo, Coburn, W. Gaffney, Garrett, _cornerback;_ V. James, Burdgess, J. Collins, B. Walker, _safety_

	Georgia	Florida
First downs	16	20
Rushes/yards	56/177	37/118
Passing yards	130	238
Return yards	77	50
Pass att/comp/int	12/8/1	26/12/2
Punts/avg. yards	5/37	5/47
Fumbles/lost	2/2	3/1
Penalties/yards	7/48	8/68

— 1979 —

Georgia 33, Florida 10

NOT SINCE THE 1946 TEAM WENT 0–9 FOR THE year had a Florida squad hit skid row as hard as the 1979 Gators readying for the November 10 free-for-all with Georgia.

The 0–6–1 Floridians of first-year coach Charley Pell had been in every contest, except a blowout to powerful Alabama, but had been unable to carve out a win. Likewise, the '79 Bulldogs were off to one of the worst starts in Georgia history.

The mediocrity of both teams gave new meaning to the popular phrase "world's largest outdoor cocktail party" as many fans welcomed the event with "the more spirits, the better," one sportswriter said.

"Forget the records! Throw the book out the window! And ready yourself for an old-fashioned Southern brawl," wrote Frank Tilton of the *Savannah Morning News*.

Coach Vince Dooley's Bulldogs were 4–4, but were unbeaten in the conference race and in the running for the SEC title. Wins over the Gators and Auburn the following week would clinch at least a tie for the championship and put Georgia in the Sugar Bowl. Yet, there was a matter of respectability.

"The 'Wonderdogs' perform in league competition while the 'Blunderdogs' are 0–4 in nonconference play," the *Atlanta Constitution* said.

Victories by the Bulldogs over the Gators in 1954, 1966, 1975 and 1976 had derailed Florida's chances of winning its first SEC crown, and the Orange and Blue wanted nothing better than to return the favor in 1979.

Georgia was embarrassed by an opening 22–21 home loss to Wake Forest, then fell 12–7 at Clemson. South Carolina followed by beating UGA, 27–20, in Athens to leave the 'Dogs 0–3. Matters improved the next month as Georgia defeated Ole Miss, 24–21; LSU,

21–14; Vanderbilt, 31–10; and Kentucky, 20–6. Then unheralded Virginia ambushed UGA, 31–0, at Sanford Stadium in one of the worst chapters in Georgia football annals.

No one knew how the 'Dogs would react to the humiliating loss to the Cavaliers and if they could close ranks in time to beat Florida.

It was no secret that the Gators were in the midst of a rebuilding year and the record showed it. Charley Pell came to Florida from Clemson where he had coached the previous two years. Pell, a lineman on Paul "Bear" Bryant's national championship team at Alabama in 1961, had led Clemson to consecutive winning seasons and Gator Bowl appearances.

The Gators lost their opener, 14–10, at Houston, followed by a 7–7 tie with Georgia Tech. Mississippi State then beat them, 24–10, before the Gators fell 20–3 at LSU; 40–0 to top-ranked Alabama in Gainesville; 20–10 to Tulsa; and 19–13 at Auburn.

"Go Gators" and "Go Dogs" signs, along with Confederate battle flags, were everywhere as game day morning dawned to the metallic drone of scores of motor homes parked near the Gator Bowl. By this year, traffic jams had become an unpleasant reality of the traditional proceedings.

A less-than-capacity crowd of about 69,000 partying fans filtered into the Gator Bowl on a windy afternoon for the traditional showdown.

Georgia was heavily reliant on the passing of quarterback Buck Belue and the receiving of Lindsay Scott and Anthony Arnold. The Gators had few heroes to cheer for, but quarterback Larry Ochab had been an offensive spark plug in the Auburn game. And all-conference wide receiver Cris Collinsworth was on his way to a career in the NFL.

The Gators won the coin toss. They chose to receive rather than take the end of the field where they would have the wind at their backs in the first quarter.

Florida, pinned deep in its own territory on the game's first possession, got off a wobbly 28-yard boot into the gusty wind, and Georgia started its first series at the UF 38. The Bulldogs came up short of a first down, but kicker Rex Robinson, with the wind behind him, nailed a 48-yard field goal to put Georgia up 3–0 with just over two minutes gone in the game.

Florida's troubles immediately accelerated. On first down after the kickoff, UF tailback Terry Williams fumbled and defensive end Gordon Terry jumped on the ball at the Gators 31. On third down, Belue hit Scott for 14 yards to the UF 17. Bulldog freshman tailback Carnie Norris then carried to the UF 7. On the next play, Norris again took a handoff from Belue, slashed outside around right end, and galloped untouched into the end zone. Robinson added his 61st consecutive PAT, tying him with former Georgia kicker Allan Leavitt for the conference record. More importantly to Robinson and his teammates, the 'Dogs were quickly up 10–0.

Minutes later, Florida's Ochab passed to Curt Garrett for a 9-yard gain. But the Gators' split end was sandwiched by several Bulldogs and the ball squirmed free. Georgia roverback Pat Collins picked the pigskin out of midair at the UF 37.

For the third time in the first period, Georgia had the ball with a first down inside the Florida 40. Sophomore tailback Matt Simon, a former quarterback from Statesboro, scampered for nine to the UF 28. Three plays later, Simon found a hole over right guard and darted 15 yards to the Florida 8. On third down, scrambling to his right under heavy pressure, Belue whipped a desperation pass toward a corner of the end zone. Seldom-used flanker Carmon Prince stretched into the sky and shagged the ball like an outfielder for a 6-yard touchdown. Robinson's 62nd consecutive extra point set a new SEC record and extended Georgia's total to 17–0 with 1:52 left in the first quarter.

Again Georgia blanketed Florida's offense and, in the opening moments of the second period, Belue hung a 30-yard pass to split end Scott with UF defender Juan Collins covering. Officials, however, ruled pass interference and Georgia had a first down at the UF 16.

The Bulldogs banged to the Gators 11 where, on fourth down, Robinson lifted a 28-yard kick through the uprights despite the tough breeze. Georgia led 20–0 with 12:39 still to go before intermission and the Sugar Bowl loomed closer for exultant UGA fans and their team.

The downtrodden Gators then finally came to life. Pell's men used 15 plays to reach the UGA 13 where, on third and eight, Ochab drifted back and flipped a pass to a Gator open in the end zone. The ball was tipped by Georgia's Jeff Hipp, but tight end Chris Faulkner pulled it in for the touchdown. Brian Clark converted and Florida had narrowed the Georgia lead to 20–7.

Unruffled by the UF offensive, Georgia started its next series on its 24 and used seven plays to reach the UF 40. Belue then rifled a pass over the middle to Scott, who wrestled away from a defender and cut across the field on a bee line for the goal line. The touchdown extended Georgia's margin to 26–7 with 1:51 left in the half. The Bulldogs went for two to extend their lead to three touchdowns, but a Belue pass didn't connect.

Florida's disaster was not yet complete. On the second play after the Georgia kickoff, fullback John Whittaker fumbled and UGA defensive guard Tim Parks recovered at the Gators 20. Simon sped for seven to the 13, followed by two more carries to the 3. Belue then hummed a strike between Florida defenders to tight end Norris Brown for the score. Robinson added the extra point to inflate Georgia's lead to a resounding 33–7 with 22 seconds left.

Many fans simply expected Florida to run out the clock and get to the locker room with no further damage done.

But UF's Darell Jones ran the kickoff back 27 yards, and Ochab passed to Terry Williams for 11 more. Two face mask penalties against Georgia moved the Gators into long field-goal range, and UF's Clark then lofted a 47-yarder as the last seconds ticked off. Georgia 33, Florida 10.

Georgia had scored on six of its seven possessions in the first half and the Gators would not recover.

In the second half, needing points, Florida's Ochab tried the air route but threw three interceptions.

The Junkyard Dogs had held the Gators offense to 40 rushing yards and 160 yards passing. Linebacker Frank Ros was the Dawgs' mainstay with 12 tackles, followed by guard Eddie Weaver with nine stops. Six Florida turnovers blew the Gators out of the water.

Offensively, Belue completed five of nine passes, three for touchdowns, and was honored as ABC's Outstanding Player of the Game and the City of Jacksonville's Most Valuable Player in the contest. Robinson not only set a new conference mark with 63 consecutive extra points, but his two field goals tied him for the all-time SEC career field-goal record of 35.

Florida lost its next game 31–3 to Kentucky, then fell 27–16 to Florida State before closing with a 30–24 loss at Miami. Pell's 0–10–1 record was the worst for the Gators since Raymond Wolf's winless campaign of 1946.

At least for this year, Georgia seemed jinxed in its own stadium as the 'Dogs lost 33–13 to formidable Auburn and, along with it, the SEC championship. They beat Georgia Tech, 16–3, in Atlanta but, at 6–5 and out of the conference race, Georgia was home for the holidays.

Rex Robinson was named to the All-America team. Robinson, UGA offensive tackle Matt Braswell, and Florida's Collinsworth were selected first-team All-SEC for the second consecutive year and were joined by Georgia center Ray Donaldson and defensive back Scott Woerner. Donaldson was drafted by the Baltimore Colts and anchored their offensive front line for over a decade. Florida linebacker Scot Brantley spent seven years in the NFL with Tampa Bay.

Scoring:

Georgia	17	16	0	0	—	33
Florida	0	10	0	0	—	10

UGA	FG	Robinson, 48 yards
UGA	TD	Norris, 7-yard run (Robinson kick)
UGA	TD	Prince, 6-yard pass from Belue (Robinson kick)
UGA	FG	Robinson, 28 yards
UF	TD	Faulkner, 13-yard pass from Ochab (Clark kick)
UGA	TD	Scott, 40-yard pass from Belue (pass failed)
UGA	TD	Brown, 3-yard pass from Belue (Robinson kick)
UF	FG	Clark, 47 yards

Georgia: *Offense:* Scott, Russell, *split end;* Braswell, Madray, *left tackle;* Hudson, Nall, *left guard;* Donaldson, Radloff, *center;* Harper, Blakewood, *right guard;* Morrison, Akacki, *right tackle;* N. Brown, J. Brown, *tight end;* Belue, Pyburn, *quarterback;* Womack, McCarthy, Guthrie *fullback;* Simon, Norris S. Kelley, McMickens, *tailback;* Arnold, Prince, Junior, *flanker;* Robinson, *placekicker;* Garrett, *punter*

Defense: Terry, Cook, *left end;* McCranie, McIntyre, *left tackle;* Weaver, Warthen, *left guard;* Parks, Creamons, *right guard;* McShea, Bouchillon, *right end;* Ros, Rogers, Taylor, Mullis, *linebacker;* Woerner, Bell, D. Williams, Fisher, *cornerback;* Collins, Elkins, Hipp, B. Kelly *safety*

Florida: *Offense:* Garrett, D. Jones, J. Gaffney, *split end;* Bennek, Hewko, *left tackle;* Subers, Redmond, *left guard;* Pharr, *center;* Plonk, Galloway, *right guard;* Hough, Wickline, *right tackle;* J. Jones, Bell, Faulkner, *tight end;* Collinsworth, S. Jackson, *flanker;* Ochab, J. Brown, *quarterback;* D. Williams, Prioleau, C. Davis, *tailback;* T. Williams, Whittaker, *fullback;* Clark, Van Wie, *placekicker;* Conover, *punter*

Defense: Golden, Brooks, *left end;* V. Jones, Luckie, *left tackle;* Fisher, Kalamaras, *noseguard;* Kreis, Ricketts, Little, F. Jackson, *linebacker;* Fike, Hinton, *right tackle;* Pratt, Voor, *right end;* Fiorillo, Peek, Burdgess, Green, *cornerback;* Hatch, James, Collins, Groves, Brodsky, *safety*

	Georgia	Florida
First downs	13	15
Rushes/yards	55/204	36/40
Passing yards	70	160
Return yards	23	14

Pass att/comp/int	9/5/0	30/16/4
Punts/avg. yards	6/43	6/38
Fumbles/lost	1/0	2/2
Penalties/yards	0/0	1/15

— 1980 —

Georgia 26, Florida 21

IN THE LATE '70S, COLLEGIATE SCOUTS FROM
Southern Cal to Ohio State were drawn to rural Wrightsville,
Ga., to watch a soft-spoken youngster who wrote poetry and shred-
ded opposing defenses as a running back at Johnson County High
School.

The feverish recruiting wars ended in April 1980 when Herschel
Walker signed with Georgia. Despite Walker's decision, few forecasters gave the Dawgs much of a chance of making a splash after a
6–5 record in 1979. Georgia was ranked 16th in preseason polls and
wasn't expected to challenge defending SEC champion Alabama for
league honors.

Yet, Herschel Walker would be the Red and Black knight of
Georgia's storybook jaunt to a national championship.

In Gainesville, the Gators of second-year coach Charley Pell were
rebounding nicely from the winless previous season and were anxious to engage the Bulldogs in the November 9, 1980, uprising in
Jacksonville. A freshman quarterback named Wayne Peace had the
Gators back on the path to respectability.

Eight games into the season, the surprising Bulldogs were unbeaten (4–0 in the SEC) and ranked second in the nation behind
undefeated Notre Dame, while Florida was rated 20th with a 6–1
record (3–1 in the conference).

Both squads were recovering from what amounted to gridiron
warfare a week earlier. The Gators had survived a 163-yard James
Brooks rushing onslaught, beating Auburn, 21–10, in Gainesville.

Georgia climbed from number four to number two in the rankings
after edging South Carolina and eventual Heisman winner George
Rogers, 13–10, in a nationally televised game. All-American Rex
Robinson kicked field goals of 57 and 51 yards, and Walker carried 43

Florida wide receiver Tyrone Young had not caught a pass in his college career until the 1980 Georgia game when he snared ten receptions for 183 yards, a series record.

times for 219 yards and a touchdown against the 14th-ranked Gamecocks.

Georgia was solid at every position. While much attention centered on Walker, junior quarterback Buck Belue and split end Lindsay Scott were back after contributing to Florida's demise in the '79 contest. Belue had already hit 52 of 105 passes for 972 yards and seven touchdowns in 1980. And the Junkyard Dogs of defensive coordinator Erk Russell were as tough and disciplined as any team in the country, ranking fifth in the nation in scoring defense.

Then there was Herschel. Walker was averaging 137 yards a game and almost six yards per carry going into the Florida contest, totalling 1,096 yards on the year to that point.

Before the season, Dooley decided the Bulldogs would revert to the silver pants worn during Wally Butts' tenure. The pants and the cry "Go you silver britches!" became trademarks of the campaign as they had been during Butts' regime.

Georgia embarked on its 1980 odyssey with a come-from-behind 16–15 thriller at Tennessee. The 'Dogs waltzed over Texas A&M, 42–0, in Athens, then beat Clemson, 20–16; Texas Christian, 34–3; Ole Miss, 28–21; Vanderbilt, 41–0; and Kentucky, 27–0. The big win over South Carolina fueled talk about a national championship in Athens.

Wide receiver Lindsay Scott (left) and quarterback Buck Belue (right) entered UGA legend when they connected on the touchdown bomb to beat Florida in 1980, arguably the most famous moment in UGA football history.

With Bob Hewko at quarterback, Florida began the season with a 41–13 win over California and a 45–12 conquest of Georgia Tech in Atlanta. The Gators then beat Mississippi State, 21–15, before losing, 24–7, to LSU at Florida Field. Wayne Peace took over at quarterback when Hewko suffered a season-ending knee injury in the LSU game.

Peace marshalled UF to a 15–3 win at Ole Miss and a 13–0 victory over Louisville before the Auburn triumph, which earned the Gators a national ranking. In addition to Peace, the Gators boasted All-SEC split end Cris Collinsworth, who was leading the league with 22 receptions for 359 yards and two touchdowns.

Some 70,000 fans crammed into the Gator Bowl and a regional television audience eagerly anticipated the kickoff.

On the game's fourth play from scrimmage, from the Georgia 28-yard line, Belue pitched to Walker running right. With fullback Jimmy Womack and tight end Norris Brown blocking, Walker churned between several Gators and suddenly broke into the open field. With the Georgia sections on their feet, Walker sprinted 40 yards downfield where he got another key block, this time from Scott who put away the last Gator defender. Walker ended his 72-yard dash in the Florida end zone, and Rex Robinson kicked his 91st consecutive extra point to stake Georgia to a 7–0 lead with only 1:51 gone in the first period.

The quick strike stunned Florida. On second down after the kickoff, Peace's pass attempt was intercepted by UGA cornerback Mike Fisher at the UF 41. The 'Dogs used three plays to gain a first down at the UF 30. Belue then passed to Amp Arnold for a nine-yard gain but the fleet flanker, trying for more yardage, was hit and fumbled. UF's Kyle Knight recovered at the Gators 21. The turn of events revitalized Florida which went on a march to the UGA 23.

Peace guided the "Run and Gun Gators" down the field using four wide receivers. When the 'Dogs stiffened, UF kicker Brian Clark nailed a 40-yard field goal to make it 7–3, Georgia, midway through the first quarter.

Late in the period, Georgia started a thrust at its 23. Belue connected with tight end Clarence Kay for eight, then found Scott for 21. With the ball at the UF 45, Belue scrambled to the UF 35 where he was tackled out of bounds. The Gators were flagged for a 15-yard personal foul, and the Bulldogs had a first down at the Florida 20. Facing third down, Belue rolled to his left behind two blocking backs

Cornerback Scott Woerner was a standout and All-American on UGA's 1980 championship team.

with Walker trailing him. Instead of pitching to Walker, Belue flicked a pass to Ronnie Stewart, who had slipped into a seam in the Gator defense at the 3. The Bulldog fullback stumbled across the goal line, and Robinson's conversion made it 14–3 barely two minutes into the second quarter.

On second down after the kickoff, Florida's Peace was tackled for a six-yard loss and fumbled. UGA defensive guard Eddie "Meat Cleaver" Weaver gathered the ball in at the UF 23 and Georgia moved from there to the 16, where they had to deal with a third and three. Belue then rolled out, was pressured, and heaved a pass that was intercepted by UF cornerback Ivory Curry and returned to the Gators 29.

The turnover inspired Florida, and Peace whipped his men downfield to the UGA 37. When the Bulldogs wouldn't budge, the Gators set up in punt formation. A pass off a fake punt failed, though, and the 'Dogs took over. But the UGA shouts died shortly afterward when Walker was crunched and committed a fumble, his first ever in a college game.

Peace and the Florida offense now dug in. Collinsworth snared a pass for 12 yards to the UGA 34. Then fullback James Jones corralled a Peace missile for 12 more before another Collinsworth reception, this one for 13 to the 'Dogs 9. On the fifth play of the offensive, Collinsworth beat Georgia's all-conference cornerback Scott Woerner, and Peace found him in a corner of the end zone for Florida's first touchdown. Clark's point after sliced the deficit to 14–10, Georgia, at the half.

Spurred by two 15-yard bursts by Walker, the 'Dogs crunched downfield on their first possession of the second half and found themselves perched on the UF 12. Belue's third-down pass fell incomplete but Robinson booted the field goal to extend Georgia's advantage to 17–10.

The Junkyard Dogs stopped the Gators offense for the second time in the third quarter, and Florida's punt left Georgia in good shape at its 47. Running a pitch to his right, Walker gained 13 to the UF 40 and Womack smashed for seven more. After a face mask violation, the 'Dogs had a first down at the UF 18. Walker knifed through for 14 more on another pitch right. From the Florida 4, Herschel was slammed for no gain on a run up the middle. He gained two on the next play but Belue lost two back to the 4 on third down. Dooley didn't hesitate, sending in Robinson. The senior kicker speared a 20-yarder that tied him with former LSU tailback Charles Alexander for

Vince Dooley takes a victory ride during UGA's undefeated season in 1980. In 25 seasons, Dooley compiled a 17–7–1 record against Florida.

the SEC career scoring mark of 254 points. Georgia had upped it to 20–10 with just under four minutes to play in the third period.

The teams swapped possessions before Florida took over on its own 19 late in the quarter. Peace heaved a pass to flanker Tyrone Young for 11 yards to the UF 30, then hit Jones for five. Two plays later, Peace again found Young slanting over the middle. Twisting and churning, the Gator receiver ripped away from three to four defenders and darted 54 yards to the UGA 11 before being tackled. Moments later, Jones slashed over right guard for an 11-yard score and Florida was back in it. Pell called time out and decided to go for the two-point conversion. The Gators went to the air, with Peace throwing a perfect pass to Young in the end zone. Just over 14 minutes remained in the game and Florida was on a roll, trailing only 20–18.

The roar from the Florida sections intensified minutes later when the Gators shut down Dooley's offense. The 'Dogs punted and Florida had a first down at its 24. They then went on a 10-play march that used up more than five minutes off the clock before reaching the Georgia 24. The drive ended there, however, and Clark came on to try a 40-yard field goal that would give Florida its first lead of the day. The kick was good and the Gators led 21–20 with 6:52 to play.

Fired-up Florida stuffed Georgia on the Bulldogs' next series and, after the UGA kick, took possession at their own 31 before grinding out two first downs. The march went down to the Bulldogs 36, as the clock ticked down on Georgia's national championship hopes. Rather than try a long field goal, Pell sent in punter Mark Dickert who deftly punched the ball out of bounds at the 8-yard line.

Georgia had 1:35 on the clock and one timeout left. Entering the huddle, Belue's intent was to get close enough for Robinson to win it with a field goal.

"I just mentioned, 'Let's give Rex a chance to win it,'" he later recalled in a *Florida Times-Union* story. The 'Dogs were confident that Robinson could hit one from as far out as 58 yards.

On first down, Belue scrambled, trying to find a receiver, and was dropped for a yard loss. A second-down pass fell incomplete and suddenly the 'Dogs were facing third and an infinity of green.

"After the second-down play, there was some frustration in the huddle," Belue remembered. "And the Florida players were taunting us, saying 'It's over.'"

On third down, Belue dropped to pass again. The Gators' defensive rush forced him to his right. Glancing over the middle he found Lindsay Scott breaking into the open at about the 25. Scott snared Belue's perfect aerial and sprinted into the annals of Georgia football history.

Based on a *Times-Union* story, Georgia radio announcer Larry Munson gave this description of the play: "Florida in a standup-5. They may or may not blitz. They won't. Buck back, third down on the 8 (actually the 7). In trouble . . . Gonna pick up a block behind him . . . Gonna throw on the run, complete to the 25! Lindsay Scott, 35, 40, Lindsay Scott, 45, 50! Run, Lindsay! 25, 20, 15, 10, 5 . . . Lindsay Scott! Lindsay Scott! Lindsay Scott!"

Scott came off his feet to catch the ball in the middle, broke to his right, then raced toward the sideline, running past Gator safety Tim Groves. In ecstasy, Dooley ran down the sideline as Scott dashed past him, clicking off the yards to glory. Ninety-three yards later, Scott crossed the Florida goal line and was engulfed by teammates celebrating as wildly as the Red and Black fans in the stands. Scott entered the UGA record books with the longest pass reception in school history, and also had his first touchdown of the season.

The end zone party resulted in a 15-yard penalty on Georgia that would be assessed on the kickoff. Leading 26–21, UGA went for two but Belue's pass was broken up.

Though stunned, the Gators still had 1:03 left to pull out a win. But on first down, Peace overthrew a receiver and was picked off by UGA senior cornerback Mike Fisher. Georgia ran off the remaining seconds to seal its incredible victory.

In defeat, the Gators still got sterling performances from Peace, who completed 20 of 37 passes for 286 yards and a touchdown in only his fourth collegiate game, and Young, who grabbed 10 receptions for 183 yards, a record for receiving yards in the series. Young's feat was even more impressive because he had not previously caught a pass in a college game.

Robinson was not the only record-setting Bulldog in Jacksonville. Herschel Walker's 237 yards on 37 carries, including a touchdown, set a new Georgia single-season rushing record. His 1,334 yards, with two regular season games still remaining, surpassed Willie McClendon's previous record of 1,312 yards.

Within hours of the Bulldogs' win, Georgia Tech tied top-ranked Notre Dame 3–3 in Atlanta. Early the following week, the 'Dogs were voted No. 1 in both polls and did not relinquish the crown.

Florida ended 1980 with a 17–15 win at Kentucky, a 31–7 loss to Miami, and a 17–13 defeat at Florida State. With a 7–4 regular season record, the Gators earned a trip to the Tangerine Bowl where they beat Maryland, 35–20, in their first bowl win since 1969.

Cris Collinsworth and linebacker David Little were named to some All-America teams for Florida and were joined by tight end

Red and black madness in the end zone as Lindsay Scott and UGA fans revel in the improbable Georgia win in 1980. [Hargrett Collection, UGA Libraries]

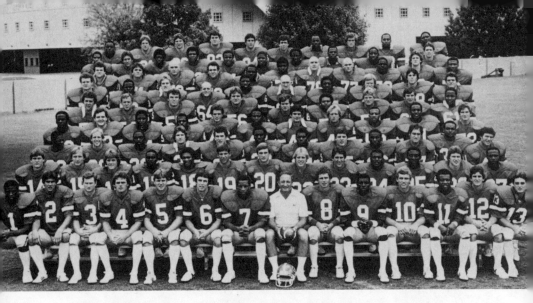

Spurred by the miraculous win over Florida, the 1980 Georgia Bulldogs went on to the national championship with a 12–0 record and a 17–10 victory over Notre Dame in the 1981 Sugar Bowl.

Chris Faulkner on the All-SEC first team. Little later was a longtime player for the Pittsburgh Steelers. Collinsworth starred for the Cincinnati Bengals, earning Rookie of the Year honors in 1981 and All-Pro distinction.

Georgia closed out the regular season with a 31–21 win at Auburn to wrap up the SEC championship and rolled over Georgia Tech, 38–20, in Athens.

Against Notre Dame in the Sugar Bowl, the 'Dogs raced to a 17–3 advantage at halftime and hung on for a 17–10 victory. Robinson, Walker, and Woerner were honored as All-Americans and named first-team All-SEC along with teammates Belue, Weaver, safety Jeff Hipp, defensive tackle Jimmy Payne, offensive tackle Nat Hudson and offensive guard Tim Morrison. Woerner was drafted by the Atlanta Falcons while Rex Robinson was selected by Cincinnati. Hudson was a New Orleans Saints draft choice.

The 12–0 Bulldogs had reached the zenith of collegiate football with a national championship due, in large part, to the miracle in Jacksonville.

Scoring:

Georgia	7	7	6	6	—	26
Florida	3	7	0	11	—	21

UGA	TD	Walker, 72-yard run (Robinson kick)
UF	FG	Clark, 40 yards

UGA	TD	Stewart, 13-yard pass from Belue (Robinson kick)
UF	TD	Collinsworth, 9-yard pass from Peace (Clark kick)
UGA	FG	Robinson, 25 yards
UGA	FG	Robinson, 20 yards
UF	TD	J. Jones, 11-yard run (Young pass from Peace)
UF	FG	Clark, 40 yards
UGA	TD	Scott, 93-yard pass from Belue (pass failed)

Georgia: *Offense:* L. Scott, Junior, *split end;* Jeff Harper, Case, *left tackle;* Blakewood, Gray, *left guard;* Radloff, Happe, *center;* Morrison, Happe, *right guard;* Hudson, Jimmy Harper, *right tackle;* N. Brown, C. Kay, *tight end;* Arnold, C. Jones, *flanker;* Belue, *quarterback;* Walker, Norris, *tailback;* Womack, Stewart, *fullback;* Robinson, *placekicker;* Malkiewicz; *punter;* Woerner, Walker, *special teams*

Defense: Miles, Bobo, *left end;* Payne, Lindsey, *left tackle;* Weaver, Parks, *left guard;* Creamons, Crowe, *right guard;* McShea, Carver, *right end;* N. Taylor, Thurson, Ros, Forts, *linebacker;* Woerner, Bell, Fisher, D. Williams, *cornerback;* Welton, Kelly, Hipp, *safety*

Florida: *Offense:* S. Jackson, Garrett, *split end;* Fike, Schultheis, *left tackle;* Plonk, Moyle, *left guard;* Redmond, D. Smith, *center;* Subers, Fraser, *right guard;* Wickline, Hough, *right tackle;* Faulkner, Marshall, *tight end;* Collinsworth, Young, *flanker;* Peace, *quarterback;* Kellom, J. Brown, *tailback;* J. Jones, T. Williams, C. Davis, *fullback;* B. Clark, *placekicker;* Sibbald, Dickert, *punter;* Curry, J. Brown, Collinsworth, *special teams*

Defense: Golden, Brooks, *left end;* Galloway, M. Clark, *left tackle;* Fisher, Whittaker, *noseguard;* Little, Wiegmann, F. Jackson, Ricketts, *linebacker;* Luckie, Coleman, *right tackle;* V. Brown, Patrick, *right end;* Curry, Vaughan, Gilliam, McKeever, *cornerback;* Knight, Pleasants, Groves, Lilly, *safety*

	Georgia	Florida
First downs	17	20
Rushes/yards	53/286	42/123
Passing yards	145	286
Return yards	29	24
Pass att/comp/int	16/7/2	37/20/2
Punts/avg. yards	5/46	7/35
Fumbles/lost	3/2	2/1
Penalties/yards	5/45	8/99

— 1981 —

Georgia 26, Florida 21

REVENGE WAS ON THE MINDS OF MANY FLORida fans traveling to Jacksonville for the November 7, 1981, tangle with fourth-ranked Georgia.

The last-minute Buck Belue-to-Lindsay Scott touchdown pass of 93 yards in the 1980 contest was a dagger in the hearts of Gator supporters who still simmered over the loss and Georgia's eventual national championship.

Herschel Walker, the Bulldogs sophomore dynamo, was a Heisman hopeful, an All-American and the spearhead of 7–1 Georgia's offense. Walker ranked second nationally in rushing with 1,309 yards and was growing in legend every Saturday afternoon. Also returning for Coach Vince Dooley were Belue and Scott, who were lionized by UGA fans for "The Play" in the 1980 contest.

Georgia would be without defensive coordinator Erk Russell, who had accepted the job as head coach at Georgia Southern, where football was being resurrected after 40 years. Russell, the architect of the Junkyard Dogs defenses, was replaced by Bill Lewis.

Third-year coach Charley Pell's Gators were 5–3 and would need a supreme effort to best Georgia. Florida's ace was sophomore quarterback Wayne Peace, already developing into one of the Gators' all-time best passers. And Pell had an additional surprise in store when the Gators took the field in Jacksonville.

With the potential to put up a strong defense of its national crown, Georgia opened the year with a 44–0 sleeper over Tennessee in Athens, then beat California, 27–13. In one of the biggest games in the South in 1981, Georgia fell, 13–3, at powerful Clemson as the 'Dogs committed nine turnovers. Georgia rebounded to defeat South Carolina, 24–0; Ole Miss, 37–7; Vanderbilt, 53–21; Kentucky, 21–0; and Temple, 49–3.

Florida's season began with a 21–20 loss at Miami and a 35–7 breather over Furman, before a 27–6 win against Georgia Tech at Florida Field. The Gators lost, 28–7, at Mississippi State; beat LSU, 24–10; Maryland, 15–10; and Ole Miss, 49–3, before being upset, 14–12, at Auburn a week before meeting Georgia.

The game was nationally televised by ABC and the usual 70,000 were in the Gator Bowl to watch the proceedings in person. A number of bowl scouts were also in attendance.

"Everywhere, there is red and black and orange and blue," the *Atlanta Constitution* said of downtown Jacksonville. The driver of an orange Cadillac stalled traffic on Duval Street as he got out and attached a "Herschel Who?" poster to his rear window.

By the pool at Georgia's hotel, Vince Dooley was approached by a woman who asked him to autograph her hand. She vowed never to wash off the signature, but a bystander quickly told Dooley, "Unless y'all lose tomorrow."

Trying to launch his Gators on an emotional high, Pell outfitted his men with orange pants, the first time a Florida team had worn the brightly-colored leggings since 1940. The ploy inflamed the Gators and their fans.

Florida, sparked by a Peace-to-tailback Steve Miller completion for 20 yards and an offside call against UGA on a third-and-four situation, early on pushed Georgia backwards. Suddenly, Florida had a first down at the Georgia 19. Just as suddenly, the Junkyard Dogs were unmuzzled. Firing through the Gators' offensive wall, the Georgians spilled Peace three times for losses of 21 yards back to the UGA 40, taking Florida out of scoring range.

Now Walker, Belue, Scott and friends would get the ball for the first time. But Florida's defense was sky high and had a bounty out for big Herschel, forcing Georgia to punt. The defenses ruled for the remainder of the first quarter.

In the early minutes of the second period, the Gators once again bulled to the UGA 19. Peace went back to pass but his toss was picked off by UGA roverback Tim Bobo at the Georgia 2.

Twice Florida had been inside the UGA 20 and come away with no points. Defensively, though, the Gators were holding Walker in check, for the most part, and keeping the volatile UGA offense blanketed.

With 6:15 left in the half, the Gators punched out to their 46 and Pell decided to go for the home run. Peace drifted back and hurled a long bomb toward Miller blazing down the sideline. The UF tailback gathered it in and streaked 54 yards to the Georgia end zone as

Florida tasted first blood. Kicker Brian Clark's extra point made it 7–0 Gators, but the first half fireworks were only beginning for both teams.

On the kickoff, the ball skidded past Walker near the goal line, and he was buried by Floridians at the UGA 2. The pigskin then popped away from fullback Ronnie Stewart on the next play when he was torpedoed by UF linebacker Fernando Jackson. Gator tackle David "Bull" Galloway recovered at the Georgia 5.

Florida bludgeoned the 'Dogs with three running plays that edged the ball to within inches of the goal line. On fourth down, fullback James Jones powered in for six. Clark's kick lengthened UF's lead to 14–0 with less than two minutes left before intermission. The Gators had struck for two touchdowns in 94 seconds.

Now Georgia's offensive unit came alive, needing just three plays to rip to the UF 24. A Belue completion to freshman Scott Williams for a 34-yard gain was the big play. Belue then hit Walker with a short pass. The potent tailback wheeled to his left, turned on the jets, and outran everyone to the end zone with 31 seconds left in the half.

"Imagine a jet-propelled, supersonic tank that turns like a Ferrari and you will begin to get the picture," Anthony Stastny of the *Savannah Morning News* wrote of Walker. Georgia kicker Kevin Butler added the extra point, and the 'Dogs had narrowed the Florida advantage to 14–7 at halftime.

Neither team did much offensively in the first half of the third quarter.

But after a Florida punt, with 7:26 left in the period, Georgia set sail on a 12-play drive that used up more than five minutes off the scoreboard clock. Norris Brown caught a Belue pass for 19, a Scott reception went for 14, and Stewart snagged a 15-yard pass. From the UF 16, Georgia then ran the same play that resulted in Walker's score in the first half. Belue flipped a short pass over the middle to the Bulldog star, who turned goalward, building steam. Gator defensive back Ivory Curry came up to make the hit, but Walker simply ran over him and rumbled into the end zone. Butler's conversion tied it at 14-all.

The impetus was with Georgia now as their defense smothered the Gators after the kickoff, forcing a punt. The kick left Georgia with a first down at the UF 47. With Walker carrying most of the load, Georgia reached the UF 4 in six plays. Walker then took a pitchout and rammed to pay dirt to give the 'Dogs their first lead of the afternoon. Butler's missed conversion left it at 20–14.

Defensive guard Eddie "Meat Cleaver" Weaver was an All-SEC performer and stalwart for the "Junkyard Dawgs" in Georgia's victories over the Gators in 1980 and 1981.

Then it was the Gators' turn to catch fire. Peace went to the air, finding receivers for gains of 27, 12, seven and 21 to surge to the Georgia 14. Steve Miller tore down to the 10 before Peace shot a pass to junior flanker Spencer Jackson in the end zone for the touchdown. Clark's extra point seized the lead back for Florida with 10 minutes left in the fourth.

The 'Dogs were penalized for clipping on the kickoff and found themselves backed up at their 5. Fate landed the teams in almost the same situation they had faced the previous year. Down 21–20 in the fourth quarter in 1980, the 'Dogs had started their 93-yard winning drive from their 7.

Georgia had substantially more time on the clock this year, but Florida was primed to pull the upset.

With Walker the workhorse, the 'Dogs steadily ground downfield. On a third-and-eight situation, Belue completed a 17-yard pass to Scott to critically keep the drive alive. By this time, the Florida defense appeared weary and Walker was punishing the Gators with sizeable gains. Ten times he ripped into the enemy line like a battering ram behind lead blocker Stewart as the 'Dogs ran more than seven minutes off the clock.

With the ball at the 1, everyone in the stadium knew Herschel would get the call.

Walker took Belue's handoff and vaulted high above the battling linemen. For an instant, he appeared suspended in air before disappearing among a mound of struggling Gators in the end zone. With

355

2:31 remaining, Georgia went for the two-point conversion to lengthen its 26–21 advantage, but Walker failed to reach the end zone again.

The grueling 17-play, 95-yard drive deflated Florida. The Gators got the ball two more times, but the Bulldogs held and ran out the clock. Emotionally and physically spent, several UGA players yelled, "It's over! Thank God, it's over!"

The win preserved Georgia's outside hope of a second consecutive national championship and SEC title.

Walker's four-touchdown performance drew raves from Dooley, as well as enhanced attention from the national media and pro scouts. Herschel carried 47 times for 192 yards and added four receptions for 55 yards. His rushing attempts set a new SEC record.

Florida's Peace completed 21 of 37 passes for 272 yards and two touchdowns with one interception, while Belue threw for 167 yards and two touchdowns, connecting on 13 of 22 attempts for Georgia. Peace's passing was offset by a Dawgs defense, headed by tackle Jimmy Payne and ends Dale Carver and Freddie Gilbert, that tagged the UF quarterback for 50 yards in losses while attempting to throw.

The Gators closed their year with a 33–12 win against Kentucky and a 35–3 pasting of Florida State to earn a Peach Bowl berth with West Virginia. The Mountaineers had too much firepower in the postseason match, downing Florida, 26–3, to end the Gators' season at 7–5.

Florida defensive tackle David "Bull" Galloway garnered All-America honors, and he and James Jones, Brian Clark and linebacker Wilber Marshall were first-team All-SEC selections. Galloway was drafted by St. Louis and started for the Cardinals into the 1990s.

Dooley's 'Dogs smashed Auburn, 24–13, to clinch the conference crown and a duel with Pittsburgh in the Sugar Bowl. A 44–7 shelling of archenemy Georgia Tech was UGA's icing on the cake. With a 10–1 regular season mark, Georgia was ranked second in the country behind undefeated Clemson, which was set to play Nebraska in the Orange Bowl. If Clemson lost and the 'Dogs beat Pitt, Georgia would have a strong argument for its second national title.

It was not to be.

Clemson defeated the Cornhuskers in Miami, and Dan Marino hit a fourth-down touchdown pass in the final minute of the Sugar Bowl as Pitt clipped Georgia, 24–20. The Bulldogs were fifth-rated in the final UPI poll and sixth in the AP rankings.

Herschel Walker was named to several All-America teams for the second year in a row and was joined on the All-SEC first squad by Buck Belue, Lindsay Scott, defensive guard Eddie Weaver, defensive tackle Jimmy Payne and placekicker Kevin Butler. Walker, Belue, Weaver and Payne all made the first team for the second consecutive year. Scott was a first-round draft pick by New Orleans.

Scoring:

Georgia	0	7	7	12	—	26
Florida	0	14	0	7	—	21

UF	TD	Miller, 54-yard pass from Peace (Clark kick)
UF	TD	Jones, 1-yard run (Clark kick)
UGA	TD	Walker, 24-yard pass from Belue (Butler kick)
UGA	TD	Walker, 16-yard pass from Belue (Butler kick)
UGA	TD	Walker, 4-yard run (kick failed)
UF	TD	S. Jackson, 10-yard pass from Peace (Clark kick)
UGA	TD	Walker, 1-yard run (run failed)

Georgia: *Offense:* Buckler, Harrell, K. Harris, *split end;* Gray, McIntyre, *left tackle;* Radloff, Blakewood, *left guard;* Happe, Case, *center;* J. Brown, Weaver, *right guard;* Harper, Hood, *right tackle;* Kay, N. Brown, S. Williams, *tight end;* L. Scott, Junior, *flanker;* Belue, Lastinger, *quarterback;* Walker, Norris, Simon, *tailback;* Stewart, Young, McCarthy, *fullback;* Butler, *placekicker;* Broadway, *punter;* Harrell, Scott, Walker, *special teams*

Defense: Carver, Hall, *left end;* Payne, Lindsey, *left tackle;* Weaver, K. Jackson, *left guard;* Crowe, Creamons, *right guard;* Gilbert, Dooley, *right end;* Taylor, Forts, Thurson, Culpepper, *linebacker;* R. Harris, D. Jones, D. Williams, S. Kelly, *cornerback;* Hoage, Bobo, S. Kelly, Dean, *safety*

Florida: *Offense:* Lang, Dixon, *split end;* Plonk, L. Brown, *left tackle;* Fraser, Moyle, *left guard;* Bromley, Allen, *center;* Schultheis, Hunt, *right guard;* Fike, Gallon, *right tackle;* Mularkey, Kurzu, *tight end;* S. Jackson, T. Young, *flanker;* Peace, Hewko, *quarterback;* Miller, C. Davis, *tailback;* J. Jones, Shannon, L. Hampton, *fullback;* B. Clark, *placekicker;* Borajkiewicz, *punter;* Curry, Hampton *special teams*

Defense: A. Johnson, Brown, W. Marshall, Clark, F. Jackson, Tolliver, Wiegmann, McCallister, *linebacker;* Galloway, Hinson, *left tackle;* Fisher, Meyers, *noseguard;* Harris, A. Jones, *right tackle;* McKeever, Vaughan, Curry, L. Smith, *cornerback;* Knight, Gilliam, Lilly, S. Marshall, *safety*

	Georgia	Florida
First downs	23	18
Rushing yards	229	36
Passing yards	167	272
Pass att/comp/int	22/13/0	37/21/1
Punts/avg. yards	7/27	7/26
Fumbles/lost	6/2	4/2
Penalties/yards	6/47	4/28

— 1982 —

Georgia 44, Florida 0

GEORGIA IRONMAN HERSCHEL WALKER HAD
the undefeated Bulldogs in the hunt for another national championship with a Heisman Trophy waiting in the wings in the fall of 1982.

Unknown to anyone, except perhaps Herschel himself, Walker
also was in the autumn of his storied career in the Red and Black.

Enlargement and renovation of the Gator Bowl meant that a
record crowd of more than 80,000 would be on hand for the November 6 Georgia-Florida brawl.

The Bulldogs of 19th-year coach Vince Dooley were 8–0, ranked
second in the UPI poll, third by the Associated Press and sitting atop
the conference standings where they had finished in 1980 and 1981.

Florida was 5–2 but virtually out of the SEC chase with losses to
LSU and Vanderbilt. Yet the Gators had a formidable cannon capable
of countering Walker's offensive menace. At a school known for its
stellar passing quarterbacks, UF's Wayne Peace soared to heights in
1982 that few had reached before him.

Peace was having a brilliant year, completing 75 percent of his
passes to lead the nation. The junior from Lakeland had hit on 126 of
170 throws for 1,458 yards and seven touchdowns. At some point
during the season, Peace was expected to pass Steve Spurrier and
move into second place behind John Reaves on Florida's career yardage list.

Georgia was gunning for its fifth straight victory over Florida, a
feat the Bulldogs had not accomplished since 1944–1948, and had
won seven of the last eight meetings between the two schools.

Walker, a two-time All-America, was the nucleus of Georgia's
return to national prominence in the '80s. The junior tailback rewrote
the record book almost every time he touched the ball. Walker owned
eight NCAA rushing records and needed only 15 yards against

All-American Jimmy Payne was a three-time All-SEC defensive tackle for Georgia from 1980 to 1982.

Florida to become the NCAA's fifth all-time leading rusher. In the Bulldogs' 34–3 bombardment of Memphis State a week earlier, Walker scored two touchdowns to give him 272 points, surpassing former UGA kicker Rex Robinson's 269 points for the new SEC career scoring record. With 1,194 yards rushing and 10 touchdowns in eight games, many fans were in awe of Herschel "Heisman" Walker, who had the benefit of running behind a strong offensive line. Two-time all-conference defensive tackle Jimmy Payne was the key to the 'Dogs defense.

Georgia downed defending national champion Clemson, 13–7, to start the season, then defeated Brigham Young, 17–14; South Carolina, 34–18; Mississippi State, 29–22; Ole Miss, 33–10; Vanderbilt, 27–13; Kentucky, 27–14, and Memphis State.

Georgia quarterback John Lastinger was trying to fill the shoes of the departed Buck Belue but was last in the conference in passing. The Gators were the worst in the SEC in pass defense but knew they had to stop Georgia's ground offensive to have a winning chance.

The Gators of fourth-year coach Charley Pell opened 1982 with a 17–14 win over Miami and a 17–9 victory against Southern California. Florida followed up with a 27–17 decision over Mississippi State, but lost 24–13 to LSU and 31–29 to Vanderbilt. The Gators then mauled West Texas State, 77–14, before upsetting Auburn, 19–17, a week before the Georgia matchup.

In addition to Peace's air force, the Gators had a strong running game of their own, led by All-SEC fullback James Jones and halfbacks John L. Williams and Lorenzo Hampton. The defensive hero was all-conference linebacker Wilber Marshall who would become one of Florida's all-time greats.

As the teams warmed up, a newly-expanded Gator Bowl with 80,700 fans, plus a CBS regional television audience, got ready for the 3:50 p.m. kickoff. The day was cool and the temperature dropped with the late fall sun.

Georgia moved 31 yards on the game's initial possession before Lastinger threw an interception. But the UF offense put the Gators in deep trouble minutes later when, on a third-down play, Peace fumbled, and Bulldog defensive end Dale Carver recovered at the UF 37. Walker crashed for seven on first down. On the next play, the Georgia jackhammer took a handoff into the right side of the Florida line, slashed through the arms of four Gators, and bolted into the end zone with only 2:23 gone in the game. The 30-yard run and kicker Kevin Butler's extra point would be all Georgia needed, but the scoring parade was just beginning.

Gator backs James Jones and Lorenzo Hampton, starting from their 20 after the kickoff, tore through the Georgia defense for substantial yardage as Florida advanced to the UGA 17. But Bulldog safety Jeff Sanchez intercepted a Peace pass on the goal line to thwart the drive with five minutes left in the first quarter. On the touchback, Georgia got the ball on its 20 and went back to work pounding it out on the ground.

Six first downs and 15 plays into the drive, Georgia was on the UF 1-yard line facing second and goal. Walker turned human javelin, cradling the ball and leaping above blockers and defenders alike before crash landing into the end zone. Butler added the conversion and Georgia led 14–0 at the 12:43 mark of the second quarter.

Florida answered with its best drive of the day. Peace ignited the Gators with a 33-yard pass completion to Hampton to reach the UGA 46. On the running of Hampton and Jones, Florida smashed to a first and goal at the UGA 5. Peace threw incomplete and Hampton ran twice to push closer, but the Gators were looking at fourth down. Pell decided to go for it, but the 'Dogs piled into Hampton inches short of the goal line.

Sanchez stopped another Florida series with his second interception later in the quarter. During the play, UF wide receiver Tyrone Young suffered a shoulder separation and was lost for the season.

Late in the half, Georgia moved inside the UF 25 before the Gators defense halted them. Butler hammered a 32-yard field goal to extend the UGA advantage to 17–0 at intermission. Florida, though barely still in the game, had the mission-impossible task of stopping Walker who already had burned them for 162 rushing yards in the first half.

The Bulldogs came out of their locker room relentless on both sides of the ball. After forcing a UF punt, Georgia went on another offensive with Walker gouging out chunks of yardage. The march sputtered at the 12, but Butler kicked a 22-yard field goal to make it 20–0.

Georgia again got the ball on another Peace fumble minutes later. With Walker running amok, the 'Dogs pushed 80 yards to the 1. Lastinger took the snap and lost his footing, bobbling the ball as he fell. The ubiquitous Walker stepped in, snatched the pigskin out of the air, and lunged over the goal line for his third touchdown. Butler's extra point gave Georgia a comfortable 27–0 margin midway through the third quarter.

Dooley began substituting freely and Herschel Walker was done for the day with 219 yards on 35 carries and three scores. Meanwhile, the 'Dogs defense, led by end Stan Dooley and Sanchez, was pulverizing Peace and the rest of the Gators. In the third period, Florida had minus yardage and did not gain a first down.

The dog-tired UF defense had been on the field much of the game. To the Gators and their backers, the night got blacker and colder by the minute, while UGA fans were already celebrating. The jubilation was fueled by news that top-rated Pitt had been upset by Notre Dame, meaning that a Georgia win would likely result in the Bulldogs moving up to No. 1 in the wire service polls.

Linebacker Wilber Marshall was the headhunter of Gator teams from 1980 to 1983 but was winless against Georgia. He was an All-American in 1982 and 1983 and was an All-Pro with Chicago and Washington.

The UGA subs didn't let up on the Gators. Second-string quarterback Todd Williams engineered a 63-yard offensive early in the fourth quarter that climaxed with Carnie Norris scoring from the 1. Butler made it 34–0.

A 30-yard field goal by Butler preceded Williams' second touchdown march. The 64-yard drive ended with Tron Jackson scooting 20 yards for the TD. Butler's kick made the final margin 44–0.

Florida did not earn a first down in the second half until only four minutes remained, and Peace had been replaced at quarterback by Bob Hewko.

Georgia amassed 391 yards rushing, with Walker's effort setting new NCAA records for career carries (936 in three years) and career rushing (4,920 in three years). He also passed Zeke Bratkowski's UGA total offense mark of 4,824 yards. And Herschel now was in fifth place on the NCAA career rushing list.

After the game, Pell described Walker as "the most dominating player in college football."

In three games against Florida, Walker had scored eight touchdowns and rushed for 649 yards, the most yards gained by any running back in the rivalry's history.

The win also left Vince Dooley with a 13–5–1 mark against the Gators.

Georgia's defense surrendered only 180 yards total offense and limited Peace to 10 completions in 19 pass attempts for just 102 yards. Florida also committed five turnovers, two interceptions and three fumbles, all by Peace. James Jones led the Gator rushers with 59 yards on 12 carries.

Florida came back from the Georgia debacle to beat Kentucky, 39–13; Tulane, 21–14; and Florida State, 13–10, to earn an invitation to play Arkansas in the Bluebonnet Bowl. The Razorbacks prevailed 28–24 but, at 8–4, Florida had its third consecutive winning season and bowl trip. Still, the fifth straight loss to Georgia and the lopsidedness of the defeat dulled the Gators' glitter.

Florida linebacker Wilber Marshall was named an All-American, and both he and fullback James Jones were honored as first-team All-SEC selectees for the second yeard in a row. Jones was a first-round draft choice of Detroit.

The Bulldogs followed their Florida triumph with a 19–14 win at Auburn to win their third consecutive SEC title and ended the regular season with a 38–18 conquest of Georgia Tech.

The Sugar Bowl would be a showdown between top-ranked, 11–0

"Heisman" Herschel Walker poses with the trophy in 1982. Walker led the Dawgs to three straight SEC titles and in three wins over Florida scored eight touchdowns.

Georgia and No. 2 Penn State, with the national championship going to the victors. The Nittany Lions snarled their way to a 20–3 second quarter lead and held off the tenacious Bulldogs for a 27–23 win.

The heartbreaking loss in New Orleans would be the end of the Herschel Walker dynasty at Georgia. Walker won the 1982 Heisman Trophy, 40 years after Frank Sinkwich captured the school's first Heisman. Herschel was consensus All-America and All-SEC for the third consecutive year. He was joined as an All-American by defensive tackle Jimmy Payne and rover Terry Hoage, who both made all-conference (Payne for the third time), along with Georgia center Wayne Radloff, offensive tackle Jimmy Harper, linebacker Tommy Thurson, defensive end Freddie Gilbert and safety Jeff Sanchez.

Walker signed with the New Jersey Generals of the new United States Football League early in 1983 and later played with Dallas, Minnesota and Philadelphia in the NFL. He was also a member of the 1992 U.S. Olympic bobsled team. Radloff later played for the Atlanta Falcons.

Georgia's faithful savor the Walker years and their 1980 national crown . . . and are occasionally caught musing about what might have been, had Herschel stayed for his senior year.

Scoring:

Georgia	7	10	10	17	—	44
Florida	0	0	0	0	—	0

UGA	TD	Walker, 30-yard run (Butler kick)
UGA	TD	Walker, 1-yard run (Butler kick)
UGA	FG	Butler, 32 yards
UGA	FG	Butler, 22 yards
UGA	TD	Walker, 1-yard run (Butler kick)
UGA	TD	Norris, 1-yard run (Butler kick)
UGA	FG	Butler, 30 yards
UGA	TD	Jackson, 20-yard run (Butler kick)

Georgia: *Offense:* Wisham, Harris, *split end;* Harper, Hood, *left tackle;* Weaver, Case, *left guard;* Radloff, K. Johnson, *center;* J. Brown, Gray, *right guard;* McIntyre, Perry, *right tackle;* N. Brown, Kay, *tight end;* C. Jones, Simmons, *flanker;* Lastinger, T. Williams, *quarterback;* Walker, Norris, *tailback;* McCarthy, Young, *fullback;* Butler, *placekicker;* Broadway, *punter;* Frix, Harrell, Montgomery, Norris, *special teams*

Defense: N. Taylor, Forts, Thurson, Culpepper, *linebacker;* Carver, M. Jones, *left end;* Gilbert, Chumley, *left tackle;* K. Jackson, Sims, *left guard;* Crowe, McAllister, *right guard;* Dooley, Hewatt, *right end;* R. Harris, D. Jones, Flack, Dean, *cornerback;* Hoage, Bobo, Sanchez, Painter, *safety*

Florida: *Offense:* T. Young, S. Jackson, Rolle, Dixon, *wide receiver;* Fike, V. Jones, *left tackle;* Hunt, Moyle, *left guard;* Redmond, Bromley, *center;* Schultheis, Moyle, *right guard;* L. Brown, Trimble, *right tackle;* Faulkner, Mularkey, *tight end;* Peace, Hewko, *quarterback;* L. Hampton, J. L. Williams, *running back;* J. Jones, N. Anderson, *fullback;* Gainey, *placekicker;* Criswell, *punter;* Hewko, Hurm, Walter, Byrd, Curry, Marshall, Williams, Hampton, *special teams*

Defense: W. Marshall, Miller, V. Brown, Patrick, F. Jackson, Pennington, Wiegmann, McCallister, *linebacker;* Harris, Whittaker, *left tackle;* R. Williams, Hinson, *noseguard;* Newton, Billett, *right tackle;* McKeever, V. Brown, Easmon, Curry, *cornerback;* Clark, Sibbald, Lilly, S. Marshall, *safety*

	Georgia	Florida
First downs	26	10
Rushes/yards	78/391	31/34
Passing yards	50	146
Pass att/comp/int	12/4/1	26/15/2
Punts/avg. yards	1/35	4/46
Fumbles/lost	1/0	3/3
Penalties/yards	5/35	3/23

— 1983 —

Georgia 10, Florida 9

Even without Herschel Walker, Georgia had a powerhouse in 1983, but Florida also was in the fight for national honors as the two antagonists headed into the November 5 disagreement in Jacksonville.

The Gators of fifth-year coach Charley Pell were 6–1–1, ninth ranked in the country and in the thick of the SEC race. Yet football fans in the Sunshine State knew Florida needed to beat fourth-ranked Georgia to earn respectability as a legitimate football force.

Florida was looking to avoid losing to Georgia for the sixth year in a row, a streak the Bulldogs had not put together against the Gators since 1931 through 1936.

Coach Vince Dooley, now in his 20th year at the UGA helm, and his 'Dogs, as well as their multitude of supporting fans, were enjoying a golden age of Georgia football in the 1980s. The Bulldogs were contending for their fourth consecutive SEC crown and had won 22 straight conference games going into the Florida battle.

Georgia All-American defensive back Terry Hoage, all-conference linebacker Tommy Thurson and defensive end Freddie Gilbert were back to lead the 7–0–1 Bulldogs. Unpredictable quarterback John Lastinger ran the Georgia offense, which was built around the running of backs Keith Montgomery, Barry Young and David McCluskey.

The 'Dogs had some problems as game day neared. Hoage was questionable due to knee and ankle injuries, and reserve running back Tron Jackson had been suspended for a week for breaking training rules.

The Gators defense was solid behind All-American outside linebacker Wilber Marshall. Senior quarterback Wayne Peace was enroute to becoming the No. 2 offensive player in SEC history behind former UF quarterback John Reaves but had yet to beat Georgia.

Still, he had thrown for 100 or more yards in 27 straight games and almost 7,000 yards in his career. Florida featured a tough offensive front and a balanced attack, averaging 212 yards passing and 192 yards rushing per game. Gator backs Lorenzo Hampton, Neal Anderson and John L. Williams were the ground threats, while wide receiver Ricky Nattiel was a favorite Peace target.

In its 1983 opener, Georgia rolled over UCLA, 19–8, and fought to a 16–16 tie at Clemson. The 'Dogs then routed South Carolina, 31–13; Mississippi State, 20–7; and Ole Miss, 36–11, before beating Vanderbilt, 20–13; Kentucky, 47–21; and Temple, 31–14, to meet Florida with a six-game winning streak.

The Gators trampled Miami, 28–3, then tied Southern Cal, 19–19, in Pasadena. Florida edged Indiana State, 17–13; trounced Mississippi State, 35–12; LSU, 31–17; Vanderbilt, 29–10; and East Carolina, 24–17, before losing, 28–21, to undefeated Auburn and Bo Jackson.

Tens of thousands of fans descended on Jacksonville for the annual frolic beside the St. Johns River.

"In this War Between the States, the weapons, before kickoff, are beer bottles and the goal is to conquer sobriety," the *Atlanta Constitution* said. "It doesn't matter if you win or lose, it's how you have a good time." Florida rooters, having suffered through five consecutive losses to Georgia, probably disagreed with the assessment.

Charged by the excitement of a clash with national rankings, bowl bids, and a conference championship on the line, more than 82,000 were packed into the Gator Bowl for the regionally televised contest.

Florida immediately put the heat on the Bulldogs defense. On the third play of the game, Peace hummed a 50-yard completion to Hampton to put the Gators in business at the UGA 15. Moments later, Peace connected on a short pass to Nattiel to the Georgia 1. The Gators were roaring at the kennel door.

Hampton tried to muscle across, but Thurson smashed him down short of the end zone. The drive died when the Gators were whistled for a procedure penalty. But kicker Bobby Raymond came on to drill a 21-yard field goal for the first score of the afternoon, climaxing the 75-yard march.

Georgia's first offensive series ended abruptly when Gator defender Bruce Vaughan intercepted a Lastinger pass at the UGA 47 and rambled 32 yards to the Bulldogs' 15. On first down, Peace completed a seven-yard pass to Hampton. From the 8, however, the senior signal-caller failed on successive throws, and Pell sent in the field-goal unit again. From the 25, Raymond guided the ball through the uprights and Florida led 6–0 midway through the opening quarter.

Lastinger regrouped the Bulldogs and steered them downfield on a 12-play, 44-yard drive that stopped at the UF 34. Placekicker Kevin Butler then came on and boomed a 51-yarder to slice the deficit to 6–3 with 1:56 left to play in the first period.

Peace continued his offensive onslaught, keeping Georgia off balance. He hit wide receiver Dwayne Dixon for five, Nattiel for four and Williams for 12. Hampton followed with a burst for 11 more to the UGA 48. Peace hooked up with Ray McDonald on a 17-yard play, then found Hampton for five more to the Georgia 24. On third down, Peace went to the end zone, but the 'Dogs' Charlie Dean was waiting and grabbed the interception.

The Florida defense ravaged Georgia the remainder of the first half, while UGA punter Chip Andrews successfully kept the Gators pinned deep with his kicks. Andrews averaged 46.2 yards per punt during the game.

But Peace and his offense again broke loose shortly before intermission. Starting from their 43, the Gators rolled to the UGA 7 in the last seconds, where Raymond booted a 32-yard field goal on the last play of the half.

Florida led 9–3, but Pell and his men were concerned. Four times the Gators penetrated inside the Georgia 25 but had only nine points to show for it. Statistics showed Florida outgaining the Bulldogs 211 yards to 86 in the first half, but the scoreboard didn't reflect the disproportionate numbers.

The Gators went on the move again early in the third quarter, with Peace's 20-yard completion to Nattiel the highlight of the drive. Raymond tried to extend the Florida lead but his 41-yard field-goal attempt missed the mark.

Georgia's offense wouldn't start up and the Gators continued their dominance on both sides of the line. Florida, however, still could not convert its advantage into more points.

The Gators embarked on another foray halfway through the third period and faced a second down at the UGA 20. Peace dropped to pass and arched the ball toward Dixon who slipped in the end zone. Georgia's Darryl Jones was there to pull it in, however, and the UGA cornerback fell out of bounds at the 1-yard line.

With 5:44 left in the third quarter, Georgia had been completely outplayed. Florida owned a three-to-one advantage in yardage and had all but strangled the 'Dogs offense. In 1980 and '81, Georgia trailed Florida late but mounted drives of more than 90 yards to pull out monumental victories. Surely the odds favored the rugged Gators defense this day and the Florida faithful were up and screaming.

Lastinger sneaked for two yards out of the shadow of the Georgia goal line to the 3 on first down. On the next snap, he tore free for a 16-yard run to give the Bulldogs some breathing room. Georgia center Keith Johnson exhorted his teammates in the huddle to "take it 99 yards," lineman Guy McIntyre said later.

Several plays after his big scamper, Lastinger backpedaled behind blockers and lofted a screen pass to tight end Clarence Kay for 25 yards. The play loomed even larger when Gator linebacker Marshall was penalized 15 yards for a personal foul, giving Georgia a first down at the UF 30. The 'Dogs muscled to the 22 on three plays, but faced a fourth and two with 82,000 people roaring. Dooley made his decision—go for the first down, forego the field goal.

Lastinger dashed outside on the option, tucked in the pigskin and lunged forward for four yards. From the UF 18, the 'Dogs punched down to the 1. From there, fullback Barry Young of Swainsboro smashed in for Georgia's lone touchdown. Butler's extra point gave UGA the edge, 10–9, with 13:18 left in the game. The 16-play, 99-yard drive is considered by many to be one of the great offensive series in the rivalry's history. "The tradition at Georgia of never giving up helped the young and old out there," McIntyre later told the *Atlanta Constitution*. "That, and a lot of pride."

The Georgia defenders were now pumped up and howling for Gator blood, but Peace coolly directed the Florida offense downfield. When the drive died, in came Raymond to try a 42-yard field goal with just under 10 minutes left. Pell later described the kick as a "chip shot," but Raymond's boot was wide right and Georgia held its slim lead. Time ticked away as the teams exchanged possessions.

Peace had one last chance to spur the Gators downfield with less than two minutes remaining.

But on third down, UGA defensive end Gilbert fought into the Florida backfield to tackle Peace at the UF 11, the only quarterback sack by Georgia all day. With a minute left, the Gators had to go for the long-odds gamble. On fourth and 19, Peace was menaced by Gilbert and threw incomplete, causing an eruption of celebration in the Red and Black sections.

Georgia roverback Terry Hoage was an All-American selection in 1982 and 1983, leading the UGA defense in victories over Florida.

Florida outgained Georgia 325 to 255, but Pell lamented two interceptions that killed Gator offensives and the missed field goal as the key plays of the game.

Demoralized Florida was haunted by six drives inside the UGA 25 that resulted in only three field goals. They also had a 51-yard touchdown run by Williams wiped away because the officials ruled the whistle had been blown before the score.

An unsung hero for Georgia was defensive back Gary Cantrell, who stepped in and played well when sophomore John Little, starting in place of injured roverback Hoage, was injured on the third play of the game.

The Gators were dumped from the SEC race with the loss to Georgia, but came back to drop Kentucky, 24–7, and Florida State, 53–14 (Raymond kicked 23 points in the FSU game to set a collegiate record), to gain a trip to the Gator Bowl against Iowa. The Gators held the Hawkeyes to two field goals in posting a 14–6 victory to close with a 9–2–1 record, Pell's fourth straight winning season.

Florida linebacker Wilber Marshall was named an All-American and a first-team All-SEC selection for the second year in a row. Other Gators honored on the all-conference first squad were defensive back Tony Lilly, wide receiver Dwayne Dixon and center Phil Bromley.

All-American kicker Kevin Butler hit a 51-yard field goal and the deciding extra point in UGA's 10–9 win over ninth-ranked Florida. Butler helped the Chicago Bears to a Super Bowl championship in 1985.

Wilber Marshall, among the elite of Florida linebackers, finished his career with a school-record 23 quarterback sacks and was a first-round draft choice of the Chicago Bears. He was instrumental in the Bears' 1985 Super Bowl win, earned All-Pro honors in 1986–1987, and later was a franchise player for the Washington Redskins before being traded to the Houston Oilers in 1993.

Wayne Peace did not earn many national honors as a Gator but remains one of Florida's career offensive leaders. He played for the Tampa Bay Bandits in the USFL.

Gator defensive back Tony Lilly went on to a pro career with the Denver Broncos, while receiver Dwayne Dixon played several years in the NFL before returning to Gainesville in 1990 as an assistant to Head Coach Steve Spurrier.

Georgia's win over Florida set up a showdown in Athens against third-ranked Auburn for the conference title. Dreams of a fourth consecutive SEC crown for the Bulldogs disappeared as the last seconds ticked off in a 13–7 Auburn win. The 'Dogs closed by whipping Georgia Tech, 27–24, to earn a bid to play top-ranked Texas in the Cotton Bowl. On New Year's Day in Dallas, Lastinger darted 17 yards for a touchdown with less than four minutes left, as Georgia shocked the Longhorns, 10–9.

The Bulldogs, 10–1–1, finished the campaign ranked fourth in the UPI and AP polls. Georgians Terry Hoage (for the second year), Freddie Gilbert and Kevin Butler garnered All-America honors. Hoage, Gilbert and Thurson were named first-team All-SEC for the second year in a row and were joined by Butler and offensive tackle Guy McIntyre. McIntyre later starred for the San Francisco 49ers, while tight end Clarence Kay and offensive tackle Winford Hood were stalwarts for Denver. Gilbert would also play as a Bronco. Terry Hoage was selected by New Orleans and also played for Philadelphia and Washington.

Scoring:

Georgia	3	0	0	7	—	10
Florida	6	3	0	0	—	9

UF	FG	Raymond, 21 yards
UF	FG	Raymond, 25 yards
UGA	FG	Butler, 51 yards
UF	FG	Raymond, 32 yards
UGA	TD	Young, 1-yard run (Butler kick)

Georgia: _Offense:_ Wisham, Hockaday, _split end;_ Hood, Harper, _left tackle;_ J. Brown, Tang, _left guard;_ P. Anderson, K. Johnson, _center;_ Gray, Holton, _right guard;_ McIntyre, Strozier, _right tackle;_ Kay, Sorrells, _tight end;_ Harris, Archie, Lane, _flanker;_ Lastinger, T. Williams, _quarterback;_ Montgomery, McCluskey, Simmons, _tailback;_ Young, S. Williams, _fullback;_ Butler, _placekicker;_ Andrews, _punter;_ Harrell, D. Jones, Moss, Ansley, _special teams_

Defense: Culpepper, Boswell, Thurson, Mitchell, _linebacker;_ Ruff, M. Jones, Loy, _left end;_ Chumley, Burroughs, _left tackle;_ Weaver, Harris, _left guard;_ Sims, Richardson, _right guard;_ Gilbert, Dooley, Hewatt, _right end;_ D. Jones, Moss, Flack, Holmes, _cornerback;_ Little, Hoage, Cantrell, Dean, Painter, _safety_

Florida: _Offensive:_ Lang, Nattiel, Dixon, _wide receiver;_ L. Brown, Ellis, _left tackle;_ Hunt, Zimmerman, _left guard;_ Bromley, Billett, _center;_ Schultheis, Hinson, _right guard;_ Ker, Trimble, _right tackle;_ Peddie, Odom, _tight end;_ Peace, Dorminey, _quarterback;_ N. Anderson, L. Hampton, _tailback;_ J. L. Williams, J. Henderson, _fullback;_ Raymond, _placekicker;_ Criswell, _punter;_ Perkins, Neal, Hampton, _special teams_

Defense: Marshall, Miller, A. Johnson, Korff, Drew, McCallister, Pennington, _linebacker;_ R. Harris, Ellison, _left tackle;_ Newton, Tinney, _noseguard;_ Cleveland, Mitz, _right tackle;_ McKeever, Stacey, Vaughan, _cornerback;_ Clark, Sibbald, Lilly, V. Brown, _safety_

	Georgia	Florida
First downs	16	16
Rushes/yards	56/194	34/139
Passing yards	61	186
Pass att/comp/int	13/8/1	29/17/2
Punts/avg. yards	5/46	3/47
Fumbles/lost	1/5	2/19
Penalties/yards	2/0	0/0
Possession time	33:20	26:40

— 1984 —

Florida 27, Georgia 0

FOR FLORIDA, THE "BIG BROTHER" OF GEORGE Orwell's novel, *1984,* seemed to be the NCAA during the nightmarish opening weeks of the football season in Gainesville.

Sixth-year UF coach Charley Pell had been forced to resign three games into the campaign after Florida was rocked by news that the NCAA expected to impose stiff sanctions for recruiting violations. Pell was replaced by interim coach Galen Hall, one of Pell's assistants who had not been implicated in the probe.

The Gators persevered, and even flourished, during the controversy as they tried to concentrate on winning football games. Indeed, Florida was 6–1–1, 10th-ranked and flying toward a midair collision with eighth-ranked Georgia on November 10 in the Gator Bowl.

The 7–1 Bulldogs of Coach Vince Dooley were aiming for an unprecedented seventh consecutive win over Florida and were riding the hot play of redshirt-freshman quarterback David Dukes, who had led Georgia to four straight wins. Georgia had a wealth of talent at running back with tailbacks Lars Tate and Cleveland Gary and fullback Andre Smith, the Bulldogs' leading rusher with a 58-yard per game average. All-American kicker Kevin Butler, the new SEC career scoring leader, also was back after booting the decisive point in the 1983 Georgia win.

The 'Dogs' miserly defense was allowing opponents an average of only 123 ground yards per outing and had accumulated 16 interceptions and 11 recovered fumbles. With Florida rushing for 257 yards a game, something would have to give.

The Gators had, what some considered, their most potent rushing force ever with Neal Anderson and Lorenzo Hampton alternating at tailback and John L. Williams at fullback. Anderson, a junior from Graceville, Fla., was averaging 95 yards a game. Florida also had an exceptional defense against the run, having allowed only three rush-

Gator tackle Lomas Brown was the key to UF's offensive line during Florida's 1984 win over Georgia. An All-American that year, Brown went on to an All-Pro career with the Detroit Lions.

ing touchdowns in eight games. The Gators, however, again were weak in the secondary.

One of the prime reasons for Florida's success was the emergence of a redshirt-freshman quarterback named Kerwin Bell, who joined the team as a walk-on. Bell won the starting job after the first-string quarterback was injured in preseason. He was a passer in the tradition of Spurrier, Reaves, and Peace, completing 74 of 135 for 1,202 yards and 11 touchdowns going into the Georgia contest.

Florida lost its 1984 debut, 32–20, to Miami and tied LSU, 21–21. The Gators then bombarded Tulane, 63–21, in Pell's last game. Hall debuted with a 27–12 win over Mississippi State, a 16–0 victory against Syracuse, and a 43–30 triumph at Tennessee. The Gators beat Cincinnati, 48–17, and were coming off a great defensive effort in a 24–3 disposal of Auburn.

The Gators were winning despite news from the NCAA on October 23 that the school was facing possibly three years of probation, which meant a ban on bowl and television appearances and a loss of scholarships.

Georgia dropped Southern Mississippi, 26–19, to begin the year, then beat Clemson, 26–23, in Athens. The Bulldogs fell, 17–10, at undefeated South Carolina but smashed Alabama, 24–14; Ole Miss, 18–12; Vanderbilt, 62–35; Kentucky, 37–7; and Memphis State, 13–3, to meet Florida with a six-game winning streak.

In a 1991 *Florida Times-Union* interview, Kerwin Bell recalled how he felt as a cocksure freshman quarterback shortly before kickoff. "I thought I had everything in control. Then I played my first Florida-Georgia game. That game will affect you like no other. . . . Your knees sort of wobble when you walk out on the field."

Bell settled down the second time the Gators had the ball. Keyed by pass completions of 17 and 12 yards to Hampton, the Gators reeled down to the UGA 26. On third and one, Williams plunged to the 25. Bell wasted little time in going for the jugular. Though pressured by UGA end Greg Waters, he hit Hampton for the 25-yard score. Bobby Raymond added the extra point and Florida enjoyed the early lead, 7–0.

The stellar defenses of both teams took center stage for the rest of the first period and into the second quarter before a damaging Georgia turnover. Minutes earlier, Florida ran a fake punt on fourth down, with defensive back Roger Sibbald completing a pass to Linzey Smith at the UGA 32. But the Bulldogs had held and UF's Ray Criswell was punting on fourth down. Georgia's Tony Flack

Outside linebacker Alonzo Johnson earned All-American honors at UF in 1984 and 1985. He later played for the Philadelphia Eagles.

fielded the ball, but was immediately hit by Florida's Pat Miller and fumbled. Gator James Massey fell on the ball at the UGA 8.

Anderson struggled for two on first down. Bell looked to pass on the next play, but Bulldog linebacker Knox Culpepper broke through and was about to level him for a loss. Bell managed to scramble away and shot a pass toward tight end Walter Odom near the goal line. Georgia's Flack was flagged for interference and Florida had a first and goal at the UGA 2. Two plays later, Anderson leaped into the line like a launched missile and landed in the Georgia end zone. Raymond kicked the point after and Florida's tally increased to 14–0.

The half ended with Georgia trying to solve the riddle of Florida's unyielding defense as well as looking for ways to stop Bell and his backfield mates. UGA quarterback Dukes had thrown for minus two yards passing and had been intercepted by Gator defensive back Jarvis Williams in the end zone. Georgia totalled only 46 yards of offense in the first half.

Dooley replaced Dukes with Todd Williams to begin the second half, but the Gators defense snuffed out Georgia's advances for most of the third period. Florida was also having problems on offense, although the Gators managed a 34-yard Raymond field goal to up their lead to 17–0.

Georgia finally got started late in the third quarter. From the UGA 30, fullback Smith pierced the Gators on three carries for 38 yards in a march to the UF 37. Williams then connected with freshman receiver Cassius Osborn for 18 yards and back David McCluskey ripped for 10 more. Two offside penalties against the Gators gave the 'Dogs a first and goal at the UF 2. What followed would be one of the finest goal line stands in the annals of the series.

Smith muscled into the line for a yard. Gary was crunched for no gain and fell on his own fumble. Tony Mangram then tried his luck but the Florida defense descended on him short of the goal, with linebacker Alonzo Johnson leading the swarm. Mangram also fumbled but Georgia recovered.

The Gators' rush was so torrid that some defenders were in the Georgia backfield before the running backs got the handoff. On fourth down, trailing by 17 with seconds left in the third quarter, Dooley gambled on the touchdown.

With the stadium a cacophony of sound, Williams handed off to Smith. But Florida manhandled the Georgia line again and the Bulldog fullback was engulfed in Gators. With fans of the Orange and Blue thundering their approval, Florida took over on offense at their

Controversial coach Charley Pell left Clemson to become head man at Florida in 1979, losing five fights with Dooley's Dawgs. He resigned three games into the 1984 season during an NCAA probe into UF recruiting violations.

1-yard line as the third quarter expired.

Florida backs punched out to the 4 on the first two downs. If Georgia expected the Gators to keep it on the ground and hope for a good punt, they guessed dead wrong. On third down and seven, Bell drifted back into his own end zone, looked over the field, and rifled a completion to split end Ricky Nattiel streaking free down the left sideline at the UF 40. Nattiel had beaten UGA cornerback Kevin Harris, who fell near midfield, and accelerated as the yard markers disappeared in his wake. The Florida half of the stadium detonated with an open-mouthed clamor pent up over the past six years as Nattiel romped 96 yards for the score. The pass completion was the second longest in UF history behind a 99-yard touchdown toss from Cris Collinsworth to Derrick Gaffney against Rice in 1977.

Raymond booted his third extra point and Florida was in command, 24–0. With about nine minutes left in the game, Georgia fans headed for the exits en masse, a sight that stoked the revelry of Gator supporters.

Late in the fourth quarter, Florida had good field position after UGA punter Chip Andrews got off an 18-yard kick. Raymond punched through a 31-yard field goal with 5:05 left to make the final score 27–0.

Galen Hall received a victory ride on the shoulders of his players at the closing whistle. UF rooters pulled down one of the goal posts and carried it jubilantly around the field, and many Florida fans were still celebrating in the bleachers an hour after the game.

The win was the most lopsided in the series for Florida since the 1956 Gators routed Georgia 28–0 and the first UF shutout of the 'Dogs since the 22–0 Florida victory in 1957. Many observers, including Dooley, agreed that the Gators dominated Georgia like no team had done for a number of years. The loss left Dooley with a 14–6–1 record against Florida and was his worst defeat ever by the Gators.

Kerwin Bell completed eight of 17 passes for 178 yards and two touchdowns to lead the onslaught. For Georgia, Williams was seven of 16 for 61 yards. The Gators defense, in addition to its goal line stand, held Georgia to 127 yards rushing on 30 carries.

Georgia ended the season with a 21–12 defeat at Auburn and a 35–18 pounding by Georgia Tech, their first loss to the Rambling Wreck since 1977. The 'Dogs' 7–4 mark was good enough for a Citrus Bowl invitation to face favored Florida State. Georgia took an early lead, but the Seminoles rallied for a 17–17 tie.

Kevin Butler garnered All-America honors for the second year in a row and was joined among the nation's best by safety Jeff Sanchez. Butler also made the All-SEC first squad for the second time, and Sanchez and linebacker Knox Culpepper were also selected to the team. Butler was drafted by the Chicago Bears and helped them to a Super Bowl win in 1985. Scott Williams was drafted by St. Louis and later played with Detroit.

The big victory over Georgia meant that a road win over Kentucky would give Florida its first league championship, a goal that had incredibly evaded them through the decades. This time, though, the Gators would not be denied, beating the Wildcats, 25–17, to cinch the 1984 Southeastern Conference title. In the euphoric Florida locker room, UF officials named Hall the new Gators coach.

Florida climaxed the season with a 27–17 victory at Florida State to finish at 9–1–1. But NCAA sanctions resulted in the Gators being declared ineligible for postseason play, and SEC members voted to strip Florida of its first-ever conference crown due to the findings.

Florida was ranked third in the final regular season Associated Press rankings, the best in the school's history. *The New York Times* and *The Sporting News* both named Florida the 1984 national champion.

Gator offensive tackle Lomas Brown and linebacker Alonzo Johnson were among All-American and first-team All-SEC honorees. Florida center Phil Bromley and middle guard Tim Newton also

Running back Neal Anderson scored a touchdown in Florida's 27–0 upset of Georgia in 1984. He was the second leading rusher in UF history and later starred for the Chicago Bears.

made the all-conference unit, Bromley for the second consecutive year. Brown was a first-round draft pick by Detroit and started for the Lions through the 1991 season. Newton was drafted by Minnesota and made the 1985 NFL All-Rookie team.

Lorenzo Hampton ended his stint at Florida as the seventh-leading rusher in UF history. He was a first-round draft choice of the Miami Dolphins a year later.

For Florida, 1984 would be a year to remember, regardless of the off-field troubles. "This is the Year of the Gator," the *Atlanta Constitution* said, "no matter what the NCAA and the SEC say."

Scoring:

Florida	7	7	3	10	—	27
Georgia	0	0	0	0	—	0

UF	TD	Hampton, 25-yard pass from Bell (Raymond kick)
UF	TD	Anderson, 2-yard run (Raymond kick)
UF	FG	Raymond, 34 yards
UF	TD	Nattiel, 96-yard pass from Bell (Raymond kick)
UF	FG	Raymond, 31 yards

Florida: *Offense:* Nattiel, McDonald, Wiechmann, Rolle, Neal, *wide receiver;* L. Brown, Gerzina, *left tackle;* Hinson, J. Davis, *left guard;* Bromley, Billett, *center;* Zimmerman, Ellis, *right guard;* Ker, Gerzina, *right tackle;*

Odom, R. Jones, _tight end;_ Bell, _quarterback;_ N. Anderson, Hampton, Massey, _running back;_ J. L. Williams, Corlew, _fullback;_ Raymond, _placekicker;_ Criswell, _punter;_ Byrd, Nattiel, Neal, Hampton, _special teams_

Defense: Moten, Miller, A. Johnson, Arthur, White, Pennington, Korff, Armstrong, Nelson, _linebacker;_ Mitz, Duhart, _left tackle;_ Newton, R. Williams, _nose guard;_ K. Williams, Garland, _right tackle;_ Easmon, Stacy, Mulberry, J. Williams, _cornerback;_ Sibbald, Adrian White, V. Brown, Knight, _safety_

Georgia: _Offense:_ Archie, Blalock, Osborn, _split end;_ Strozier, Perry, _left tackle;_ Stephens, Burroughs, _left guard;_ P. Anderson, K. Johnson, _center;_ Holton, K. Stephens, _right guard;_ Weaver, Adams, _right tackle;_ S. Williams, Strozier, _tight end;_ Hockaday, Lane, _flanker;_ Dukes, T. Williams, _quarterback;_ Mangram, T. Jackson, _tailback;_ A. Smith, McCluskey, _fullback;_ Butler, _placekicker;_ C. Andrews, _punter;_ Messer, Harrell, Lane, Blalock, _special teams_

Defense: Culpepper, Brantley, Boswell, Mitchell, _linebacker;_ Ruff, Loy, _left end;_ Chumley, Lovelace, _left tackle;_ H. Harris, L. Brown, _middle guard;_ Sims, Auer, _right guard;_ Hewatt, Waters, _right end;_ Flack, Willis, K. Harris, _cornerback;_ Sanchez, Little, Ruff, _safety_

	Florida	Georgia
First downs	14	11
Rushes/yards	50/142	30/127
Passing yards	191	59
Pass att/comp/int	18/9/0	21/8/2
Punts/avg. yards	4/41	7/39
Fumbles/lost	1/1	2/1
Penalties/yards	5/22	6/50

— 1985 —

Georgia 24, Florida 3

WITH A 15–0–1 RECORD, FLORIDA FANS WERE hailing Coach Galen Hall as a gridiron messiah for leading the Gators to the pinnacle of the collegiate football world the week before the UF-UGA tangle.

For the first time in school history, Florida was ranked No. 1 in the Associated Press poll as they prepared for the November 9, 1985, battle with the 17th-ranked Bulldogs.

The 7–0–1 Gators were serving two years' NCAA probation: no live television, a loss of scholarships, and no shot at the conference title or a postseason bowl. But they were in a prime position to be voted national champions if they remained undefeated. The Gators had not lost a game since a defeat to Miami in the 1984 season opener. Their 18-game unbeaten string was the longest in the nation.

Sophomore quarterback Kerwin Bell was drawing national acclaim, leading a Gators offense averaging 392 yards per contest and almost 29 points. Going into the Georgia tilt, Bell had thrown for more than 1,700 yards and 17 touchdowns and was second in the country in passing efficiency. On the ground, backs Neal Anderson and John L. Williams had combined for 1,364 yards rushing. All-American linebacker Alonzo Johnson was the enforcer of the Gators defense which ranked seventh in the nation.

Florida's season began with a 35–23 road win over Miami. The Gators jumped out to a 21–0 lead over Rutgers a week later, but the Scarlet Knights charged back to tie it. The Rutgers deadlock dropped UF from third to 11th in the AP poll, but the Gators climbed back steadily with a six-game winning streak. Mississippi State fell 36–22; LSU, 20–0; Tennessee, 17–10; Southwestern Louisiana, 45–0; and Virginia Tech, 35–18. A week before meeting Georgia, the Gators kayoed Auburn and Bo Jackson, 14–10. The win, coupled with top-rated Iowa's loss to Ohio State, resulted in Florida being voted the best in the country in the Associated Press poll released on the Tuesday before the Georgia contest.

Bulldog coach Vince Dooley had the Peach State abuzz in the offseason with news that he might leave UGA to run for the U.S. Senate. After much consideration, Dooley announced in July that he had decided to stay at Georgia.

Alabama spoiled 6–1–1 Georgia's 1985 debut, dropping the 'Dogs 20–16 in Athens. The Bulldogs then beat Baylor, 17–14; Clemson, 20–13; South Carolina, 35–21; and Ole Miss, 49–21, before a 13–13 tie at Vanderbilt. Georgia rolled over Kentucky, 26–6, and butchered Tulane, 58–3, at UGA homecoming a week before the Florida game.

Bulldog quarterback James Jackson had taken over from Wayne Johnson as the starter after the Alabama game. Jackson, the MVP in the 1984 Citrus Bowl, was a running and passing threat who had been averaging 125 yards in total offense per game. The 'Dogs had a pack of young running backs, including junior Lars Tate and freshmen Keith Henderson and Tim Worley.

Harrah's installed Florida as 5½ point favorites for the game, and more than 82,000 were in the Gator Bowl to see it.

In the dressing room, Georgia freshman lineman Todd Wheeler, who would later be a UGA team captain, remembered the thunder of thousands of feet overhead and the tradition related by the Georgia recruiters. "The first thing I think about is sitting in the locker room and hearing the stands rumble above you," he said in a 1991 _Florida Times-Union_ interview. "I think it's one of the greatest things I've ever heard. Sitting in that locker room, it feels like the stands are going to fall on top of you. That's a game that every kid that comes to Georgia is told about. You'll never hear anything like the fans there."

From the game's outset, the Bulldogs fired off the line and took the fight to the favored Gators. Bell found himself under a mad dog rush, yet spurred the Gators to the Georgia 16 after UGA's Jackson had fumbled, only to see kicker Jeff Dawson's 33-yard field-goal attempt sail wide right.

With Georgia in possession on its 24, the Gators were zapped by a Red and Black lightning bolt who gave the 'Dogs all the points they would need this day. Fullback Keith Henderson, on his first carry of the afternoon, knifed into the line, wheeled to his left and lunged free in the Gators' secondary. Gaining speed and distancing himself from the orange hats, the flying freshman ripped for big yardage. By now it became a test of speed, with a Gator trying to intercept him inside the UF 20. Henderson was hit by cornerback Curtis Stacy around the 5, stumbled, and dove across the goal line for the touchdown. The 76-yard scoring play electrified the UGA throng as placekicker Steve Crumley added the extra point for a 7–0 Georgia lead.

Georgia's fired-up defense stonewalled Florida's runners and Bell and the UF offense couldn't get anything started. Early in the second quarter, UGA went on the prowl again.

A 16-yard run by freshman tailback Tim Worley propelled the 'Dogs to the UF 32. Then Henderson speared into the heart of the Florida defense, much as he had done on the touchdown run. Eluding Gators, the charging fullback made it to the sideline and scampered downfield, hurdling the flag at the goal line for his second touchdown. Crumley's conversion extended the 'Dogs' lead to 14–0 with 11:39 remaining in the half. A tomb-like atmosphere enveloped the UF faithful, while frenzy shook the Georgia sections.

Bell, shortly thereafter, hit a series of short passes to move Florida past midfield, but again the 'Dogs stiffened. Dawson came on for a three-point attempt from 46 yards out but pulled it wide right again.

Though the scoring drive had produced no points, Florida seized some momentum and crunched the 'Dogs on UGA's next offensive series. Georgia freshman punter Cris Carpenter, who would keep the Gators backed up all afternoon with booming kicks, then skyed the ball deep to Ricky Nattiel, who gathered it in and juked upfield for a 31-yard return to the UGA 30. The Gators couldn't get it much closer and Dawson came on for his third field-goal attempt of the half. With the ball spotted on the 36, Dawson's kick was true and the Georgia lead was trimmed to 14–3.

Having stuffed the 'Dogs offense on its previous series, the Gator defenders now pinned Georgia near their goal line after the kickoff. With the Bulldogs operating from their 8, it appeared Florida might have a chance to force a punt and score again in the closing minutes of the half. But that was before Tate stormed into the line, broke free, and rumbled for 40 yards. 'Dogs' quarterback Johnson, substituting for Jackson, quickly hit receiver Fred Lane for a 17-yard completion. With little time left, Crumley kicked a 32-yard field goal to make it 17–3 at intermission.

Georgia had played its finest half of the season. The formidable stable of Gator running backs was being silenced, and, although Bell was completing some passes, the Gators had yet to connect for a big play. With a national championship hanging in the balance, Florida knew it had 30 minutes to mount a comeback.

But Dooley and his assistants had Georgia fine-tuned and sky high. No Georgia squad had ever beaten a top-ranked team, an added incentive for the Bulldogs.

Georgia took up in the third quarter where it had left off in the first half. Florida's rushing game was flattened and Bell was compelled to throw on practically every down. Completions to Williams, Anderson, Raymondo McDonald and Frankie Neal rolled up yardage and kept the statisticians busy. But Florida wasn't able to push the ball into scoring range. Meanwhile, Georgia's offense, resting on a two-touchdown lead, was bottled up by the Gators. Georgia punter Carpenter continued his kicking feats and the third quarter ended with no scoring.

The stalemate wore on halfway through the final period, and Florida's dreams of everlasting glory dimmed with each tick of the scoreboard clock. The Gators finally put together a drive with about seven minutes left. Bell, under a rabid Bulldog rush, as he had been all afternoon, managed to guide the Gators inside the UGA 10. Florida's last stand ended when fullback Williams fumbled at the 8 and the ball was claimed by Georgia's Steve Boswell.

With five minutes left, the game appeared to be all over but the shouting. And perhaps Worley shouted loudest of all. On second down, the freshman back took a pitch and darted out on a sweep to the right. Following his blockers, Worley swerved back inside and turned it on. The Gators were bunched in a short-yardage defense when the big tailback sprang free. It turned into a one-man track meet, with Worley clicking off 89 yards to the UF end zone. Only 4:47 remained on the clock when Crumley's extra point lengthened Georgia's lead to 24–3, and Florida's hopes of a national championship flew in the breeze fanning off the St. Johns River.

Hundreds of excited UGA fans rushed the field, intent on tearing down the goal posts. Jacksonville police and security officers formed a protective ring around each goal, but several officers were injured slightly in the mayhem, and a number of rowdier fans were taken into custody. Some Georgia rooters ripped up chunks of stadium turf as souvenirs.

Florida student Chris Weaver, better know as "Albert the Alligator," the UF mascot, was attacked by a mob of Georgia students who beat him and ripped his costume.

On the day, police made about 100 arrests at the stadium, including 39 apprehended for scalping tickets before the game.

The tale of the Georgia defense, along with the long runs of

Coach Galen Hall led UF to its first number one ranking in 1985 before the 24–3 upset by Georgia. Hall resigned during the 1989 campaign amid an NCAA investigation. He was 2–3 against Georgia.

Henderson, Worley, and Tate, was Florida's epitaph. Georgia rushed for 344 yards, while the Gators were held to 28.

Bell had a spectacular day in defeat. Sacked three times, buried under a rush, and hurried on numerous plays, he still completed 33 of 49 passes for 408 yards, a new Florida single game passing record. Bell was also the only quarterback ever to pass for more than 400 yards in the series. Bullish UF back John L. Williams also set a series record with 12 pass receptions.

The loss to Georgia dropped the Gators to 11th in the polls, while the 'Dogs jumped to 12th. The Florida express got back on track a week later, beating Kentucky, 15–13, and ended the regular season with a 38–14 rout of Florida State. Florida finished fifth in the final AP rankings.

Linebacker Alonzo Johnson and offensive lineman Jeff Zimmerman made All-America and first-team All-SEC (Johnson for the second year on both levels). Other Gators selected for the all-conference first team were Kerwin Bell and running back Neal Anderson. Anderson went on to a starring role with the Chicago Bears as a first-round NFL draft choice. Johnson was a finalist for the Butkus Award, given to the nation's top linebacker, and would be a rookie starter for the Philadelphia Eagles a year later.

John L. Williams ended his UF career as the first Gator to rush for over 2,000 yards and total over 700 yards in pass receptions. He was a first-round draft pick of Seattle and a durable starter for the Seahawks through 1992.

The Bulldogs followed the win over Florida with a 24–10 home loss to Auburn and wrapped up the regular season with a 20–16 defeat at Georgia Tech. With a 7–3–1 record, UGA accepted a bid to play Arizona in the Sun Bowl, the 'Dogs' sixth consecutive post-season appearance. Georgia came back from a 10-point deficit to tie the Wildcats, 13–13, and finish out a disappointing year, other than the trip to Jacksonville. The 'Dogs were not ranked in the Top 20 in the final AP and UPI polls.

Georgia center and team captain Peter Anderson and roverback John Little were honored as All-Americans and first-team All-SEC selections. They were joined among the conference all-stars by teammates safety Tony Flack and defensive end Greg Waters.

Scoring:

Georgia	7	10	0	7	—	24
Florida	0	3	0	0	—	3

UGA	TD	Henderson, 76-yard run (Crumley kick)
UGA	TD	Henderson, 32-yard run (Crumley kick)
UF	FG	Dawson, 36 yards
UGA	FG	Crumley, 32 yards
UGA	TD	Worley, 89-yard run (Crumley kick)

Georgia: *Offense:* Hockaday, Blalock, Archie, *split end;* Perry, Tate Warren, *left tackle;* Burroughs, Tang, *left guard;* Anderson, Abram, *center;* Stephens, Wheeler, *right guard;* Strozier, Adams, *right tackle;* Sadowski, R. Smith, *tight end;* Tate, Worley, Jackson, *tailback;* McCluskey, Henderson, *fullback;* Jackson, Johnson, Dukes, *quarterback;* Lane, Osborn, *flanker;* Crumley, *placekicker;* Carpenter, *punter;* Little, Lane, Blalock, *special teams*

Defense: Ruff, Loy, *left end;* Williams, Giles, *tackle;* Harris, L. Brown, *left guard;* Richardson, Sims, Stewart, *right guard;* Waters, Chubb, *right end;* Mitchell, Webster, Brantley, Boswell, Guthrie, *linebacker;* Flack, Williams, Hammonds, Moss, Mangram, *cornerback;* Little, W. Jones, M. Brown, M. Smith, Fromm, Beasley, *safety*

Florida: *Offense:* Nattiel, Wiechmann, J. Jones, McDonald, Neal, *wide receiver;* Gerzina, Hiott, *left tackle;* J. Davis, Pinner, *left guard;* McCarthy, Daniels, *center;* Zimmerman, Sills, *right guard;* D. Williams, Garland, *right tackle;* R. Jones, Peddie, *tight end;* N. Anderson, W. Williams *running back;* J. L. Williams, A. Williams, *fullback;* Bell, *quarterback;* Dawson, *placekicker;* Criswell, *punter*

Defense: Miller, Moten, A. Johnson, Charlton, Pennington, Dickens, Armstrong, A. White, *linebacker;* Mitz, Duhart, *left tackle;* Roth, H. Brown, *noseguard;* K. Williams, Tinny, *right tackle;* Stacy, Mulberry, A. White, V. Brown, *cornerback;* J. Williams, Glover, Oliver, Knight, *safety*

	Georgia	Florida
First downs	13	23
Rushes/yards	47/344	30/28
Passing yards	31	408
Return yards	7	31
Pass att/comp/int	8/3/0	49/33/1
Punts/avg. yards	7/50	5/44
Fumbles/lost	1/0	3/2
Penalties/yards	6/41	3/20
Possession time	27:43	32:17

— 1986 —

Florida 31, Georgia 19

KERWIN BELL HAD NOT PLAYED IN ALMOST A
month when he limped off the bench to lead Florida to an upset of
ninth-ranked Auburn a week before the Gators' fracas with 19th-
rated Georgia.

Bell, the All-SEC first team quarterback, had been out of action
with a sprained knee until he came on to spark Florida to a touchdown and score the winning two-point conversion over the Tigers.

In fact, both Georgia, 6–2, and Florida, 4–4, were concerned
about key injuries as they readied for the November 8 game in
Jacksonville.

Yet, there was another and even bigger story in Athens this year
stemming from the 1982 firing of Jan Kemp, a coordinator in the
University of Georgia's developmental studies program. Ms. Kemp
had filed a civil suit claiming her dismissal resulted from her protests
over systematic preferential treatment of some students, including a
number of UGA athletes. As the story unfolded, Ms. Kemp identi-
fied nine Georgia football players she alleged had been given preferential treatment and improperly promoted out of the developmental
studies program. In a monumental decision, a jury ruled in her favor
and awarded her $2.57 million in damages as well as reinstated her at
the university. In May 1986, Ms. Kemp settled out of court for $1.08
million. The Kemp episode rocked the world of collegiate athletics
and forced many institutions, including Georgia, to reassess their
academic standards regarding student-athletes.

Although UGA president Fred Davison resigned under pressure a
month after Ms. Kemp's legal victory, Vince Dooley weathered the
typhoon of controversy and got on with the 1986 season.

The top Dawg had more immediate problems heading into the
Gator Bowl ruckus. Georgia backs Tim Worley and Keith Henderson, who had gutted the Gators with long touchdown runs in the

387

Bulldogs' 1985 upset, were expected to be out with knee injuries. Georgia was depending on shifty quarterback James Jackson, who had already thrown for 1,353 yards, and Lars Tate to be the running workhorse. Despite the injuries to Henderson and Worley, the UGA offense was ranked ninth in the nation, averaging 426 yards per game.

In addition to Bell, Coach Galen Hall's Gators were worried about the status of wide receiver Ricky Nattiel, who sustained a shoulder separation against Auburn. He did not practice in preparation for Georgia and was listed as questionable. Florida running backs Anthony Williams and Octavious Gould were trying to fill the big void left with the graduation of John L. Williams and Neal Anderson, both playing in the NFL, but the Gators were next to last in the conference in rushing.

Buoyed by All-American tackle Jeff Zimmerman, who had been moved from guard, the UF offensive line averaged 274 pounds per man to outweigh the Bulldogs defensive front. Georgia's defense was led by All-American defensive back John Little and linebackers John Brantley and Steve Boswell, while linebacker Clifford Charlton and back Jarvis Williams headed the UF defensive unit.

With a 3–1 SEC record, Georgia was vying for another conference title, while Florida was 1–3.

In its season opener, Florida beat defending Division 1-AA national champion Georgia Southern, 38–14. The Eagles were coached by Erk Russell, Vince Dooley's longtime assistant, who already had become a living legend in Statesboro.

The Gators then lost, 23–15, to Miami; 21–7 to Alabama; 16–10 at Mississippi State; and 28–17 to LSU, before burying Kent State, 52–9, and Rutgers, 15–3. No one knew what to expect after the Gators pulled the 18–17 shocker over Auburn at Florida Field.

Georgia's campaign began with a 31–7 win over Duke followed by a 31–28 loss to Clemson in Athens. The Dogs beat South Carolina, 31–26, and Ole Miss, 14–10, before a 23–14 setback at LSU. Georgia pounded Vanderbilt, 38–16, and Kentucky, 31–9, but was less than impressive in a 28–13 homecoming win over Richmond a week before the Florida game.

Nattiel's status was not decided until the pre-game warmups when he decided to try to play. It would prove to be a bad decision—for Georgia.

The drunken mayhem at the end of the previous year's game prompted Jacksonville officials to crack down on partying in 1986.

About 400 law enforcement officers were assigned to the stadium and adjoining parking lots. Plainclothes officers mixed in with the crowds to arrest ticket scalpers. The law against alcoholic beverages in the stadium was so strictly enforced that one reporter suggested the descriptive "World's Largest Outdoor Cocktail Party" be changed to the "North Florida Milk and Cookie Festival."

With a relatively sober 82,000 in the stands, Georgia immediately went on the march. The Bulldogs offensive line was controlling the line of scrimmage, and a 13-play drive ensued from the UGA 32 with Tate carrying eight times. Fans on both sides were surprised to see Keith Henderson, wearing a leg brace, enter the Georgia backfield. Jackson completed a 15-yard pass to John Thomas then, on first down from the UF 14, heaved a 12-yarder to Troy Sadowski. Moments later, Tate ended matters with a 1-yard sweep to his right. Steve Crumley booted the extra point and the favored Bulldogs had the first knockdown, 7–0.

Bell and his Florida boys were shut down on their first series and had to punt. Taking over on the UF 49, Georgia again churned downfield. An 11-play offensive died at the 7-yard line, but Crumley came on and hit a 24-yard field goal to make it 10–0 Georgia at the 3:45 mark of the first quarter.

At this point, the Bulldog linemen were having their way offensively and defensively. The trend continued into the second quarter

Gator Jarvis Williams was an All-SEC defensive back in 1986 and 1987, garnering All-American honors in 1987.

until Florida, starting from its 26, used 12 plays to reach the UGA 6. The drive climaxed with a 23-yard field goal by Jeff Dawson—10–3, Georgia.

Georgia struck back with an eight-play incursion to the Gators 19, where Crumley came on and kicked a 35-yard field goal to make it 13–3, Bulldogs.

On Florida's next possession, UGA cornerback Miles Smith intercepted a Bell pass, returning it five yards to the UF 34. From there, Crumley nailed a 45-yarder to extend Georgia's lead to 16–3. The 'Dogs had been moving almost at will to this point but had only penetrated the end zone once.

Georgia had another chance to add to its lead moments later when cornerback Greg Williams jarred the ball loose from UF wide receiver Darrell Woulard at the Florida 29. After logging minus four yards on three carries, the 'Dogs trotted out Crumley for another field-goal attempt, but this time the ball veered wide from 50 yards out.

As Georgia rooters had been surprised to see Keith Henderson enter the game, so, too, were UF fans astonished when Ricky Nattiel joined the Gators' huddle on UF's second possession. Floridians held their collective breath when Nattiel went down hard on his shoulder in front of the Bulldogs bench. Nattiel got up slowly but remained in the game.

The fleet receiver made his presence felt when Bell cranked up the offense in the final minutes of the first half. Starting from his 36, Bell hit five passes to slingshot the Gators to the UGA 8. Nattiel then ran a post pattern, working free from 'Dogs cornerback Williams who was playing him one-on-one. Bell put it up and Nattiel snared it for Florida's first touchdown. Dawson's extra point cut Georgia's lead to 16–10. With the half coming up, the Gators and their fans were back in it.

The defenses ruled much of the third quarter until Georgia's offense sputtered to life. The Bulldogs marched 47 yards to give Crumley his fourth field goal of the afternoon, this one from 43 yards, and Georgia a 19–10 count with just over five minutes left in the third. The Bulldogs had had their chances to apply the knockout blow. Now Florida came off the mat.

From his 23, behind an almost impenetrable line, Bell began to stretch the Bulldogs defense. Passes to Woulard, wide receiver Erik Hodges and Nattiel propelled the Gators to the UGA 9. Georgia was blitzing desperately in a futile effort to pressure Bell, leaving the

Ricky "The Rocket" Nattiel caught three touchdown passes from UF quarterback Kerwin Bell in Florida's 1986 upset of Georgia. A year later he was playing for the Denver Broncos.

'Dogs secondary in one-on-one coverage which Bell riddled with his passing.

From the 9, Nattiel evaded defender Williams' coverage and grabbed a Bell pass for his second TD reception. Dawson's conversion kick pulled Florida to within two, 19–17.

Henderson returned the kickoff 35 yards to the UGA 45 to give Georgia good field position. But on first down, Tate was drilled by UF linebacker Arthur White and fumbled. Gator end Steve Stipe recovered at the UGA 41.

In five plays, the Gators roamed to the Georgia 3-yard line. On the first play of the fourth quarter, running back James Massey banged over the goal line and the Orange and Blue had their first lead of the day. Dawson made it 24–19, Gators.

With about seven minutes left, Florida took possession on their 33. In four plays, Florida reached the UGA 42, chiefly on Bell's passing. From there, the Gators' all-conference quarterback drifted back, well protected, and drew a bead on Nattiel, again working one-on-one against UGA's Williams on a post pattern. Nattiel slipped inside, avoided the cornerback's contact, and turned on the speed as Bell hurled the ball high and hard. The pigskin hung in the sun and Nattiel lost it for a second, then made a stretching, fingertip catch and darted into the end zone. Dawson's PAT was the game's last point and the 31–19 score was chiseled in stone.

Georgia failed to pull out one of its miracle finishes, and Florida had its second win over the Bulldogs in three years.

Named UF's most valuable player for the game, Bell finished the day with 20 completions on 31 attempts for 272 yards and the three touchdowns to Nattiel, whom many, including Bell, considered the MVP. Bell attributed his success to the superb protection from his offensive line.

Including his touchdowns, Nattiel had seven catches for 97 yards and became Florida's second all-time leading receiver (behind Carlos Alvarez) with 2,032 yards. He also became the only Gator wide receiver in the history of the series to catch three touchdown passes in a game.

The victory was a milestone for Galen Hall, who became the first UF coach in history to beat Georgia and Auburn in the same year twice (1984 and 1986).

For the Bulldogs, quarterback Jackson had his worst passing effort of the season, completing only four of 17 for 50 yards. With 86 yards on 23 carries, Tate was tabbed as Georgia's MVP. Henderson finished with six rushes for 68 yards, averaging over 11 yards a carry.

Georgia regrouped to drop Auburn, 20–16, and Georgia Tech, 31–24, for a trip to the Hall of Fame Bowl and a match-up with Boston College. The Eagles scored a touchdown with 32 seconds left to nip the Bulldogs, 27–24, and end Georgia's campaign at 8–4.

Defensive back John Little garnered All-America and All-SEC honors for the second consecutive season. Offensive captain and tackle Wilbur Strozier also earned All-America and all-conference recognition. Lars Tate and defensive guard Henry Harris rounded out UGA's contingent on the All-SEC first squad. Strozier went on to play for Denver and Seattle.

Florida followed the Georgia triumph with a 10–3 loss at Kentucky, but ended the regular season with a 17–13 road win over rival Florida State to finish at 6–5. Galen Hall was now 2–1 versus Georgia.

Jeff Zimmerman made All-SEC and All-America first teams for the second straight year. He was joined among the all-conference elite by Ricky Nattiel, Clifford Charlton, Jarvis Williams, defensive back Adrian White and defensive tackle Keith Williams. Nattiel was drafted by Denver in the NFL's first round and caught a 56-yard touchdown pass on the first offensive play of Super Bowl XXII as one of the Broncos' "Three Amigos." Zimmerman was a third-round draft choice of the Dallas Cowboys; White a second-round draft pick by the New York Giants.

Scoring:

Florida	0	10	7	14	—	31
Georgia	10	6	3	0	—	19

UGA	TD	Tate, 1-yard run (Crumley kick)
UGA	FG	Crumley, 24 yards
UF	FG	Dawson, 23 yards
UGA	FG	Crumley, 35 yards
UGA	FG	Crumley, 45 yards
UF	TD	Nattiel, 8-yard pass from Bell (Dawson kick)
UGA	FG	Crumley, 43 yards
UF	TD	Nattiel, 9-yard pass from Bell (Dawson kick)
UF	TD	Massey, 3-yard run (Dawson kick)
UF	TD	Nattiel, 42-yard pass from Bell (Dawson kick)

Florida: *Offense:* Nattiel, S. Simmons, E. Hodges, Woulard, E. Frazier, *wide receiver;* McGriff, R. Jones, C. Reynolds, *tight end;* Zimmerman, D. Williams, *tackle;* B. Sims, C. Wright, J. Davis, *guard;* McCarthy, *center;* A. Williams, Gould, J. Massey, W. Williams, C. Smith, T. Lomack, *running back;* Bell, *quarterback;* Dawson, *placekicker*

Defense: Stipe, Charlton, Byrd, Lamberth, *end;* K. Williams, Roth, Weston, H. Brown, Pinner, W. Burnett, *linemen;* S. Armstrong, A. White, Gatlin, P. Moorer, *linebacker;* J. Williams, Mulberry, A. White, L. Oliver, Glover, Lang, T. Jones, Watkins, *defensive back;* McAndrew, *punter;* J. D. Francis, Byrd, S. Ewing, Watkins, McGinty, DeWitt, Benjamin, Bartruff, Loden, D. Ferguson, Vorwerk, Corlew, *special teams*

Georgia: *Offense:* J. Thomas, Osborn, N. Lewis, D. Dukes, *wide receiver;* Sadowski, Warner, *tight end;* Strozier, Perry, *tackle;* Stephens, Burroughs, *guard;* Wheeler, K. Johnson, *center;* Tate, McCluskey, Lane, Henderson, *running back;* Jackson, *quarterback;* Crumley, *placekicker*

Defense: Chubb, Tardits, *end;* H. Harris, L. Brown, T. McClendon, Goldberg, R. Smith, Lovelace, *linemen;* J. Brantley, Boswell, T. Webster, Guthrie, C. Ruff, *linebacker;* W. Jones, Little, Moss, G. Williams, M. Smith, *defensive back;* C. Carpenter, *punter;* B. Collins, F. Cook, D. Douglas, R. Beasley, S. Harmon, H. McCrary, J. Smith, P. Simmons, H. Berry, K. Brown, M. Guthrie, *special teams*

	Florida	Georgia
First downs	20	14
Rushes/yards	38/126	47/221
Passing yards	272	50
Return yards	19	16
Pass att/comp/int	31/20/2	17/4/0
Punts/avg. yards	4/42	6/45
Fumbles/lost	2/1	1/1
Penalties/yards	4/17	5/39
Possession time	30:30	29:30

— 1987 —

Georgia 23, Florida 10

FLORIDA SENIOR QUARTERBACK KERWIN BELL was a preseason Heisman Trophy favorite, but freshman running back Emmitt Smith captured most of the headlines and the glory in the weeks before the November 7 Georgia-Florida grapple.

Smith's running had given the pass-minded Gators another offensive dimension and made their onslaught more balanced. His ground production had taken some of the heat off UF's young receiving corps and Bell, who was having a subpar campaign.

Against Temple, in the seventh game of the year, Smith went over 1,000 yards earlier than any freshman in college history to set a new NCAA record. Indeed, Smith was the nation's leading rusher with 1,083 yards and 11 touchdowns.

Bell's Heisman stock had been diminished by average statistics. He had completed 101 of 176 passes for 1,333 yards but had only six touchdowns.

Georgia was tied with Clemson at No. 10 in the AP poll. The 6–2 'Dogs were 3–1 in the SEC and had the top running game in the league, averaging almost 290 yards per contest. The land rush was led by All-SEC senior tailback Lars Tate with 778 yards for the year and freshman Rodney Hampton with 680 yards.

The UGA offense was averaging 412 total yards and more than 28 points a game, but the quarterback question was unsettled. James Jackson, who could run but whose passing ability was much maligned, was the starter. His backup, Wayne Johnson, was seeing some playing time and threatening to replace Jackson.

The 17th-ranked Gators were 5–3 overall and 2–2 in the conference. The UF defense was ranked among the best in the SEC, allowing less than 100 yards a game rushing and under 12 points per outing.

Georgia's defense, headed by linebacker John Brantley, had the

Florida outside linebaker Clifford Charlton was All-SEC in 1986 and 1987 and an All-American in 1987. A first-round NFL pick by Cleveland, Charlton later played for Miami.

unenviable task of trying to pressure Bell and key on Smith at the same time. Many observers expected the Gators to test a suspect Bulldog secondary early and often when Smith was not carrying the ball.

Georgia was seething to get at Florida after a Jacksonville newspaper columnist said UGA's defensive backs were so bad they "couldn't cover their mouths when they coughed." Another Florida paper quoted UF receiver Willie Snead as saying the UGA secondary was "mediocre."

The Bulldogs started the year with a 30–22 win at home over Virginia and a 41–7 pasting of Oregon State. Georgia then lost a 21–20 decision at Clemson, but took a 13–6 verdict against South Carolina and a 31–14 victory at Ole Miss. The 'Dogs fell, 26–23, to LSU; outlasted Vanderbilt, 52–24; and slipped by Kentucky, 17–14, at homecoming a week before facing the Gators.

Florida's 1987 season debuted with a 31–4 loss at Miami, before a 52–0 butchery of Tulsa in Gainesville. The Gators beat Alabama, 23–14, in Birmingham and Mississippi State, 38–3, before a 13–10 defeat at LSU. Florida then bombarded Cal State Fullerton, 65–0, and Temple, 34–3, before losing, 29–6, at Auburn.

A crowd of almost 82,000 packed the Gator Bowl for the game being televised nationally on cable by WTBS. A strong breeze would make the kicking game unpredictable.

With the wind at their backs, the Gators clawed downfield on their first possession of the afternoon. Georgia's defense awoke and stopped the drive after five plays, and UF coach Galen Hall elected to go for a 52-yard field goal. Kicker Robert McGinty toed the ball which soared on the wind blasts and through the uprights. Florida was up 3–0 on the longest field goal in the history of the rivalry and McGinty's personal best.

The Gators' ranks were thinned about five minutes into the game when outside linebacker Jeff Reuter went down with a serious knee injury.

Later in the first period, Georgia faced a fourth down and sent in David Dukes to punt. Dukes executed a perfect coffin corner kick, skillfully dropping the ball out on the UF 2. Trapped against their goal, the Gators couldn't dent the 'Dogs and punter Jamie McAndrews only got off a 29-yard kick. Georgia had a first down at the Gators' 34.

The 'Dogs stayed on the ground with Hampton and Tate carrying the load. Three running plays and a face mask penalty later, Georgia had a third and four at the UF 13. Tate then made what some observers consider the best run of his college career. Barreling into the Florida defense, Tate bulled over four Gators before he was hauled down just short of the goal line. On first and goal, Tate muscled over the middle for the score. John Kasay's extra point made it 7–3, Georgia, with 1:27 to play in the quarter.

Bell tried to lead the Gators back but faced a terrific UGA defensive rush. The 'Dogs were smothering the UF runners, forcing Bell to go to the air on almost every down. Emmitt Smith was finding few niches in the Bulldog wall.

Georgia, with the wind advantage in the second quarter, capitalized after cornerback Ben Smith intercepted a Bell pass at the UGA 29. The 'Dogs forged into Gatorland, with Hampton, Tate and Jackson taking turns on a 10-play drive that sputtered at the UF 34. UGA's other placekicker, Steve Crumley, trotted on to attempt a 51-yard field goal which, if successful, would be the longest of his career. Much as McGinty's had done earlier, Crumley's kick rode the wind through the goal posts, and Georgia led 10–3 midway through the second quarter.

Georgia's harassment of Bell continued, but the Gators defense also played tough. In fact, Florida's rush was so strong that Georgia exploited it by running misdirection plays. The second period ended with no further scoring and Emmitt Smith had been held to 27 yards.

Bell had a horrendous half, sacked twice by defensive end Richard Tardits and once by linebacker Vince Guthrie. On practically every pass, the Gator quarterback was hurried or buried under the Bulldog rush as he threw.

Bell tried to loosen the UGA defense in the third quarter by going to the run with backs Emmitt Smith and Wayne Williams. The strategy worked as the Gators drove to the UGA 29. But Bulldog cornerback Ben Smith made a diving interception in front of wide receiver Darrell Woulard at the UGA 22 to snuff out Florida's march.

On the running of Hampton and Tate, Georgia reached the Gators 19, before Florida stiffened. Kasay kicked a 35-yard field goal into the wind to extend UGA's lead to 13–3.

In the closing minutes of the period, Georgia recovered a UF fumble at the Florida 34 and, with Tate, Hampton and Jackson grinding for yardage, the Bulldogs reached the UF 1. The Gators battled and held to force a fourth and goal. Carelessly, the 'Dogs suffered a delay of game penalty and were backed up to the 6, where Crumley entered to boot a 21-yard field goal, making it 16–3 with just over nine minutes left.

The Gators still hadn't found a way to deal with the Red and Black defenders, some of whom were in the UF backfield as much as the Florida runners. Tardits got his third sack of the day in the second half as Bell and his offense were mauled. The Gators only had the

Defensive back Louis Oliver was a first-team All-American and All-SEC performer for Florida in 1987 and 1988. He was a first-round pick of the Miami Dolphins.

ball three minutes in the fourth quarter.

With its defense in control, Georgia stomped on a 44-yard drive that put the 'Dogs on the UF 1. The grim Gators buckled as Tate ripped over for the touchdown. Kasay's conversion pushed the tally to 23–3 with 2:38 remaining.

By now, many UF fans had left the stadium only to miss Florida's best showing of the afternoon. On the kickoff, Wayne Williams streaked upfield and was finally tackled after a 70-yard return, the longest for Florida since Cris Collinsworth ran a kickoff back 97 yards against LSU in 1978.

Inspired by the runback, the Gators' offense came up with the big play shortly afterward, Bell connecting with Stacey Simmons for 17 yards and Florida's only touchdown. McGinty's extra point brought the final score to 23–10.

Georgia quarterback James Jackson was named the game's most valuable player with only 70 yards rushing, but several gains came at crucial times. Jackson credited the Bulldogs offensive line and players on both teams agreed that Georgia's linemen dominated.

Rodney Hampton ran for 103 yards and Tate added 89, including his touchdown plunges. Tate's second score gave him 34 TDs for his career, good for second place on UGA's career touchdown list behind Herschel Walker with 52.

Georgia put the wraps on Emmitt Smith, holding the Heisman hopeful to 46 yards on 13 carries, his lowest rushing output of the season. Florida was limited to 204 yards in total offense. The 'Dogs terrorized Bell, who had faced Georgia for the last time to the relief

Tailback Lars Tate plunged for two touchdowns as UGA beat Florida 23–10 in 1987. Tate earned All-SEC honors that year.

of many Bulldog fans. Georgia's defenders sacked the Gator passer four times for losses totalling 41 yards. Bell completed 15 of 22 attempts for 162 yards and a touchdown but had two interceptions, both by Ben Smith. His yardage total was the lowest in his four games against the Bulldogs.

Kerwin Bell ended his four-year career against Georgia with a 2–2 record, a total of 1,020 passing yards and six touchdowns. The Gator who made the team as a walk-on was the SEC's all-time leader in passing yardage (7,581) and touchdown passes (56). He played two years in the NFL, in 1988 with Atlanta and 1989 with Tampa Bay, and later debuted a piece of sports video technology, the infamous "helmet cam," while playing in the WLAF.

Jacksonville law enforcement authorities reported 42 arrests before, during, and after the game, but noted that alcohol was not much of a problem with only five people arrested for disorderly intoxication and two for resisting arrest.

Florida eased the pain of the loss to Georgia with a 27–14 win over Kentucky, but ended the regular season with a 28–14 loss at home to Florida State. With a 6–5 record, the Gators accepted a bid to play UCLA in the Aloha Bowl in Honolulu and fell 20–14.

Gators linebacker Clifford Charlton and defensive backs Jarvis Williams and Louis Oliver were honored as All-American selections and Charlton and Williams were named to the first-team All-SEC squad for the second year in a row. Other Gators selected first-team all-conference were Oliver, defensive tackle Rhondy Weston, middle guard Jeff Roth and running back Emmitt Smith. Charlton was a first-round draft choice of Cleveland.

Smith ended his freshman year with 1,341 yards on the ground to make him Florida's all-time single season rushing leader, a record he would shatter two years later.

Auburn brought the Bulldogs back to earth a week after the win over Florida, beating UGA, 27–11, in Athens to short-circuit any chance of an SEC title for Georgia. The 'Dogs routed Georgia Tech, 30–16, to end the regular season and secure a berth against Arkansas in the Liberty Bowl. In a thriller, Kasay drilled a 39-yard field goal with no time left as Georgia emerged with a 20–17 victory and a 9–3 record.

Lars Tate made the All-SEC first team for the second consecutive year and was joined by linebacker John Brantley and offensive guard and team captain Kim Stephens. Tate was a second-round draft pick by the Tampa Bay Buccaneers.

Georgia was ranked 13th in the final Associated Press poll and 14th in the UPI standings.

Scoring:

Georgia	7	3	3	10	—	23
Florida	3	0	0	7	—	10

UF	FG	McGinty, 52 yards
UGA	TD	Tate, 1-yard run (Kasay kick)
UGA	FG	Crumley, 51 yards
UGA	FG	Kasay, 35 yards
UGA	FG	Crumley, 21 yards
UGA	TD	Tate, 1-yard run (Kasay kick)
UF	TD	Simmons, 17-yard pass from Bell (McGinty kick)

Georgia: *Offense:* Thomas, Hummings, *split end;* Adams, Anderson, *left tackle;* Burroughs, Henderson, *left guard;.* Wheeler, Mrvos, Abram, *center;* Stephens, Wainwright, *right guard;* Mull, Tellis, *right tackle;* Sadowski, Warner, *tight end;* Osborn, Lewis, *flanker;* J. Jackson, W. Johnson, Talley, *quarterback;* Tate, Hampton, K. Brown, *tailback;* Ellis, Cleveland, R. Jackson, *fullback;* Crumley, Kasay, *placekicker;* Hester, Dukes, *punter;* M. Lewis, Bowen, Osborn, Hampton, N. Lewis, *special teams*

Defense: Guthrie, M. Lewis, Brantley, Collins, Webster, D. Douglas, *linebacker;* T. McClendon, Hickey, *tackle;* Goldberg, Giles, *left guard;* L. Brown, Dotson, *right guard;* Chubb, Guthrie, Tardits, *end;* B. Smith, Russaw, Vincent, Hargett, *cornerback;* W. Jones, M. Brown, Beasley, Harmon, *safety*

Florida: *Offense:* Simmons, Snead, Mills, Woulard, *wide receiver;* D. Williams, Hatcher, *left tackle;* Sims, Birch, *left guard;* Daniels, Bromley, *center;* Starowesky, Wright, *right guard;* Davis, Durden, *right tackle;* Odom, McGriff, *tight end;* Bell, *quarterback;* E. Smith, W. Williams, J. Massey, *running back;* A. Williams, McGrady, *fullback;* McGinty, *placekicker;* McAndrews, *punter;* J. Williams, Lomack, K. Watkins, Simmons, *special teams*

Defense: Reuter, Speer, Charlton, Richardson, Dickens, Odom, Murray, Moorer, *linebacker;* H. Brown, Pinner, *left tackle;* Roth, Burnett, *noseguard;* Weston, Seager, *right tackle;* Mulberry, Glover, Watkins, T. Jones, *cornerback;* J. Williams, Loden, L. Oliver, Fain, *safety*

	Georgia	Florida
First downs	22	11
Rushes/yards	66/306	28/42
Passing yards	47	162
Return yards	30	34
Pass att/comp/int	13/4/1	22/15/2
Punts/avg. yards	4/35	4/38
Fumbles/lost	1/0	2/1
Penalties/yards	5/35	7/35
Possession time	37:06	22:54

— 1988 —

Georgia 26, Florida 3

GATOR TAILBACK EMMITT SMITH AND HIS Bulldog opposite, Tim Worley, were expected to be the gunslingers in the November 5, 1988, duel in Jacksonville.

Georgia coach Vince Dooley was in his silver anniversary year as king of the kennel, and Georgia was hoping to crown his 25th and final season with another victory against the detested Gators.

Five weeks into the season, Florida had been 5–0 and climbing in national prominence under fifth-year coach Galen Hall. The Gators butchered Montana State, 69–0; won 27–15 at Ole Miss; beat Indiana State, 58–0; downed Mississippi State, 17–0; and upset 14th-ranked LSU, 19–6, to replace the Tigers at No. 14 in the AP poll.

But Florida's star dimmed suddenly with consecutive losses to Memphis State, 17–11; Vanderbilt, 24–9; and Auburn, 16–0, going into the Georgia game. The Gators fell out of the rankings during their three-game slide, which spawned rumors that Hall was on the way out.

Some of Florida's misfortune was due to Smith not being able to play against Vanderbilt and Auburn. The sophomore All-SEC tailback, the nation's leading rusher with a 125-yard per game average, was recuperating from a sprained knee. Gator freshman quarterback Kyle Morris sat out most of the Auburn contest with a hand injury, but both he and Smith would be back for Georgia.

The Bulldogs knew that Smith, an early season Heisman candidate, would be anxious to atone for the 1987 contest when he was held to 46 yards rushing.

Georgia faced Florida with a 6–2 record and was tied with Auburn for the SEC lead at 4–1. The 19th-ranked Dawgs were 3½ point favorites to whip Florida. Behind the potent running of Worley and his backup, Rodney Hampton, Georgia was averaging close to 425 yards in total offense a game and leading the SEC in rushing.

401

The Dawgs opened 1988 with a 28–17 victory over Tennessee in a nationally televised game, downed Texas Christian, 38–10, and Mississippi State, 42–35, before being dominated by South Carolina, 23–10, in Columbia. Georgia rebounded to batter Ole Miss, 36–12, and Vanderbilt, 41–22, before being surprised, 16–10, at Kentucky. In overwhelming William & Mary, 59–24, at homecoming, the Bulldogs' unpredictable defense had given up more than 400 yards, a matter of great concern to Dooley.

Florida was particularly strong on pass defense, its secondary built around senior All-American safety Louis Oliver. And the massive UF line was nicknamed "the Great Wall" for good reason. Overall, the Gators defense ranked second in the country, surrendering an average of only 226 yards per game.

Georgia, meanwhile, had shown itself vulnerable to the pass throughout the season. Adding to Dooley's problems was a linebacking corps that was thin in numbers. Georgia would be without Brent Collins, and Richard Tardits was questionable with a sprained ankle. Florida would also be without ace wide receiver Stacey Simmons, who suffered a season-ending knee injury against LSU. Several other Gators, including Oliver, would play hurt.

An intense thunderstorm enveloped Jacksonville before dawn on game day, but the rain abated and the sun came out little more than an hour before kickoff. Still, the bad weather diminished the number of UGA rooters who attended the annual Bulldogs Barbeque Brunch in Metropolitan Park. And choppy waves on the St. Johns River made it rough on boaters docking near the Gator Bowl.

Vice President George Bush and Democratic challenger Michael Dukakis were less than a week away from a Tuesday showdown for the presidency. Dukakis supporters were not in evidence but Republicans were handing out "Bulldogs for Bush" or "Gators for Bush" posters in the stadium parking lots.

Just under 82,000 were wedged into the Gator Bowl for the nationally televised game on WTBS.

The Gators' Oliver psyched himself up by watching UGA fans chewing on toy alligators.

To curtail rowdiness, Jacksonville had enacted an ordinance prohibiting the carrying of alcoholic beverages in open containers near the stadium. City police were also enforcing an ordinance against "obscene" or "offensive" bumper stickers or signs in vehicles.

Everyone was frisked for alcohol as they entered the stadium. "I don't care if it's Mother Teresa, I'm gonna search her," an unidentified officer told the *Atlanta Constitution.*

"Despite the best efforts to control alcohol at the gate, the entire stadium had the unmistakable smell of bourbon," a reporter noted.

Finally the game was underway. To almost everyone's surprise, UF freshman tailback Willie McClendon, not Emmitt Smith, trotted onto the field for the Gators' first possession. But Smith, wearing a bulky knee brace, entered the game on the Gators' second possession and was greeted by a raucous ovation from the UF sections.

As in so many Georgia-Florida games, the defenses were the story of the first quarter, despite the bevy of good running backs. While the Dawgs were containing Smith, the Gators were stopping Worley.

Georgia's deepest penetration in the period was to the UF 37, where the Bulldogs faced a fourth down. Kicker John Kasay came on and guided a 47-yard field goal through the stiff wind to give Georgia the early lead at 3–0.

The first break of the day came in the second quarter. Florida's Morris, gunning for one of his wide receivers cutting over the middle on a curl pattern, was intercepted by UGA junior linebacker Demetrius Douglas who returned it to the UF 35. Georgia used four plays to reach the 22. On third and nine, quarterback Wayne Johnson was pressured, scrambled to his right, and fired the ball toward the end zone. Senior split end John Thomas, guarded closely by UF strong safety Bill Lang, managed to make the catch as he fell down. The 22-yard touchdown and Kasay's extra point gave the Bulldogs a 10–0 lead that they took with them into the locker room at halftime.

The highlight of the third quarter came when Georgia marched to the UF 28 and set up for a field goal on fourth down. The Dawgs faked the kick with Worley attempting a pass to Keith Henderson, but the ball was overthrown and Florida had held.

The Gators returned the Bulldog deception with their best drive of the afternoon. Smith ripped off a 17-yard gain on first down. On the next play, he hauled in a swing pass from Morris for 19 more.

On third and seven at the UGA 27, Georgia linebacker Morris "Mo" Lewis hurried UF's Morris into a pass incompletion and Florida settled for a field-goal attempt.

Despite the tricky wind, J. D. Francis' squarely hit kick floated over the crossbar from 44 yards out to draw the Gators to within a touchdown at 10–3 with 3:18 left in the third quarter.

If Florida could stuff Georgia here, emotion's pendulum would swing to the Gators.

But the UF kickoff was short and Georgia tight end Chris Broom returned it 14 yards to the Dawgs 42. Johnson flipped a pass to Henderson for 11 and tailback Hampton plowed for 17 to move Georgia deeper into Gator territory. Johnson then slithered around end for 11 yards to the UF 5 on the last play of the third period. On third down from the 1, Worley took the handoff and was stopped momentarily by a wall of Gators at the goal line before falling into the end zone. Kasay's extra point try caromed off the goal post, but Georgia was resting easier with a 16–3 lead.

Georgia's defense took the stage, holding Florida without a first down, including a nine-yard loss when Morris was sacked by Bulldog noseguard Bill Goldberg.

Florida was still very much in the contest when it regained possession minutes later. But on first down, a short pass by Morris glanced off the helmet of intended receiver Mark McGriff, and Georgia's Douglas was there to snatch it out of the air at the UF 38. Three plays later, Kasay nailed a 45-yarder to widen the gap to 19–3 with 6:49 remaining.

The Gators' woes continued after the kickoff. Near midfield with less than two minutes left, Douglas blitzed, crunching Morris from behind. The ball came loose and Georgia defensive tackle Wycliffe Lovelace made the recovery at the UGA 43.

On third down at the UGA 49, Worley plunged off left tackle and suddenly found himself in the clear. The big, swift tailback cut back and raced 51 yards for his second touchdown. Kasay's conversion made it 26–3 to complete the rout.

UGA fans began chanting "We Want Auburn!" in anticipation of the game a week later. A win over the Tigers would clinch at least a tie for Vince Dooley's seventh SEC championship at Georgia.

As the final seconds ticked off, Bulldog lineman Scott Adams, a Lake City, Fla., native, fell and kissed the turf, knowing he could go home with his head held high, at least for this year.

In the last minutes, about 100 policemen, some on horseback, surrounded the field to keep fans from rushing out of the stands as they had done in droves in 1984 and 1985. The tactic worked but many of the officers were pelted by plastic cups thrown from the seats.

Georgia had held Florida to 219 yards total offense and a field goal, in what Dooley would describe as "the most complete game we've played all season." The Bulldogs had all but smothered Emmitt Smith again, holding him to 68 rushing yards.

Worley, carried from the field on the shoulders of his joyous teammates, was the Georgia hero, romping for 135 yards and two touchdowns. He was voted the game's most valuable player, though Douglas was equally worthy of the honor.

The Gators finished the season with a 24–19 win against Kentucky, a 52–17 whipping by Florida State, and a 14–10 victory over Illinois in the All-American Bowl. Galen Hall had his first bowl win and Florida had a 7–5 (4–3 in the SEC) record. Florida's Louis Oliver and defensive tackle Trace Armstrong garnered first-team All-America honors.

Emmitt Smith, Oliver, Armstrong, offensive tackle David Williams and middle guard Jeff Roth made the 1988 All-SEC squad.

Oliver, one of three finalists for the Thorpe Defensive Back of the Year Award, was a first-round draft pick by the Miami Dolphins, while Armstrong was chosen in the initial round by Chicago and Williams by Houston. The Dallas Cowboys drafted both defensive tackle Rhondy Weston and middle guard Jeff Roth.

Georgia lost, 20–10, at Auburn to fall out of contention in the SEC race. The Dogs grounded Georgia Tech, 24–3, for Dooley's 200th coaching win in the final regular season game, putting him in hallowed company as only the ninth Division 1-A coach in history to reach the milestone. Dooley ended with a 17–7–1 record against Florida.

Tim Worley and Troy Sadowski were honored as All-Americans; and Worley joined center Todd Wheeler, noseguard Bill Goldberg, linebacker Richard Tardits and cornerback Ben Smith on the All-SEC team. Fullback Keith Henderson was drafted by the San Francisco 49ers, and Worley went to the Pittsburgh Steelers as a first-round pick. Tardits was chosen by the Phoenix Cardinals and Sadowski went to the Atlanta Falcons.

In the Mazda Gator Bowl against Michigan State on New Year's Day, 1989, the Dawgs held off the Spartans, 34–27, to close Dooley's illustrious career in triumph. The next day, 33-year-old Ray Goff, the 1975–76 Bulldog quarterback and team captain, was named Dooley's successor in a move that surprised many UGA supporters and football experts.

Georgia was ranked 15th in the final 1988 AP poll. The coming year preceding the next Florida-Georgia game would hold a number of surprises for both teams.

★   ★   ★

Scoring:

Georgia	3	7	0	16	—	26
Florida	0	0	3	0	—	3

UGA	FG	Kasay, 47 yards
UGA	TD	Thomas, 22-yard pass from Johnson (Kasay kick)
UF	FG	Francis, 44 yards
UGA	TD	Worley, 1-yard run (PAT failed)
UGA	FG	Kasay, 45 yards
UGA	TD	Worley, 51-yard run (Kasay kick)

Georgia: *Offense:* Thomas, Maxwell, *split end;* Colley, DeFoor, *left tackle;* Anderson, Henderson, *left guard;* Wheeler, Mull, Sanders, *center;* Adams, Simmons, *right guard;* Mull, DeFoor, *right tackle;* Sadowski, Warner, Broom, *tight end;* Johnson, Talley, *quarterback;* Worley, Hampton, *tailback;* Ellis, Henderson, *fullback;* Marshall, Hummings, *flanker;* Kasay, *placekicker;* Hester, *punter;* M. Lewis, Carswell, Cleveland, *special teams*

Defense: M. Lewis, Chubb, Cowins, D. Douglas, Webster, Allen, *linebacker;* Lovelace, Cole, *tackle;* Goldberg, Bell, *middle guard;* Giles, Wainwright, *end;* B. Smith, Wynn, Hargett, Carswell, *cornerback;* Guthrie, Hargett, Beasley, Harmon, *safety*

Florida: *Offense:* Snead, Barber, Lomack, Sullivan, T. Ellis, *wide receiver;* Williams, Dixon, *left tackle;* Starowesky, Sills, *left guard;* Daniels, Dixon, *center;* Bromley, Ismail, *right guard;* Durden, Hatcher, *right tackle;* McGriff, Kirkpatrick, *tight end;* Morris, *quarterback;* McNabb, McGrady, *fullback;* McClendon, E. Smith, C. Smith, *running back;* Francis, *placekicker;* Perry, *punter;* Bromley, Morris, Barber, Lomack, Sullivan, *special teams*

Defense: Bartruff, Bartley, Richardson, Murray, Moorer, Odom, Nicoletto, Paulk, Ellis, *linebacker;* Weston, McCoy, *right tackle;* Roth, Culpepper, *middle guard;* Armstrong, Neeley, *left tackle;* Fain, T. Jones, Watkins, Young, *cornerback;* Lang, White, Oliver, Spierto, *safety*

	Georgia	Florida
First downs	14	13
Rushes/yards	48/237	35/120
Passing yards	65	146
Pass att/comp/int	12/6/0	27/14/2
Punts/avg. yards	4/42	7/32
Fumbles/lost	1/1	3/1
Penalties/yards	5/40	5/30
Possession time	31:19	28:41

— 1989 —

Georgia 17, Florida 10

Florida was 20th ranked, had Heisman candidate Emmitt Smith in the backfield, and the country's stingiest defense; but the Gators' off-the-field woes were also a major part of the 1989 clash with Georgia.

The 6–2 Gators were jarred on October 9 when sixth-year coach Galen Hall resigned under pressure in light of an investigation by the NCAA and a federal grand jury concerning allegedly illegal payments made to assistant coaches. Hall also was accused of arranging for a player to receive money to help make child support payments. There was some speculation that the NCAA might impose the "death penalty" on Florida, meaning the school would not be allowed to play football for at least a year.

Then on October 16, starting quarterback Kyle Morris and his backup, Shane Matthews, were suspended from the team for placing bets on college and professional games.

The November 11 tussle in the Gator Bowl had to be one of the most unpredictable of the series.

With a 5–3 record, first-year Georgia coach Ray Goff was off to a less than spectacular start in trying to live up to the tradition Vince Dooley had forged in Athens. Many of Goff's assistant coaches, some brought on during the Dooley years, were UGA letterman: Bill Hartman, a Georgia All-American in the 1930s, Willie McClendon, Dicky Clark, John Kasay, Frank Orgel, Charles Whittemore, Steve Greer and Joe Tereshinski all had firsthand experience "between the hedges."

The 1989 game was billed as a war between the Dawgs' hard-charging junior tailback Rodney Hampton and Emmitt Smith, considered by many to be the best backs in the nation.

Smith, a junior from Pensacola, had a rushing average of 151 yards per game, tops in the country. He had gained over 1,200 yards in the

Gators' first eight games and established himself as Florida's all-time leading rusher. Georgia took pride in holding the Gator runner to 114 total rushing yards and no touchdowns in the 1987 and 1988 games.

Hampton's slashing runs accounted for two-thirds of the Bulldogs' 1989 ground attack with a 116-yard per game average, even though he had missed the Mississippi State game with an ankle injury and been hampered by a bad knee.

The Gators defense, spearheaded by junior linebacker Huey Richardson, was leading the nation in total defense and had Hampton in its cross hairs. Yet, many Florida fans wondered if the nightmare that had gripped Gainesville for the past five weeks would affect the Gators' play.

With the cloud of NCAA sanctions looming again, interim UF coach Gary Darnell was trying to hold the team together and depending heavily on freshman quarterback Donald Douglas. Douglas made his first collegiate start in Florida's loss at Auburn a week before. His baptism by fire would continue against the Bulldogs.

Florida began the year with a 24–19 home loss to Ole Miss before mauling Louisiana Tech, 34–7. The Gators then beat Memphis State, 38–13; Mississippi State, 21–0; and LSU, 16–13, before Hall resigned. Under Darnell, who had been Hall's defensive coordinator, Florida scuttled Vanderbilt, 34–11, and New Mexico, 27–21, before a 10–7 loss at Auburn.

Georgia opened '89 with a 15–3 home win over Baylor and followed with a 23–6 victory against Mississippi State. But South Carolina handed the Bulldogs a 24–20 defeat in Athens and the skid was on. Georgia lost at Tennessee, 17–14, and 17–13 at Ole Miss before besting Vanderbilt, 35–16, and Kentucky, 34–23. The unranked Bulldogs celebrated homecoming by beating Temple, 37–10, although they hadn't been particularly impressive.

More than 81,500 fans jammed into the Gator Bowl on a sunny Saturday for the nationally televised encounter. As usual, thousands of fans partied along Haines Street outside the stadium, throwing toy alligators or stuffed bulldogs under the wheels of passing vehicles.

The Gators quickly forced a punt after an initial Georgia first down. With Douglas at the helm, Florida marched from its 5 to the UGA 37 and appeared to be headed for a score. On the next play, however, the 'Dogs pressured the Gator quarterback as he tried to pass, and UGA inside linebacker Curt Douglas made the interception at the Georgia 37.

The Florida drive was the only serious offense of the first quarter.

With the UF program in turmoil, Gary Darnell led the Gators after Galen Hall resigned during the 1989 season. Darnell lost his only game as UF head coach against Georgia, in Ray Goff's first coaching win over Florida.

For the remainder of the period, the teams battered each other in a gridiron version of trench warfare, both squads playing spine-cracking defense.

Georgia outside linebacker Morris "Mo" Lewis continually harassed UF's Douglas on passing attempts, while the stunting Gator linemen put heavy pressure on Bulldog quarterback Greg Talley. Hampton and Smith were paying with their bodies for the yardage they gained.

The Bulldogs broke the ice in the second quarter after a grinding drive mired at the UF 26. From there, junior kicker John Kasay hit a field goal to give Georgia a 3–0 lead.

The defensive combat continued until the closing minutes of the half when the Gators came back. Douglas fired a pass to wide receiver Ernie Mills for a 37-yard gain into Georgia territory and UF fans were on their feet. From the UGA 19, four plays later, Douglas again found Mills, who made a leaping catch for the touchdown. Senior kicker J. D. Francis tacked on the extra point, and Florida was up 7–3 as the half ended.

Georgia had given up 117 yards on the ground in the first half, including 66 to Smith. But the Bulldogs were more surprised by the effectiveness of Florida's passing.

Florida took the second half kickoff at their 30 and immediately put together its third sustained drive of the game. In six plays, the Gators moved to the UGA 22 where they faced a third and one. Smith was leveled for no gain and, on fourth and one, Darnell decided to go for it rather than attempt the field goal.

It was high noon for a Heisman hopeful, and everyone in the stadium knew Smith would likely get the call. He did, but a bevy of fired-up red hats, led by middle guard Robert Bell, buried him inches away from the first-down marker. Douglas had slipped during the handoff, throwing off the timing of the crucial play.

Georgia's ecstasy ended momentarily. On first down, a short pass by Talley was picked off by linebacker Ephesians Bartley, and the Gators were back in business at the UGA 46.

Again the 'Dogs defense came through. On the first play after Bartley's interception, Douglas passed over the middle to wide receiver Stacey Simmons near the UGA 25. Georgia free safety Ben Smith came up fast and cracked him with a bone-jarring lick. The ball popped free and Bulldog linebacker Matt McCormick recovered the fumble at the UGA 24.

Georgia then drove to its 47, highlighted by a 15-yard sweep by Hampton around right end. On third down, needing only inches for a first down, Georgia, instead of running, set up to pass. The ball

Power running back Emmitt Smith, Florida's all-time leading rusher, was an All-American in 1989. A first-round draft pick by Dallas and member of their Super Bowl championship team, he was 0–3 against the Bulldogs.

tumbled out of Talley's hand and spun slowly toward Hampton, who caught it and raced 29 yards before being hauled down at the Florida 15 by UF cornerback Richard Fain. Goff later described the pass as the "ugliest I had seen."

From there, Hampton tore through for five and, on second down, knifed through to pay dirt. With Kasay's extra point Georgia regained the lead, 10–7, with about five minutes left in the third quarter.

Florida then went to the air, as Douglas tried to connect with tight end Kirk Kirkpatrick down the middle. But the throw was high and 5–11 safety Ben Smith was there again, outjumping the taller Kirkpatrick to make the interception a the UF 37.

A 15-yard pass to UGA receiver Kevin Maxwell and a personal foul on Florida moved Georgia to the UF 11. Hampton carried it to the 2 before torpedoing over the pile for the score. Kasay's conversion built the Georgia margin to 17–7.

With less than eight minutes left in the fourth quarter, Douglas was replaced by redshirt UF freshman Lex Smith, who completed six of 11 passes for 66 yards. The Gators' last chance ended with a drive to the UGA 8. Florida couldn't punch it in from there, so Francis kicked a 24-yard field goal to whittle the lead to 17–10 with 3:18 remaining.

With only 29 seconds left, Florida got the ball back but Ben Smith intercepted a Lex Smith pass on the last play of the game.

The Gators won the statistics battle, though not the one that counted: the final score. Florida had 25 first downs to Georgia's 15, outrushed the Bulldogs, 191 to 103, and enjoyed a 247- to 175-yard passing advantage.

Gator quarterback Douglas had a good day for a freshman thrust into such a sea of intense adversity, but his failures to convert in the second half proved costly. He completed 12 of 20 passes for 181 yards, a touchdown, and three interceptions, two by Ben Smith.

In addition to his two touchdowns, Hampton won the rushing battle against Emmitt Smith, outgaining his counterpart 121 to 106 on 29 carries. Indeed, Hampton *was* the Georgia ground assault. Talley and his backup, Preston Jones, combined for the 'Dogs other five rushing attempts that resulted in minus 18 yards.

Georgia had won its third in a row over Florida, and Ray Goff tasted victory against the Gators for the first time as a head coach.

The Bulldogs lost, 20–3, at home to 12th-ranked Auburn and 33–22 to Georgia Tech in Atlanta to finish at 6–5 overall and 4–3 in the conference. They accepted a Peach Bowl invitation but lost, 19–

Tailback Rodney Hampton thrived on Gator meat in UGA wins from 1987 to 1989. He turned pro after his junior year and was drafted by the New York Giants.

18, to Syracuse to finish at 6–6 in Goff's first campaign. Defensive back Ben Smith went on to play for the Philadelphia Eagles, and Rodney Hampton decided to forego his senior year, turning pro and being quickly gobbled up by the New York Giants in the first round.

Florida downed Kentucky, 38–28, and lost 24–17 to sixth-ranked Florida State, but still earned a Freedom Bowl bid against Washington. The Huskies dominated, winning 34–7 to finish Florida's eventful year at 7–5 (4–3).

Emmitt Smith was named SEC Player of the Year and was consensus first-team All-America. He was a first-round pick by the Dallas Cowboys after deciding to turn pro at the end of his junior year. Still, he is a prominent figure in the UF record books as Florida's career rushing leader with 3,928 yards. He also holds records for most yards in a season and game, as well as carries in a career, season, and game for the Gators. Georgia fans like to note that he was 0–3 against the 'Dogs.

Smith was honored as a first-team All-SEC selection for the third consecutive year and was joined on the honor squad by Gator offensive tackle John Durden, linebacker Huey Richardson and defensive back Richard Fain. Georgia defensive back Ben Smith also made the elite squad.

On December 31, the day after the Freedom Bowl, former Gator quarterback and Heisman Trophy winner Steve Spurrier was named Florida head coach. A first-round draft pick by San Francisco in 1967, Spurrier played with the 49ers and Tampa Bay Buccaneers and later was head coach of the Tampa Bay Bandits of the United States Football League from 1983 to 1985. As head coach at Duke from 1987 to 1989, his pass-oriented teams compiled a 20–13–1 record.

Spurrier brought John Reaves, another Gator quarterback luminary, with him as an assistant coach on his return to Gainesville. Twenty-four years after he lost his last game as a player against Georgia in 1966, Spurrier would haunt the Bulldogs with a vengeance.

Scoring:

Georgia	0	3	14	0	—	17
Florida	0	7	0	3	—	10

UGA	FG	Kasay, 26 yards
UF	TD	Mills, 19-yard pass from Douglas (Francis kick)
UGA	TD	Hampton, 10-yard run (Kasay kick)
UGA	TD	Hampton, 2-yard run (Kasay kick)
UF	FG	Francis, 24 yards

Georgia: *Offense:* Hummings, Evans, McCoy, *split ends;* Colley, Fellows, *left tackle;* Sadler, Wynn, *left guard;* Swan, Lane, *center;* DeFoor, Rosenberg, *right guard;* Mull, Cole, *right tackle;* Warner, Broom, Etheridge, *tight end;* Marshall, Maxwell, *flanker;* Talley, P. Jones, *quarterback;* R. Hampton, Strong, Ware, *tailback;* Cleveland, Ellis, *fullback;* Kasay, *placekicker;* Hester, *punter;* Cole, Wallace, *special teams*

Defense: M. Lewis, Gantt, C. Douglas, McCormick, G. Jackson, D. Douglas, Evans, Cowins, Thompson, *linebackers;* Goldberg, Brewer, *left tackle;* Bell, *noseguard;* Berry, Steele, *right tackle;* Wynn, Andrews, C. Wilson, A. Jackson, *cornerback;* M. Jones, Rinard, B. Smith, Andrews, *safety*

Florida: *Offense:* Simmons, Lomack, A. Sullivan, Mills, Barber, T. Jones, *wide receiver;* Neely, Hatcher, *left tackle;* M. White, Ismail, *left guard;* Dixon, Bromley, *center;* Bromley, Starowesky, *right guard;* Durden, Taotoai, *right tackle;* D. Douglas, L. Smith, *quarterback;* E. Smith, McClendon, McNabb, *running back;* C. Smith, Perry, McNabb, *fullback;* Thomas, Kirkpatrick, *tight end;* Francis, *placekicker;* Francis, Rone, *punter;* Bromley, Neely, Nichols, Lomack, Barber, Watkins, *special teams*

Defense: Myles, Speer, Richardson, Miles, Moorer, Baldwin, Odom, Paulk, Ellis, *linebacker;* Murray, Gunter, *left tackle;* Culpepper, P. Johnson, *middle guard;* McCoy, Rowell, D. Smith, *right tackle;* Watkins, Scavella, Fain, Spencer, *cornerback;* Bartley, M. Oliver, W. White, Grow, Grandison, *safety*

	Georgia	Florida
First downs	15	25
Rushes/yards	34/103	45/191
Passing yards	175	247
Pass att/comp/int	26/12/1	31/18/3
Punts/avg. yards	8/44	4/35
Fumbles/lost	0/0	2/1
Penalties/yards	8/75	10/63
Possession time	25:34	34:26

— 1990 —

Florida 38, Georgia 7

WITH FLORIDA FAVORED BY AT LEAST 18 points, even the most pessimistic UF fan had to agree that the Gators had one of their best chances ever to whip the Dawgs in 1990.

First-year Florida coach Steve Spurrier, the former Heisman-winning quarterback, and his 10th-ranked Gators were fresh from a 48–7 thrashing of then fourth-ranked Auburn a week earlier at Florida Field.

The Gators defense was second in the nation only to Clemson, which had manhandled Georgia, 34–3, earlier in the season.

Under second-year coach Ray Goff, the 1990 Bulldogs were among the youngest and most inexperienced UGA teams in more than 20 years.

Florida came into the November 10 Gator Bowl rumble at 7–1 (4–1 in the SEC) with only a 45–3 loss to high-powered Tennessee in Knoxville marring its campaign. Spurrier's team owned wins over Oklahoma State, 50–7; Alabama, 17–13; Furman, 27–3; Mississippi State, 34–21; LSU, 34–8; Akron, 59–0; and Auburn. The Gators were a preseason pick to battle Auburn and Tennessee for the SEC title.

Casting a pall over the season, however, was a one-year NCAA probation stemming from the Galen Hall investigation. The Gators were prohibited from going to a bowl game or winning the conference.

Georgia, meanwhile, was 4–4 (2–3) and had dropped three of its previous four games coming into the showdown. Before the season the team's youth had made it a question mark for the forecasters. So far, the schedule had been highlighted by a come-from-behind 17–16 win over Alabama in Athens, an 18–17 victory over Southern Mississippi, and home triumphs against Vanderbilt, 39–28, and East Carolina, 19–15. In addition to Clemson, the Dawgs had fallen to

LSU, 18–13; Ole Miss, 28–12; and Kentucky, 26–24, the latter defeat coming two weeks before the Florida game.

Oddsmakers said the 18-point spread for the Gators would have been higher except for Florida's history of underachievement in the series.

Both teams were missing stellar running backs who had left college early to play professional football. Georgia's Rodney Hampton signed with the New York Giants and the Gators' Emmitt Smith went to the Dallas Cowboys. Smith was Florida's all-time leading rusher.

Compounding the Dawgs' problems was the team's decimation by injuries and academic shortcomings. Flanker Arthur Marshall had broken his leg in the LSU game. Nine defensive players, including safety David Hargett, linebackers Demetrius Douglas and Norman Cowins, and noseguard Robert Bell were among those out.

An estimated 81,529 fans descended on the Gator Bowl under overcast skies. Cold, blustery winds at times lowered the wind chill factor to about 44 degrees.

The massive deployment of U.S. forces to the Persian Gulf region and the threat of impending war with Iraq put the game in perspective for many fans.

Despite the odds seemingly stacked against them, Georgia had beaten the Gators the past three years. The record also showed the 'Dogs had won 10 of the last 12 and 15 of the last 19 games against Florida.

But Spurrier had waited 24 years to avenge the 27–10 loss Georgia handed him during his senior season.

Florida took the opening kickoff and drove 47 yards to the Georgia 17 before Gator junior tailback Willie McClendon fumbled, and the Dawgs recovered to snuff out Florida's first invasion.

But on Georgia's second down, fullback Alphonso Ellis fumbled it back to Florida at the UGA 15. The Gators' McClendon crashed into the end zone three plays later from two yards out, and Arden Czyzewski's extra point gave UF the 7–0 lead.

Pinned near their goal line after the kickoff, the 'Dogs went to the air. Quarterback Greg Talley hit wide receiver Sean Hummings with a hard pass at the UGA 36, but the ball glanced off the Woodbine senior's shoulder pads and into the hands of Florida inside linebacker Tim Paulk, who spun and rumbled down the sideline into the end zone.

"When I looked up, I saw nothing but blue shirts in front of me,"

Florida inside linebacker Tim Paulk returned an interception for a 36-yard touchdown against Georgia in the first quarter of the 1990 UF win.

Paulk later said of his TD run. "I've never had a game like I had those first five minutes."

The Gators defense stuffed Georgia, and Florida threatened again late in the quarter. But on third and goal from the UGA 1, UF sophomore quarterback Shane Matthews lost the snap, and Georgia cornerback Mike Jones fell on it at the 3-yard line.

The turnover awakened Georgia which embarked on a seven-play drive. Talley connected with flanker Kevin Maxwell for 22 yards, then found tight end Chris Broom for 25 more. Aided by a 15-yard pass interference penalty, Talley, from the Florida 23, passed to freshman end Andre Hastings in the center of the field near the goal line. Hastings was sandwiched by at least two Gators but lunged into the end zone. John Kasay's extra point trimmed Florida's lead to 14–7 with less than a minute left in the first quarter.

Florida used up about five minutes on a 12-play drive highlighted by quarterback Matthews' passes of 30 and 17 yards to tight end Kirk Kirkpatrick and an 11-yard toss to McClendon. When the 67-yard drive stalled, Czyzewski speared a field goal from the UGA 23 to extend Florida's margin to 17–7.

Georgia's much-heralded freshman Garrison "Doobie" Hearst hauled in the kickoff at his 1 but stumbled down at the 6, putting the

Bulldogs in another hole. On the next play, Talley rolled right, eyeing Maxwell for a short pass only to find him blanketed by UF cornerback Richard Fain. The junior signal-caller tried to throw the ball out of bounds, but it hung high in the wind and Fain snared it at the UGA 6, stepping out of bounds.

Two plays later, Matthews passed to wide receiver Ernie Mills for a touchdown. Czyzewski's PAT made it 24–7 and Florida was rolling.

Goff replaced Talley with freshman Joe Dupree on the next series but he was ineffectual, leading the team to minus 16 yards on Georgia's final three possessions of the first half.

Florida lost a couple of other opportunities when Gator freshman tailback Errict Rhett was stopped for a loss on fourth and one at the UGA 20. Czyzewski then missed a 35-yard field goal on Florida's next possession after the Gators again nosed inside the 'Dogs 20.

Seconds before halftime, Gator tight end Greg Keller caught a pass but was tackled in bounds at the UGA 19, allowing time to run out before a field goal could be attempted.

Despite the lead, Florida fans knew the margin should have been more. Five times in the half the Gators had advanced inside the Georgia 20 and emerged with no points.

All-SEC wide receiver Ernie Mills snared two touchdown passes from Shane Matthews to help destroy Georgia 38–7 in 1990. He later played for the Pittsburgh Steelers.

Defensive end Huey Richardson was among Florida's stars in the 1990 romp over Georgia. The effort helped him earn All-American honors and a draft selection by the Pittsburgh Steelers.

Yet, the damage had been done to Georgia, and the Gator defenders continued their handiwork in the second half. Talley returned to guide the Bulldogs but couldn't muster a first down in the third quarter against the overpowering Floridians. In addition, he was without Hastings, his top receiver, who injured an ankle on the touchdown lunge. And the orange hats were swarming like angry hornets on defense.

Taking over at its own 49 after a Georgia punt, on first down, the Gators ran a flea-flicker. Matthews pitched to Rhett who handed the ball back to Matthews who then passed to Terence Barber all alone at the Dawgs 5. The Florida receiver tumbled into the end zone, completing the 51-yard scoring play and burying Georgia's hopes. Czyzewski's kick swelled the UF margin to 31–7.

Later in the third period, Florida got the ball at its own 46. Matthews hit Monty Duncan for 17 yards and Kirkpatrick for 12. The eight-play drive culminated with Matthews' toss to Mills for a TD from 16 yards out. Czyzewski's PAT accounted for the final margin, 38–7.

There was an array of Gator stars this day. Matthews threw for 344 yards and three touchdowns, including two to Mills, and completed 26 of 39 attempts with no interceptions. His aerial bombardment and running accounted for 377 yards of total offense, a new record in the series.

Kirkpatrick, Florida's leading receiver going into the contest, caught eight passes for 112 yards, a school record for receptions by a Gator tight end in a game. His effort against Georgia also set a UF season record for catches by a tight end.

On defense, Paulk and ends Huey Richardson and Mark Murray were among the many Florida standouts.

The 31-point loss was Georgia's worst ever to the Gators. Dawg outside linebacker Morris Lewis summed up the UGA viewpoint in an interview with the *Savannah News-Press:* "No matter what the rankings are, it's always going to be a grudge match between us. Today it wasn't that. They came to embarrass us."

The Saturday that brought the Gators' biggest win ever in the series also saw Southern Mississippi shock Auburn 13–12 at home and top-ranked Notre Dame hold off No. 9 Tennessee before more than 90,000 at Knoxville.

Florida torpedoed Kentucky, 45–17, on November 17 to claim the unofficial SEC championship, but fell, 45–30, to powerful Florida State to close Spurrier's first season at 9–2.

Shane Matthews was named the 1990 SEC Player of the Year and was well on his way to becoming one of the greatest passing quarterbacks in Gator history.

Gator defensive back Will White and defensive end Huey Richardson were honored as All-Americans; and, along with Matthews, linebacker Tim Paulk, flanker Ernie Mills, and tight end Kirk Kirkpatrick, were named to the first-team All-SEC squad, Richardson for the second consecutive year.

Richardson and Mills were drafted by the Pittsburgh Steelers and cornerback Richard Fain joined the Cincinnati Bengals. Georgia kicker John Kasay went to the Seattle Seahawks.

Georgia was pounded, 33–10, by Auburn and fell, 40–23, to eventual co-national champion Georgia Tech to end the campaign at 4–7, their first losing season since 1977. Both teams looked to 1991 as THE year.

Scoring:

Florida	14	10	14	0	—	38
Georgia	7	0	0	0	—	7

UF	TD	McClendon, 2-yard run (Czyzewski kick)
UF	TD	Paulk, 36-yard interception return (Czyzewski kick)

UGA	TD	Hastings, 23-yard pass from Talley (Kasay kick)
UF	FG	Czyzewski, 23 yards
UF	TD	Mills, 6-yard pass from Matthews (Czyzewski kick)
UF	TD	Barber, 51-yard pass from Matthews (Czyzewski kick)
UF	TD	Mills, 16-yard pass from Matthews (Czyzewski kick)

Florida: *Offense:* Matthews, Fox, Morris, *quarterback;* McNabb, *fullback;* McClendon, Rhett, *tailback;* Mills, *flanker;* Kirkpatrick, Keller, *tight end;* Barber, *split end;* White, *left tackle;* Ismail, *left guard;* Dixon, *center;* Bromley, *right guard;* Rowell, *right tackle;* Czyzewski, *kicker*

Defense: Murray, Richardson, *ends;* Culpepper, *left tackle;* Brandon, *right tackle;* Bartley, Odom, Paulk, *linebackers;* Speer, Fain, *cornerbacks;* White, Myles, *safeties*

Georgia: *Offense:* Talley, Dupree, *quarterback;* Ellis, *fullback;* Hearst, Ware, *tailback;* Maxwell, *flanker;* Mitchell, Broom, *tight end;* Hummings, Hastings, *split end;* Rosenberg, *left tackle;* Sadler, *left guard;* Swan, *center;* Wynn, *right guard;* Tellis, *right tackle;* Kasay, Armstrong, *kicker*

Defense: Lewis, Allen, Jackson, Simmons, *linebackers;* Steele, *noseguard;* Jennings, *right tackle;* Coney, *left tackle;* Carswell, Wynn, *cornerback;* Jones, Thompson, *safeties*

	Florida	Georgia
First downs	27	11
Rushes/yards	40/111	35/99
Passing yards	359	110
Return yards	59	7
Pass att/comp/int	42/28/0	23/8/2
Punts/avg. yards	4/32	10/31
Fumbles/lost	4/2	2/1
Penalties/yards	7/55	4/55
Possession time	34:24	25:36

— 1991 —

Florida 45, Georgia 13

GEORGIA'S INCONSISTENT DEFENSE WOULD have to slow Florida quarterback sensation Shane Matthews and the rest of the Gators' "Fun and Gun" offense if the Bulldogs were to have a chance in the November 9, 1991, game in Jacksonville.

At 7–1 and 5–0 in the SEC, the sixth-ranked Gators knew a win over the 'Dogs would clinch at least a tie for the conference championship, a crown that always had eluded them through bad luck and probation.

Matthews, the 1990 SEC Player of the Year, was the triggerman for the Gators who were ranked in the Top 10 in most preseason polls and had remained there throughout the season.

Second-year Florida coach Steve Spurrier was trying to go 2–0 against third-year UGA coach Ray Goff, both former quarterbacks for their respective teams. Goff was 1–1 against Florida but the Gators were 12-point favorites to win their second in a row over the Dawgs, a feat not accomplished since 1962–1963.

No. 23 Georgia still was an enigma at 6–2 (3–2 in the conference). The Bulldogs played superbly in a nationally televised upset of then sixth-ranked Clemson, but hit bottom with a loss at Vanderbilt. Georgia started the year with veteran Greg Talley and hightly-touted freshman Eric Zeier sharing playing time at quarterback, but Zeier's performance against Clemson earned him the starting role.

Georgia flattened Western Carolina, 48–0, in its season opener, then pummeled LSU, 31–10, in Athens. The Bulldogs were ranked 25th in the AP poll before Alabama edged them 10–0. Georgia struggled to beat outclassed Cal State-Fullerton, 27–14, before tomahawking Clemson, 27–12. Zeier's scrambling and passing were keys in the shocker that catapulted Georgia to 22nd in the AP poll. The 'Dogs then beat potent Ole Miss, 37–17, before calamity set in.

Georgia, 17th-ranked, jumped out to a 14–0 lead at Vanderbilt's homecoming, but the Commodores came back to sink UGA in a stunner, 27–25.

The Bulldogs regained their stride with a 49–27 pounding of Kentucky in which Zeier threw for 302 yards, the first 300-yard game for a UGA passer since Larry Rakestraw in 1963. But the defense that had carried Georgia against Clemson had been shot full of holes by Vanderbilt and Kentucky and was a major concern for the UGA staff.

Florida opened the year big, maiming San Jose State, 59–21, as Matthews passed for five touchdowns to tie the SEC single-game record. Sixth-rated Florida smashed 16th-ranked Alabama, 35–0, in a nationally televised game in Gainesville, then traveled to Syracuse as the fifth-rated eleven in the country. The 18th-ranked Orangemen surprised the Gators, 38–21, dropping them to No. 13 in the AP ratings.

Florida drilled No. 21 Mississippi State, 29–7, a week later as Matthews tossed two touchdown passes to tie him for third place with Steve Spurrier on Florida's career-passing touchdown list. Matthews passed his coach a week later, throwing for a touchdown as Florida outlasted LSU, 16–0, in Baton Rouge.

The Gators then rolled over fourth-ranked Tennessee, 35–18, swamped Northern Illinois, 41–10, and kayoed Auburn, 31–10.

Matthews had received little attention in the Heisman Trophy race despite his numbers: 157 completions in 260 attempts for 2,257 yards, 20 touchdowns, and 12 interceptions. At Air Florida where the passing of Spurrier, Bell and Reaves was legendary, the young Mississippian was rewriting the flight plan. Wide receiver Willie Jackson, whose father, Willie Jackson, Sr., was one of UF's first black athletes in the early 1970s, was Matthews' favorite target with 34 catches and seven touchdowns.

Florida had few weaknesses other than a secondary that was among the league's worst in pass defense. Matthews was putting up big numbers every Saturday, but the UF assault was balanced with a strong running game headed by backs Errict Rhett, Willie McClendon and Dexter McNabb. The Gators had a rock-solid offensive line and an overlooked, but ferocious, defensive front, headed by tackles Brad Culpepper and Tony McCoy.

The Gator defenders knew they would have to pressure Zeier, who came in with 109 completions in 192 attempts for 1,438 yards, six touchdowns, and only two interceptions.

Kickoff was moved to 4 p.m. to accommodate a national telecast

With his laser-sharp passing, Shane Matthews led the Gators to three consecutive wins over Georgia. Twice named SEC player of the year, he threw for more than 9,000 yards and 74 touchdowns.

by ESPN and the 81,679 fans that poured into the Gator Bowl shivered through one of the coldest Florida-Georgia matchups ever. Rain threatened from gray skies as temperatures dipped into the 40s, with a torturous breeze dropping the wind chill factor into the 20s.

Florida was as cool as the weather in showing no jitters in the opening drive. Starting from the UF 25, Rhett rammed for four and Matthews hit wide receiver Willie Jackson for 12. Two runs by Rhett gained seven before Matthews connected with wide receiver Harrison Houston for 12 to the UGA 39. A short pass over the middle to Rhett netted 11 more, and Matthews threw to Jackson for 12 to the UGA 16. On a draw, Rhett stormed to the 5 for a first and goal. On third and goal, with Dawg fans screaming for defense, Matthews hit Willie Jackson who had beaten cornerback Chuck Carswell just inside the end zone. Gator kicker Arden Czyzewski added the extra point and Florida led 7–0.

Georgia now cranked up its offense for the first time. On third down, Zeier rolled left and lofted his first pass of the day toward flanker Andre Hastings, running down the sideline in front of the Florida bench. Hastings made the grab for a gain to the UF 36. Running back Garrison Hearst burst through for six, and a personal foul penalty on the Gators gave Georgia a first down at the UF 25. Hearst swept left end to the 20 but Zeier was tackled for a loss back at the 25 by UF end Darren Mikell, and the 'Dogs were forced to go for the field goal. Kicker Kanon Parkman drilled a 41-yarder to trim the UF lead to 7–3 midway through the quarter.

Fans on both sides were beginning to sense a high-scoring shoot-out when Larry Kennedy returned the Georgia kickoff 58 yards to the UGA 38. But two Matthews incompletions and a penalty foiled the series. With Georgia in possession, back Larry Ware caught a Zeier pass at the UGA 20 but the 'Dogs couldn't earn a first down. Punter Scot Armstrong got off a kick under a heavy rush and was smashed by two Gators. Florida was flagged for roughing the kicker and UGA had a first down at its 35. The hit aggravated a knee injury Armstrong suffered in practice earlier in the week and eliminated him from further action.

Georgia could not kindle its offense and had to punt minutes later.

The Gators got the ball again at their own 29, and Matthews zeroed in on fullback Dexter McNabb over the middle, who broke several tackles after the catch and thundered to the UGA 43 for a 29-yard gain. Three plays later, Duncan caught a first-down pass at the 30. Matthews found Rhett at the 26 and clicked with wide receiver Alonzo Sullivan for a first down at the 'Dogs 13. Rhett then slashed through the Georgia line, broke a tackle in the secondary, and romped into the end zone for Florida's second score. Czyzewski's kick made it 14–3 Florida with only 27 seconds gone in the second period.

On Florida's next possession, starting from the UF 30, Matthews passed to Sullivan for 13. Five plays later, he threw to fullback Kelvin Randolph at the UGA 37. Another two plays and Matthews went airborne again. Drifting back, he saw Harrison Houston work free in the end zone and nailed him despite the effort of Dawgs safety Mike Jones. Czyzewski's extra point widened the Gators' advantage to 21–3.

Georgia took a turn on offense with Zeier passing to split end Arthur Marshall at the Georgia 37. After Zeier was tackled for a loss to the 29, he again went to Marshall, this time to the UGA 42. Three plays later, a personal foul call on Florida put Georgia at the UF 35 with a first down. Goff called a reverse. Zeier handed off to Ware as flanker Andre Hastings streaked across the backfield to take a pitch from the running back. But Ware was leveled by Gatorback Ephesians Bartley as he let fly and the pigskin sailed away from Hastings. A mad dash for the live ball ensued with several Gators in pursuit. Hastings got to it first and was immediately tackled by Florida safety Will White for a 19-yard loss. The play shattered UGA's impetus and Armstrong's replacement, Stuart Saussy, punted minutes later. Georgia got a break when the ball was downed on the UF 4.

Florida's Rhett, ignoring the field disadvantage, tore out to the 16. Runs by Rhett, Matthews, and a short pass to tight end Charlie Dean, soon had the Gators out to their 39. On the next play, Matthews threw to Sullivan, open on the sideline at the UF 45 in front of the Georgia bench.

No Bulldog was within five yards of the senior Gator receiver when he made the catch, dodging away from converging cornerback George Wynn to race down the sideline untouched for a 61-yard touchdown. It was the first TD of Sullivan's career, and Czyzewski's conversion lengthened the margin to 28–3 with 2:19 to play in the half.

Georgia's offense flickered to life after Marshall returned the Florida kickoff to the 'Dogs 38. A screen pass from Zeier to Hearst went all the way to the UF 38. Two plays later, Mack Strong gathered in a shovel pass and galloped to the 28. Hearst ran to the 24 and Strong bulled to the 15 with 33 seconds left. On a second-down play, Zeier found Marshall at the 8, but, on the next snap, his pass to Marshall in the end zone was broken up. On fourth down with two seconds left, many Bulldog fans booed as Goff sent in Parkman for the field-goal try. The 25-yard kick bounded off one of the uprights and through the goalpost to make it 28–6, Florida, at halftime.

Hastings ran the second half kickoff back to the UGA 41. On first down, Zeier, in the act of passing, was bumped by a Gator. The ball was intercepted by defensive back Myrick Anderson who fell forward to the UF 49. Matthews' passes to Houston and Rhett, plus his 6-yard run, moved the ball to the UGA 8. The Bulldogs retreated no further and Czyzewski was good on a 25-yard field goal to extend Florida's lead to 31–6.

By this time, the cold weather and the hot Gators were sending many Red and Black rooters toward the exits. But the 'Dogs took over on their 36 and went on their best drive of the night. On second down, Hearst took a shovel pass from Zeier and darted to the UF 43 for a 22-yard gain. Zeier scrambled and hit Marshall at the UF 19, before another personal foul on the Gators moved the ball to the 9. Three plays later, Zeier was incomplete on a pass to Hastings in the end zone; but the Gators again were flagged for a personal foul, giving the Dawgs a first down at the 4. On second down, Zeier drifted back, looked to his left and fired to Hastings, who made the catch at the 3 and went in untouched. Todd Peterson's extra point trimmed the Florida lead to 31–13 with 6:51 remaining in the third quarter.

Wide receiver Willie Jackson caught three touchdown passes against UGA in 1991 and another in 1992.

With Georgia bent on stopping the UF offense and trying to maintain some momentum, Florida took over at its 26. Rhett ran to the 30 and Matthews passed to Willie Jackson at the UF 43. Three runs by Rhett brought UF to the Georgia 37, and Matthews connected with Houston on a pass to the UGA 21. But the drive died and Czyzewski's field-goal attempt failed when the ball hit the upright and bounced away. Still, Florida used up several minutes and held their big lead.

Three Zeier incompletions and a punt gave UF possession again at the UGA 47. Spurrier put McNabb to work. On three punishing runs, the Gator fullback propelled Florida to the UGA 24 as the third period ended. A draw play to Rhett reached the 'Dogs 10. On second down, Matthews went to a well-covered Willie Jackson who, despite having Wynn as a shadow, came up with the ball in the end zone. Czyzewski's conversion made it 38–13.

Now, most of the remaining Georgia rooters were filtering out of the stadium. The Gators' faithful gave them a warm sendoff by chanting "S-E-C! S-E-C!" and barking at the Georgia players on the sideline.

The teams traded punts before Florida began first and ten at the UGA 44 with Brian Fox replacing Matthews at quarterback. McNabb rushed to the 40 and Rhett gained two more. Fox, aided by a personal foul against Georgia that put the Gators on the UGA 24, then passed over the middle to Jackson running a post pattern. The ball was tipped by a defender but Jackson grabbed it and tumbled over the goal line for Florida's sixth touchdown. Czyzewski's kick ballooned the lead to 45–13 with 6:22 left and just enough time for the Gator second- and third-teamers to get in a little exercise.

With the Gator Bowl all to themselves, Florida fans revelled in their school's biggest victory ever over Georgia. After the final whistle, many of them took up the derisive shout of "Keep Ray Goff! Keep Ray Goff!" Gator players waved packets of sugar signifying the sweetness of the win and a probable date in the Sugar Bowl.

Three touchdown catches by Willie Jackson and the passing magic of Matthews grabbed the headlines, but Florida's offensive line and headhunting defense put the game away. Gator defenders held Georgia to 220 yards total offense, including only 25 yards rushing, and sacked Zeier three times. Matthews threw for four touchdowns, completing 22 of 32 attempts for 303 yards. His scoring tosses tied him with former Florida star quarterback John Reaves for the single-season record of most touchdown passes in the SEC.

Zeier threw for 195 yards, completing 18 of 35, including the lone Bulldog touchdown.

After the cold calamity in Jacksonville, Georgia beat Auburn, 37–27, and accepted a bid to play Arkansas in the Independence Bowl. The Bulldogs closed the regular season by taking Georgia Tech, 18–15, then downed the Razorbacks, 24–15, in the bowl. Georgia was rated 17th in the final AP poll and 19th in the *USA TODAY*-CNN rankings.

For Florida, the win over Georgia put them in position to win the SEC title outright with a home victory over Kentucky a week later. The Gators rose to No. 5 in both polls and tamed the Wildcats, 35–26, to stand alone atop the SEC.

Already tasting the Sugar Bowl, Spurrier's men further sweetened their year with a 14–9 whipping of archrival and third-ranked Florida State.

Florida then faced 18th-ranked Notre Dame in New Orleans on New Year's Day, but the dream year soured somewhat as the Irish rallied for a wild 39–28 decision. Florida finished seventh in the AP poll and eighth in the *USA TODAY*-CNN final rankings.

Shane Matthews became only the second player in SEC history to pass for 3,000 yards in a season. He and defensive back Will White were named to the all-conference team for the second consecutive

Safety Will White was an All-American in 1990 and an enforcer in UF victories against UGA from 1990 to 1992. An All-SEC player, he was drafted by the Phoenix Cardinals.

year and were joined by teammates Errict Rhett, guard Hesham Ismail, center Cal Dixon, tackles Brad Culpepper and Tony McCoy, linebacker Tim Paulk and punter Shayne Edge. Georgia linebacker Dwayne Simmons also made the squad.

Culpepper, whose father, Bruce, was a Florida team captain in the early 1960s, was honored as a first-team All-America pick.

Nine Gators were selected in the 1992 NFL draft. Culpepper was chosen by Minnesota and Paulk was selected by Atlanta. Others picked were center Tony Rowell by the Los Angeles Raiders; McCoy and defensive end Michael Brandon by Indianapolis; Dexter McNabb by Green Bay; Ismail by Pittsburgh; Dixon by the New York Jets; and linebacker Ephesians Bartley by Philadelphia.

Scoring:

Florida	7	21	3	14	—	45
Georgia	3	3	7	0	—	13

UF	TD	Jackson, 4-yard pass from Matthews (Czyzewski kick)
UGA	FG	Parkman, 41 yards
UF	TD	Rhett, 13-yard run (Czyzewski kick)
UF	TD	Houston, 36-yard pass from Matthews (Czyzewski kick)
UF	TD	Sullivan, 61-yard pass from Matthews (Czyzewski kick)
UGA	FG	Parkman, 25 yards

UF   FG   Czyzewski, 25 yards
UGA TD   Hastings, 4-yard pass from Zeier (Peterson kick)
UF   TD   Jackson, 9-yard pass from Matthews (Czyzewski kick)
UF   TD   Jackson, 24-yard pass from Fox (Czyzewski kick)

Florida: *Offense:* H. Houston, W. Jackson, Sullivan, *wide receiver;* Dean, Duncan, T. Jackson, *tight end;* M. White, Golden, *left tackle;* Ismail, D. Smith, *left guard;* Dixon, Monk, Crouch, *center;* Watson, Swain, *right guard;* Rowell, Taylor, Fisher, *right tackle;* Rhett, McClendon, Ackerman, *running backs;* Matthews, Fox, Dean, Mangus, *quarterback;* McNabb, Randolph, Bilkie, *fullback;* Czyzewski, Edge, *kickers;* Nichols, *holder*

Defense: Brandon, H. Thomas, Gunter, *left end;* Culpepper, E. Johnson, *left tackle;* McCoy, Gaines, *right tackle;* D. Mikell, K. Carter, L. Smith, *right end;* E. Bartley, T. Paulk, C. Miles, E. Robinson, K. Freeman, M. Oliver, *linebackers;* M. Anderson, W. White, Archie, *safeties;* L. Kennedy, D. Speer, Scavella, L. Hatch, Pouncy, *cornerbacks*

Georgia: *Offense:* Marshall, *split end;* B. Williams, D. Rogers, *left tackle;* Swan, Sadler, *left guard;* DeFoor, Rissmiller, David, *center;* Tellis, Duggins, *right guard;* Millen, Rosenberg, *right tackle,* Hastings, J. Thomas, *flanker;* Mitchell, Etheridge, *tight end;* Hearst, Ware, Strong, Harvey, *running backs;* Zeier, *quarterback;* Peterson, Armstrong, Parkman, Saussy, *kickers*

Defense: Douglas, Brewer, *left tackle;* W. Jennings, Barnum, *nose guard;* Maib, C. Ware, *right tackle;* M. Davis, Simmons, J. Allen, C. Butler, T. Jones, D. Ward, Hambrick, *linebackers;* M. Jones, Hargett, A. Jackson, R. Thompson, *safeties;* Carswell, G. Wynn, C. Wilson, Pledger, *cornerbacks*

	Florida	Georgia
First downs	29	14
Total yards	512	220
Rushing yards	185	25
Passing yards	327	195
Pass att/comp/int	33/23/0	35/18/1
Fumbles/lost	0/0	1/0
Penalties/yards	10/86	7/73
Punts/avg. yards	2/32	7/33
Possession time	34:27	25:33

— 1992 —

Florida 26, Georgia 24

WHEN THE GATORS AND DAWGS TANGLED ON Halloween 1992, Georgia was hoping to exorcise the ghosts of two straight embarrassing defeats to Florida.

The Gators began the year with visions of a second consecutive SEC crown and a Heisman Trophy for quarterback supreme Shane Matthews. But Florida's express train to these summits, much less a possible national championship, had been derailed by the time Georgia invaded Jacksonville.

With the addition of South Carolina and Arkansas, the conference expanded to 12 schools and was divided into Eastern and Western divisions for the first time in 1992.

Months before the season opened, many forecasters believed the Florida-Georgia proceedings would decide the king of the SEC's new Eastern Division. The division winners would vie for the SEC title in the conference's first-ever championship game.

The Gators had been a good bet to take their third straight win over Georgia (a feat not accomplished since the four-game UF winning streak of 1960–1963) when the season began, but on-field fortunes cast the big game in a different light. Early losses to Tennessee and Mississippi State stunned Coach Steve Spurrier's highly-touted team, which had been rated in the top five in virtually every preseason poll.

Yet, by game week, it was Georgia ranked seventh in the Associated Press poll with tailback Garrison Hearst coming from nowhere to become the Heisman Trophy front-runner.

The 7–1 Bulldogs were favored to skin the 20th-ranked Gators in the regionally televised game by ABC. More than 82,400 fans were in the stands to see it.

The versatile Hearst, a junior from Lincolnton, was one of the

431

prime reasons for Georgia's success. Through eight games, the headline back was the nation's leading rusher and was posting numbers even better than those of Herschel Walker during the latter's 1982 run to the Heisman. Going into Jacksonville, Hearst had 152 carries for 1,232 yards and 16 touchdowns. He had caught 15 passes for 203 yards. Hearst was outshining Walker's meteoric season and it appeared Georgia had a great shot at its third Heisman Trophy winner.

Shane Matthews had not had a great season, but was on a pace to bag even more SEC passing records in 1992 after throwing for 3,130 yards and 28 touchdowns his junior year. The Mississippian had led the conference in passing the past two years and won SEC Player of the Year honors for the second consecutive year in 1991. Through Florida's first six games of 1992, Matthews had completed 133 of 225 passes for 1,523 yards, 12 touchdowns and nine interceptions. He had had better years, but at a school known for its passing quarterbacks, Matthews would be among the best.

His prime receivers, Willie Jackson and Harrison Houston, made the Florida air attack a fearsome weapon. On the ground, junior tailback Errict Rhett had been the SEC's premier runner in 1991 when he was an all-conference performer. Rhett had been slowed early in the '92 campaign by an injured ankle, but was expected to be at full throttle against Georgia.

On defense, Florida, 4–2, was armed with eight returning starters, including safety Will White, a 1990 All-American and two-time All-SEC honoree. Linebackers Carlton Miles and Ed Robinson were solid behind a young Gator defensive line.

Georgia was celebrating its football centennial in 1992, and the Bulldogs of fourth-year coach Ray Goff had been rated as high as seventh by one preseason publication. They had lived up to the billing. With a pack of good running backs headed by Hearst and Mack Strong, Georgia also was a passing menace. Sophomore quarterback Eric Zeier was a proven leader whose throwing prowess had opened up the UGA offense. The duo of Zeier and flanker Andre Hastings was considered one of the top passing tandems in the SEC and among the best in the country. Zeier had struggled during the season despite his talent. He had completed 106 of 183 passes for 1,615 yards and nine touchdowns but had thrown eight interceptions.

The "glue" holding the Dawgs defense together, according to Goff, was junior free safety Greg Tremble, who was second on the team in tackles. Tackle Greg Jackson and linebacker Randall Godfrey also were mainstays.

Florida had little trouble in its season opener, dropping Kentucky, 35–19, as Matthews threw for four touchdowns. But a week later, the Gators drowned 31–14 in a rain-drenched affair at Tennessee. The nightmare intensified with a 30–6 loss to Mississippi State as Matthews' Heisman hopes dimmed with five interceptions. A 28–21 win over LSU helped matters, but Florida had plummeted to No. 23 in the AP poll. The Gators whipped Auburn 24–9 and Louisville 31–17, with Matthews moving ahead of Kerwin Bell as Florida's career passing leader with 7,605 yards.

Georgia started the '92 campaign with a 28–6 win at South Carolina, but No. 20 Tennessee surprised the Bulldogs 34–31 in an Athens thriller despite three touchdowns by Hearst. The upset overshadowed a 354-yard passing day by Zeier, the second-best effort in Georgia history. The loss also dropped the 'Dogs to 19th in the AP rankings. They then pulverized Cal State-Fullerton, 56–0, and beat Ole Miss, 37–11, before a 27–3 win at Arkansas. A 34–7 victory over I-AA Georgia Southern drove the Bulldogs to a No. 10 ranking, before Georgia beat Vanderbilt, 30–20, and crushed Kentucky 40–7 to head to the Gator Bowl with a six-game winning streak.

Fans on both sides figured the passing eye of Matthews and the Heisman heart of Hearst would likely decide the game. The role of sophomore Zeier could prove equally as decisive.

Georgia won the coin flip and decided to kick off. The Gators wasted little time in going for a bundle. On the second play from scrimmage, Matthews set up and fired long over the middle to receiver Willie Jackson, who made a leaping grab at the UGA 31. The 41-yard gain had Gator fans roaring. Rhett reached the Georgia 25 and, two plays later, caught a Matthews pass for a first down at the 20. After another first down at the 8, though, the drive died. Kicker Bart Edmiston came on to hit a 21-yard field goal and the Gators led 3–0.

Georgia's retaliation was swift. After a touchback on the kickoff by Florida's Ryan Ruland, UGA's offense came on for the first time. In the backfield at running back was Frank Harvey, a junior from Dawson, Ga., who was replacing the injured Mack Strong. On first down, Harvey took a handoff from Zeier, sidestepped behind a block by tackle Bernard Williams, and slipped through the grasps of two Gators at the line. Suddenly he was in the clear, outracing the UF defensive backs to the end zone. The 80-yard romp stunned Florida and set off euphoria in the Georgia sections. Todd Peterson's extra point gave the Bulldogs a 7–3 lead with 10:01 to play in the quarter.

On Georgia's second possession, despite a pass interference penalty on Florida, the Dawgs set up to punt at about their 32. But Gator cornerback Larry Kennedy slipped through to partially block Scot Armstrong's kick, the ball careening out of bounds at the UGA 39. Matthews hit Houston for 12 on an out pass and, two plays later, connected with Rhett. The pass completion plus a face mask call on Georgia gave Florida a first down at the 13. A 9-yard scramble by Matthews, a short burst by Rhett, and a quarterback sneak put the Gators at the 1. On second down, Rhett, the UF workhorse, swept to his right after taking a pitchout from Matthews and beat a diving Bulldog back to the goal line. Edmiston's kick was partially blocked, but the ball wobbled over the crossbar for a 10–7 Florida advantage.

Georgia got no further than its 33 on its next series and had to punt. On second down from the UF 27, Matthews found Willie Jackson for 13 and Rhett bulled out to the UF 45 as the quarter ended. Three plays later, tight end Charlie Dean caught a Matthews pass for a first down at the UGA 35. The Gators earned another first down at the 22 on a fourth-down surge by Rhett. Florida reached the 7 but was pushed back to the UGA 27 on an illegal block penalty. The setback was temporary. Matthews passed to Dean at the 9, then spotted wide receiver Jack Jackson uncovered in the end zone, hitting him for the score. Edmiston's kick failed but Florida lengthened its lead to 16–7 with 11:11 left in the half.

The Gators defense, specifically left end Kevin Carter, zeroed in on Zeier on UGA's next possession, sacking the stellar sophomore QB for an 8-yard loss and Georgia had to punt again.

The Gators got good field position when Monty Duncan returned Armstrong's kick to the UGA 38. Fullback Kelvin Randolph hauled in a Matthews toss at the 26 and Rhett banged to the 18 as the Gators threatened again. Two plays later, Matthews lofted a pass to Willie Jackson who had worked free in the back of the end zone. Edmiston's kick made it 23–7 and some jubilant Floridians believed they had sealed the victory.

Georgia, needing a score, came to life, in a roundabout way, on its next series. On second down, Hearst finally ran free of the stubborn Gators, breaking out to the UGA 31. Zeier then rolled out and fired a strike to wide receiver Ha'son Graham to the UGA 49. Two runs and an offsides call on Florida pushed the 'Dogs to the UF 36. But then a Zeier pass skipped off the hands of Hearst into the arms of UF linebacker Ed Robinson. The Gators, though, could not get a first down and punter Shayne Edge kicked to Hastings, who was tackled

Georgia tailback Garrison Hearst was held to 41 yards by the UF defense, dashing his Heisman Trophy hopes in the Gators' 26–24 victory in 1992. The Phoenix Cardinals picked him in the first round of the draft.

at the UGA 38 after a 15-yard return. Zeier was dropped for a loss again by Carter on first down. Undismayed, he calmly found Hastings on a middle screen pass, which the flanker turned into a gain to the UF 37. Zeier then rifled a throw to Damon Evans at the Gators 18. On third and four from the 13, Zeier again went to the air, connecting with Graham over the middle for the touchdown. Peterson's PAT cut Florida's lead to 23–14 with 3:26 before intermission.

The Bulldogs defense was fired up. Rhett was leveled for a loss by noseguard Casey Barnum and the Gators had to kick. Georgia had the momentum, but little time starting from its 27. Hastings snared a Zeier throw for 19 with less than a minute left but Harvey dropped a pass at midfield. Hearst then corralled a Zeier toss at the UF 39. The Bulldogs reached the 32 where, with 13 seconds left, Peterson nailed a 49-yard field goal to end the half's scoring. At 23–17, Georgia was right back in it. And the Dawgs would get the ball first in the second half.

But the Florida defense reasserted itself on UGA's first possession of the third period. Hearst was smothered for a four-yard loss by right end Johnie Church and the 'Dogs had to punt.

Matthews went for more points, starting from his 45 when he hit Aubrey Hill on a pass to the UGA 36. Runs by Kedra Malone and Willie Jackson moved the Gators to the Georgia 24. A personal foul call on the Bulldogs helped Florida reach the 5, but Rhett fumbled and Georgia's Greg Jackson recovered the ball at the 9.

Later in the period, Florida gained possession on a UGA punt to the Gators 20. Rhett rambled for 13 on a draw and, two plays later, burst over center to the UF 47. Matthews then went to the air, hitting Chris Bilkie at the UGA 41, Hill at the 24, and Jack Jackson at the 18. But Georgia shut it all down, yielding only one more yard, and Florida had to settle for a 34-yard Edmiston field goal and some breathing room at 26–17.

On runs by Harvey, Hastings and Hearst, plus a Zeier pass to Jeff Thomas, Georgia drove to the UF 34 before being stymied by an offensive pass interference call. The Dawgs, punting on the first play of the final period, almost got a huge break when the Gators' Duncan fumbled the kick. But Duncan managed to recover the loose ball for Florida at the UF 19. Rhett hauled in a Matthews pass at the 31 but had to limp off the field, having reinjured his left ankle. His replacement, Malone, fumbled on the next play and UGA's Barnum pounced on the pigskin at the UF 31. A holding penalty moved the 'Dogs back to the UF 39.

It was there, as the Halloween dusk settled over the Gator Bowl, that Georgia may have suffered its backbreaker. Zeier stepped back to pass, was flushed from the pocket, and scrambled to his right. Tripped by a blue-shirted pursuer, Zeier threw as he fell. The slingshot pass hit Florida bandit back Ben Hanks in the numbers, and the Gators had the ball again at their own 40. Both teams then swapped possessions before Florida, from its 22, began to gain yardage and work on the clock. Houston caught a Matthews pass at the UF 40 and Rhett ran three times for short yardage but came up short of the first down. With a little over five minutes left in the duel, the Gators had to kick.

Georgia went to work with its fans screaming for a rally. In shotgun formation from his 22, Zeier rocketed a pass to Hastings, who slipped a tackle at the 35 and broke away for another 12 yards to the UGA 47. Again from the shotgun, Zeier dodged an oncoming Gator and found Hearst running open at the UF 45. Showing Heisman flair, Hearst raced down the sideline before being bowled out of bounds at the UF 24. With the Red and Black throng going wild, Zeier retreated into the pocket and launched a high spiral toward the end zone. Split end Brian Bohannon ran under the ball, clutched it with both hands over his head, and got a foot in the end zone before tumbling out of bounds. Peterson kicked the extra point and the Dawgs trailed only 26–24 with 4:05 to play.

The stage was set for another Georgia miracle ending in the Gator Bowl. Goff would later say he had considered an onside kick attempt but decided to let his defense get the ball back.

The game hinged on a Georgia last-stand effort to contain Spurrier's offense. With the stadium rocking, Rhett took a shovel pass on first down but was leveled behind the line by Greg Jackson. From his 14, Matthews calmly whipped a pass to Willie Jackson at the 29, but the Gators still faced third and short. Matthews burrowed into the line for a first down at the 31.

Rhett reached the 34 and Georgia called a time out with 2:21 left. A long incompletion and delay-of-game penalty left Florida with a third and 13. Matthews, on a gutty, clutch play, drilled a pass to Houston for a first down at the 43, and the 'Dogs were running out of time and tactics. The pass by Matthews set a new Gator record for career completions (611) to pass Wayne Peace, but nobody was browsing through history books at the time.

Georgia called its last time out with less than two minutes to play. If the defense held Florida here, Georgia still had a shot. But Matthews killed the last Bulldog hope with a surprise quarterback draw, pushing up the middle to the UGA 43.

In the hoopla and heartbreak after the final whistle, a group of Gator players cavorted in the southeast corner of the stadium, taunting Georgia fans who bombarded them with a cascade of ice, plastic cups, boos and curses from the stands. The situation could have turned ugly but other Gator teammates hustled them off the field. On Sunday, Steve Spurrier apologized for the taunting incident. "What our players did was just uncalled for. There is a lot of jawing in football games between players . . . but when players taunt the opposing team's fans, that's wrong."

The game was so intense, said UF's Matthews, that he was actually bitten by a Bulldog during a pile-up. Much of that intensity was due to the work of Florida's young defensive line, which had helped limit Hearst to a mere 41 yards on 14 carries. The Georgia star had been averaging 8.1 yards per carry and 154 yards per game.

Matthews completed 28 of 45 passes for 301 yards and two touchdowns. It was the last time he would face Georgia as a player, and no one in Red and Black was sorry to see him go. In three games against UGA, Matthews had thrown for 948 yards, nine touchdowns, and had not been intercepted.

Zeier had put his team in position to win, but Florida's offense had come through on its final possession. The Georgia passer was 15 of 28 for 238 yards, two touchdowns, and two interceptions.

The loss to Florida dropped the Bulldogs to 15th in the AP poll while the Gators climbed to No. 14. Coupled with South Carolina's upset of 16th-ranked Tennessee, the win in Jacksonville vaulted Florida into prime position to clinch the SEC East.

The Bulldogs won a thriller, 14–10, at Auburn on November 14 with the Tigers mired in a pile at the UGA half-yard line as time expired.

Georgia closed its regular season with a 31–17 thrashing of hated Georgia Tech to finish at 9–2 and awaited a bowl invitation.

A week after the madness on the St. Johns, Florida, now 14th ranked, survived a scare from Southern Mississippi in Gainesville with a 24–20 win. Spurrier's men slipped by South Carolina, 14–9, at home a week later for their sixth straight win.

Florida won the SEC's Eastern Division by whipping Vanderbilt 41–21, winning for the first time in Nashville since 1966 and extending its winning streak to seven. The Gators, now sixth-ranked, closed the regular season at third-ranked Florida State, getting shelled 45–24.

With its 8–3 mark, Florida faced second-ranked Alabama in the conference's first championship game with a berth in the Sugar Bowl on the line. The Gators were in the tussle until the final three minutes when a Matthews pass was intercepted for a touchdown and a 28–21 Crimson Tide triumph. Despite the disappointment, Florida remained in the bowl picture.

Garrison Hearst finished third in the Heisman voting behind Miami quarterback Gino Torretta and San Diego State running back Marshall Faulk and was a consensus All-American. The Bulldog back had marquee statistics including 21 touchdowns to snap an SEC single-season record, set by Herschel Walker, and lead the nation in scoring. He won the Doak Walker Award as the country's best running back among juniors and seniors and rushed for 1,537 yards on 228 carries. But a black day in Jacksonville likely cost him the Heisman. "Hearst may have left the Heisman on the floor of the Gator Bowl in late October," Tony Stastny of the *Savannah News-Press* wrote on November 29. "Playing the Gators, Hearst not only needed a big game personally, but Georgia needed a big game from him. Neither got what they needed."

Eric Zeier was the SEC's passing leader, based on his efficiency rating, completing 151 of 258 throws for 2,248 yards and 12 touchdowns. But he was 0–2 against Florida and Goff was now 1–3.

The Bulldogs earned an invitation to the Citrus Bowl and clipped No. 15 Ohio State, 21–14, as Hearst rushed for 168 yards and two scores. With its 10–2 record, Georgia finished at No. 8 in the polls and enjoyed its 11th 10-victory season in the school's history.

Andre Hastings ended the year as the league's leading receiver and set UGA single-season records for receptions (52), receiving yards (860), and touchdown catches (13).

Hearst led the Bulldogs contingent honored on the All-SEC team.

Steve Spurrier returned to Gainesville as the UF head coach in 1990 and promptly won three consecutive games over Ray Goff's Bulldogs. UF won its first official SEC title in 1991 and narrowly missed in 1992.

Teammates joining him were wide receiver Hastings, left tackle Alec Millen, outside linebacker Mitch Davis and defensive back Tremble.

Hearst and Hastings both decided to skip their senior years at Georgia and enter the NFL draft, meaning the Bulldogs would have significant holes to fill on offense before 1993. Hearst was a first-round selection of the Phoenix Cardinals, the third pick overall, while Hastings was tabbed in the third round by the Pittsburgh Steelers. Two other Dawgs were chosen in the seventh round: offensive tackle Millen (New York Jets) and kicker Todd Peterson (New York Giants).

No. 14 Florida received a bid to the Gator Bowl and whipped 12th-ranked N.C. State, 27–10.

Shane Matthews, described by Spurrier as the greatest quarterback in UF history, passed for 9,287 yards and 74 touchdowns and won 28 of 36 games he started. Although he was not selected in the NFL draft, he entered Gators legend as one of the greatest passing quarterbacks of all time.

Matthews and defensive back White were All-SEC selections for the third year in a row. Wide receiver Willie Jackson and inside linebacker Carlton Miles also won all-league laurels.

Florida cornerback Lawrence Hatch was chosen in the sixth round of the draft by the New England Patriots and All-American safety Will White was picked in the seventh round by Phoenix.

The taunting incident, the coolness between Ray Goff and Steve Spurrier, and the sting of a third consecutive defeat to Florida would have Georgia out for Gator blood when the schools collided again. In the Halloween chill after the '92 drama, no one on either side could know that the game would undergo a major transition in the first months of 1993.

Scoring:

Florida	10	13	3	0	—	26
Georgia	7	10	0	7	—	24

UF	FG	Edmiston, 21 yards
UGA	TD	Harvey, 80-yard run (Peterson kick)
UF	TD	Rhett, 1-yard run (Edmiston kick)
UF	TD	J. Jackson, 9-yard pass from Matthews (kick failed)
UF	TD	W. Jackson, 14-yard pass from Matthews (Edmiston kick)
UGA	TD	Graham, 13-yard pass from Zeier (Peterson kick)
UGA	FG	Peterson, 49 yards
UF	FG	Edmiston, 34 yards
UGA	TD	Bohannon, 24-yard pass from Zeier (Peterson kick)

Florida: *Defense:* Church, Smith, *right end;* McMillian, Barnard, *right tackle;* Gunter, Barnard, *left tackle;* K. Carter, Riggins, *left end;* E. Robinson, Daniels, Pearson, Miles, Freeman, *linebacker;* Kennedy, Hatch, Speer, Lake, *cornerback;* Hanks, M. Anderson, Grow, Oliver, *safety*

Offense: Green, Golden, *left tackle;* Swain, Golden, *left guard;* Crouch, Johnson, *center;* Watson, Carey, *right guard;* Odom, R. Taylor, *right tackle;* Keller, Dean, *tight end;* W. Jackson, J. Jackson, A. Hill, Houston, Everett, Duncan, *wide receiver;* Rhett, Malone, T. Davis, *running back;* Bilkie, Randolph, *fullback;* Matthews, *quarterback;* Edmiston, Ruland, *placekicker;* Edge, *punter*

Georgia: *Defense:* G. Jackson, T. Jones, *right tackle;* Barnum, McKever, *nose guard;* Wallace, Kaiser, *left tackle;* M. Davis, Ledbetter, Clemons, Ward, Godfrey, Evans, Butler, Harrell, *linebacker;* A. Jackson, Pledger, Chris Wilson, Chad Wilson, *cornerback;* Tremble, Stephens, M. Jones, A. Jackson, *safety*

Offense: Mitchell, Etheridge, *tight end;* Millen, Fredenburg, *left tackle;* Taylor, O'Neal, *left guard;* Swan, Weeks, *center;* Roberts, Chosewood, *right guard;* B. Williams, Stark, *right tackle;* Bohannon, Graham, *split end;* Hastings, Evans, *flanker;* Harvey, *running back;* Hearst, T. Davis, *scatback;* Zeier, *quarterback;* Peterson, *placekicker;* Armstrong, *punter*

	Florida	Georgia
First downs	27	17
Rushes/yards	48/136	29/143
Passing yards	301	235
Return yards	37	37
Pass att/comp/int	45/28/0	28/15/2
Punts/avg.	5/36	7/32
Fumbles/lost	3/2	1/0
Penalties/yards	7/61	8/68
Possession time	37:24	22:36

Epilogue

Even while the dust and fur flew at the 1992 Florida–Georgia game, another issue was threatening to completely change the complexion of the rivalry for years to come.

Rumblings that the game, played in Jacksonville since 1933, would be switched to a home-and-home format were intensifying. In the days after Florida's 26–24 win in 1992, the issue became more direct, particularly in Athens. While some UF fans claimed Georgia wouldn't have brought up the prospect of moving the game if Florida had not won the three previous years, UGA officials said they had other concerns.

Georgia athletic director Vince Dooley was concerned that UGA played only five home games in 1995, one less than desired. He raised the possibility of playing the Florida game in Athens that year as part of a larger plan that might move the series to Athens and Gainesville.

Fueling Dooley's fire was a UGA survey of season-ticket holders showing that 53 percent wanted the game played in Athens. But a survey among UGA students showed a slight majority in favor of keeping the game in Jacksonville.

Negotiations among officials from both universities and the city of Jacksonville culminated on March 22, 1993, when Dooley announced a plan backed by Florida.

The schools would play in the Gator Bowl through 1994 when a two-year contract between them and Jacksonville ended. The 1995 game would be played in Athens for the first time since 1932 when Georgia won a 33–12 victory. The universities agreed to a new contract to continue the series in Jacksonville from 1996 to 2002.

Florida made a concession vital to the agreement. The 1995 game was technically the Gators' home game, but UF athletic director Jeremy Foley agreed to switch in order to solve Georgia's problem of having only five home games that year.

Both universities made it clear that the plan was contingent on whether the city of Jacksonville followed through on a $49 million renovation of the Gator Bowl. The construction would be completed by fall 1995.

As an important aside, Georgia also asked Jacksonville officials to address the problem of price-gouging by some hotels, plus parking and security problems.

So it appeared one of the Southland's richest and fiercest football rivalries had weathered another crisis. And the Gators and Bulldogs counted the days before the next legend was born on the field where he would earn his glory yards.

Appendixes

Series Through the Years

1992 Florida 26, Georgia 24
1991 Florida 45, Georgia 13
1990 Florida 38, Georgia 7
1989 Georgia 17, Florida 10
1988 Georgia 26, Florida 3
1987 Georgia 23, Florida 10
1986 Florida 31, Georgia 19
1985 Georgia 24, Florida 3
1984 Florida 27, Georgia 0
1983 Georgia 10, Florida 9
1982 Georgia 44, Florida 0
1981 Georgia 26, Florida 21
1980 Georgia 26, Florida 21
1979 Georgia 33, Florida 10
1978 Georgia 24, Florida 22
1977 Florida 22, Georgia 17
1976 Georgia 41, Florida 27
1975 Georgia 10, Florida 7
1974 Georgia 17, Florida 16
1973 Florida 11, Georgia 10
1972 Georgia 10, Florida 7
1971 Georgia 49, Florida 7
1970 Florida 24, Georgia 17
1969 TIE 13–13
1968 Georgia 51, Florida 0
1967 Florida 17, Georgia 16
1966 Georgia 27, Florida 10
1965 Florida 14, Georgia 10
1964 Georgia 14, Florida 7
1963 Florida 21, Georgia 14
1962 Florida 23, Georgia 15
1961 Florida 21, Georgia 14
1960 Florida 22, Georgia 14
1959 Georgia 21, Florida 10
1958 Florida 7, Georgia 6
1957 Florida 22, Georgia 0
1956 Florida 28, Georgia 0

1955 Florida 19, Georgia 13
1954 Georgia 14, Florida 13
1953 Florida 21, Georgia 7
1952 Florida 30, Georgia 0
1951 Georgia 7, Florida 6
1950 Georgia 6, Florida 0
1949 Florida 28, Georgia 7
1948 Georgia 20, Florida 12
1947 Georgia 34, Florida 6
1946 Georgia 33, Florida 14
1945 Georgia 34, Florida 0
1944 Georgia 38, Florida 12
No game in 1943
1942 Georgia 75, Florida 0
1941 Georgia 19, Florida 3
1940 Florida 18, Georgia 13
1939 Georgia 6, Florida 2
1938 Georgia 19, Florida 6
1937 Florida 6, Georgia 0
1936 Georgia 26, Florida 8
1935 Georgia 7, Florida 0
1934 Georgia 14, Florida 0
1933 Georgia 14, Florida 0
1932 Georgia 33, Florida 12
1931 Georgia 33, Florida 6
1930 SCORELESS TIE
1929 Florida 18, Georgia 6
1928 Florida 26, Georgia 6
1927 Georgia 28, Florida 0
1926 Georgia 32, Florida 9
1920 Georgia 56, Florida 0
1919 Georgia 16, Florida 0
No games in 1917 or 1918
1916 Georgia 21, Florida 0
1915 Georgia 37, Florida 0
1904 Georgia 52, Florida 0★

★Series records: Georgia 43 wins; Florida 25 wins with 2 ties after 1992 game (Florida doesn't count the 1904 game because UF wasn't incorporated until 1906).

The Coaches' Records

FLORIDA	Games	Won	Lost	Tied
*M. O. Bridges	1	0	1	0
Charles McCoy	2	0	2	0
A. L. Busser	1	0	1	0
William Kline	1	0	1	0
H. L. "Tom" Sebring	2	0	2	0
Charles Bachman	5	2	2	1
D. K. "Dutch" Stanley	3	0	3	0
Josh Cody	4	1	3	0
Tom Lieb	5	1	4	0
Ray Wolf	4	1	3	0
Bob Woodruff	10	6	4	0
Ray Graves	10	6	3	1
Doug Dickey	9	3	6	0
Charley Pell	5	0	5	0
Galen Hall	5	2	3	0
Gary Darnell	1	0	1	0
Steve Spurrier	3	3	0	0

*Various accounts of the 1904 game list M. O. Bridges as either the coach or the team captain of the Florida Agricultural College team. Whatever his status, the University of Florida does not recognize the game in its official records.

GEORGIA	Games	Won	Lost	Tied
Charles Barnard	1	1	0	0
★W. A. Cunningham	3	3	0	0
H. J. Stegeman	1	1	0	0
George Woodruff	2	2	0	0
Harry Mehre	10	6	3	1
Joel Hunt	1	1	0	0
Wally Butts	21	12	9	0
Johnny Griffith	3	0	3	0
Vince Dooley	25	17	7	1
Ray Goff	4	1	3	0

★W. A. Cunningham is given credit for the 1919 UGA win although he was recovering from broken ribs sustained in a fall. The Georgians actually were led to victory by assistant coach H. J. Stegeman.